Music Editing for Film and Television

D1610358

University Campus Oldham

5909685197

Music Editing for Film and Television

The Art and the Process

UniversityCampus
Oldham

A partnership between
the University of Huddersfield & Oldham College

ıan, MPSE

Library & Computing Centre: 0161 344 8888
UCO Main Reception: 0161 344 8800
Cromwell Street, Oldham, OL1 1BB

**Text renewals: text `renew' and your UCO ID number to
07950 081389.**

Class No: 781.542137

Suffix: SAL

WITHDRAWN

This book is to be returned by the date on the self-service receipt.
Your library account can be accessed online at:
http://www.uco.oldham.ac.uk/library/catalogue.aspx
Follow UCO Library on Twitter: www.twitter.com/ucolcc

RECEIVED 1 3 DEC 2016

First published 2015 by Focal Press
70 Blanchard Road, Suite 402, Burlington, MA 01803
and by Focal Press
2 Park Square, Milton Park, Abingdon, Oxon OX14 4RN

Focal Press is an imprint of the Taylor & Francis Group, an informa business

© 2015 Steven Saltzman

The right of Steven Saltzman to be identified as author of this work has been asserted by him in accordance with sections 77 and 78 of the Copyright, Designs and Patents Act 1988.

All rights reserved. No part of this book may be reprinted or reproduced or utilized in any form or by any electronic, mechanical, or other means, now known or hereafter invented, including photocopying and recording, or in any information storage or retrieval system, without permission in writing from the publishers.

Notices
Knowledge and best practice in this field are constantly changing. As new research and experience broaden our understanding, changes in research methods, professional practices, or medical treatment may become necessary.

Practitioners and researchers must always rely on their own experience and knowledge in evaluating and using any information, methods, compounds, or experiments described herein. In using such information or methods they should be mindful of their own safety and the safety of others, including parties for whom they have a professional responsibility.

Product or corporate names may be trademarks or registered trademarks, and are used only for identification and explanation without intent to infringe.

Library of Congress Cataloging in Publication Data
Saltzman, Steven.
Music editing for film and television : the art and the process/Steven Saltzman.
pages cm
1. Motion picture music—Production and direction—Vocational guidance.
2. Film soundtracks—Production and direction—Vocational guidance. I. Title.
ML3795.S2326 2014
781.5'42137—dc23

2013045953

ISBN: 978-0-415-81757-8 (pbk)
ISBN: 978-0-203-58278-7 (ebk)

Typeset in Palatino LT Std
By MPS Limited, Chennai, India

UNIVERSITY CAMPUS
OLDHAM

MIX
Paper from
responsible sources
FSC® C014174
FSC
www.fsc.org

Printed and bound in the United States of America by Sheridan Books, Inc. (a Sheridan Group Company).

This book is dedicated to my mother,
Muriel Saltzman.

Who was an inspiration for all my musical endeavors.

And in memory of my father whose life as an artist greatly
influenced my connection to the visual and teaching.
William Saltzman.

Bound to Create

You are a creator.

Whatever your form of expression — photography, filmmaking, animation, games, audio, media communication, web design, or theatre — you simply want to create without limitation. Bound by nothing except your own creativity and determination.

Focal Press can help.

For over 75 years Focal has published books that support your creative goals. Our founder, Andor Kraszna-Krausz, established Focal in 1938 so you could have access to leading-edge expert knowledge, techniques, and tools that allow you to create without constraint. We strive to create exceptional, engaging, and practical content that helps you master your passion.

Focal Press and you.

Bound to create.

We'd love to hear how we've helped you create. Share your experience:
www.focalpress.com/boundtocreate

Focal Press
Taylor & Francis Group

Contents

Acknowledgments

Many people were influential in the creation of this book. My composing and music editing has been enriched by many colleagues and mentors. I would particularly like to recognize Don Wilkins for his inspirational teachings at Berklee College of Music, as my first film-scoring and music editor instructor. I also want to acknowledge Modern Music for opening the door to the world of music editing.

I will be forever indebted to two colleagues, J.J. George and Joel Krantz, for their expert editorial work on this manuscript. Joel, an assistant professor in the Department of Cinema and Television Arts at California State University Northridge, was my choice to line edit for both grammatical corrections, and Pro Tools and postproduction clarity. As an educator and author of textbooks himself, Joel's intimate knowledge of Pro Tools and postproduction were invaluable.

J.J. George, an expert music editor, and my good and very patient friend, guided me with his incisive critique and his keen sense of all the nuances of music editing. With his many years of experience in the field he was able to clarify and add important insights. Indeed, he is the author of the PAX Quotes ("Professional Audio mX") which appear throughout this book. Humor has been a connection for J.J. and me, helping to dissipate frustrations or tensions on tough projects. When he suggested his tips be anonymous, we began to play with acronyms. Pax is actually the name of my dog, an Australian Shepherd, who spends his time at my feet, keeping me company during long hours of editing. So the inside joke is that J.J.'s authorship was credited to a very smart and beloved dog.

The interviews collected in this book are from some of the most high-profile and respected professionals in Hollywood. Their insights not only describe their perspectives on and experiences of the world of postproduction music editing, they also illustrate the thick technical content, particularly shedding light on the creative and interpersonal collaborations that are so important in enabling and supporting postproduction workflows. I would like to thank all those interviewed, including Carli Barber, Gary Bourgeois, Bob Bowen, Joseph S. DeBeasi, John Debney, Patrick Don Vito, Bobby Fernandez, Scott Martin Gershin, Kevin Kaska, Christopher Kulikowski, David Rennie, William Ross, Frank Salvino, Kevin Tent, and Jon Turteltaub.

I am also greatly appreciative of the help of Jim Cooper, Alex Gibson, Richard Grant, and Ron Grant, who carefully reviewed and contributed to several important sections. Many thanks to the composer Charles Bernstein for lending his wonderful article on spotting notes. My special gratitude is also due to William Ross for his enthusiasm in writing the foreword to this book. His contribution brings with it a authoritative credibility based on his established worldwide influence as a composer and conductor.

Thanks are also due to Anais Wheeler, the previous acquisitions editor for Focal Press, whom I first approached with the idea for a book about music editing. She had faith that this type of book would successfully fill a need in the emerging area of postproduction education. Production Editor Emma Elder and copy editors Kate Manson and Sarah Steele were invaluable for their contribution of countless hours and detailed work that really helped pull this book together. I am most appreciative of the help of Meagan White, the Focal Press editorial project manager who supported this first-time writer at every stage—she was always patient and informative; and of Megan Ball, the current acquisitions editor, who did not hesitate to show her excitement and support for the book's success.

Finally, I would like to thank my family for their love and support. My brother-in-law Leonard Jacobs, a publisher, generously guided me through my first entrance into the publishing world. My daughter, Julia Barnes Saltzman, an artist in her own right, influenced the cover design and shot my photograph. I very much appreciate the help of my son Benjamin with writing, grammar, and style. Above all, I would like to express my deepest appreciation to my wife, Katherine, for her love and compassionate support. Throughout our 34 years of marriage she has guided and sustained us, as I followed my dreams as a film composer, music editor, and now as writer of this book.

About the Author

Photo credit Julia Barnes Saltzman

Music editor and composer Steven Saltzman has a unique take on music and film. His diverse background and his passion for teaching give him the ability to create a new way of understanding the world of music editing. He earned a Bachelors of Music in composition and film scoring from Berklee College of Music in Boston. Leading up to this degree, he also attended the Comprehensive Musicianship Bachelors program at Moorhead State College, one of ten such programs in the United States. Steven also studied composition with Boston Conservatory composer John Hess, and while on the East Coast he composed music for WGBH and ABC Television, independent films, and a variety of commercials, as well as for the theatre. He moved to California to pursue his dream of composing in the film industry. There he continued to study composition and orchestration with Dr. Albert Harris, and he attended the BMI Film Scoring workshop with Earl Hagan. He composed the scores for numerous independent feature films, commercials, and syndicated television shows. One of those films went on to receive a nomination for an Academy of Motion Picture Arts and Sciences Award of Merit for best animated short film.

For the past eighteen years Mr. Saltzman has focused his career on music editing for films and television. His work includes: *Brick Mansions, Movie 43, Priest, Seven Days in Utopia, Straw Dogs* (remake), *Born to be a Star, The Hole, The Answer Man, Dragonball Evolution, WAR, Inc., Ghost Rider* (additional editing), *Bewitched, A Guy Thing, Heartbreakers*, and *Hyperion Bay*, a Warner Bros. television series. He has worked with many composers, including Klaus Badelt, Mark Mothersbaugh, Nathan Furst, Robert Revell, J.A.C. Redford, and Larry Groupé. He has also received a Golden Reel Award and two nominations for his music editing.

Mr. Saltzman is a certified expert Avid Pro Tools instructor and has created a music-editing course, which he has been teaching for the past nine years. He has taught at UCLA Extension, Moviola Digital Arts Institute, Video Symphony, Community Colleges in Los Angeles and Riverside, California and is presently an instructor at Musicians Institute in Hollywood. He has lectured at the Motion Picture Editors Guild, Ex'pression College in San Francisco, Media Institute in Minneapolis, and most recently joined the faculty at the Palomar Film Music Workshop. He serves on the Board of Directors for Motion Picture Sound Editors (MPSE), and the Advisory Boards of Los Angeles City College and the University High School Recording Arts Program. He is a member of the Motion Picture Editors Guild, the Society of Composers and Lyricists, the MPSE and the Local 47 Musicians Union. He is married with two children, and he remains a Midwestern boy and a California dreamer.

Foreword

I love the concept of learning. What a wonderful experience to be exposed to ideas and information that can transform our ability to make sense of the world around us. While we may live in a time where the reference book is being replaced by a search engine, a website, a link, a hard drive, or files on our computer desktop that contain more information than any encyclopedia, the concept of a learning resource ... whatever form it takes ... may be more important than ever.

Regardless of how we access an information resource, the potential end result remains the same: a transformative experience that changes the course of our thoughts, our perceptions, and possibly our lives. Such is the power of information. Such is the power of Steven Saltzman's book, *Music Editing for Film and Television: The Art and the Process*.

For anyone interested in the world of film and music, and the marriage of these two that has been going on since the invention of moving pictures, Steven Saltzman's book has the potential to be one of those transformative sources of information.

Music editors, with the knowledge and craft they possess, have been a critically important part of the emotional synergy that can happen when film and music are linked together. Simply by the nature of when they often begin work on a project, music editors are often in a position to profoundly affect the final musical direction and score for a film.

There are many composers who rely on their music editor to help point them in the "right" direction ... or, as is sometimes the case when the paper is blank, in any direction!

The knowledge, skill, craft, and artistry it takes to be a good music editor is substantial and formidable. Like any art, it can take years to learn ... and as with any art, the forces of change, and what those forces mean for the aesthetic of that art, transcend the life of any one individual.

Steven's book is a masterful exposition of the skill set and knowledge it takes to be a music editor in today's world. The chapter titles alone read like a checklist of the things that need to be addressed and dealt with in the creation of a musical score: the Team, Spotting, the Temp, Songs, and Source, to name just a few. These are all things that are a part of the daily life of anyone working with music and film.

On a more personal note, I want to take the opportunity to thank Steven for the tremendous time and effort it takes to write a book such as the one he's written.

I am profoundly grateful to those who have the ability, and take the time, to compile and explain an area of knowledge in a way that is useful and helpful to those whose interests and curiosity can be stimulated and propelled by that knowledge.

One of my favorite quotes is by T.S. Eliot. It may have a certain relevance to all of this. Eliot writes, "We shall not cease from exploration. And the end of all our exploring will be to arrive where we started and know the place for the first time."

After reading Steven's book, the truth of those words once again reminded me of why I love that quote so much. In some instances, I felt like I was discovering things about music editing for the first time. The power of knowledge and information to continually change and shape our lives is one of the profound truths of being human.

I hope that anyone who reads Steven's book will enjoy the experience, be open to the ideas he presents and discusses, and be transformed in their understanding of what a music editor does and how they do it.

William Ross
Los Angeles, California

Preface

Welcome to the world of music editing: it's the invisible element that enables music to bring motion pictures to life. Working in the music industry with motion pictures of all types—films, television shows, games, videos, webisodes, and commercials—is challenging and rewarding. On the surface music editing may seem straightforward and simple; in fact it is quite complex and dynamic. Each project takes twists and turns that can keep even the most experienced editors on their toes. This book is designed to introduce the reader both to the principles of editing music and to some of those challenges he or she might encounter.

The book is written for the person working in postproduction audio, committed to the marrying of music to picture in its many forms. It will also be of value to those in other postproduction sound fields, such as sound effects, dialogue, and sound design, since it details the music editor's workflows and techniques. Directors and film editors may also find it of interest, as it will help them to gain a better understanding of the inner workings of the music editor's job within the postproduction process. Perhaps the postproduction supervisor, sound supervisor, music supervisor, or producer will turn to these pages as a guide to working more effectively and efficiently with music editors. Certainly, composers and their teams can appreciate the workflows and relationships the music editor has with all the other members of the production. Above all, this book is geared towards those that want to learn this professional craft, either as the focus of or as an ancillary to a postproduction sound career. For the curious non-professional sound aficionado this book might also be of interest.

This book is the culmination of my many years of music editing. It is not a collection from other sources but a series of tutorials based on my professional experience and teaching in this field. I certainly would not claim to be the sole bearer of this knowledge. Many music editors, film editors, composers, mixers, directors, and music supervisors have supported my career and guided me along the way, and they have influenced both the creation of this book and my music editing courses.

The reader will notice that this book does not have a glossary or bibliography; I have found that the extensive postproduction resources available on the Internet render these sections largely redundant. Instead, I have clarified some terms and abbreviations in the body of the text and provided a list of a few online resources in the last section of the introduction.

Much of the material in this book is based on my own experiences and those of other contributors. While a textbook with definitive answers to every question would be invaluable, no book, let alone this one, could anticipate all the possible scenarios. Attentive readers will also notice that the book contains contradictions, with many proposed workflows being followed by apparently conflicting alternatives. Far from sacrificing clarity or professionalism, such alternatives show that there are many equally valid solutions to the various problems inevitably posed by postproduction work. The process naturally gives rise to multiple scenarios, obstacles, and puzzles, and resolving them requires creative and experience-based innovations. I have attempted to share many true-to-life as well as hypothetical examples. As the reader encounters new and unforeseen situations in their own work, I hope he or she will resolve them with resourcefulness and imagination: the two greatest tutors of all.

Another important element in this book is its interviews. I sought out a few of the most distinguished professionals to share their viewpoints. I asked questions with a focus on music editing and the interviewees expanded the conversation to include workflows, personal experiences, and comments on the industry at large. I consider these interviews to offer the most important lessons, as they provide true and diverse insight into the interviewees' professions and the postproduction industry. I hope that readers will recognize the common threads linking these interviews with the technical and practical guidance offered throughout the book. In addition to the interviews, readers should take note of the article by Charles Bernstein reprinted in Chapter 3, on spotting, it offers a unique point of view.

Studying this book, even with all the information it contains, will not instantly make you a music editor. As with most careers, the only true means to success is experience, diligence, and focus. This book will, however, help to set you on the path to building a career in the field of music editing. To succeed, you must: learn your craft by practicing; know Pro Tools inside and out; keep up with new technologies; attend courses taught by professionals in the field and gain from their experience; start small but think big (that is, work with passion and professional commitment on even the smallest of projects, no matter how low paying); and network, network, network—not just online or via email, but by getting out there and personally making (and keeping) friends in the industry. While these friends may be able to include you on their projects as their own careers develop, more importantly they will often provide personal support which is priceless in a tough industry. Be willing to ask for guidance or advice. Even the seasoned music editor knows to ask for help in situations that prove overwhelming or when they feel stumped.

I sincerely hope you find this book informative, intriguing, educational, and entertaining. May these writings contribute to your success in the postproduction audio industry and help you avoid cataclysmic mistakes you might fear most. In the end, enjoy the journey and have fun.

Steven Saltzman
Los Angeles, California

Introduction

I.1 WHAT IS MUSIC EDITING?

Music editing, simply stated, is the artistic and technical craft of working with music placed with and married to a motion picture medium. Essentially, music editing is manipulating and shaping music to fit the motion picture and delivering music tracks for a mix. Motion picture media include Hollywood feature films, independent low-budget films, television shows, made-for-cable shows or films, and made-for-Internet or streaming shows and games.

Music editing is not a new art or process: the synchronization of sound and music with motion pictures has been explored and developed since the late 1800s. According to an informative web site on early film sound:

> From the inception of motion pictures, various inventors attempted to unite sight and sound through "talking" motion pictures. The Edison Company is known to have experimented with this as early as the fall of 1894 under the supervision of W.K.L. Dickson with a film known today as *Dickson Experimental Sound Film*. The film shows a man, who may possibly be Dickson, playing violin before a phonograph horn as two men dance.
>
> *From the article "Early Edison Experiments with Sight and Sound" on the Library of Congress web site Inventing Entertainment: The Early Motion Pictures and Sound Recordings of the Edison Companies (http://lcweb2.loc.gov/ammem/edhtml/edmrrg.html)*

Figure I.1 Frames from the Edison Company's *Dickson Experimental Sound Film*.

In fact, even before the use of technology for synchronizing talking and sound effects with a motion picture became widespread, music guided the emotional shape of a film. Recall the organist or pianist, and later the orchestra, playing live in the theater to accompany silent motion pictures, and so enhance their emotional effect.

The requirements and aesthetics of music for film have changed little over time. What has changed, however, are the tools we use to meet those requirements and create those aesthetic effects; and as the tools have evolved so have the challenges of using them. This book explores the traditional and current elements of music editing with the hope of serving all those interested in this art and professional craft.

1.2 THIS BOOK

Why read this book? You may be reading these introductory pages to find out whether the book has value for you. Or perhaps the book has been purchased as a course text. In any case, this introduction will give you an overview of music editing, its multiple facets and applications, and the challenges of creating a music soundtrack for motion picture films, television shows, webisodes, direct-to-DVD films, games, or visual content for streaming.

This book is designed to communicate the aesthetic effects and techniques necessary to place, build, and synchronize music with visuals effectively. It is important to understand that although most of the techniques and examples are based on "Hollywood"-type film productions and workflows, this in no way limits the reader in using the information. While it is the reality of postproduction work that a wide range of puzzles and problems are likely to arise—and it is impossible to examine all the potential challenges that might confront the person editing or compiling the music for a particular project—the breadth of information presented here should enable the reader to extrapolate and apply a variety of solutions in a way that suits their own situation.

1.3 WHY IS MUSIC EDITING IMPORTANT?

Before I discuss the techniques of music editing, it is important to consider music and its psychological effects, specifically those pertaining to music embedded in a visual product. I do not claim to be an expert in the field of psychology and music, but there are a multitude of articles and theses on the subject. The box that follows contains an extract by Stuart Fischoff that I feel captures the relationship between music and the story-embodied emotion communicated by motion pictures. When music is paired with or married to visuals, it takes on a new and often more complex life. This is the magic and mystery of music and films, and a major consideration for music editors, composers, and songwriters.

> *I feel that music on the screen can seek out and intensify the inner thoughts of the characters. It can invest a scene with terror, grandeur, gaiety, or misery. It can propel narrative swiftly forward, or slow it down. It often lifts mere dialogue into the realm of poetry. Finally, it is the communicating link between the screen and the audience, reaching out and enveloping all into one single experience.*
>
> **Film composer Bernard Herrmann**

Films are generally fantasies. And by definition fantasies defy logic and reality. They conspire with the imagination. Music works upon the unconscious mind. Consequently, music works well with film because it is an ally of illusion. Music plays upon our emotions. It is generally a non-intellectual communication. The listener does not need to know what the music means, only how it makes him feel. Listeners, then, find the musical experience in film one that is less knowing and more feeling. The onscreen action, of course, provides clues and cues as to how the accompanying music does or is supposed to make us feel.

Let us distinguish between scoring a movie, a movie *score*, and writing songs for a movie, a movie *soundtrack*. Many of us know about a soundtrack, and can sing songs from movies. But, few of us are even aware of the score of a film unless someone produces a breakaway or break-out hit, like Celine Dion's singing "My Heart Will Go On," from *Titanic* (1997). Some films combine the two. *Platoon* (1986) has both scoring and a soundtrack, as does *The Big Chill* (1983), where hit songs of the era are included in the film to establish time, place, and psychological mood.

Since the 1930s, most orchestrations for movies are composed directly for the screen and, as we'll see, cannot easily exist independent of the movie without much fleshing out. This is in contrast to a film using in its score the hit songs of an era, songs which existed independently, before the movie, and will exist independently after the movie is long gone[,] even though [they] might be singularly associated with the film henceforth. Think of Roy Orbison's classic hit, "Pretty Woman," from the film *Pretty Woman* (1990). Or all the films with songs by Dean Martin, such as *Moonstruck* (1987), [where they are used] to establish both time and, often, place, such as Las Vegas or New York's Little Italy.

How would we like movies without music or soundtracks? Would we miss them? In the 50s a movement toward realism led some directors to exclude music scores from their films because, they contended, in life there is no music which accompanies our day and punctuates the ebbs and flows of our dialogue with the world.

This rebellious movement didn't last long. No music is a problem when the film is flat, or worse, dead. When a director needs [a] music score to fill in and enliven a dead script, we may be painfully aware of music being used inappropriately, compensatively.

This no-music, cinematic "purism" resurfaced more recently with the European-inspired *Dogma* style of filmmaking, which also excludes all music scoring. The only music allowed is *source* music, i.e., music, say, from an on-screen radio, that's part of the ambience of the scene. A recent French film, *Va Savoir* (2001), is entirely without music. So is the Danish film, *The Celebration* (2002). Every once in a while you can have a film with *sound effects* but no music (*Grapes of Wrath* [1940], *A Tree Grows in Brooklyn* [1945], *Diabolique* [1955] and, most recently, *The Blair Witch Project* [1999]); but it's rare.

For the most part, this move to remove music from films because music is unnatural, is frowned upon, naturally, by film composers (and directors). Films need music, they insist. Even silent movies had (live) musical accompaniment. Because of the "work" a musical score does in augmenting a film's aural effects on the visual–emotional experience, eliminating a musical score or musical commentary accompanying onscreen activity would be hazardous to a movie's impact and, likely, audience engagement and enjoyment.

Further, the argument goes, music is the simplest and most direct way of making a statement, even though it is often registered subconsciously, since a viewer, paying attention to events taking place on screen, hears but ordinarily does not (consciously) listen to the accompanying score. The interplay between the visual and the aural or auditory experience can be fascinating indeed.

To comprehend fully what music does for films, one should see a picture before and after it [is] scored, first in *rough cut* and then in *final cut*. Not only are dramatic effects heightened by the addition of music and, frequently, sound effects, but in many instances the faces, voices, and even the personalities of the players are experientially altered. Music adds something we might call *heightened realism* or *supra-reality*. It is a form of theatrical, filmic reality, different from our normal reality. That, of course, may be the point entirely. Because films are two-dimensional, extra-ordinary experiences, they may need help, as it were, from music. After all, in real life when you're scared you don't need scary music to tell you. Absent repressions your body, your nervous system, your cognitions, tell you that. So, perhaps heightened realism merely levels the playing field[,] enabling films to draw us in and, as the saying goes, suspend disbelief.

Indeed, according to film composer Miklos Rozsa (who composed the scores for biblical epics like *King of Kings* [1961], *Sodom and Gomorrah* [1963], and *Ben Hur* [1959], but also more contemporary films like Steve Martin's *Dead Men Don't Wear Plaid* [1982]), the role of musical background is clear; the music serves the drama and creates in the subconscious an idealistic and sometimes irrational dimension against which the naturalistic components play. One could compare the music's function with the role of a Greek chorus, painting the drama and underlining and psychologically enhancing the action.

Finally, on the subject, according to film composer Lawrence Rosenthal,

Film, unlike theater, is essentially a visual–aural rather than verbal–intellectual medium. Even though film and the stage play obviously share certain properties, such as dramatic action, dialogue, and character, the basic nature of the film is quite different.

One of the chief differences is that in a film, sound becomes a highly expressive sensory element, whether it be music, sound effect, or speech. Total silence is an unnatural vacuum in a film. The ear seems to insist on filling it—whether with a few harp notes, the rustle of clothing, or a human voice. Of course, a great express train could race by on the screen, accompanied by perfect silence or with its natural sound replaced by that of a plaintive woodwind, and that might be enormously effective, but the point is that SOME SOUND—or silence in relation to preceding and subsequent sounds—seems essential. In principle, dialogue plays a lesser role in the aural complex of a film than it does on the stage, where, of course, it enjoys complete supremacy. Hence, the correspondingly greater importance of music and sound in motion pictures.

To summarize the major functions of film music:

1. Provides a sense of narrative continuity
2. Reinforces formal and narrative unity
3. Communicates elements of the setting
4. Underlines the psychological states of characters
5. Establishes an overall emotional tone or mood or a film or scene
6. Can be an identification of or signature of a character

Stuart Fischoff, PhD

From "The Evolution of Music in Film and Its Psychological Impact on Audiences," a reading for Stuart Fischoff and Alan Bloom's course on the psychological impact of film at California State University, Los Angeles (http://web.calstatela.edu/ faculty/abloom/tvf454/5filmmusic.pdf)

The painter Wassily Kandinsky also made some interesting observations relating to music. According to him, "All the arts derive from the same and unique root. Consequently, all the arts are identical." Comparing music and painting, he said:

> It is very simple at first glance. Music expresses itself by sounds, painting by colors, etc. facts that are generally recognized. But the difference does not end here. Music, for example, organizes its means (sounds) within time, and painting its means (colors) upon a plane. Time and plane must be exactly "measured" and sound and color must be exactly "limited." These "limits" are the preconditions of "balance" and hence of composition.
>
> *Quoted in S.D. Yadegari (1992) "Self-Similar Synthesis: On the Border Between Sound and Music" (http://yadegari.org/MasterThesis)*

I.4 CONTEMPORARY POSTPRODUCTION

"Postproduction" can be defined as the stages that take place after the shooting or filming of a film has been completed. These can include video editing, special effects, sound design, ADR (automated dialogue replacement), Foley, color correction, music, and countless other elements of visuals and sound; basically, postproduction is anything that happens after the film has been shot which is needed to complete it. This book discusses specifically the music-related aspects of postproduction. Readers are encouraged to familiarize themselves with postproduction practices in general, including the related terminology. It is not possible to cover all the necessary topics here; the amount of information would certainly overwhelm and detract from the main focus of the book, which is music.

The web sites listed here provide a range of information resources for postproduction, both for audio and video:

- http://www.filmsound.org
- https://www.editorsguild.com
- http://www.pro-mpeg.org
- http://encyclopedia.thefreedictionary.com
- http://en.wikipedia.org/wiki/Post-production
- http://www.digitalrebellion.com/glossary.htm
- http://joyoffilmediting.com
- http://www.indiedcp.com/broadcast-industry-terminology.html

I.5 PREREQUISITES

A short list of topics in postproduction appears below; though some are covered in the book, I also assume readers are familiar with many of these. Readers should be aware of and prepared to learn about all of these areas:

- The various film and video speeds
- Technical specs for audio:

- Sample rates
- Bit rates
- Audio file formats
- Pull down and pull up
- Technical specs for film and video:
  - Video codecs
  - Commonly used frame rates
  - Traditional 35 mm film specs
- OMF (Open Media Framework) and AFF (Advanced Authoring Format)—for transferring sequence or timeline information, including video files, audio files and sound mixing data, from one application to another
- Basic audio mixing formats and layouts
- Basic re-recording techniques
- Basic editing techniques
- Basic musical terms and workflows for composition
- The techniques and aesthetics of composing music for film
- Moderate- to expert-level Pro Tools operations

For readers using the Avid Pro Tools audio coursework as a guide, the following courses are important: 101, 110, 201, 210P, and 201M. Also useful are 310P and 310M. All these Avid audio courses are designed to enhance the inner workings of Pro Tools and can greatly help the user in postproduction and music. You can find trainers and training centres all over the world (see http://www.avid.com/US/support/training/curriculum).

I.6 CARRY ON

As we continue our work in postproduction audio, we can learn from the past, avoid the pitfalls, enjoy the elation of successfully marrying sound and picture, and avoid the ever changing technological and political minefields.

> Sound is 50 percent of the moviegoing experience, and I've always believed audiences are moved and excited by what they hear in my movies at least as much as by what they see.
>
> *George Lucas*

Chapter 1
Postproduction

1.1 WHAT'S WHAT

Most audio-visual entertainment projects including films, television shows, online sit-coms, or computer games, have many facets to their production and there are many steps needed to ensure their success.

Production is generally divided into three parts:

- **Part one: preproduction** This is when a script is written, visual design concepts are formulated, and the project is "green lit," meaning it has the go-ahead to proceed to the next stage. At preproduction there should also be financial backing, at least enough to proceed to and complete the next production stage. Many people in the industry feel that preproduction often needs careful attention and this is where some low-budget projects falter, as startup money is difficult to find.
- **Part two: production** The actual "working" stage of the project, as it would be recognized by most people outside the industry: actors are cast, for example, and shooting takes place.
- **Part three: postproduction** As the name indicates, this stage comprises the processes followed "after" production.

The descriptions given here are necessarily very brief, and I encourage students to familiarize themselves with these production stages using the many books and Internet resources available, particularly those relating to postproduction.

1.2 THE NUTS AND BOLTS OF POSTPRODUCTION

Postproduction tasks include the following (listed in no particular order):

- Video or film editing
- Sound effects editing
- Sound design FX audio
- Dialogue editing
- Music editing
- Composing
- Composer's music demo or mock-up presentation

- Score recording
- Music mixing
- Visual effects or special effects editing
- ADR (automatic dialogue replacement, sometimes referred to as additional dialogue recording) and voiceover recording and editing
- Foley recording and editing
- Color correction
- Telecine (film only) or digital transfers
- Re-recording mixing (final dub)
- Print master and film out

The elements most pertinent to the music editor are video or film editing, sound editing, composing, score recording, music mixing, and the final dub. This book will cover in depth how the music editor's work interfaces with and relates to each of these topics. The remainder of this chapter gives an overview of each.

1.3 VIDEO OR FILM EDITING

The music editor interfaces with the film editor at many points during a project. If there is a "temp" (temporary) score edited by the music editor, then there are significant technical and creative interactions with the film editor. As the film editing progresses, the music editor has to keep up with revisions to the "cut" and edited versions of the cut, making music changes as the film changes. This is called "conforming." The film editor or their assistant will continually update the sound departments, including the music editor, with changes in the film, which are known as "turnovers."

Consideration needs to be given to the technical workflow between the film editing systems and Pro Tools or DAW (Digital Audio Workstation) music systems, including maintaining and matching the film frame rate, or speed. This is achieved digitally via the sample rate, the file type, and importing and exporting using various exchanging protocols, such as AAF (Advanced Authoring Format).

The working relationship with the film editor is key. He or she will act as a conduit for valuable information and communication involving the director, music supervisor, postproduction supervisors, and other pertinent executives. The film editor will often see the project through the final dub, as well as color corrections and final delivery.

1.4 SOUND EDITING

Sound editorial is one of the critical partners working with music and dialogue editorial; together, these three departments will produce the three main elements of the film's final soundtrack. Sound effects are often described as being musical in nature because of their ability to evoke emotions, such as fear or surprise, in much the same way as music. Taking this one step further, sound design can provide a sonic environment that is demonstrated by "hard" or real "background" effects. Consider the imaginary sound of *Star Trek's Enterprise* jumping to warp speed. Just as visual special effects editors have through their work become a creative force in the industry, so sound design experts have been developing their craft. Many sound effects editors and mixers are musicians, and have similar creative influences.

In a film mix, the most important element, the one which must stand out most clearly, is the dialogue; the music and sound effects must therefore be balanced with the dialogue track. However, music can be of primary importance—for example during a montage—and may occur either with or without sound effects. A successful soundtrack is therefore a matter of achieving an often delicate balance between music, sound effects, and dialogue; as noted elsewhere, it is critical for the sound effects department and the music department to work together successfully. At present I am working on a film project for which the sound designer is sharing sound effects as they are created, and the composer is in turn sharing music demos with the sound effects editors. This is an ideal method of collaboration between sound and music, but it is a rare luxury to have the time and opportunity to work in this way.

1.5 COMPOSERS AND SCORING

As a primary member of the composer's team, the music editor has multiple responsibilities, including technical and communications tasks, creative support, and acting as bridge communicator with relevant parties, such as the director, film editor, music supervisor, and re-recording mixer. The music editor also works with the score to make sure it is tracked correctly and presented properly for the re-recording mixer. Finally, he or she can make any necessary editorial changes at the final mix or dub.

1.6 THE MUSIC MIX

The music for a project may be recorded live, with musicians, then mixed specifically to the picture. Alternatively the score could be recorded and mixed simultaneously. In either case, the music editor can advise the mixer in relation to the musical balance to be struck, on creating "stems" and which musical elements might benefit from being on their own track (ways of recording similar instruments as single tracks or multitrack stems, to allow for easier mixing and editing), and on keeping track of cues. (Stems are audio tracks containing either a combination of musical instruments or sounds of isolated separate instrument[s] into one audio track or output path. For example, a woodwind section of an orchestra, including flutes, clarinets, and oboes might be recorded or mixed into one stem that would be titled 'wood winds', rather than a separate track for each. Although a single stem may also be an important solo instrument that perhaps plays a key melody. Stems are useful both for the music editor for easier editing as well as the re-recording mixer to manage the music for a dub.) Alternatively, and particularly for low-budget projects, a score may be produced, mixed, and mastered completely on computer; this is known as mixing "in-the-box." While this precludes recording with a large group of musicians, many of the music editor's responsibilities remain the same.

In relation to the music mix, the music editor will also manage any technical "sync" issues and delivery requirements for the re-recording mixer.

1.7 THE FINAL DUB

At the final film mix or dub, the music editor presents the music stems to the re-recording mixer, and makes sure that the music is played correctly, from a technical standpoint, and balanced in a way that respects the composer's creative ideas.

This final stage of the postproduction process can present the music editor with some challenging situations; even with the best of intentions and much preparation, many things can put you to work. For example:

- The director wants to change one or more music cues, either completely or by editing and manipulating various stems.
- The songs are changed at the last minute and need to be recut.
- The studio producers have questions and concerns regarding the music or certain music cues.
- The film has been recut and the music needs conforming to the new cut.
- The music tracks need to be converted, reordered, or relabeled for the re-recording mixer.
- The music delivery from the composer is lagging behind; this is sometimes referred to as "chasing the mix."
- During the mix at the dub, new music cues need to be checked and placed.

This is not, of course, an exhaustive list; the challenges are different for every project.

1.8 INDUSTRY INSIDER: CHRISTOPHER KULIKOWSKI, POSTPRODUCTION SUPERVISOR

1. **How would you describe your role as it relates to the overall success of a film or television show? What are some of the key skill sets your job requires?**

   Back during the days of the studio system the associate producer was responsible for most if not all facets of the filmmaking process at the time of production wrap. In addition, he or she was often involved with managing and interfacing between the production crew and the film lab during the dailies process. I have always regarded post-production supervisors as post producers … that is what we do and that is what we are. Those of us working in the field oversee editorial, sound, the lab, VFX, and music crews, to name a few. We manage budgets, vendor bids, schedules, problem solving, and creative egos. In terms of my own personal skill set, it stems from years of experience making films as a kid, attending university as a film student, and working under Douglas Trumbull's post supervisor, Jack Hinkel, whom I owe a great deal.

2. **What are some of the similarities and differences between working on low-budget and high-budget films? And between a supervisor working in a staff position in a film company and an independent post supervisor?**

   From my own experience the difference between working on a lower-budgeted film or higher-budgeted film is simply a matter of time, money, and workload. I find that lower-budgeted films are far more stressful and challenging; one has to wear more hats and complete everything with lesser resources and time. On the flip side, the smaller projects tend to build tighter relationships between the post super and the producers and director. I have found that I am much more creatively involved with the overall storytelling and finishing process and that alone can make it more enjoyable and rewarding.

As for working in a staff position with a larger company, one has the luxury of having to deal with far less minutia … if, of course, the supervisor allows that to happen. The downside is often the responsibility in managing more people, strict schedules, and larger budget expenditures.

3. **How do you see the music editor's role, as it pertains to the overall involvement of music production? Particularly in terms of how it relates to your job, with regard to their technical, musical or interpersonal skills, or any other qualities?**

Mmm … from my standpoint the music editor's role is far more creative than that of most post supers. I mean, they are editing and shaping music on a daily basis. Television music editors really seem to have all the fun (well, maybe). One can look at the work done on such shows as the original 1960s *Star Trek* to see how music editors shaped and spliced cues together so brilliantly.

Most of the time my involvement with the music editor starts at the beginning of the editorial process—making sure that they have everything they need to execute their work (equipment, schedules, a pat on the back, etc.)—and at the end of the mix, [when] a music editor will hand over [the] final music cue sheet and score elements such as compact discs or music score files, which are all part of the final delivery.

With any position or job there's always the need for specific technical and interpersonal skills. The thing that post supers and music editors have in common is that we work with the same people—director, producers, music supers, mixer—and are part of the same family.

4. **How do you envision your role in postproduction evolving in future, particularly in terms of budgets and expectations?**

In all honesty, I see the demands on post supervisors growing much more in the future. With technology ever evolving, expectations are much higher and, as is often the case, post budgets and *time* are much tighter. My personal feeling on all of this is simply this … there are far fewer producer-filmmaker types left in this world, people who really understand what it takes to finish a film. The business is run by fewer artists and more bottom-line types. The post supers are the field generals, the "Pattons" that get dirty and bruised while keeping the parts moving along and under control … well … most of the time.

5. **Is there a situation in the postproduction industry where it's appropriate or even advantageous for the composer to mix and produce his or her own music, perhaps without the help of a music mixer, orchestrator, programmer, music editor, or other team members?**

Yes, absolutely there are times when a composer can take it all on, so to speak. It's simply a matter of time, talent, and keeping an open mind. I've had the good fortune of working with a handful of composers who are extremely hands-on with their work from beginning to end. This issue is no different than a director who also takes on the role of producer and editor. What can be lost is perspective, and again keeping an open mind to change. Artists often get locked in with their work.

6. **From your experience of working with many music editors, what are the skill sets that are crucial for their success in this industry?**

Well, taking creative direction is certainly a crucial factor and being able to execute those requests seamlessly and beautifully is a talent. The other key to a music editor's success is simply the relationship he or she has with director, producer, and music supervisor. The "frequencies" between people have to work—it's that simple. This applies to everyone in this business and many other businesses.

7. **Is there a story or two relating to your working relationships with composers, producers, music editors, or directors, whether about positive or difficult situations, which you can share as something we might learn from?**

I have to say that over the years I've worked with some amazing directors, producers, editors … all types of people and situations. I've experienced the joys and rewards of working in the film business as well as some of the darkest moments of my professional life. Some of my fondest experiences stem all the way back to my high-school years when I met a young composer by the name of Stephen Melillo. At that time I was a saxophone player in a completion (marching) band in which Stephen wrote original music, much of which was extremely filmic. As it turned out, Stephen was a heart-and-soul film composer. Since that time we've successfully collaborated on three projects together, with hopefully more to come.

Back to the question at hand, I could spend days reflecting and writing all that I've experienced while working in "Hollywood" but if I could give some advice I would simply say: absorb as much as you can, watch everything and everyone, be patient and learn and take in every facet of postproduction. It is in post that the narratives are put to the final test and are shaped, not only in terms of the picture [and] performance but also in terms of the music choices. I believe it was the composer Bernard Hermann who said that the composer can do far more than any actor, director, or editor, in that they (along with the music editor) can manipulate and guide the narrative and emotions felt by the viewer. When it all works, it's a rush—magic—and makes the ninety percent of hard work, stress, and aggravation melt under the ten percent of love and accomplishment.

1.9 INDUSTRY INSIDER: FRANK SALVINO, POSTPRODUCTION SUPERVISOR

1. **How would you describe your role as it relates to the overall success of a film or television show? What are some of the key skill sets your job requires?**

Postproduction supervising is akin to line producing. It plays a key role in keeping a film or television show on schedule and budget. The line producer starts the race and passes the baton to the postproduction supervisor, who brings it across the finish line. And like line producing, postproduction supervising requires several distinctly different skill sets, which include:

a. **Accounting** Staff postproduction supervisors usually generate the post budget. Freelance postproduction supervisors, on the other hand, often inherit a budget that they had no hand in creating. Then during postproduction and sometimes even during production the PPS writes all the POs (purchase orders), tracks all the costs, approves and submits timecards, analyses and approves all the invoices, and regularly meets with the postproduction accountant to review and make changes, if necessary, to the cost report. In the event a potential overage might be looming, as is often the case during reshoots or additional photography or if the post schedule gets extended or compressed, it's the PPS who calculates the costs and submits an overage memo to the producers and studio for approval. The PPS also keeps track of all the equipment and assets on the film.

b. **Project management/scheduling** The PPS creates the postproduction schedule (which needs to match the budget and cost report) and keeps the crew and studio apprised of all the key dates and potential changes and deadlines. In accordance with the schedule the PPS books the ADR stages, actors, re-recording stages, and crew for the temp dubs, pre dubs, and final mix; coordinates with all the departments, including editorial, music, visual effects, titles and graphics design, laboratories, and all vendors and facilities involved in the project. And it's ultimately the PPS who inspects, approves, and provides all the final delivery elements to the studio(s) and/or distributors per the contractual delivery schedule(s).

c. **Technical proficiency** The PPS must have a solid understanding of the filmmaking process and postproduction workflow as well as all the technologies involved.

d. **Legal and contract knowledge** Much of what happens during the course of a production is driven by legal contracts. The PPS has to coordinate with the legal or business affairs department regarding matters that range from actors' salaries to signatory agreements to licensing contracts, which could include music, stock footage, artwork, and the like. The PPS notifies the business affairs department regarding certain delivery dates that trigger payments to talent and companies. And in the case of music, the PPS makes sure that an accurate music cue sheet is delivered to the studio at the completion of the film so that all residual payments can be correctly calculated.

e. **Artistic sensibility** Much like the vast majority of any crew on a production, they are there to help support the creative vision of the director. As such, it is paramount that the PPS understands the artistic intentions of the director, and within the confines of the budget and schedule does everything he or she can to help the director realize that vision.

2. **What are some of the similarities and differences between working on low-budget and high-budget films?**

   The process of post supervising a production is very similar regardless of budget. The main difference stems from the limited resources inherent in a low-budget project, requiring everyone on the production to be more efficient, disciplined, and innovative.

3. **How do you see the music editor's role, as it pertains to the overall involvement of music production? Particularly in terms of how it relates to your job, with regard to their technical, musical or interpersonal skills, or any other qualities?**

   A good music editor is invaluable to the post process and an immense help to the PPS, and an integral part of the success of a film. Most good music editors have the perfect combination of musical talent and technical proficiency. They have an almost encyclopedic knowledge of music, a high degree of technical expertise, and great interpersonal skills. They can quickly and accurately identify the musical taste of the director and filter it through their own artistic sensibilities to find and/or cut the perfect cue for a scene. A music editor, especially while creating the temp track, helps to shape the final form of the project. This can sometimes lead to "temp love," when the director keeps wanting to go back to the temp track. And from a postproduction supervisor's point of view, a music editor who also grasps the importance of deadlines and budgets is a real pleasure to work with.

4. **How do you envision your role in postproduction evolving in future, particularly in terms of budgets and expectations?**

   Technology has had a huge impact on film and television production and postproduction. As such, the primary role of the postproduction supervisor has and will continue to evolve into that of a data manager. It's the PPS's responsibility to coordinate the transfer, manipulation, and delivery of a massive amount of data that ultimately will allow the filmmakers to tell their stories. And much like the economy as a whole, film and television production has not been immune to the constant downward pressure on costs, and ultimately salaries. More and more seasoned and talented professionals are making less and less with each passing year. I hope this trend is cyclical, but with the rapidly changing landscape of film and television distribution and the uncertainty it breeds, the cycle might prove to be a prolonged one, if not a permanent one. The changes will most assuredly bring new opportunities as well. But, as always, the expectations are to make more impressive-looking and -sounding films and television shows for less money and in less time.

5. Is there a situation in the postproduction industry where it's appropriate or even advantageous for the composer to mix and produce his or her own music, perhaps without the help of a music mixer, orchestrator, programmer, music editor, or other team members?

Low-budget projects are well-suited [to this], and oftentimes require that the composer mix and produce the entire music track. Many composers started off music editing, and with the ever-improving technologies they can compose, produce, edit, and mix everything right in their studios. Economic pressures will probably make this more and more common in the future.

6. From your experience of working with many music editors, what are the skill sets that are crucial for their success in this industry?

Talent, tenacity, and passion. They need the musical talent to do their job, the tenacity to find the job, and the passion to sustain the drive to succeed. And as mentioned earlier, good music editors should be technically astute, have plenty of musical talent or knowledge, and possess the interpersonal skills to get along with a wide variety of people. Being able to work under pressure and/or long hours is also a trait that will undoubtedly be expected of them.

7. Is there a story or two relating to your working relationships with composers, producers, music editors, or directors, whether about positive or difficult situations, which you can share as something we might learn from?

As in illustration of how composers and music editors have to constantly deal with changing schedules, I remember on one film I was working with the composer Bruce Broughton. He and I were walking to the scoring stage on the Sony lot for the first day of recording and he turned to me and with a hint of astonishment in his voice said, "This is the first film that I've actually recorded the score on the date that was indicated on the first postproduction schedule I was given." It was one of those rare films that tested well at the first preview and the studio decided not to preview the film again. And as is often the case with previews, the high scores had little bearing on the success of the film at the box office. The film bombed.

Chapter 2
The Team

2.1 WHO'S WHO?

Music is perhaps the most universal of the arts—it is the most performed; it is listened to, commented on, loved, hated the world over. Reflecting this universality, all of those involved in the production of a film often become involved in one way or another with the music. In this chapter I describe a wide range of production roles and their typical influences, functions, and responsibilities in relation to the music. Keep in mind, however, that the boundaries of decision-making power regarding music can at times be gray and unclear.

2.2 THE DIRECTOR

The director is the boss and the creative impetus behind a film, with decision-making involvement spanning all aspects of production and postproduction (this is generally less the case in television, though, where the producer is often "the boss"). It is not uncommon for a film's director also to be its writer, particularly on low-budget projects; and this is also often the case for documentary films. For low-budget films, documentaries, and computer-animated films, the director's role is often synonymous with that of filmmaker.

The director or filmmaker may begin thinking about music early in the process of writing the story, considering songs or even a style of score. Songs are sometimes intrinsic to a film, with an actor or a particular artist performing a song on-camera in order to create or reinforce emotional impact or contribute to the story. The director should be very careful of tying a specific song into the story, particularly early in the scriptwriting process, since licensing it may constrain the film's budget, and it may be too expensive altogether.

The other major considerations regarding the director's involvement with the music in a film are choosing a temp score (see Chapter 4), and choosing and working with the composer (see Chapter 7).

2.3 INDUSTRY INSIDER: JON TURTELTAUB, DIRECTOR

1. **From your experience working with many music editors, how important is a music editor as a collaborative part of your creative and editorial team? Do you enjoy working with a music editor?**

   On rare occasions, the right music for a movie will be obvious from the beginning. In most cases, however, finding the right music for a film is a treasure hunt. It's this wild goose chase where we have to try everything under the sun to nail exactly what each scene needs. But much more importantly, we are trying to find the right *style* of music for a film. It's not just finding the specific cues for specific scenes that gets tricky, it's landing the right overall tone that's hardest to do. And this is where the music editor is vital. I count on music editors to have a massive inventory of cues, songs, styles, shapes, and genres, not just in their hard drive but in their head. They're there to do what I can't. The actual editing is the easy part. It's capturing the right tone that's tough.

   Working with the music editor, when things are clicking, is one of the most enjoyable parts of the entire process. When the music editor finds just the right cue and cuts it to hit just the right moments, suddenly the movie comes to life. It's the difference between believing a scene works and knowing a scene works. That's the best feeling there is for a director.

   It's also enjoyable to work with a music editor because they tend to be a lot less precious about their work. They didn't write the music, or edit the picture, so they tend to be very amenable to making changes without taking things too personally. Translation: I can boss them around without worrying about their feelings getting hurt!

2. **What technical skills and personality style do you expect a music editor to have in order to work well and in a collaborative way?**

   I find that music editors who really listen tend to be the best. The ones who really hear not just what I'm saying but what I'm *meaning* do the best work for me. They get it quicker, which means fewer changes, which means fewer discussions, which means more time for everything. And for all that to happen, a music editor has to be fast with the use of the hardware. Waiting days to hear a cue kills the creative process. Someone who is quick usually is going to make the entire creative process move better.

3. **What do you view as the value of the temp score and what contribution does it make to your projects? Do you feel it helps your communication with the composer and others? If so, can you mention any specific, unique ways in which it does this?**

   There is no way to avoid having a temp score these days. In fact, there's usually a temp score on the film before I ever see it because the editor has put one on the film by the time the assembly is finished. It always makes me laugh when people see a movie or a scene without the music on it and later, after seeing it with music, they comment on how having music really helped. Of course it helped! Did they think that there wasn't going to be music as part of the overall construction of the film? Most of the time, not having music is like not having sets. It has to be there, not as an afterthought, but as a vital creative element in the construction of a film. So if there's no music when looking at rough cuts, the movie feels "off." That's why we need temp scores. Back in the olden ancient times, there weren't that many people who watched the rough cuts so you could leave a lot to someone's imagination. Nowadays, so many people see early cuts that you have to show a much more refined product early on. And that means having a temp score.

4. **Very often the film editor and the director start building temp music tracks early in the editorial process, without a music editor. Do you feel this is a good way to work or would you prefer to have a music editor on the project at the start of editorial?**

It would be great to have a music editor there from the start … but not just for creative reasons. Most editors are usually pretty decent music editors because they know exactly where the emotional beats of a scene hit and how to punctuate them with music. The problem is, they don't have the time to spend editing music all day. There's too much picture editing to do. So it would be terrific to have someone else there to create the temp score so that the editor could focus on picture and dialogue.

2.4 THE PRODUCER

The producer can also be the boss, though this is usually the case for television rather than for feature films. The producer generally oversees the entire production budget. He or she can also be very involved in the logistics of shooting, production, and postproduction, as well as casting and choosing creative talent for the project. On low-budget productions the producer is often closely tied to the director, providing support and advice for their creative decisions. In this situation, they can certainly influence musical decisions.

2.5 THE MUSIC SUPERVISOR

Traditionally music supervisors work as independents with specific, limited responsibility for searching, choosing, and clearing or making the license deals for songs in films and television shows. This is no small task, as they have to know past and current song artists, musical genres and recordings, be able to negotiate fees and financials with the song publishers, and ensure the director is satisfied with the song choices for the project. They also need to be able to work as a creative businessperson, bringing songs to the project on or under budget. Very often their importance is underscored by the appearance of their name in the opening or main-on-end credits, alongside those of the director, producer, actors, composer, and so on, as well as on the advertising "billing block."

The role of music supervisor has developed into a very influential one, and can involve oversight of many aspects of the music for a project. A music supervisor who is on-staff in a film company or media group may have their responsibilities reach into all the aspects of the music, not limited to songs. And they are often working on many projects at one time.

2.6 THE COMPOSER

The composer writes original music specific to the creative and technical needs of the film. This kind of composition is very different from songwriting, composing for live performances, or recording outside the filmmaking world. It requires a specific set of skills, and an intuitive sensitivity to film as a medium and how it conveys emotions (see Chapter 7 for more discussion). These skills sometimes come quite naturally to a composer, and sometimes they are learned and acquired through experience. There are a number of schools that guide and teach composers in this area, including USC (University of Southern California), UCLA (University of California, Los Angeles), and Berklee College of Music, to name a few.

Some of the skills and attributes a composer needs to achieve success in the film world are:

- Understanding of filmic emotions, as evoked through storytelling, and how to use music to help convey these emotions.
- People skills, including the ability to communicate musical ideas and emotions to the director, producers, editors, and others.
- Extreme self-confidence, passion, and dedication to the musical goals of the project.
- Complete understanding of postproduction workflows, including picture editing, dialogue, sound effects, and music editing, and, most importantly, an understanding of how each of these processes interacts with the music.
- Knowledge of the technical aspects of contemporary film scoring, including computer-based music sequencing, MIDI (Musical Instrument Digital Interface), sample-based instruments, digital audio, and digital video.

2.7 THE MUSIC MIXER

The music mixer is highly skilled in all aspects of the recording arts, and specifically in working with composed music for film. They record and mix the composer's music, and combine all the musical elements into cohesive audio tracks known as "stems." Music for films requires particular treatment, both technically and aesthetically. The music tracks to be mixed into a film soundtrack must be set up specifically for the dubbing of the film and for the re-recording mixer. (The re-recording mixer is a specialist skilled in balancing the three elements of a film soundtrack—dialogue, sound effects, and music; the mix of these elements is called the "dub.")

A music mixer is likely to be concerned, among other things, with the following:

- Mixing in 5.1, 7.1 (surround sound) Unity gain; preparation for Dolby Atmos™ master tracks.
- Mixing sections of the music in various stem configurations: 5.1, 5.0, Quad, LCR, stereo, mono, and so on.
- Track limitations for the final dub of the film must be known before the dub. These are usually communicated among the music editor, re-recording mixer, and composer via email or phone.
- The mixed music needs to sound complete on its own, before being added to the film. In addition, the music needs to play well with the film, with respect to the dialogue and sound effects. The music mix is usually adjusted to improve the balance with these two primary elements of the soundtrack.
- Melodies and percussion elements can if necessary be made more effective, with respect to the music's role in the overall effect of the soundtrack, by raising and/or lowering their volume in the mix, or moving or deleting isolated parts. It is important to take this overall effect into account, and to make the necessary changes, before the music is delivered to the dubbing stage.

- In the end, the music mixer should make the music sound just as the composer conceived it and deliver the tracks at unity gain, or "0 VU," to the music editor.

This list of concerns is certainly relevant to many composed film scores for high- or medium-budget projects. Low-budget films often cannot afford a mixer, though, nor sometimes a music editor, and the composer may be required both to mix the music and to deliver it to the dub stage. If this is the case, many of the concerns remain the same, however, and should be taken into account.

2.8 INDUSTRY INSIDER: BOBBY FERNANDEZ, MUSIC MIXER

1. **How would you describe your role as it relates to the overall success of a film or television show? What are some of the key skill sets your job requires?**

    We all like to think that what we do relates to the overall success of the film we're working on, and in a way it does. A good score and a great music mix contribute to the overall sound and elevate a film.

    Skill sets As a film-scoring engineer the skill sets range across:
    - Knowing and understanding the recording process, knowing how to record live musicians.
    - Having a knowledge of microphones—how they work, which ones to use and when to use them.
    - Acoustics—walking onto a scoring stage and being able to get the best sound possible out of the room.
    - Mixing a score for a film, which is very different than for mixing a music CD. This requires knowing how music works in a film and understanding that "dialog is king."
    - Knowing how a score should be delivered to the dub stage.
    - The ability to record, mix, and edit in Pro Tools (which has become the de-facto "standard" for mixing) and other music production programs.
    - Above all to respect and work with others as a team.

2. **What are some of the similarities and differences between working on low-budget and high-budget films?**

    Most low-budget films nowadays are packages. The composer is given a budget, which includes his or her fee. The scoring mixer's fee is usually paid out of the composer's package, which is a set fee for all work done on the film. So, working as quickly and efficiently as possible is essential. (This is where communication between the mixer and music editor is very important. Keeping the mixer informed of all changes saves having to go back and remix a cue and speeds up the mix process.) Normally the scoring mixer's fee would be paid by the production company and would include overtime and union benefits. Some low-budget studio films do include overtime and union benefits, but overtime is really kept to a minimum. The music editor's fee is usually paid by the production company.

    On a low-budget film you don't have the luxury of time that you would have on a big budget. Having said that I'll point out that this is a gray area, in that big-budget films sometimes don't have time as well, due to a compressed schedule.

    The schedule: this is the one big similarity. "Chasing the stage" has become a common saying these days. Dubbing schedules and picture release dates are sometimes so tight that we are literally mixing around the clock to keep up with the dub stage. This means we're mixing in the order the dub stage is dubbing. If they start on reel 3, that's where we start. Cues are sent off to the stage as fast as they're mixed. The difference here is that with a big-budget film overtime costs are covered. On most low-budget films that I've worked on there is no budget for overtime.

I find myself wearing more than one hat on low-budget projects. By that I mean I'm doing things I would not normally do on a large-budget film. For example on a big budget you would have a music editor, an assistant music editor, Pro Tools operator, and a mixer. So the scoring mixer's job would be to just concentrate on mixing the score. Low-budget films usually don't have the budget for an assistant music editor or Pro Tools operator, just a music editor and scoring mixer. The music editor is on the dubbing stage overseeing the music dub. This leaves the mixer to edit, mix the score, and prepare the dubbing reels for the dub stage (wearing more than one hat).

3. **How do you see the music editor's role, as it pertains to the overall involvement of music production? Particularly in terms of how it relates to your job, with regard to their technical, musical or interpersonal skills, or any other qualities?**

Involvement The music editor's involvement in the production starts early in the process, before a note of music is ever written. He or she works closely with the composer and director in the "spotting" of the music for the film. (This is where the director points out to the composer where he or she wants music to start and end, and the type of score he or she wants for the film.) [The music editor's] timing notes are what the composer goes by when writing a cue for a scene.

He or she also keeps track of all picture and timing changes and keeps the composer up to date on any changes the director has made. Nothing is more frustrating for the composer than to be on the podium recording a cue only to find out the picture has been edited and the music no longer matches the scene.

The music editor is also the scoring mixer's ears on the dub stage. He or she communicates any changes being made and any requests the dub stage may have, related to the mix or mix delivery.

Technical and musical skills These two go hand in hand. A music editor's knowledge of the programs the composer uses is absolutely necessary (i.e. Digital Performer, Logic, etc.). This is where the skills of the music mixer and music editor come together. A good example would be: If there were changes in a cue that could be addressed by editing, the music editor could make the changes on the dub stage. This saves a remix or, in the worst-case scenario, a rescore.

4. **How do you envision your role in postproduction evolving in future, particularly in terms of budgets and expectations?**

With the job distinction line between the music editor and scoring mixer pretty much disappearing. I see mixers doing much more than just mixing the score and editors doing much more than just editing. As I mentioned for the difference between big-budget and low-budget films, from a budget standpoint this may benefit the producers, but puts more of a workload on the editor/mixer. More work for less money.

5. **Is there a situation in the postproduction industry where it's appropriate or even advantageous for the composer to mix and produce his or her own music, perhaps without the help of a music mixer, orchestrator, programmer, music editor, or other team members?**

Yes, if it's a package budget and a small, simple score that does not require multiple "stems." No one knows the music better than the composer. If he has the time and expertise to create a multi-stem surround film mix, yes, do it.

6. **From your experience of working with many music editors, what are the skill sets that are crucial for their success in this industry?**

Communication, the ability to work in a team, and knowledge of music and programs used in the process of film scoring and music production.

2.9 THE RE-RECORDING MIXER

The final mixing of the film soundtrack, including combining and balancing the dialogue, sound effects, and music, is the responsibility of the re-recording mixer. Whether the film is a high-budget Hollywood-type production or a small, fifteen-minute student film, there needs to be a re-recording mixer. The techniques a mixer will acquire over many years of experience are too many to describe here, and a bit off-topic as far as the role of the music editor goes, but the music editor is intrinsically involved in the delivery of the music to the re-recording mixer for the final dub and there is much collaboration between the two. They share opinions regarding the edits, mix levels, and any technical issues of concern.

To give a little bit of history, in the not-too-distant past there would have been three re-recording mixers working on a film. You guessed it: one for dialogue, one for sound effects, and one for music. This is the ideal set-up for teamworking. Because of financial considerations, though, it is now usual for studios to budget for only two mixers: one for effects, and one for both dialogue and music. I have also been involved in low-budget projects that have one mixer for everything, and one mixer is also becoming more common for temp mixes. On very low-budget and independent productions, the re-recording mixer is often asked to edit all of the sound for the film as well. The considerations and techniques for dialogue, sound effects, and music, however, are the same, regardless of the budget. The question becomes: What level of sound quality does the filmmaker expect, and what can he or she afford? There is often a conflict between expectation and affordability. Many of us will have heard the famous industry saying: "You can have your project delivered fast, cheap, or good … but you can only pick two." Whichever two options you pick will exclude the third.

2.10 THE PICTURE EDITOR

While it may not sound like the picture (or film) editor is part of the music team, their role has evolved over many years to become an important element in the musical direction of a film. The picture editor's influence extends to placing temp music, introducing songs, and recommending potential composers. Many discussions in this book concern the collaboration required between the picture and music editors to realize the technical and aesthetic aims of a film. For low-budget and independent films, the picture editor will often be wearing many other hats—director, writer, producer, and so on.

2.11 INDUSTRY INSIDER: PATRICK J. DON VITO, FILM EDITOR

1. **How would you describe your role as it relates to the overall success of a film or television show? What are some of the key skill sets your job requires?**

    I would say that my role is to try to make the director's vision come to life. When there are story problems I have to make changes that best serve the story. The start is the script, but once you receive the shot footage, you frequently have to rethink the story.

I know that many people say that editing is rewriting and that is true. You have to reimagine the story that the script is telling and make it work as best as possible with the footage that you have. You have to figure out what scenes or parts of scenes are non-essential to the story. As far as skill sets, besides having a strong story sense, you need to have good people skills to be able to navigate well between director, producers, and studio. Strong troubleshooting skills are necessary as well.

2. **What are some of the similarities and differences between working on low-budget and high-budget films?**

As far as the job goes there is really no difference between budget levels. You still have to perform all the same work that you normally do. The only difference may be that you have to figure out inexpensive ways to do things that you normally do. Visual effects have to be done cheaper and with a lower budget, and music suffers as well. It can be difficult to get songs at a budget if your film requires it. A good music supervisor can help with this.

3. **How do you see the music editor's role, as it pertains to the overall involvement of music production? Particularly in terms of how it relates to your job, with regard to their technical, musical or interpersonal skills, or any other qualities?**

Having a good music editor is a crucial key to a smooth postproduction experience. Having a music editor with a large knowledge of film soundtracks is very helpful for temping a movie. I have worked with music editors that have been able to successfully temp a movie in a short amount of time. Part of this is the knowledge of score and the ability to communicate well with the director and editor and understand the tone they want to create. This can be especially helpful with directors that have a hard time putting their feelings into words musically.

4. **How do you envision your role in postproduction evolving in future, particularly in terms of budgets and expectations?**

Budgets seem to be going down and down while expectations rise and rise. Producers expect picture editorial to cover a lot of different ground—picture editing, music editing, visual effects temps—all with a stripped down crew that usually consists of just an editor and one assistant. This can put more pressure on editorial. I only see this getting worse and worse. Now, on some films, we have to work as the "lab" as well, having to convert all the raw footage ourselves and sync clips in the Avid. Having a good music editor can take some of this pressure off of picture editorial; that is, if the producers are willing to hire a music editor early enough to give him or her time to help shape the movie with music.

5. **Can you briefly discuss the workflow between the film editor and music editor? Perhaps include some dos and don'ts, and what to watch out for?**

I like to give the music editor lots of room to experiment with music, in order to help tell the story. Being a musician myself, music is very important to me. I like to give the music editor good temp music to fall back on if needed and to help guide them. Some films are more difficult to temp than others, so that sometimes doesn't happen. Or sometimes the schedule is so short that I don't have a lot of time to pull temp music.

6. **From your experience of working with many music editors, what are the skill sets that are crucial for their success in this industry?**

A wide knowledge of film score is crucial. The ability to look at a scene and immediately have an idea of what scores they would go to in order to temp the film is so important. Also being able to read the director and editor. Sometimes people have a hard time communicating what they want, or just don't know. Having the ability to not take too many things personally is important as well. Some people can be curt or impatient, and being able to ignore that and keep pushing through is helpful. This goes for picture editors as well.

7. **What are some of the technical issues that you as an editor come across with regard to music? Has a music editor helped resolve any of these?**

Sometimes it is hard to find enough time as a picture editor to make good music cuts all the time. It is helpful to have someone who works with music all the time take over and solve those issues. Also, some movies have a character sing live in a scene and when you cut it all together they have slightly different pitches, and having someone tweak and fix that is helpful. On some films I have had music editors give me frame-cutting suggestions to put correct musical rhythms and counts back in the picture, to help keep a live singing scene in the correct time signature.

8. **Do you have any insights into how someone who feels they have a knack for music editing might break into the business? Of course the question of whether there will be a need for music editors in the future also needs to be asked.**

I think someone who wants to get into music editing should talk to music editors. If possible assist them and get to know more people in the business. Hard work is always rewarded. It can be tough, but those people who persevere are the ones who succeed in getting continuous employment. If getting in the union is an issue, try to seek out non-union work or even web-based productions.

9. **Can you comment on the film editor being asked to temp the music as they are cutting the film. Do you see this as a positive industry standard workflow or perhaps a distraction from the film editorial process, better left to the music editor?**

I love music and don't mind cutting in temp music. Although on some films it is hard to find the time. I am always thinking of music. In fact, sometimes I will find a piece of music to play while I am cutting a scene to give myself inspiration while working. Even if the piece of music isn't perfect it can help give you a rhythm for a scene.

10. **Is there a story or two relating to your working relationships with composers, producers, music editors, or directors, whether about positive or difficult situations, which you can share as something we might learn from?**

I have worked with a composer who was working with a director for the first time and created a great working environment. When the director would express concerns about a certain piece of score, he would listen and really address his concerns and come back quickly with modifications. On the other side I have worked with composers who don't take criticism very well and make the finishing of a film very contentious and difficult. I think that you have to use a bit of psychology in order to get along with the very creative people in this business. On a difficult film, it sometimes helps to remember that you are serving the story as much as you are serving the director, producers, and editor.

2.12 THE ASSISTANT FILM EDITOR

An assistant film editor may be hired for a low-, medium- or high-budget film. This person is worth their weight in gold, acting as an invaluable cog in the wheel of the film-music machine. Very often the assistant employs technical information and skills that the film editor does not, or more often does not have time to deal with and implement. The assistant is the technical bridge between the dialogue, sound effects, and music departments. They deliver turnover and change notes for conforming to all three of these departments (see Chapter 9). In addition, they receive file transfers and various workflows from the film editor.

2.13 THE ORCHESTRATOR

Although working for the composer, the orchestrator is key to making the composed score work for the film soundtrack. Many orchestrators are composers in their own right. And on low-budget films the composer often orchestrates the music themselves.

An orchestrator takes the composer's musical ideas and sketches, often in the form of MIDI data, expands them, and assigns instruments to the melodies, harmonies, and percussive elements of the score. A skilled film-score orchestrator can elevate the music and its impact in the film through their manipulation of the instrumentation and the balance of the music. There is also an invaluable connection between the music editor and orchestrator, in particular during music recording.

If the budget does not allow for "live" musicians to perform the music, the score may be composed and orchestrated "in the box," that is, on computer only. Some orchestrators are also skilled at reproducing and interpreting the composer's music by this method. A good orchestrator can bring a score to life in a way that would not have been possible, had they not brought their skills and sensibilities to the scoring process.

2.14 INDUSTRY INSIDER: KEVIN KASKA, ORCHESTRATOR AND COMPOSER

1. **How would you describe your role as it relates to the overall success of a film or television show?**

    George Lucas once said that sound is 50 percent of your movie. If the music and sound effects are created by amateurs, then 50 percent of your movie will suffer greatly. Music is enormously important in order to convey emotion in a film. There have been many great films throughout the decades with instantly recognizable scores. Could you imagine *Gone With the Wind*, *Lawrence of Arabia*, *The Magnificent Seven*, *Psycho*, or *Star Wars* without its musical score? The music to each one of those films has become so recognizable that it has also been parodied many times. This kind of iconic score elevates the movie to a far greater level than any director or audience can imagine. Composers who can write memorable melodies have always been welcomed in Hollywood; producers know that a score is the "perfume" that lasts after people leave the theater.

2. **What are some of the key skill sets your job requires?**

    As a composer working in film, the most important skill required to work (and continue working) in film is teamwork. A classical composer can write a concert piece in solitude and has no need to collaborate with anyone to finish his music. In film, there are several people working on all the different elements of the movie; and in the end, all these parts have to work together harmoniously. If you cannot collaborate or work with others in a positive and flexible way, you will not get very far in the film business. Oftentimes you will work with a producer or director that has a very limited knowledge of music, yet they understand its impact on the movie. They may ask you to change your music to accommodate the film, even for scenes that you believe have your "best" music. Being flexible not only applies to the composer, but to music editors, orchestrators, musicians, and everyone working on the film. Every so often someone's ego can get the better of them, but in the entertainment industry, it is best to leave that out when dealing with a team of professionals.

3. **How do you see the music editor's role, as it pertains to the overall involvement of music production? Particularly in terms of how it relates to your job, with regard to their technical, musical or interpersonal skills, or any other qualities?**

    A music editor is extremely important and a crucial member of a composer's team. The one thing I learned about the business is that it is so important to be flexible—elements of the film can change from day to day. Making a film is not an exact science. There are many opinions and uncertainties involved in the creative process, so a movie can evolve on a day-to-day basis owing to adjustments made by the director and producers. Oftentimes there are changes made in the editing room that greatly affect the scene that a composer is scoring. A music editor needs to keep track of these different "versions" and inform the composer of which version is current. Due to time constraints, a composer may not have the time to keep up with the evolving aspects, because his or her job is to focus on composing the score. Frames are omitted, scenes are cut, and new versions arrive daily. The music editor has to be up on this and generate new click tracks, cue sheets, and keep logs of source music and background score.

4. **How do you envision your role in postproduction evolving in future, particularly in terms of budgets and expectations?**

    I often hear from many people in the business that "budgets are shrinking!" This belief may have some validity, but many parts of the business are changing. Film is being replaced by video, CGI is replacing live action, and orchestras are being replaced by synthesizers. Businesses are always trying to find ways to save money, and this will continue to happen not just in film, but in many different industries. There is still a tremendous amount of work in the movie industry, so I would not be discouraged by this mentality. Expectations have more or less stayed the same, too—"Please do your best as fast as you can." Eventually a production company will have a successful film and the profits from it will be channeled to make more movies. Producers like to use the same crew of people that created the successful film, it gives them hope and faith that their "formula" can create a new hit.

5. **Is there a situation in the postproduction industry where it's appropriate or even advantageous for the composer to mix and produce his or her own music, perhaps without the help of a music mixer, orchestrator, programmer, music editor, or other team members?**

    Sound is a very complex science—possibly more complex than visuals. I have learned a set of compositional skills in order to compose my music, but if I were to mix my own music, I believe I would fail miserably at it. Mixing music (as well as mixing the overall sound of a movie) is an extremely sophisticated skill that should be left to great mixers and engineers. Composers may know when certain instruments should be louder or softer in their score, but a trained engineer is the one who knows all the ins and outs of making your music sound better. The right EQ, reverb, and balance are the icing on the cake for finishing a piece of recorded music. Obviously, it is beneficial to attend the mix and give input, but it takes decades to master this skill, so I would leave that to a great engineer.

Chapter 3
Spotting Music

3.1 INTRODUCTION: COMMUNICATION AND ORGANIZATION

Effective communication and documentation workflows are extremely important in any film, television, or media project. And although this is most obviously true for large-scale, large-budget projects, it also applies to low-budget films; all projects benefit from being well organized and documented. The postproduction meeting known as the "spotting session" is the main forum for exchanging ideas and making decisions about the music for a project. Following this meeting the music editor compiles "spotting notes," and this document then becomes central to the work of producing the music. Spotting is more than just a technical or organizational task—it also has aesthetic and creative aspects, as outlined in the excellent article by composer Charles Bernstein which appears at the end of this chapter.

3.2 THE SPOTTING SESSION

The three main sound elements of a film soundtrack are dialogue, sound effects, and music. Each of these elements has its own spotting session, at which the "spots" in the film that need attention from the different departments are identified. The spotting for dialogue usually revolves around ADR (automated dialogue replacement). For sound effects, it is often concerned with sound design and Foley. (Taking its name from Jack Foley, the Hollywood sound editor regarded as the "father" of these effects, Foley effects are sounds that are created by recording [usually] everyday movement while watching the edited picture. Different from the environmental backgrounds ["BGs"] and hard effects [FX], Foley effects are sounds like footsteps, object handling, the rustling of clothing, etc. The people involved in this process are the Foley Walkers or Artists who perform those sounds and the Foley Mixer who records them.) The music spotting session covers all musical issues.

The composition of this meeting can vary greatly, depending on where the film is in its postproduction schedule and how it is progressing. It is likely to involve the music editor, director, film editor, composer, music supervisor, producers, and others. Primarily, however, the people needed are the film editor and director (for a feature film) or the film editor and producer (for episodic television), and the music team.

At the time of the spotting session a composer may not have been hired. If this is the case there will most likely be a second session, to enable the composer and director to share and respond directly to each other's ideas and feelings about the music.

It is very important that the film be played from beginning to end, in real time, in the spotting session. Even though the editor and director will by then have seen it many times, often it will be only the first or second time for the music editor and composer, and playing the whole film is a valuable opportunity for all concerned to take a fresh look at it and listen to the music. It also allows the music editor, music supervisor, and composer to ask questions about specific musical pieces or spots. The music editor may pick up on an actor singing or humming on-camera, which needs to be included as a musical cue and perhaps investigated by the music supervisor—a moment of improvisation in the acting may actually mean a song has to be cleared or licensed. Instances of source music may need to be interrogated for the same reason. On occasion a need for an additional piece of source music may be identified, having been missed during the film editor's playback.

This is not to suggest that playback shouldn't stop for discussion; discussion is what the spotting session is for, after all. But the whole film does need to be viewed, without skipping any sections. If necessary, the session can be extended beyond the planned time to ensure everything is seen. During playback a timecode or feet and frames "window burn" (a visual overlay on the digital picture playback monitor) should also be visible to everyone in the room, as this indicates the position in the reel, and provides a means of referencing specific points in the film accurately, in particular when a piece of music should start and end.

3.3 THE SPOTTING NOTES

The spotting notes are important from both creative and technical standpoints. They provide various pieces of information for each music cue, and this information must be kept up to date and accurate throughout the project. Database software can be used for this, and one such program—output from which can be seen in the figures for this chapter—is CueChronicle, which in turn is based on FileMaker Pro software. Written by Vincent Cirilli from Los Angeles, it is not available in stores but has a small but viable market among music editors and composers. It has many features that can assist with audio postproduction, particularly in relation to organizing music editing, music composition, and scoring. Other programs such as Cue Tracker can also provide some of the basic layout and functions for music spotting notes, and you can write and format your own versions in Microsoft Excel or Word.

It is important to realize that the spotting notes can and often do change in the course of music composing, postproduction editing, and through the final dub (the film mix). They are in many ways quite fluid, and the composer, music supervisor, or director may make changes to the film that affect them. The music editor may need to make changes to the actual score to address the director's wishes even after the music is composed, in addition to conforming music to the re-edited film.

Tip

Spotting notes can be shared between the composer, music editor, orchestrators, and others as an interactive document. The Google Drive service is one possible route for this important communication. This can be quite dynamic: documents similar to those shown in the figures in this chapter, once uploaded to a server, can be changed and updated, for example with the addition of notes, color codes, and so on.

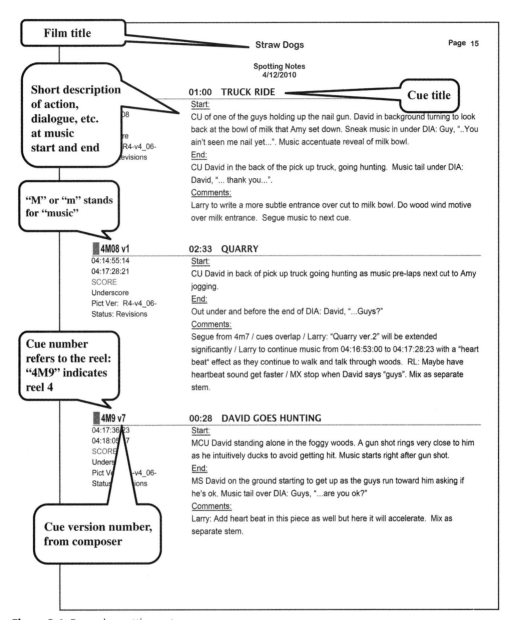

Film title

Straw Dogs

Page 15

Spotting Notes
4/12/2010

Short description of action, dialogue, etc. at music start and end

01:00   TRUCK RIDE

Cue title

Start:
CU of one of the guys holding up the nail gun. David in background turning to look back at the bowl of milk that Amy set down. Sneak music in under DIA: Guy, "..You ain't seen me nail yet...". Music accentuate reveal of milk bowl.
End:
CU David in the back of the pick up truck, going hunting. Music tail under DIA: David, "... thank you...".
Comments:
Larry to write a more subtle entrance over cut to milk bowl. Do wood wind motive over milk entrance. Segue music to next cue.

"M" or "m" stands for "music"

■ 4M08 v1
04:14:55:14
04:17:28:21
SCORE
Underscore
Pict Ver: R4-v4_06-
Status: Revisions

02:33   QUARRY

Start:
CU David in back of pick up truck going hunting as music pre-laps next cut to Amy jogging.
End:
Out under and before the end of DIA: David, "...Guys?"
Comments:
Segue from 4m7 / cues overlap / Larry: "Quarry ver.2" will be extended significantly / Larry to continue music from 04:16:53:00 to 04:17:28:23 with a "heart beat" effect as they continue to walk and talk through woods. RL: Maybe have heartbeat sound get faster / MX stop when David says "guys". Mix as separate stem.

Cue number refers to the reel: "4M9" indicates reel 4

■ 4M9 v7
04:17:36:23
04:18:05:17
SCORE
Underscore
Pict Ver: -v4_06-
Status: Revisions

00:28   DAVID GOES HUNTING

Start:
MCU David standing alone in the foggy woods. A gun shot rings very close to him as he intuitively ducks to avoid getting hit. Music starts right after gun shot.
End:
MS David on the ground starting to get up as the guys run toward him asking if he's ok. Music tail over DIA: Guys, "...are you ok?"
Comments:
Larry: Add heart beat in this piece as well but here it will accelerate. Mix as separate stem.

Cue version number, from composer

Figure 3.1 Example spotting notes.

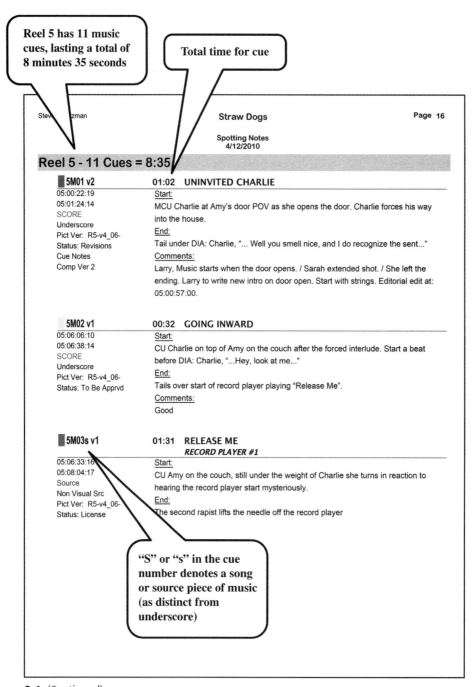

Reel 5 has 11 music cues, lasting a total of 8 minutes 35 seconds

Total time for cue

Stev___zman   Straw Dogs   Page 16

Spotting Notes
4/12/2010

Reel 5 - 11 Cues = 8:35

■ **5M01 v2**   01:02   **UNINVITED CHARLIE**

05:00:22:19   Start:
05:01:24:14   MCU Charlie at Amy's door POV as she opens the door. Charlie forces his way
SCORE   into the house.
Underscore
Pict Ver: R5-v4_06-   End:
Status: Revisions   Tail under DIA: Charlie, "... Well you smell nice, and I do recognize the sent..."
Cue Notes   Comments:
Comp Ver 2   Larry, Music starts when the door opens. / Sarah extended shot. / She left the
                                   ending. Larry to write new intro on door open. Start with strings. Editorial edit at:
                                   05:00:57:00.

■ **5M02 v1**   00:32   **GOING INWARD**

05:06:06:10   Start:
05:06:38:14   CU Charlie on top of Amy on the couch after the forced interlude. Start a beat
SCORE   before DIA: Charlie, "...Hey, look at me..."
Underscore
Pict Ver: R5-v4_06-   End:
Status: To Be Apprvd   Tails over start of record player playing "Release Me".
                                   Comments:
                                   Good

■ **5M03s v1**   01:31   **RELEASE ME**
                                           RECORD PLAYER #1

05:06:33:16   Start:
05:08:04:17   CU Amy on the couch, still under the weight of Charlie she turns in reaction to
Source   hearing the record player start mysteriously.
Non Visual Src
Pict Ver: R5-v4_06-   End:
Status: License   The second rapist lifts the needle off the record player

"S" or "s" in the cue number denotes a song or source piece of music (as distinct from underscore)

Figure 3.1 (Continued).

The remainder of this section describes the main features of spotting notes, and discusses various alternatives and potential issues.

3.3.1 The Film Title

The film title can change at any time during the post editing process, up until release. Big Hollywood projects may use an "AKA" (also known as) title for security reasons, to fend off unwanted publicity and piracy. Often this does not work, and the Hollywood news media acquires some kind of "buzz" about a film. The title of a lower budget film may change if the film is sold; the choice of title may then become the buyer's prerogative.

A title is usually changed for marketing reasons. As an example, the spotting notes in Figure 3.2 are for a film which had the working title *Dream of the Romans* throughout the scoring process; later, the company that bought the film changed this to *The Answer Man*.

3.3.2 Cues

Each piece of music or musical content in a film is listed as a separate music "cue." Whether this is a composed score piece or a song, or even a person humming a nondescript tune while walking down the street, it is labeled as a cue in the film and given its own cue number. Occasionally the spotting notes can include a reference to the scene number or range of numbers where the music is occurring. While not shown in these examples it would be labeled as simply 'SC 125' or 'SC 125–128' to denote a range of shots that make up the emotional arc of the scene. This additional information can greatly help connect the world of the picture to the world of music.

3.3.3 Cue Numbers

Cue numbers have a typical, standard structure: the number of the reel in which the particular cue occurs, followed by "M" or "m" to indicate it is a music cue, followed by a number indicating its position in the sequence of music cues. So "2m25," for example, would be the twenty-fifth cue, and in reel 2.

Cue numbers may either follow in sequence through to the end of the film, or begin again at "1" with each new reel. Using the former system, if the final cue in the film was 6m75 (for example), this would indicate that there were 75 pieces of music in the film. In the latter system, if 2m25 were the last cue in reel 2 this would indicate 25 pieces of music in this reel; the next cue—the first in reel 3—would be 3m1. The choice of which of these systems to use is up to the composer; or, if a composer has not yet been hired, to the music editor. I have used both systems while working with various composers, and each has its advantages and disadvantages. John Williams and Larry Groupé seem to prefer starting at "1" for each reel, while Teddy Castellucci and others prefer continuous numbering. I tend to use continuous numbering more often, as it can avoid confusion when there is a rebalance or a scene is moved.

It is also common to include "s" after the cue number to indicate when the cue is a song or source piece of music. So "3m14s" would indicate that 3m14 is a song, most likely a source piece, and therefore that it does not need to be composed but does need

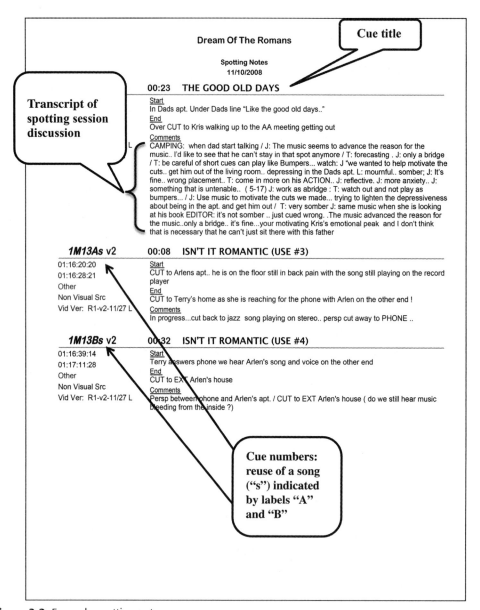

Figure 3.2 Example spotting notes.

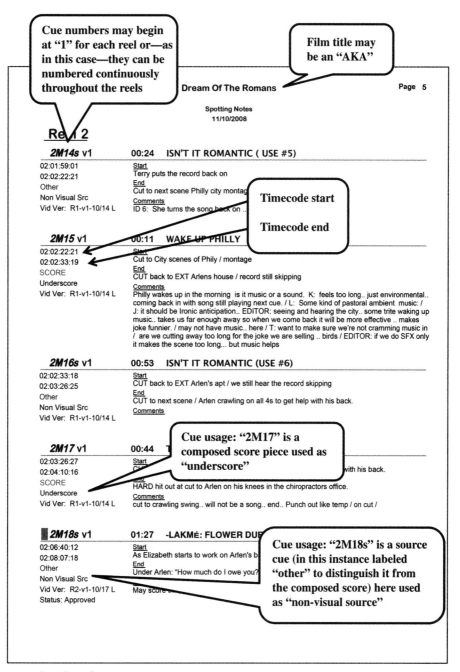

Cue numbers may begin at "1" for each reel or—as in this case—they can be numbered continuously throughout the reels

Film title may be an "AKA"

Dream Of The Romans   Page 5

Spotting Notes
11/10/2008

Reel 2

2M14s v1   00:24   ISN'T IT ROMANTIC (USE #5)

02:01:59:01	Start
02:02:22:21	Terry puts the record back on
Other	End
Non Visual Src	Cut to next scene Philly city montage
Vid Ver: R1-v1-10/14 L	Comments
	ID 6: She turns the song back on ..

Timecode start

Timecode end

2M15 v1   00:11   WAKE UP PHILLY

02:02:22:21	Start
02:02:33:19	Cut to City scenes of Phily / montage
SCORE	End
Underscore	CUT back to EXT Arlens house / record still skipping
Vid Ver: R1-v1-10/14 L	Comments

Philly wakes up in the morning is it music or a sound. K: feels too long.. just environmental.. coming back in with song still playing next cue. / L: Some kind of pastoral ambient music: / J: it should be Ironic anticipation.. EDITOR: seeing and hearing the city.. some trite waking up music.. takes us far enough away so when we come back it will be more effective .. makes joke funnier. / may not have music.. here / T: want to make sure we're not cramming music in / are we cutting away too long for the joke we are selling .. birds / EDITOR: if we do SFX only it makes the scene too long... but music helps

2M16s v1   00:53   ISN'T IT ROMANTIC (USE #6)

02:02:33:18	Start
02:03:26:25	CUT back to EXT Arlen's apt / we still hear the record skipping
Other	End
Non Visual Src	CUT to next scene / Arlen crawling on all 4s to get help with his back.
Vid Ver: R1-v1-10/14 L	Comments

Cue usage: "2M17" is a composed score piece used as "underscore"

2M17 v1   00:44   T

02:03:26:27	Start
02:04:10:16	Cut ... with his back.
SCORE	End
Underscore	HARD hit out at cut to Arlen on his knees in the chiropractors office.
Vid Ver: R1-v1-10/14 L	Comments
	cut to crawling swing.. will not be a song.. end.. Punch out like temp / on cut /

2M18s v1   01:27   -LAKMÉ: FLOWER DUE

02:06:40:12	Start
02:08:07:18	As Elizabeth starts to work on Arlen's b
Other	End
Non Visual Src	Under Arlen: "How much do I owe you?
Vid Ver: R2-v1-10/17 L	May score
Status: Approved	

Cue usage: "2M18s" is a source cue (in this instance labeled "other" to distinguish it from the composed score) here used as "non-visual source"

Figure 3.2 (Continued).

to be licensed by the music supervisor. In this way, the notation helps a reader quickly determine who has responsibility for each piece.

Distinguishing the source from the score music is also important because a separate total time is needed for each: the composer needs to know the total duration of the score music so that he or she knows how much to write, while the source music total helps the music supervisor work out the song licensing budget. (For more detailed discussion on this topic, see Chapter 5.)

There are some alternative cue referencing systems, which label score and source cues separately, so that, for example, the source cue "3s14" might appear as well as the music cue "3m14." One composer I know prefers to label the score cues with a number and the source cues with a letter, so "3m1," "3m2," and "3m3" would refer to score cues only, while "3mA," "3mB," and "3mC" would be source cues.

Letters might also be added to a cue reference to distinguish cues which, because they are related, are given the same number—for instance a series of source music pieces following each other in close sequence, either different pieces or perhaps the same one repeated. Figure 3.2 includes an example of the same piece of music treated as being used more than once in the same scene. In this film, the song "Isn't It Romantic" is heard many times, and here it is labeled as occurring in two separate but related cues, "1m13As" and "1m13Bs." As "A," the song plays on a phonograph while the main character makes a phone call; "B" follows when the song is heard at the other end of the phone line, playing in the background. This is an example of "diegetic" music, used as an intrinsic, on-camera element in the story, or as a means of identifying a character or indicating they have particular qualities. In this instance there are two separate cues for the song because it is briefly interrupted (notice the start timecode of 1m13Bs is about ten seconds after the end timecode of 1m13As)—this is important because the license fees for a piece of source music are typically charged according to how many uses there are or how many separate times it is heard in the film. The same number might similarly be given to several pieces of source music heard coming from a radio or television, say for a scene in which a character is flicking between channels, with "A," "B," "C," added to the cue numbers to distinguish them. Each piece of music that is heard, no matter how short, is labeled with a separate cue number.

It is important that once the spotting notes are compiled and agreed upon the original music cue numbers are maintained and remain associated with the same pieces of music and scenes, even though some of the related information, such as cue duration or title, may change. Cues are sometimes deleted, but in this case their numbers are not reallocated—usually they appear in the notes without a cue name, and often with the term "omitted." Cues can also be added, and a new cue is often given the same number as the one immediately before or after it, with the addition of a further letter to distinguish it. Which of the numbers is used for the new cue is often determined by the scene it occurs in. So, if 3m20 (for example) occurs in a scene where the main character is being chased by the bad guys, and new content is then added which occupies the same visual space and may involve similar action, the new music cue added to go with the new content might be labeled 3m20A, the "20" indicating it occurs in the same scene.

> **Tip**
> Once a cue gets a number, it keeps it. Changing the reel number or adding a letter to the reference is okay, but the cue number should stay the same. This is the case even if other cues are added or deleted around it. This ensures that same piece of music is always identifiable by the same number and scene, so avoiding confusion among the composer, music editor, orchestrators, programmers, and others.

3.3.4 Cue Titles

Each music cue is given a title, and whereas song cues should keep their original titles, the composed cues need to be named. These names often reflect the scenes the cues occur in. They are most often created by the music editor, though the composer may also have some ideas; they are usually finalized by the end of the "dub" or by the time of the recording (or "scoring") session. While the choice of title for a music cue may seem unimportant, it can be significant. First, each title will eventually end up on the written score that is archived with the cue audio, as well as on the music cue sheet (see Chapter 11), providing a reference that identifies the specific piece of music as unique for legal purposes (for example for the collection of royalties and copyright protection). Second, the title can be a means of providing immediate recognition, identifying not just the cue's location in the film but also its relationship to the emotion of a scene. For example, 1m12 in *Dream of the Romans* (see Figure 3.2) has the title "The Good Old Days," echoing one of the first lines of dialogue in the scene in which it is used.

Other titles may be more casual or even humorous. Cue 2m17 in *Dream of the Romans* (Figure 3.2 again) is called "The Bad Back Crawl"—a play on words and a wry name for an upbeat, jazzy piece that plays as the main character, unable to walk upright because of the pain in his back, is crawling down the sidewalk toward the soon-to-be-revealed co-star's chiropractic office.

3.3.5 Timecode Start and End

For readers with a basic understanding of postproduction this topic is more or less self-explanatory. The timecode start is the exact point in the current edit of the reel at which the first sound or modulation of the music cue starts with frame accuracy. This may change as the result of changes to the film, or if the composer decides to move the start of the cue. The exact ending timecode is more flexible and of less concern; a piece of music will often tail off—what we call "ring-off." I often have the end timecode at the very last sound of the music, found by listening to the composer's demo, or "mock-up" (for more on this topic, see Chapter 7 on composing).

A note is needed here about how timing is indicated: for feature films, the start and end timing is most often given in 35mm feet and frames; projects following current trends and using exclusively digital filming will likely use only timecode, usually 24-frame timecode. Television projects almost exclusively use timecode.

For practicality in communicating with the composer and music supervisor, spotting notes seem in general to favor timecode (though the music editor may make notes in feet and frames during the spotting session and later convert). On the dub stage, it is common to have both a feet and frames counter and timecode. In summary, these numbers are essentially interchangeable in describing the placement and synchronization of the music cues relative to the picture, and one should be well versed in both.

3.3.6 Total Time

The total time for a music cue is simply the length of the piece of music in minutes and seconds. This is calculated by finding the difference between the starting time-code and the ending timecode. These calculations can be done with pencil and paper, but are more usually made and automatically updated in database software (mentioned at the beginning of this section).

3.3.7 Cue Usage

"Cue usage" refers to how music is used in the film. In general, cues are either "underscore" (or just "score") or they are "source." Score music is not heard by the characters. Source music (diegetic music) is, and is depicted as coming from a source in the film, such as a TV, radio, or DJ (more subtly, it can also be an implied source, not necessarily seen on camera). A third possibility, a hybrid of sorts, is a combined dramatic usage of "song" and "score," or "song-score." "Scource," a term combining "score" and "source," is discussed later, in Chapter 5.

Cue usage information is included by the music editor in the spotting notes. Some examples of this appear in Figure 3.3; a fuller list is as follows:

- BI   Background Instrumental   (score or source)
- BV   Background Vocal   (score, source or scource)
- VV   Visual Vocal   (source)
- VI   Visual Instrumental   (source)
- TO   Theme Open   (score or song)
- TC   Theme Close   (score or song)
- EE   Logo(s)   (score)
- EC   End Credits (can also be TC)   (score and/or song)

Chapter 11 provides more detail on the uses of music in a project, as it affects the music cue sheets and royalties for composers and artists.

3.3.8 Cue Start and End Descriptions

Most spotting notes should contain a short description of the start of the music cue and what is happening in the scene at that point. The start, and its timecode, falls at the exact moment the first sound in the music cue is heard. The cue's end spotting is often a little "looser"—allowing the end of the music to "ring over" the endpoint of the scene—but it can also be defined very precisely, as desired. Someone reading the start and end descriptions should be able to visualize the scene and what is happening in it at the relevant moments. Acquiring the knack of writing effective start and end descriptions often takes some practice.

The trick—and purpose—of these descriptions is to give a quick-reference reminder of the scene's action, for the use of the composer, director, music supervisor, editor, music editor, and anyone else involved with the music. The use of abbreviations and note-style language is very acceptable: "cam pushes thru" rather than "camera pushes through," for instance. And most often these notes will include a variety of industry-specific terms and abbreviations, many describing camera movements or positions. (Some of these have quirky or jokey origins. "MOS," for example, is thought to have originated with a German director's mispronunciation of the English phrase "without sound"—see the box) A few of these are:

- LS   long shot
- MS   medium shot
- CU   close up
- INT   interior
- EXT   exterior
- MOS   without sound (or offstage sound)
- POV   point of view
- DISS   dissolve

Many online resources provide definitions, lists, or glossaries of industry shorthand. Useful sites include:

- http://encyclopedia.thefreedictionary.com
- http://en.wikipedia.org/wiki/Post-production
- http://www.digitalrebellion.com/glossary.htm
- http://www.indiedcp.com/broadcast-industry-terminology.html

---

"MOS" in film industry jargon means "without sound," or offstage sound. Various theories have been put forward for its origin, including the story of a German director recently arrived in twenties-era Hollywood—perhaps Ernst Lubitsch or Fritz Lang—who, when asked how he wanted a scene to be shot, replied in his broken English, "mit out sprechen!"

Over time MOS has also been made to work as an acronym for "motion on screen" or "man on the street," the latter referring to the short interviews of members of the public which are a common feature of fact-based and reality TV shows.

3.3.9 Cue Commentaries

Saving the best for last in this section, cue commentaries are, in general, one of the most important parts of the spotting notes. These are the music editor's notes on and direct transcriptions of what is said and decided at the spotting session. The film editor may at this stage have included music as (almost literally) a "sounding board" for discussion about musical direction, helping to reveal the director's creative aims and expectations about how the music should contribute to the film (for further discussion of temp editing, see Chapter 4). At the same time, many parts of the film may not have music at all, and whether and where to include it is also a matter for discussion. By providing a record of these discussions, the cue commentaries help to guide the composer in writing the music, ensuring that it will best fulfill the director's requirements. They can

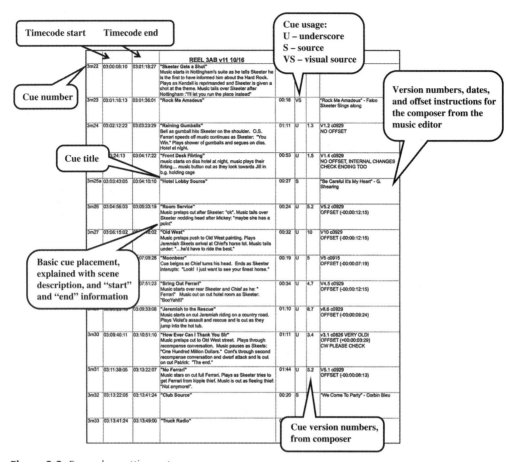

Figure 3.3 Example spotting notes.

also serve as a reminder to the composer about their own creative ideas, as discussed during the spotting session. Many valuable comments are made and ideas put forward in this environment; the cue commentaries are designed to include all of the musical ideas, likes, dislikes, and expectations expressed during spotting session discussions.

The director is not usually expected to have musical expertise or to be able to express their ideas in specifically musical terms (though many experienced directors do have excellent musical understanding and skills—John Turteltaub is a good pianist, for example, and Clint Eastwood creates many of his own musical ideas). All directors will most likely have a musical concept, however, as well as particular ideas about how the film should communicate emotions or actions. It is therefore the job of the music editor, in their notes, to communicate the expectations and desires of the director in both filmic and musical terms.

Clearly, accurate note-taking and transcription for cue commentaries is important. Since spotting session discussions often move fast and involve multiple contributors, hand-writing or typing notes is mostly too cumbersome and inaccurate. I usually record the conversations and transcribe them later (using initials to denote the different speakers). Examples of cue commentaries, including some direct transcriptions, are shown Figures 3.1 and 3.2.

It is also possible, however, that spotting notes may not be based on meetings or discussions; this is particularly likely on low-budget or independent projects. Here, the music editor may be working to some extent in isolation, with only basic temp music from the film editor to guide them in placing cues. They must therefore rely on their filmic and musical sensibilities to create the spotting notes. The result will be basic start and end cue information and a few notes, as well as timecode starts and ends, title, and cue number, similar to the example shown in Figure 3.3. Since there is in this situation no real discussion or commentary involving the director or editor, the music editor should be careful *not* to make notes about the creative intent or emotions to be conveyed, but to stick to the camera movements and significant action.

Finally, although simplified spotting notes are particularly suited to low-budget projects, the example in Figure 3.3 is in fact from a very high-budget film. This illustrates that the style of spotting notes depends on the individual music editor's preferred approach, and that postproduction workflows can vary greatly from project to project.

3.4 IN THE ROOM: KEY ISSUES FOR SPOTTING

Some of the key questions and issues which should be covered in the spotting session are described below; if these are not discussed, the music editor may need to follow up later with the director or composer to make sure the spotting notes are complete:

- Does the director, film editor, or composer like or dislike the temporary music cues?
- What about the temp music does the director like or dislike, love or hate? This may involve aspects of style, tempo, hits or accents, instrumentation (including specific instruments used or not used), notes or chords that produce particular effects, or elements that enhance or detract from the music's impact.
- For sections without temporary music, what is the emotional effect the director wants to achieve, and what is his or her concept or vision for the music? What opinions or comments about these sections have been voiced in the spotting session?
- Are there any scenes in the film that would be better off without music; that play better without it?

3.5 CONCLUSION

The music placement and the musical direction for a project have their origins in the spotting session. As a source of both technical and creative information, then, spotting is valuable to all types of project, at all levels of budget. A full set of accurate, detailed spotting notes doesn't guarantee that issues won't come up, but it will make them easier to deal with. For the independent or solo filmmaker, formalizing the process of note-taking to the extent described in this chapter may seem like overkill, but, regardless of the level of budget, every composer, music supervisor, or entertainment attorney will appreciate and may require some kind of documentation which gives details of the music to be used.

Film Music: Spot On!

There is one thing we can say about every piece of music that's ever been written or played. At some point it starts and at some point it stops.

This simple reality confronts and confounds film composers. It is the first question that comes up when a score is about to be written. All music starts and stops, but deciding exactly where in a film to begin and end the music is always a dilemma for the composer. No matter how softly the score may "sneak in" to a scene, it can be felt instantly, even when we are not consciously aware of its arrival. When music starts, something changes. We just feel it in our bones. Likewise, when any film music stops, there is a loss, a substantial or a subtle void. These musical starts and stops require skillful planning. Something in the story must "invite" the music to begin, and then, something must "justify" the music ending. The composer faces the eternal question … *Why*? Why *this* music? Why *here*? Why *now*? Why should it start? Why should it stop? And, of course, the music itself must supply the answers.

The process of choosing when and how to use music in a film has come to be called "spotting" in the official jargon. The term may have originated early on, when the editor would take a grease pencil and put a "spot" on a frame of film where music comes in, and another one where the music goes out. A "spotting session" is still the name for that often-tortuous meeting where the filmmakers and the composer (sometimes refereed by a knowledgeable music editor) struggle over the precise spots where they "hear" music. Spotting a film can be a particularly tense process for the composer, who will have to create the music from scratch, and who knows how crucial the placement of the cues can be in determining the ultimate style and character of the score. For example, the director of a tough, urban action thriller may surprise everyone by wanting all the fights and chases to be "naturalistic" (with only sound effects and no music), leaving the score to cover the slower/softer parts of the film, perhaps the love scenes and flashbacks of the main character's childhood. That "tough action" score could end up sounding like it came from a nostalgic love story. The fact is, what we call the score of a film is really the sum total of the spotted sections, and it may not necessarily reflect the overall character of the movie. In David Shire's tasteful score for the 1976 political expose, *All the President's Men*, we don't hear a lot of snappy cues reflecting the Washington D.C. newsrooms, nor do we find noble anthems depicting the nation's capital and its institutions. The sparse spotting focused the music on the quieter undertones and dark implications of an unraveling presidential scandal. The spotting of Claude Lelouch's romantic classic, *A Man and a Woman* (1966), confines the instrumental score to portions of the film that don't reflect the lovers' tragic losses or their conflicted attempts at intimacy, but rather it concentrates on the more lyrical outdoor montage sequences or Jean-Louis Trintignant's exciting world as a race car driver.

Since so much of a score's identity will be determined at the spotting session, we might expect filmmakers to lavish plenty of time and attention on such a crucial process. Unfortunately, this is not always the case. Too many films are already "pre-spotted" when the composer comes on board by virtue of the temporary score. Oftentimes, a bit of music that was "slapped in on the fly" to help an editor in cutting, may remain and serve to dictate where a composer should begin a newly spotted cue. Even if the temp score is long gone, it can still be difficult for filmmakers to let go of a "spot" that once contained music. But it is not only the previously temped areas that can drive a composer crazy. There those scenes that every composer instinctively knows *should not be scored*. A director might say, "We couldn't find any temp music for this scene, but you'll know what to do." In such a case, the composer may realize that the scene simply doesn't work, that adding music can only make things worse (or even make the composer look responsible for the problem). The director might then lean on the composer with the dreaded words, "I think we could *really* use something here." Of course, the "something" that is so badly needed is usually a better script, a better actor, or a miracle. But, too often, the composer will have to fill the space with "meaningless" music anyway. It can be quite difficult indeed to compose music that fills up space, and yet carefully "says nothing" in a film. (Or, as the great American poet/playwright, Edna St. Vincent Millay, once had a character exclaim in exasperation, "I have nothing to say … and I'm saying it!")

There is no rulebook or checklist that tells composers how to spot music for films. Knowing how to place music strategically throughout a film is a special skill and an art. It is very much a part of what makes some composers excel as musical dramatists. There is a rhythm and an intuitive quality to spotting music. Most people in their daily lives will choose to start and stop music many times during the day. In that sense, non-composers have a small taste of spotting musical cues in their lives. The Drive Home, The Morning Jog, The Backyard Bar-B-Q, The Dinner Party, The Love Scene or The Seduction, these are all occasions when people may choose music to "score" their lives. But the similarity ends there. Aside from actually creating the music, the film composer will have to deal with countless additional issues, like planning the film's musical identity, how frequently the musical themes should reoccur, how the score will develop and change over the course of the film, and whether the budget (or schedule) will allow for all the grand and glorious sounds that the director is suddenly expecting.

In spotting, some films may seem to require a lot of music, densely placed—perhaps highly synchronized with the action (as in some broad physical comedies or animated pictures). Other films may suggest a more sparse treatment (journalistic, documentary or realistic stories), or a film may call out for a more vague, unsynchronized and somewhat random kind of spotting (perhaps some "European" styled films or more dreamy atmospheric projects). And, on vary rare occasions, the director and the film may conspire to demand something so preposterous, so outlandish and so unimaginable that all bets are off. Such a case might be Jean-Luc Godard's 1961 New Wave comedy, *Une femme est une femme*, scored by the wonderful Michel Legrand. The offbeat use of music in this film defies any conventional idea of spotting. Cues start and stop abruptly, swells or accents may suddenly punctuate the action or dialogue, incongruous choices abound. For example, there is a soft-spoken and heartfelt discussion in a café inexplicably accompanied by comedic-styled chase music. Nothing about the placement and use of music in this film seemed familiar or conventional at the time it was made. Godard decided to turn traditional film spotting on its ear, and this score still baffles audiences, composers and critics alike.

As we have seen, spotting the music is fundamental to the art of film scoring. Spotting is that special "liquid" moment in the creation of a score when anything is still possible and nothing is yet tangible. It is also the crucial juncture where the three great forces—the composer, the filmmaker and the film itself—all converge to negotiate the role of music in the storytelling. Of course, in the end it is always the filmmaker who has the final word about where music will start, where it will stop, and what it must do. A composer can try to make a persuasive case at the spotting session, but moviemaking is still a director's medium. And, as composers learn time and again, a leopard may be far more likely to change its spots than some directors.

Charles Bernstein
www.charlesbernstein.com

© *2012 Charles Bernstein*
Permission to reproduce granted on behalf of Charles Bernstein

Chapter 4
Temp Editing

4.1 WHAT IS TEMP EDITING?

Music: beautiful, used, abused, and then thrown out. This is what the skillful, creative, and tough-skinned music editor loves, hates, and endures with temp editing (also known as temp scoring). The "temp" here is short for "temporary," but can also be understood to mean "template," in reference to its role as a guide for the director, editor, and composer; although, as discussed in Chapter 7, composers may have issues with treating the temp as a "template" for their writing. Whether or not this is the case, this wonderfully crafted musical score will eventually be tossed aside and replaced by the newly composed music.

It is important to note that preparing temporary sound does not just happen in the music department: sound effects and dialogue editors also develop their tracks, honing and smoothing them out as each new temp mix is presented. All three elements of a movie's soundtrack can elevate the emotional, dramatic, or comedic qualities of the film—as Steven Spielberg recently said, "The eye sees better when the sound is great." So the focus here is of course on music, but the overall soundtrack and the importance of achieving a balance between its different elements should not be underestimated. (Though there are different views on what the right balance is. Recently a well-known composer pulled me aside at a film's final mix and, in response to the treatment of his music, said, "If they want more emotion in the scene, bring up the volume of the music!")

The music editor creates the temp score not by writing or recording music as a composer would, but by editing pre-existing pieces of music together while thinking like a film composer. In this chapter, I will explore both the creative and the technical challenges involved in this process. But first: Why does a film need a temp score?

4.2 WHY IS A TEMP SCORE NEEDED?

The practice of temp scoring is thought to have begun in the early twentieth century. It continues to be used today in the early stages of film editing, to help filmmakers determine how their film sounds and, more specifically, how an audience is likely to react to it. The temp music also helps the film editor and director by demonstrating how music can enhance the emotional and creative directions of the film. First-time filmmakers will often be nervous about how the film is progressing, but even experienced directors and filmmakers benefit from a skillfully created temp score. The goal here is to present a "preview" audience with the most complete and realistic movie-going experience possible. From this point of view, studios, producers, directors, and everyone with a stake in a film understand the need for and value of a successful temp mix: preview audiences' opinions are often make or break, in terms of producers' and studios' support for a film.

4.2.1 Audience Previews

Playing a film to test audience reaction is called a "preview." Here, the audience is solicited to see an unfinished movie for free, in exchange for their opinions; most of us love free things, so you can imagine how easy it is to fill the theater. After watching the film the audience members complete a questionnaire or survey. Often they are videotaped during the preview, and the picture is then re-edited with the video in sync in 'the Avid' (a video and audio editing and recording system) so the filmmakers can see the audience reaction—or lack of it—frame by frame. This is particularly helpful for judging timing in a comedy, for example when allowing time for laughter, before the next joke is delivered.

Often a small focus group of 15 to 20 volunteers is invited to stay after the preview to share their opinions in more depth. Questions might include:

- Did you like the movie?
- Do you like the actors?
- Would you take your mother, brother, or sister to this movie?
- Did you like the ending?
- Did you like the music?

The feedback from the audience and focus group is analysed and assigned a rating score from 1 to 100, with a further ratings breakdown according to basic age and gender demographics. These statistics are a little like the film's midterm test results, and the producers and director can use them to decide how to improve and change the movie. A good score for a comedy is around 65 to 75, while a great score would be 80 or higher. As with many art forms, predicting how the audience will respond is difficult, if not impossible—even the pros are still learning, trying to figure out what scares an audience, and what makes them laugh or cry.

4.3 FINDING THE RIGHT TEMP MUSIC

The temp music ideas often come from the film editor and director when they are tackling the first director's cut of the film. Ideally a music editor should be brought in early in the film-editing process to start building the temp score; and recently there has also been a trend for composers to get involved at an early point, to save themselves from having to compete with a well-established and beloved temp score. Their big themes are sometimes passed to the music editor from day one in an attempt to preserve the concept of an "original score."

Over the past few years, though, it has become more common for the film editor to find, cut, and edit the temp music. Many film editors have an excellent musical sensibility and good musical communication skills. Their choices of music can often be just right for a film's musical direction. They also have a significant amount of creative control over the musical direction simply because they are most involved at the start of the editorial process. The film editor is strongly guided by the director, and together the editor and director will often create a complete temp score. However, while many film editors like to create a temp score and find it valuable, this is only one of the many aspects of their work, and they can get overwhelmed. They often appreciate the input of a music editor, who can pick up where they have left off—there may be places where the director feels music is needed that haven't yet been addressed, for example. This leads us back to the beginning of the music editor's job: the music spotting session (see Chapter 3).

It is also important to note that the music editor has a significant technical advantage over the film editor. Picture editing systems such as Avid Media Composer and Final Cut Pro can only edit sound to the closest frame boundary—either a thirtieth or a twenty-fourth of a second, commonly for North American productions, depending on the frame rate. Avid Pro Tools and other Digital Audio Workstations (DAWs) can edit or cut the audio much more precisely—to a 192,000th of a second, depending on the sample rate chosen. Currently the sample rate most commonly used in postproduction work is 48,000 samples per second. This allows a skilled music editor to achieve better musicality and improved synchronization with the film; editing to the nearest frame is not consistent with good music editing.

In addition, temp editing, like all music editing, demands the full range of editing skills and sensibilities. As well as editing precisely at the sample level, the music editor must use their expertise and ear to consider the overall feel and effect of the music.

4.4 CONSIDERATIONS FOR THE TEMP SCORE

Almost all of the questions listed here are relevant, and should be asked in relation to the director's personal preferences, ideas and emotional responses to the music. The music budget, studio's influence, and occasionally the music supervisor may also be relevant to the decisions to be made.

- Why does a given scene need music?
- What emotion is the scene conveying?
- Who or what in the scene is the music responding to?
- What kind of music is appropriate (a score from another movie's soundtrack, a classic song, …)?
- Where in the scene should the music cue start and end?

4.5 TEMP EDITING CONSIDERATIONS

Many music cues may have been cut in before the music editor arrives on the scene, but due to limits on the film editor's time and source material some silences may have been left where music is needed. Alternatively, too much music may have been cut in.

At the other extreme, there may be no music in the film at all, giving the music editor a blank slate to work from. This is how temp scoring was traditionally approached, and, more than simply relieving the film editor of responsibility for the temp music, this allows the music editor to use their expertise creatively, and to achieve a continuity and flow in the temp scoring process. The music is more likely to feel designed for the movie if it is the result of a process like this, where it comes from a consistent source.

Whatever the scenario facing a music editor at the time they are hired, though, they will face some unique challenges. They should approach the technical and creative process of designing a temp score as if they were a composer scoring the film; the difference being that they are using pre-recorded pieces rather than creating new music. Various considerations specific to this process are discussed in the subsections that follow.

4.5.1 Musical Resources

Listening to music is the first, most obvious, and most important step in creating the temp score. Often it takes longer than actually cutting the music. The most commonly used resource for a temp score is existing film scores. This is for the simple reason that a piece of music written by a skilled film composer for a particular type of scene—whether involving love, horror, action, murder, sadness, or happiness—is likely also to work for another, similar scene. For example, if you are working on a big action movie, the scores of Hans Zimmer or James Newton Howard might be appropriate. If it's a drama or a romantic comedy, consider Alan Silvestri or Randy Newman. You will likely find that a small selection of composers will provide a wide choice of cues to fit your scenes.

For a more intimate film, with a small cast and few locations, a simple score is often most appropriate, perhaps using acoustic guitar, strings, or piano. Both strings and piano have the ability to convey romance, drama, and intimacy, as well as darker and scarier emotions (darker effects can be created by dissonance, which the music editor might look for in existing examples or create themselves, by combining non-dissonant tracks).

Here are some listening suggestions—examples of instrumentation and film scores—for a variety of cinematic situations and emotions:

- Heroic—French horns
  - *Legends of the Fall*, James Horner
  - *Starship Troopers*, Basil Poledouris
- Military—martial-sounding snare drums
  - *Glory*, James Horner
  - *The Patriot Games*, James Horner
- Sensitive, romantic, and sad—piano, acoustic nylon guitar
  - *One True Thing*, Cliff Eidelman
  - *I Am Sam*, John Powell
  - *The Devil Wears Prada*, Teddy Shapiro
- Scary—synthesizer pads, high string tremolo, percussion
  - *The Hole*, Javier Navarrete
  - *The Uninvited*, Christopher Young

- Loneliness—strings, solo trumpet (sometimes muted)
  - *Losing Isaiah*, Mark Isham
  - *The Bodyguard*, Alan Silvestri
- Action—brass and percussion
  - *Tomb Raider*, Alan Silvestri
  - *Mr and Mrs Smith*, John Powell
- Sneaking around
  - *Clear and Present Danger*, James Horner
  - *Casino Royale*, David Arnold
- Comedy—woodwind: clarinet, flute, bassoon, bass clarinet, and so on
  - *Herbie Fully Loaded*, Mark Mothersbaugh
  - *Lilo and Stitch*, Alan Silvestri
  - *As Good as it Gets*, Hans Zimmer
- Comedy—light percussion: triangles, woodblock, and other hand-held instruments
  - *Curious George*, Heitor Pereira
  - *A Guy Thing*, Mark Mothersbaugh
  - *Last Vegas*, Mark Mothersbaugh

That said, some music editors find that matching music from similar scenes is effective less than half the time, while a piece of music may fit a scene that bears little or no relation to the one it was originally composed for.

> **Tip**
> You might "tie your own hands" if you focus too much on what the source was originally written for.

You also need to be careful if using popular movie music for your temp. Music which is too familiar to the audience will lose its impact, and may come across as corny. For a scary, tense scene in a serious drama it's probably best to avoid those two alternating notes from *Jaws* or the high, screeching strings from *Psycho*. This doesn't necessarily mean you need to look far for something more suitable: there are a number of pieces of music in both *Jaws* and *Psycho* that most people won't recognize, making them better choices.

> **PAX Quote**
> "Don't be afraid to think outside of the genre when picking temp music. *Jaws* and *Psycho* are hilarious in the right comedic scenes! We used *Psycho* when Eddie Murphy had to make a diaper change in *Daddy Day Care*."

Of course, the musical elements in any piece of score music will most often need to be manipulated, cut, and mixed to create a new piece to fit your particular scene. Making these choices and changes in an appropriate and creatively effective way is one of the many very specialized skills of a music editor—though some film editors are also highly skilled in this respect.

It's also important to note that temp music is not limited to scores. Source (or "diegetic") music is also needed, most commonly in the form of songs which the characters hear on-camera, as part of the story. Other instances might include classical instrumental pieces, or music from on-camera or implied sources, for instance a video game soundtrack. (Working with songs, source music, and pre-recordings is discussed in detail in Chapters 5 and 6.)

4.5.2 Musical Continuity

You need to consider the style of music, and try to maintain a consistent sound "palette"—the analogy here is with an artist's color palette, and indeed composers often talk about the "colors" in music. Whether your musical "painting" involves a large orchestra, or only a piano (as in Dave Grusin's score for *The Firm*), then as much as possible keep that sound throughout the movie. This can often be achieved by using a small number of film scores with similar palettes, or using only one or two composers.

> **Tip**
> If a composer's score is working, stick with him or her. Look at their other scores—even if the subject matter of the films they were written for is different, the compositional style may be compatible, and a good fit for your film.

4.5.3 Important Scenes

Select a few of the most important scenes in the movie where you want the audience to cry, to laugh out loud, or cover their eyes in fear. These scenes require the strongest music, carrying the central "thematic" or "melodic" part of the score. Often when you find the appropriate music for these few key scenes, the score for more incidental scenes will fall into place—for example other pieces from the same score or by the same composer may then become obvious choices.

4.5.4 Working with the Film Editor's Temp Music

It is important to work within the musical direction that has been established by a film editor's previous musical choices. For the music editor starting on a project where temp music has already been cut in, the challenge becomes to understand and fit into the workflow and relationship already established between the director and film editor. The music editor needs to work and contribute ideas in a way that feels comfortable for all concerned, including when suggesting alternatives to music already placed.

> **Tip**
> Once a piece is in the cut, and everyone is getting used to it, it can become increasingly difficult to persuade them that there's something that will work better.

As I've already mentioned, the music editor can also often improve on existing temp music for the simple reason that the film editor's time and technical resources are limited. In addition to its much finer editing resolution, Avid Pro Tools has audio processing capabilities such as pitch shifting and time stretching, cross-fading, a variety of plugins, and precise mixing and volume graphing.

4.5.5 The Composer and the Temp Score

PAX Quote

"There are many different responses to a good temp score, right? Good, bad, indifferent. Jerry Goldsmith refused to listen to one of mine. The director tried to play it and he put his fingers in his ears!"

A composer is likely to appreciate the music editor having given some thought to the "size" and production values of the temp music used, in relation to the likely cost of producing a score on a similar scale from scratch. The composer may not have the budget to reproduce a "big" musical sound.

The music editor may therefore need to dissuade the director from using a big-orchestra sound and move toward a more budget-friendly soundtrack. A smaller soundtrack might use percussion samples or a small string section, or a basic sonic palette of sample-based instruments combined with a few live players. Although less desirable than recording live instrumentalists, another alternative is to create a larger sound using virtual (software-based) orchestral instruments. Often a skillful music editor can create a temp score that achieves the same emotional drama as an expensive, big-sounding movie score, but using a smaller or more efficient musical palette.

Tip

If you place temp music which uses a large orchestra or has particularly high production values you may be making a composer's task difficult, if their budget is limited.

If the music editor is creating the temp score after the composer has been hired, it is wise to ask whether or not they would like their previous work included in the temp score, as this can be a double-edged sword: the composer is likely to have been hired on the basis of what they've done before, but using it in the temp score can place the composer in the creatively difficult position of having to recreate or reinvent the same music. This is a challenge for any composer, and best avoided if possible. On the other hand, a composer might be more comfortable hearing their own rather than another composer's music in the temp (otherwise the question might be: "Why did they hire me if they want his music?").

4.5.6 Placing Temp Music

For both the experienced professional and the first-time filmmaker, the aesthetics of music has the potential either to elevate and reinforce a film's artistic impact or to undermine it, having a direct impact on the audience's experience. A sound supervisor recently reminded me that less experienced filmmakers, in particular, tend to put in too much music, and in inappropriate places. This all-too-common situation dilutes the effect of good acting, storytelling, and sound design. It is an easy mistake to make, however, especially as the movie-editing process begins without music. In particular, the difficulty of achieving the right pacing when cutting a movie from raw dailies (the unedited footage) may mean there is an over-reliance on music for pacing.

Good film and music editors are adept at choosing and working with music in a way that helps with decisions about a film's editing and pacing. Some pieces of music obviously work well with the editing, for example source music, music for a montage, or an opening or closing song. It is advisable to step back from the temp scoring process from time to time, play the film through from beginning to end, and think very critically about where you have placed the music. Ask yourself: Is each piece really necessary? Could the scene play better without music? If there are too many music cues playing too close to one another, the soundtrack will feel crowded. Most film and music editors are fully aware of these pitfalls. They remind us of the humorous industry saying: You cannot fix "bad" acting by adding music.

All the considerations discussed in this section, and many others, will continue to influence the music editor's work as editing progresses; it's a moving target. Often the musical decisions for a project go through multiple changes and transformations as the film is re-edited. The music editor (and sometimes the film editor) will constantly revisit the music, modifying and conforming it to the film as other changes are made.

4.6 FINDING MUSIC

So far, we've established what a temp score is and why it is important, and discussed some of the main creative issues involved. At a practical level, the music editor needs to find music to use for the temp. The strongest and most common source of temp music comes from previous film scores and soundtracks. Film scores and soundtracks, songs, and other material can come from almost any source, including the director's best friend and the studio president's nephew's band—everybody loves music and many interested parties often get involved. Some of the more usual sources are listed below.

- As a music editor you build your own library of film scores, either by purchasing them or directly collecting composed scores from projects you work on.
- The music supervisor may have a number of their own sources (specifically related to songs).
- Other music editors may be able to give you scores from their film projects.
- Composers' agents are usually more than happy to send in their clients' music, particularly if they are likely to be considered for scoring the movie.
- ASCAP and BMI maintain databases of many composers' and songwriters' music.
- Downloads are often available on composers' web sites.
- "Stock" music libraries can be a useful source of inexpensive music, though typically they have more songs and less score material.
- iTunes and other commercial sites are often a very efficient route for sourcing music.

If you are considering buying a film soundtrack, take care to review it first to make sure it contains what you are looking for. It might consist mainly of songs and other source music, with only some score material, or indeed just songs.

4.6.1 "Free" Sources of Music

A few web sites and other places claim they can supply music for free. These should be treated with caution, though, because this is rarely truly the case: there will most likely be an up-front fee or terms that limit songs' usage—for example to particular geographic regions—or even stipulate royalties.

4.6.2 Copyright for Temp Music

There are, in general, few or no copyright issues related to music used in a temp score. You can use any music in the world as temp music without risk of infringing copyright, as it is not going to be used in the final film. The preview audience do not pay to see the movie and, with no money exchanged, there are in most instances no copyright issues.

Clearly, if songs used in the temp are to be kept for the final dub, then they must be licensed and cleared. In this situation, it is customary for the music supervisor to contact the production company's legal department to verify that the correct licenses are in place.

4.7 BUILDING A TEMP SCORE IN PRO TOOLS

A temp score is usually built in Pro Tools in one of two ways (or sometimes a combination of both, depending on your workflow requirements): you can make one session for each reel of the movie, or use a "super session." A super session contains all the separate reels, with each one set to start at its corresponding timecode or feet and frames ruler position. Television or long-form TV movies usually start at First Frame of Action (FFOA), which equals 1:00:00:00 in timecode, and continue in one session through to the end of the show.

4.7.1 Working in a Super Session

The super session is excellent for temp editing because you have the whole movie in one place, and can access music from one clip bin for all of the reels. In addition, your music can easily be imported into the re-recording mixer's session, if they are mixing from a super session.

In a super session the feet and frames locations have to be reset for each reel, as you work in it. This is done in Pro Tools by placing the insertion cursor in the timeline at the desired hour start location (for instance at "02" for timecode 02:00:00:00), and then choosing Setup > Current Feet + Frames Position, and entering the desired position in the dialog box. It is standard industry practice to match timecode to the reel hour you are working in, and to restart the feet and frames numbering from zero for each new reel or hour. For example, timecode 02:00:00:00 will align with 000 feet + 00 frames (35 mm film).

4.7.2 Working in One Session for Each Reel

This type of Pro Tools session usually has the session start time code 'hour' equal to the Academy Leader's 'start mark' for each reel film. The Academy Leader is a specific length of film stock (or digitally created) to count backwards from the start mark equal to 000 + 00 (feet and frames) for 8 seconds up to the FFOA (First Frame of Action). (So, for example, if we are looking at Reel 5, it's Academy Leader will begin at 5:00:00:00 representing the time code start and 000 + 00 for the feet and frames start.) Remember, film speed is 24 frames per second and there are 16 frames in each foot of 35 mm film, therefore 3 feet equals 2 seconds. The "2 pop" occurs at 5:00:06:00 or 9 feet + 00 frames and the FFOA starts at 5:00:08:00 or 12 feet + 00 frames. This format is found in all feature films and will be in each single-reel DAW's (digital audio workstation) session and each new reel of a super session. Whether using a single session per reel or a super session, it is also important to maintain the sync with the film editor's multi-track Open Media Framework Interchange (OMFI) or Advanced Authoring Format (AAF) export.

4.7.3 HD Video Frame Rate

Many films are now in HD (high definition) digital video and can be set to shoot with a variety of frame rates. A common HD frame rate is 23.976 FPS (frames per second), sometimes given as 23.98. In the Pro Tools session, make sure you check the Session Setup window, ensuring that it shows the proper timecode and feet and frames rulers. It is possible to have the feet and frames ruler set to 23.976 FPS and the timecode ruler set to the SD (standard definition) value of 29.97 FPS—that is, both can be used in the same Pro Tools session—though it's more usual for both to be set to the HD value. Setting the timecode ruler to 23.976 FPS will mean that the audio and video run 0.1 percent slower than the actual film speed of 24 FPS. The digital picture in this case also shows 24 FPS, not 30 FPS. While it's possible to receive projects from an Avid picture editor running at either HD video speed (23.976 FPS) or film speed (24 FPS), the audio frame rate should ideally match the frame rate of the digital picture. HD video speed (23.976 FPS) seems to be the most common HD project frame rate right now. It is a good idea to verify the project frame rate and speed with the film editor's assistant in advance.

4.7.4 3-perf

While many films are still shot with traditional 35 mm film stock, and not digitally, we are seeing a change from the traditional 4-perf film stock to 3-perf, aimed at saving money; 4-perf has four sprocket holes per frame and 3-perf has three. This is not usually a concern, since the speed of the film is the same for both, at 24 FPS. However, at this time Pro Tools can only show a feet and frames ruler for 4-perf. Until Avid adjusts their software, if the film stock is 3-perf you should use the timecode ruler to identify locations of frames.

4.7.5 Organizing the Music

In a Pro Tools session, new tracks are added as stereo tracks, since almost all commercial music is distributed in stereo. The number of tracks to use in the temp score is up to the music editor; however, when the time comes to audition musical ideas the tracks and audio files need to be organized and ready, so as not to waste the director's time. Some editors like to place markers at each cue position or even make playlists for multiple versions.

When delivering the super session or single-reel material to the re-recording mixer, make sure your tracks are concise (that is, there are no extraneous tracks or audio files that the mixer does not need to consider) and organized clearly, so that they can be reviewed at a glance. It is common practice to place score material at the top of the session and source music at the bottom. However, track layout may be at the discretion of the music editor or requested in a certain way by the re-recording mixer. The re-recording mixer is also free to move tracks around as they see fit. (I just finished a film where I placed source material at the top and the score underneath, and the re-recording mixer imported my music, placing the source and score in an pre-existing mixing template.) The dialogue and sound effects tracks are usually delivered separately to the mixer by their relevant specialist departments. If this is the case, the music editor should either not deliver these elements with their temp tracks, or should hide, mute or make them inactive. The film editor's temp music tracks should be also hidden but need to be available in case the mixer or director wants to hear them.

4.7.6 Listening to and Loading Music

There are many ways to import audio and monitor music in Pro Tools; I prefer to listen from the workspace browser (see Figure 4.1). In this window you can do a detailed music search, select cues very quickly and click on different locations in the file's waveform view to hear various sections; you are not limited to listening from the beginning. You can also recognize what the music might sound like from the peaks and valleys of the waveform. For example, regular sharp peaks indicate a rhythmic track, while longer, smoother waveforms usually represent legato or sustained music, as produced with, say, strings or synthesizer pads.

4.7.7 Critical Listening

As you begin the process of selecting the temp music, it is important to imagine how music might work in a scene, to "visualize" the scene with music—that is, it is important to think like a film composer, and begin to consider how music might work even before listening to any. Consider the musical criteria discussed with the director and film editor and the overall musical style, pay close attention to the spotting notes, and keep in mind the creative and practical issues specific to the project (see Section 4.5). The listening process can take longer than actually cutting the music. When you find a piece that seems like it will work, you can drag it directly from the workspace browser window and drop it into either an empty audio track or into the clip bin in the Pro Tools session edit window.

At this early stage of listening and finding appropriate music, don't be too concerned with editing or placing the cues in the proper track or sync location. Often I find there is a serendipitous thing that happens when temp editing, where you drag and drop a cue in the general area you imagine it's going to fit, and somehow much of the music turns out to be in just the "right" emotional place in the scene. Give this a chance to happen—sit back and listen. Be open, but also critical: critical listening and thinking

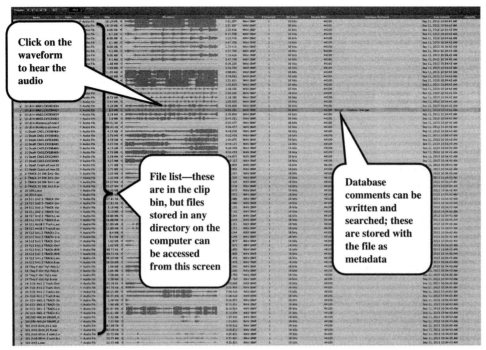

Figure 4.1 The workspace browser in Pro Tools 11. This shows information and metadata associated with files currently available on the computer. (The files shown in this example are in the Pro Tools session clip bin.) Note that you can start listening to a clip at any point in the file, not just from the start. You can also control the listening volume, search comments fields, and even alter the sample rate from this window.

are crucial to a successfully edited score. You may discover there are particular sections of a piece that work best. The music will most certainly still need to be edited and finessed.

PAX Quote

"Sometimes a piece that is perfect in your mind falls on its face when you put it to picture. But when it's right you will feel a new depth of emotion when you watch it."

Another interesting thing that often happens as you listen is that a piece strikes you as perfect for a scene in a totally different part of the movie. When this happens, "throw" the music in a track in that scene or, if it's in another reel, make a note to do it later. (Of course, if you are working in a super session, you have access to all the reels and can move the music around in a very fluid way.)

Finally, while listening, it is important to skip around within the cue's waveform—the midpoint, beginning, ending, and points in between. You may discover even small portions of a piece can be useful. The end of a cue is of particular importance because it can be edited with other material to help it sound as if it has been composed for the scene.

> **Tip**
> **Important:** It's better to edit music precisely to fit a scene, rather than using fade or volume graphs to start or end it.

4.8 IMPORTING AND WORKING WITH THE FILM EDITOR'S MUSIC

Effective workflow and exchange of music, dialogue, and sound effects tracks between the film editor and music editor is critical. Although there will always be new and improved ways to exchange data between computers; currently the most commonly used are the AAF (newer) or OMFI (older) file exchange protocols. Either of these will allow the music editor to receive accurate synchronized tracks and edits originating from the film editor's picture editing system (usually Avid Media Composer or Apple Final Cut Pro). When building Pro Tools sessions for temp score editing make sure you import and keep in sync all the tracks from the AAF or OMFI files.

A pending revision of workflows between Avid Media Composer and Pro Tools will soon allow the Pro Tools user to access in real time the video and audio media that the Avid editor is using; a current alternative is the Avid ISIS, a network interface that enables this workflow. Other, third party systems may also be available.

4.9 MUSIC EDITING TECHNIQUES AND FILM CONSIDERATIONS

Once you've selected the music you'll eventually be presenting to the director, it's time to cut. The subsections that follow discuss some important points about making your edits with the film in mind.

> **PAX Quote**
> "If you believe the audience might hear your edit, it is a poor edit. The object is always to create what sounds like a natural, unaltered piece. The best music editor's work will go unnoticed by all but the most careful listeners. Also, the better known a piece is the more difficult it is to 'hide' your edits."

4.9.1 Camera Movements

Notice when the camera "pushes in" or "pulls back"; that is, when it moves closer to or further from a fixed object or view. When this happens, emotion is being expressed visually, and music can be highly effective in supporting and enhancing the effect. Edit in an emotionally appropriate melody or a chord change or tonal shift that helps express the emotion of the moment. Similarly, the moment when one scene dissolves into another often marks an important emotional transition which can be supported with a musical transition or tonal chord shift.

4.9.2 The Emotional Arc

The director and the music editor need to use their expertise and musical sensibilities to shape the music appropriately to the movie's "emotional arc." The emotional arc of a movie, in terms of film editing and music, is a collection of consecutive scenes that are shaped to follow a particular trajectory in relation to emotional expression and/or actions. Music cues which trail or carry over the cut to the next scene or which start before the cut ("prelap") are often effective in helping shape scenes in this way. They bridge the scenes, so helping the audience "stay in the movie." Oddly placed or mixed musical elements or sound effects can have the opposite effect, distracting the audience and causing them to be "taken out of the movie." Starting or ending music abruptly on the cut (sometimes referred to as "biting the cut") can do the same, although it's not always a bad thing: Quentin Tarantino loves to use this effect.

> **Tip**
>
> Music editors look for and use the downbeats of the music when editing, but it doesn't necessarily follow that a downbeat is the best place to cut. It can be better to "hide" an edit in the bar.

4.9.3 Looping or Repeating

Repeating can be a useful tool if you need to extend a piece of music, or make a section within the music play longer or act as a bridge between two parts. I generally limit this to two or maybe three literal repeats. I usually prefer to make a third repeat a slight variation on the previous two, which is similar to what a composer might do when writing music; think of a theme and variations, as a traditional composing technique. If you want to repeat a looped section at a later time in the emotional arc of a scene, try to vary it slightly from the first hearing.

> **Tip**
>
> You can help hide a too-obvious repeat by overlaying music on another track. Also, the longer the repeated section, the easier it is to hide.

Often, repeating a sustained section or a sound that holds on one pitch or chord results in an obvious and offensive "bump" or pulsing sound at the repeat. One way of avoiding this is to "reverse" the audio file loop:

1. Select a section for which there is as little bump or pulse sound as possible, when played with Loop Playback.
2. Apply reverse AudioSuite digital processing to the section. This is most effective for a sustained note played by strings, or perhaps a synthesizer pad sound.
3. Build a longer section, alternating between the unprocessed and reverse processed clips.
4. Overlap the clips and use wide, equal-power cross-fades to smooth one into the next, until you fill the gaps.

To make this sound natural, you're likely to need to spend a significant amount of time moving the clips, experimenting with different cross-fades, and sometimes applying volume graphing.

4.9.4 Using Fades-Ins and -Outs

Do not simply fade cues in or out while music continues to play in the underlying clip—this is not how a good film composer would write their music, and usually results in a sloppy-sounding music track that can fail to follow the emotional arc of the scene in a natural and elegant way. Consider each situation on its merits, edit the beginnings and endings of cues, and use fade-ins and -outs only when they're genuinely desirable—in conjunction with a visual dissolve, for example.

4.9.5 Edit around the Dialogue

Shape the music around the dialogue. You do not have to stay clear of dialogue completely—that would most likely be musically awkward. If you are stating a melody, whether at the beginning or in the middle of a piece, have that melody "start" either before or after the "start" of a line of dialogue. This will allow the mixer to avoid having to lower the volume of the music drastically at the point the dialogue starts.

Pay particular attention to melodies, chords, and phrasing in positions where they respond to the dialogue; a kind of "call and response" technique. Similarly, the music might "comment" before a specific line is spoken. These two techniques can be particularly effective for comic dialogue, and should be used more sparingly in dramatic scenes. Working around dialogue is of particular importance while editing songs with lyrics, as we shall see in the next chapter.

4.10 ADDITIONAL EDITING TECHNIQUES

This section describes some helpful principles and techniques for editing score cues; some are also applicable to songs and source cues. The figures show Pro Tools, as the industry's DAW (Digital Audio Workstation) of choice, but the methods are applicable across other audio editing systems.

> **Tip**
> In contrast to audio editing systems, picture editing systems such as Avid Media Composer and Final Cut Pro cut audio to the frame, which limits their usefulness for editing music.

4.10.1 Matching Similar Musical Phrases, Tones, and Lyrics

To edit parts within the same or similar pieces of music, it's good practice to place them on separate tracks, one above the other, then alternate between the two and listen for notes, chords, orchestrations, lyrics, or musical phrases which are similar or exactly the same. Select and edit the appropriate sections, then move the material on

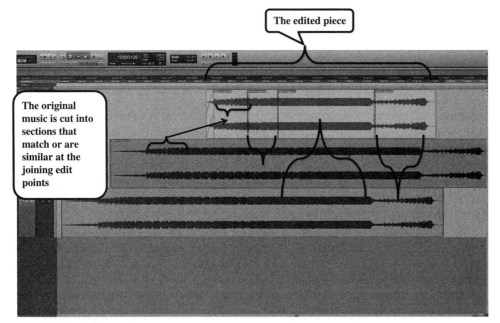

Figure 4.2 Here, the two lower tracks are the full, original pieces of music, sections from which have been edited together to create the piece at the top. When editing pieces together, the first step is to match sections which are the same or similar, in terms of orchestration, instrumentation, melody, and percussion elements. When combining sections it is critical to maintain the rhythmic consistency of the original music.

the lower track around to match it up with corresponding sections in the track above, before editing them together (see Figure 4.2).

PAX Quote

"If you must change a phrase or melody, make every effort to do so in the spirit of the original composition. Follow the composer's lead."

Tip

Important: When editing together different instruments, listen for pitches which are the same, and orchestration or chords which are the same or similar.

Pitch changes or modulations, whether occurring naturally in the music or created by the editor, can make a musical edit sound better, smoother, and more natural. Creative editing like this is often used to make a musical phrase or melody match a specific section or cut of a scene. To achieve good music editing you need to be aware of and use some of the same scoring and sensibilities a film composer would.

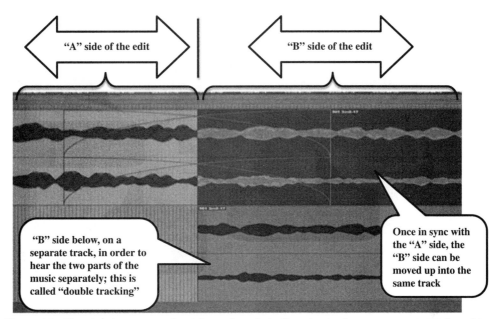

Figure 4.3 Often it is best to match sections of music by listening to them on separate tracks—this is called "double tracking." Once matching sections have been found, the "new" section—the "B" side of the edit—can be dragged into the same track as the "A" side and the two parts edited together. A music edit is often smoothed out with an equal-power cross-fade, using material from both sides of the edit. Further experimentation with various types of cross-fade may improve results.

Tip

Hide your work in the most graceful way.

4.10.2 Cross-fades

Cross-fades are one of the most common ways of smoothly blending one section of music with the next. Many editors set their cross-fade default in Pro Tools to "equal-power." This style of cross-fade is suitable where the material is similar, or it can be used as a starting point for exploring creative next steps, and choosing from the various other cross-fade styles in order to make the edit sound natural (see Figures 4.3, 4.5, and 4.6).

If you want to cross-fade sections of music from within the same piece, it can be easier to split the sections onto two adjacent tracks (the "double tracking" described previously), then match the waveforms that represent the pitches, notes, chords, or tonalities for the cross-fade (see Figure 4.7).

It is common to use the smart tool in Pro Tools to center the fade directly over an edit selection boundary. Musically, this can sometimes work well, but often after critical listening you'll find you need to adjust the cross-fade position (see Figures 4.8a–c).

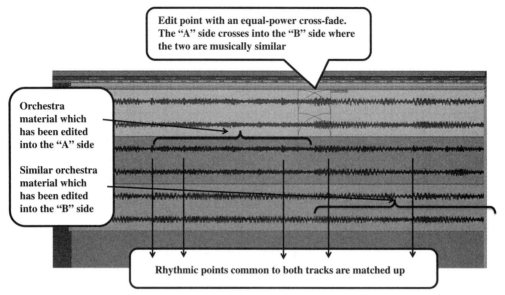

Figure 4.4 Two similar sections from different tracks combined using an equal-power cross-fade to make a consistent, smooth, and musically appropriate edit.

AU1

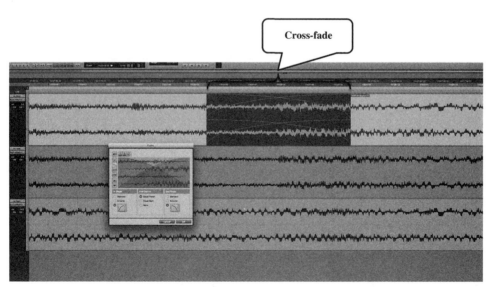

Figure 4.5 An equal-power linked cross-fade highlighted, with settings shown in a dialog box.

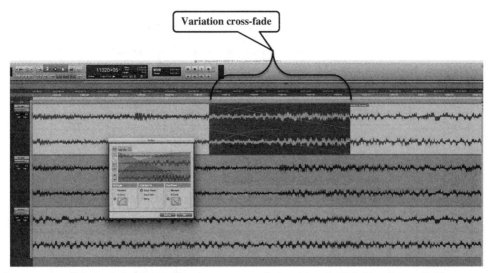

Figure 4.6 A slight variation on an equal-power cross-fade, giving the "A" side of the edit (the left-hand, outgoing side) a little less emphasis to create a smoother, more natural-sounding transition to the "B" side.

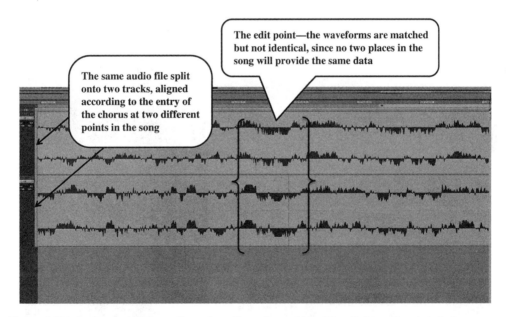

Figure 4.7 It is often helpful to split tracks to listen for and identify suitable edit points, before placing the music on a single track and creating a cross-fade.

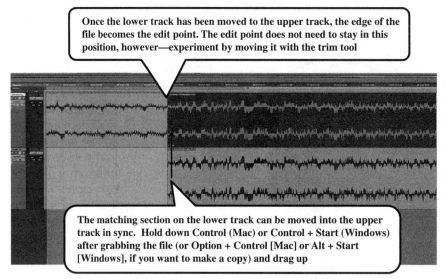

Figure 4.8a Editing together two parts of the same song (as shown in Figure 4.7). Once the two sections have been synchronized and an edit position found, the two audio files can be placed in the same track and a cross-fade created.

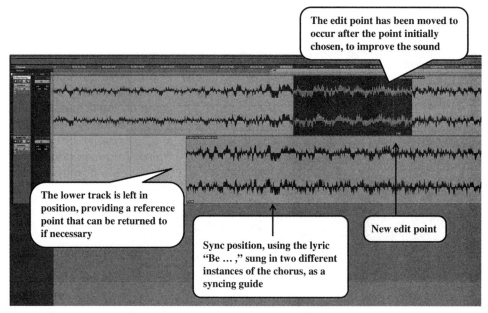

Figure 4.8b A smoother edit can be created by placing a cross-fade an uneven distance before and after the edit point.

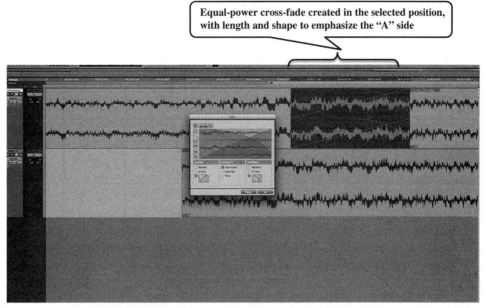

Equal-power cross-fade created in the selected position, with length and shape to emphasize the "A" side

Figure 4.8c Adjusting the lengths and shapes of the "incoming" and "outgoing" parts of cross-fades can also help smooth an edit, and make the music sound natural and flowing.

Tip

Moving a cross-fade using the grabber tool, either to the right so that it occurs later (a "retard") or to the left so it comes earlier (an "advance"), often creates a smoother musical transition.

4.10.3 Checkerboarding

In most situations you should keep the edited music on the same track. This makes it easier for the mixer to view and mix the music. However, pieces are sometimes placed on alternating tracks. This is called "A.B.-ing" or "checkerboarding" the tracks, or sometimes "two-tracking," as the Pro Tools screen takes on the appearance of a checkerboard. Splitting tracks in this way can be useful to the mixer, who then has control over pieces of music that play for particular scenes or overlapping sequences of scenes.

4.10.4 Multitracking

A music editor should not be limited to two stereo tracks. For certain types of films, such as action films, and projects for which the musical direction is a bit more experimental, it can be desirable to multitrack the temp music. With this approach, sections of music are edited so that they overlay on multiple tracks which then play at the same time.

> **Tip**
> If editing multiple tracks to be played together, Pro Tools track grouping and clip grouping functions can be used to help keep the musical elements in sync with each other.

This approach works best when different musical elements are being combined, for example percussion with synthesizer or string beds, pads, solo instruments, a solo voice, or choir. As you construct pieces in this way, pay attention to the overall sound and whether it emulates what a composer might do. For example, consider the key and tonal relationships—you may want to change the pitch of some parts to keep them in relative keys. On the other hand, it can be appropriate to have conflicting sounds—dissonance can be very effective at heightening the sense of drama or in scary scenes.

4.10.5 Sweeteners

Multitrack editing, in particular, can be assisted by the addition of "sweeteners." To help musical transitions sound smoother, or to accentuate a film dissolve, transition, or cut, sounds such as cymbal swells, cymbal rolls, timpani rolls, or synthesizer pads can be included. Non-pitched percussion sounds can be used to great effect because they don't create any unwanted dissonance with more tonal, consonant musical elements.

4.10.6 Hits

A musical "hit" is an edited or composed element in a piece of music which is designed to accent a visual moment or picture shift—maybe a monster attacking, the sudden appearance of a hand reaching out to grab the girl—or a cut. Hits are used by composers and music editors to help create the emotional shape of a scene, and provide musical drama or comedy. Often hits are composed of a chord or percussive elements, though they can also be more subtle—they don't necessarily need a full orchestra or a loud bang. A sweetener can be used, and edited in using multitrack editing (see Figure 4.9).

Creating multiple hits for a scene, accenting lots of cuts and action moments, is often tempting and exciting. However, although hits in these places can be effective, they can also conflict with the sound effects and the drama created by sound design.

> **PAX Quote**
> "An effective score should be felt more than noticed. I recall watching the film *Meet Joe Black* and being absorbed in the emotion of it but having almost no recollection of the music. But when I listened to the score on its own it was gorgeous. It's a fine line when temping. You can draw attention away from the drama by being overly dramatic and you can hurt the comedy by trying to be funny. Being too literal and trying to hit too many things can present your cue with the dreaded 'cartoony' label."

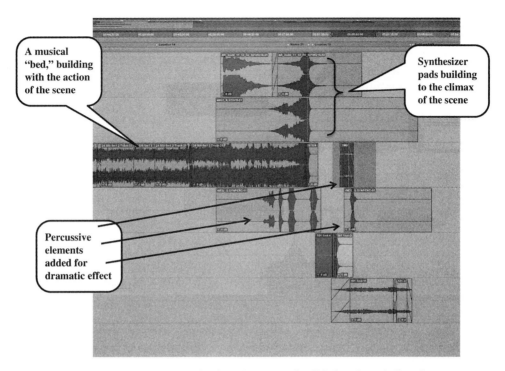

Figure 4.9 A multitrack temp score which includes percussive "hits" and cymbal swells to accentuate action or transitions. Note here the various edits of the musical parts.

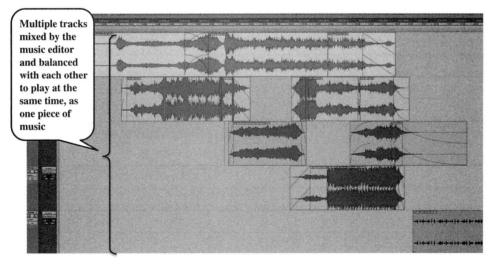

Figure 4.10 An example of multitrack temp score editing. Several different tracks from movies and TV shows have been edited to play together and create a dramatic, effective score. This is very creative work, and a different approach to composing by editing.

In particular, do not place a loud hit on an important line of dialogue. This will dilute the musical effect and make it difficult for the mixer to balance the dialogue, sound effects, and music. Additionally, hits at the same time as important sound effects will often be lost in the soundtrack, and rightly so—the sound effect in this case should "win." In summary, use hits sparingly, reserving them for those few truly emotional moments when you want the audience to jump out of their seats, gasp in horror, laugh, or be shocked.

4.11 PRESENTING MUSIC FOR THE DIRECTOR OR PRODUCER

Presenting musical ideas and edits to the director or producer involves striking a delicate balance: too few options, and they may get the impression you are having difficulty coming up with ideas; too many, and they may think you're "shooting in the dark"—either way, they may feel that you lack confidence in your work, and perhaps that you're failing to understand what the film demands, musically speaking. So how many ideas are too few, and how many are too many? It's not possible to give a definitive answer, but some of the questions to think about include:

- How many pieces of music has the film editor already cut in successfully?
- Has any thematic musical material already been chosen, perhaps by the director or editor?
- Have you played any pieces for the director or producer? If so, did they like the direction you were taking?
- How much interest does the director or producer have in the music? How much time do they have to spend on it?
- How many different scenes do you need to present at any one time?
- Has the director or producer asked to see any specific scenes (even though you may have much more to show)?

On a practical note, the director may have you send the film editor your cuts and ideas, and listen to them with the film editor rather than with you in your cutting room or studio. This can simply be a function of your location—you may be working in Los Angeles while the film is being edited in New York. (Ideally, though, the music editor should be in or near the same suite of offices or cutting rooms as the film editor, allowing them to develop the temp music quickly and effectively.)

If auditioning your music with the director present, however, you will be faced with the following dilemma: Do you take the time to fix and edit while he or she is there, or do you do it later and wait to present the fix? You might ask the director if they have time to listen to a quick fix, but keep in mind that you must be able to do this perfectly and quickly, on the spot.

Playing your music on speakers is the preferred option—for many editors headphones are reserved only for the dub stage. However, if you are making corrections to the edit while someone else is in the room, headphones can be desirable, as the scrubbing and repetition of sections of music can be very annoying to a listener.

4.11.1 Less is More

When presenting music, less is often more; though it is important to have some alternatives in your back pocket in case the director does not like your initial presentation. It's a good idea to begin by presenting two to three edited pieces that contain the main thematic ideas for the most important scenes in the film. These might include a climactic fight or love scene, or the movie's opening or final scenes.

PAX Quote

"Take 'yes' for an answer. Don't play other options after they 'buy' one. They will question your opinion of the choice."

You will have an opportunity to talk about each of the edits, and what you think works well, and what doesn't work so well. Note that all your pieces must have the effect of enhancing the film and be edited to perfection, even if you're convinced one works better than all the rest.

You may have some alternate edits—perhaps one version ends slightly earlier or another has a shorter midsection—which have the same basic effect. In this case, you can save time and avoid redundancy by playing just the altered section. Do so, however, only if the director likes the piece overall: slight changes in your edits are unlikely to change his or her mind.

When the director, producer, or film editor dislikes a piece of music or an edit, you have a perfect opportunity to find out exactly what it is they don't like. This will help you adjust your subsequent work to match their aims and ideas more closely; and it's also possible there's a simple change you can make. Perhaps there is one cymbal "hit" you think is great, but that the director hates, and if it is a sweetener it can be easily deleted or muted.

4.11.2 A Cautionary Tale

One experience of auditioning music was negative at the time, but provided me with a good lesson. I had been editing a musical idea: the beginning and end of the piece were done to my liking, but the midsection was unfinished, and still contained "bad" or "rough" edits. I had planned to fix this, but hadn't had time before the director and editor arrived. I clarified that I wasn't done and that the middle section would not sound good, but given a bit more editing time the piece would be presentable. They said not to worry and they would take this into account, and asked that I play it anyway. So I played the piece through, and when we reached the "bad" area they were visibly taken aback.

This is a perfect example of how poorly edited music can "take an audience out of the movie." Needless to say, in hindsight I should have played only the sections that were edited to my satisfaction, and skipped the unfinished part. It certainly left a bad taste in their mouths. Something else this experience emphasized for me was that there is a great difference between editing film and editing music. I can understand how an unfinished section of a film, perhaps with a "black" section or an unrendered dissolve, could be acceptable to a director. But when something doesn't sound right, no matter how you present it or how much you warn the listener, it will sound bad and wrong, and they will feel uncomfortable with what they hear. In this respect, music is one of the most "untouchable" and mysterious parts of the movie-making process.

> **Tip**
> Know your listener. Some are better than others at imagining a finished piece.

4.12 INDUSTRY INSIDER: JOSEPH S. DEBEASI, MUSIC EDITOR

1. **How would you describe the role of a music editor creating a temp score, as it relates to the overall success of a film? What is the value of a temp score, in your opinion? How has this changed over the years, and how might it change in the future?**

   The role of a music editor as it relates to the temp score is crucial to the success of the score and the film. As you work closely with the director, your work plays a critical role in shaping and defining the voice of the score. You're ultimately laying out a blueprint for the composer to follow when it comes time to complete the final score. Yes, you are adding music for screenings and for the director to see how well scenes work; however, this process is more important than just that. You get to experiment. Many times the process reveals which music doesn't work. In a sense you get to fail as you rule out styles and genres. If this were your composer's demos, especially this early on in the process, the director could begin to lose confidence and start to question his choice of composer. As music editors, we do our best to prevent a situation like that from happening.

   Always involve your composer in the temp process. My latest project I was fortunate to play all my temp choices for my composer before I ever sent them onward to the director. It was unusual for me to do that but in this case it worked really well for us. Additionally, never temp a style of music that is not in your composer's wheelhouse. If you find yourself in a situation where the director wants to temp music that is outside your composer's voice, you absolutely edit that music into the film. It's your job. It's also your job to inform your composer of the situation and facilitate the communication between your composer and director about the cue. They will work it out. Lastly, always work to get your composer and director communicating. The more that relationship builds, the better the score will meet the director's expectations. That was how I handled it.

   Temping can become very political. "Temp love" can prevail and very often composers are asked to write music similar to the work you've done in the temp. Some say this is the most creative time and process in the making of the score. Honor it. Respect it. And again, always involve your composer in the process as much as possible.

2. **What are some of the similarities and differences between working on low-budget and high-budget films?**

   When it comes to working on a low-budget project as compared to high-budget film, I find that the expectations of the work are the same. It must be great. It boils down to the cost of labor and not to the cost of materials. We still use Pro Tools. We still use our developed skills and aesthetics when it comes to editing music to film. We still must prepare music for the dub. In the end, we are responsible for the work of our hands, and our reputations are on the line no matter what our salary ends up being. Some producers know this and take advantage of that knowledge, but we always have choices and we can walk away and say no thank you to the project should we feel the need to do so. It is up to us to retain our own value in the eyes of the producers. It's our lesson to learn, not theirs. Not everyone can do what we do and I do believe "you get if you pay for." That being said I also believe that in certain situations 75 percent of something is better, at times, than 100 percent of nothing. It's a balancing act.

3. **How do you see the music editor's role, as it pertains to the overall involvement of music production? Particularly in terms of how it relates to your personal workflow, and with regard to your technical, musical or interpersonal skills, or any other qualities you bring to your work?**

This is extremely important. Our involvement in the music production is crucial. In the end we are ones "who know where the bones are buried." Many times on the dub stage one has to make an edit and had I not been involved throughout the whole process of the making of the score I would not have been able to pull off the type of edit that was needed.

On the dub stage of *The Book of Eli*, I needed to make a major edit. It was a scene where the directors decided that they were not happy with the cue that was recorded. I was asked to make a change. Because I was involved in the entire music production, I knew that we recorded some "grab-bag" material that the orchestrator prepared should we have time in our recording session to record it. I knew that material was a perfect choice for a critical scene in the cue. I cut it together along with other cue pieces and parts and everyone loved it … including the composer. Had I not been involved, that edit would not have come together as well as it did.

4. **How do you approach your temp score work with regard to preparation, and to collaborating with the director, film editor, music supervisor, and studio music directors or producers?**

My approach to temp scoring is the same as how I would approach composing for a scene. It starts with a lot of investigative work. I, in a sense, "interview" the director for what he's looking [for in terms of] emotionality for the scenes. I also find out the style of music he is wanting. With one director, I found that he didn't like high instruments, particularly high sustaining strings. Another director hated piano and wanted no solo piano in the temp. Asking questions before starting really helps facilitate the process. I do the same with the picture editor too. Most music supervisors I've worked with really collaborate regarding the temp score, and help with scores I may need and don't have access to. I also get a lot of songs for the scenes where songs are called for or to try. My experience with studio music directors is minimal during the temp phase. It's not until a composer is on board [that I] have a lot of interaction with them.

5. **From your experience of working in postproduction music, what are the skill sets that are crucial for a music editor's success in this industry?**

Be a musician. Understand music theory and production. I've heard music edits that were cut rhythmically correct be harmonically incorrect. In other words, the edit did not follow typical musical progressions or resolutions and it sounded weird to a trained ear. Had the editor known some theory that edit would not have happened. I've been asked to make bad edits where the music doesn't edit properly in rhythm or harmonically and when pointing it out the producer says "We'll just fade the music at that point and hide it under sound effects." OUCH. This is where the skill of diplomacy really helps.

Chapter 5
Editing Songs and Source Music

5.1 SONGS IN MOVIES

Songs have been a big part of the movie-making process ever since the beginning of "talkies," with Al Jolson singing "My Mammy" in *The Jazz Singer* (1927)—a prime example of an on-camera featured song in a movie. Songs have always been an important part of entertainment, and their attraction, interest, and "pull" for an audience mean a unique connection has been forged between songs and movies. The emotional connection between the film's visual storytelling power and the magic of music and lyrics is cherished as an art form and valued as a powerful moneymaker. The music supervisor, music editor, film editor, and director are all intrinsically involved in nurturing this emotional and financial connection between song and film. The music supervisor deals with the creative aspects of song selection as well as the financial and legal matter of licensing. The music editor is concerned with the inner workings of the relationship between the songs and the film, often from very early on in the temp editing process, and must use their creative skills to marry the two. As a team, the music supervisor and music editor have the responsibility of choosing and using songs so as to build a wonderful, effective, and emotionally resonant soundtrack of songs.

5.2 FINDING THE RIGHT SONG

Songs can be selected from many different sources. Our lives are inundated with music—on the radio and Internet, in stores, offices, and elevators. The question of how to find suitable songs for a film or television show might therefore seem like a simple one with obvious answers, but in practice the process is not quite so straightforward. The right material has to be found, and then legally acquired.

On large-budget projects, the music supervisor has room to reach out to artists for material that will make the director and studio happy. And individual artists, record labels, and music libraries are constantly trying to get their songs heard by music supervisors, due to the potential for lucrative music licensing deals; music editors can also be targeted in this way, as they often have a key role in placing songs in a movie. At the other extreme, on a low-budget film produced, written, directed, and edited by one person, that one person must search out music that is both creatively right for the film and affordable, and wade through the legal detail. That said, the sources they use are often the same as those for big-budget films.

5.2.1 Music Libraries

Music libraries represent a good, inexpensive source of song material, and even the biggest movies utilize their services. They include companies like 5 Alarm, MasterSource, FirstCom, BMG, APM, Beyond, Killer Tracks, and Omni Music, among many others. They collect and record music, and contract with composers and song-writers to license their music to television and film productions. Most of the music they provide is song-form, with some dramatic underscore also available.

While songs provided by music libraries will not be from the *Billboard* top ten, it is possible to license "soundalike" songs, and at a much lower cost. These often achieve writing and production values, and sound quality that match those of the hits, old and new, and they are often used by films and TV shows to provide background diegetic music and to create ambience, for example in a bar or restaurant scene. As a rough guide, a license to use one instance of such a song in a film might cost between $1,700 and $2,500 (for exact rates, contact the music libraries—most can be found online). In addition to soundalike music, some libraries acquire the songs of better-known artists in order to make additional revenue through royalties.

Music libraries often have recordings of songs both with and without lyrics. This is a great advantage for the music editor because he or she can cut between lyrics and instrumental sections, and combine and edit as needed. (This requires good editorial technique, of course—this is discussed later in the chapter.)

5.3 SONG LICENSING

The low-budget filmmaker wearing many hats needs to be careful when venturing into the world of song licensing. Studios and music supervisors have the knowledge base and resources to handle the many potential pitfalls and legal traps. Questions to ask include:

- Who owns the song? There are two parts to this: the licensing of the recording to be used, and the licensing of the song itself from the owner of the intellectual property rights. This latter is usually—but not always—a publisher and/or the creator of the song.
- How long will the license last? "In perpetuity," or does it run out after a certain length of time?
- Are there limits on how the song can be used? For example, a license might only allow for festival play, or it might apply only to a specific geographical area. If you want your film to be available in theaters worldwide, or for types of public performance other than those specified, you may need to pay more. The license needs to state the terms of usage clearly.

- How much of the song are you intending to use in your movie? Generally the initial contract with the publisher will state a certain length of time, say 38 seconds, for which the song will play in the film. The contract and the amount paid therefore only cover the use of 38 seconds or less, even if it's a 3-minute song. If the film is recut and the length of time the song plays increases as a result, a renegotiation will likely be needed.
- How many times will the song be used? Each separate time the audience hears the song, this is considered one usage—so a character switching off a radio on which a song is playing then switching it back on again (with the same song still playing) represents two uses of that song. Cutting between locations might have the same result. This is traditionally called a "needle drop," a term from the days of phonographs: each time you put the needle down was counted as one use of the song.
- Can you edit the song in the way you want to? The contract should contain some statement to the effect that the film production has the right to edit the song as they deem necessary. While this seems obviously part of the deal, it is a good idea to have it in writing; some artists are very protective of their material.
- Is there any performing rights organization attached to the composers or publishers of the song? While this is not necessarily a factor in the contract, it is something the music editor will need to know for the finished preliminary music cue sheet, which is part of the delivery requirements.

5.4 SONGS AS SOURCE MUSIC AND SONGS AS SCORE

As mentioned previously, there are two basic types of music usage in a project: underscore (or score) and source music. Underscore is the non-diegetic music which only the audience hears, and is usually specially composed. Source music is diegetic music that the characters also hear, for example on a radio or iPod, or as background music in a scene set in a restaurant or club. Most often these source pieces are previously recorded songs which were not written or performed with the movie in mind. Occasionally a song may be recorded specifically for the project, however, and some songs can take the form of an on-camera performance by one of the actors or by a "live" artist appearing in the movie. An artist might also be contracted to write a song for a film's opening or end credit sequence, or for a montage or particular collection of scenes. On-camera music is discussed in more detail in the next chapter.

Songs can also be used as score, and be mixed in to support the action, emotion, or storyline; this is a "song-score." Similarly, "scource" music is usually a song which the audience understand as coming from a source such as a radio, but which nevertheless develops and is mixed so as to underscore the scene.

5.5 EDITING SONGS

Where songs are used as source music, the music editor will need to cut them to fit the scene in a certain way. At a basic level, they might need to lengthen or shorten a song, fade it in and let it end as recorded, have it begin as recorded then fade it out, or have it begin "in progress" (that is, as if it had already been playing)—this last is common where a song is playing as background, say in a bar scene. These initial decisions are made by the director, and he or she will often also request that particular lyrics or instrumental sections play at particular moments. Editing a song doesn't just mean trimming or extending it to fit, however—that's the easy part. It also involves shaping the music and lyrics for dramatic impact. It is the music editor's task to cut the song to match the particular effect the director is looking for, and to achieve the optimum impact.

Figure 5.1 provides an example of this. Here, a source song has been "sweetened", or modified, by overlaying an extra drum section and a guitar part taken from the body of the song, creating a "prelap" and extending the introduction. Using separate tracks is usually simpler and gives the editor more control, so here the parts have been "two-tracked," or "split off." The drum intro has been mixed with the guitar part, the end of which has been processed with reverb to make it "ring," creating a natural-sounding introductory chord. This reverb has been blended with the guitar piece using a short cross-fade. Finally, slight volume graphing has been used to help balance the two tracks. Pro Tools also supports "clip gain" controls, which allow you to adjust and shape the volume of any individual clip. Using clip gain adjustments in conjunction with cross-fades, as well as volume graphing, gives you detailed creative control over your editing.

As this example helps to show, the song editing process and workflow can be complex and challenging. The next few subsections provide some specific guidance, and describe various song editing techniques and principles.

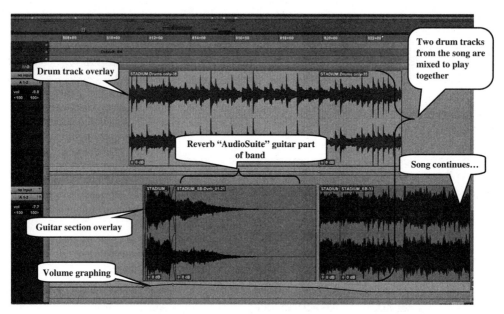

Figure 5.1 Two-tracking drum parts of a song to mix and blend with a short guitar intro.

5.5.1 Using Split Tracks

If you are editing a song that is used as source or scource it is very helpful to have split tracks. ("Scource," as mentioned, is music which functions both as source and score. An example is a source song on an on-screen radio which then changes for dramatic effect, being given a score-style treatment so that it sounds fuller and louder.) The kind of split will likely depend on what the music editor needs and what the song engineer or publisher can supply. It's common, however, to be able to get full-mix tracks and an instrumental-only track. This is particularly useful if the song is used as scource and must play along with and be cut around dialogue. Other splits that it can be helpful to acquire are separate vocal and instrumental tracks, or even separate tracks for drums, guitars, keyboards, bass, and so on—though unless the song is featured as a main title or an on-camera performance this type of multiple split is rarely needed.

The first step is to check that the split stems play in sync. There's a detailed discussion on syncing in Chapter 6, but essentially the process is simplified if the stems start at the same sample location, meaning they can be synced simply by "snapping" them to the same start point. If this is not the case, you can sync the vocal or instrumental track (or both) to the master mix track by matching waveforms and checking their phase relationship. You then need to consolidate all vocal and instrumental stems, which essentially "freezes" the sync relationship between the tracks in new, separate audio files. It's a good idea to rename the files to indicate they are to be edited together. For example:

- Song Title_Artist_Mstr_sync_VOX
- Song Title_Artist_Mstr_sync_INST

You can then place and edit the song following the director's instructions or preferences. Here, mixing, matching, and alternating between the full mix track, the instrumental track, and the vocal track can be very effective. Similarly, you might create or enhance impact in a scene by having a chorus enter where there is no dialogue, or perhaps where a character makes an emotional statement. This can also be a useful technique for the opening of the movie (the main title) or the end credit section, where you are shaping a song to provide a dramatic beginning or a climactic ending. At the same time, it is necessary to keep in mind the integrity and continuity of the song—for example, you should avoid making edits in the middle of a chorus or phrase which is particularly characteristic of the song. Figures 5.2 and 5.3 show examples of songs edited for use as source and scource.

5.5.2 Minimizing Edits

When lengthening or shortening a song to fit a director's requirements and a scene's dramatic shape, it is best to use as few edits as possible (see Figure 5.4, for example). The aim is to maintain the song's musical integrity and to respect the artist's original intent. While it is not possible to avoid some editing, the song should be recognizable to the audience, both in form and lyrical content. This is even more the case—and an even greater challenge—where the song is an old classic or a hit you can expect the audience to be familiar with.

It is usually preferable to use a song's natural beginning and ending, rather than fading it in and out, although different directors may have different preferences. You

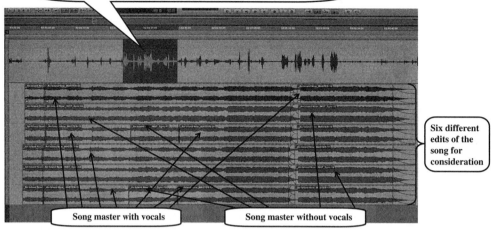

Figure 5.2 A song to be used first as a source piece, coming from a car radio, then as scource, when it is used to emphasize the drama and emotion of a moment between two young characters in love. The highlighted section in the top track represents important dialogue. Below this track are six different edits of the song for the director, editor, and mixer to discuss and choose between. These have been created by the music editor using the full master mix (with vocals) and an instrumental version (without vocals). The third and sixth edited versions, in particular, include instrumental sections where the highlighted section occurs in the dialogue track, to ensure the song doesn't compete too much

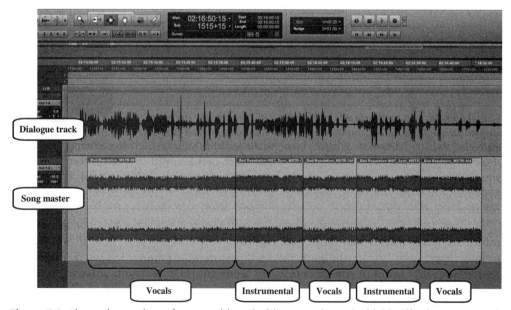

Figure 5.3 Alternating sections of a song with and without vocals can be highly effective. Here vocals are included as the song begins, when there is little drama on screen—the characters are hanging out in a bar. It is then cut with instrumental sections where there are verbal confrontations between characters, the vocals returning in the end scene, where the tension has been resolved. This avoids interference with the dialogue and makes for a better film mix

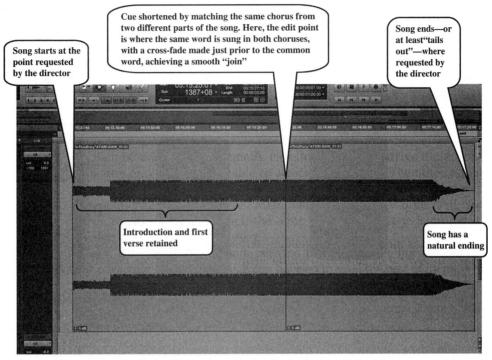

Figure 5.4 A song edited to fit the film and match the director's aims, but retain the essential character and content of the original

may be able to follow the film editor's lead in this respect, if the song in question has already been cut and shaped during the film editing process, but take care not to base too many assumptions on this.

Tip

Never assume anything in postproduction work. It is best to get confirmation if you are unsure. (Don't overdo it, though—asking too many questions may give the impression of a lack of confidence.)

Sometimes a song, as originally recorded, will fade out at the end with the band playing a repeated section; this is called a "record fade." Where this is the case, it may be necessary to edit the song to give it a one-chord ending, so that in shape and length it follows the emotional arc of a scene and matches its conclusion, or a segue into the next scene. To create an ending that sounds natural and as the band might have played it, the editor can use pieces from different places within the song, often short instrumental sections from the introduction, bridging verses or choruses, or drum fills.

5.5.3 Identifying Where to Edit

The starting point for achieving controlled editing is listening for the places in a song where lyrics, syllables, verses, choruses, bridges, or solo sections are similar. This identifies key points within the instrumental and voice parts where cuts and joins can be made without losing the song's structure or creative integrity. Introductions are a common place to start looking for these key points.

> **Tip**
> Pay attention to chord progressions and try to preserve them.

You can often shorten a song by cutting out a verse or chorus. While this may not immediately give you a song of the right length or structure, or one with all the lyrics in exactly the right place, it provides a starting point for constructing the desired edit. See Figures 5.5 and 5.6.

When editing out a repeated section of a song, it can be best to avoid cutting on an even bar. For example, in a phrase of eight bars it might be best to edit out bars 3, 4, 5, and 6 instead of bars 1 through 8. This way you can share the leftover bars 1 and 2, as the "A" side of the edit, with the leftover bars 7 and 8 as the "B" side. A further example is shown in Figure 5.7a–c.

> **PAX Quote**
> "All things being equal, cut on beat 2 or 3 of a bar—it's less obvious than the downbeat. If someone notices your handiwork you aren't doing it correctly."

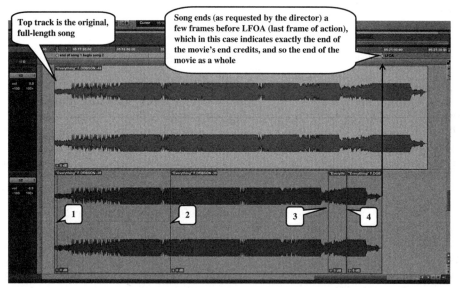

Figure 5.5 A song shortened with four edits—the track at the top is the original song, while the edited version is below. 1. Introduction shortened, as there are no vocals. 2. Edit within a verse, matching lyrics with the same syllable ("styling" and "smiling"), though the actual edit point and cross-fade come before the lyrics start. 3. An eight-bar phrase is here cut to four bars, with the edit on the word "ready," which is used in both the third and sixth bars. 4. The chorus plays three times in the original, but only twice in the edit.

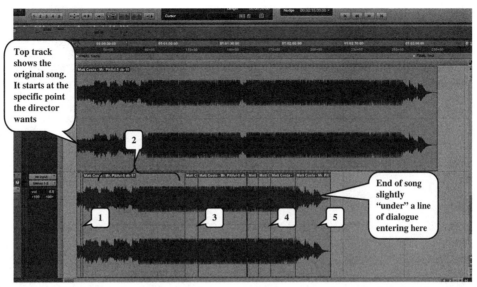

Figure 5.6 Another example of a shortened song—again, the track at the top is the original and the edited version is below. 1. Introduction shortened, as there are no vocals. 2. In general, it's a good idea to keep the first verse of a song. 3. Edit using the word "hope," which is repeated in different verses. 4. Repeated phrases can be deleted—if the same phrase is played three times, for example, you might cut the second iteration. 5. Song edited to end naturally, slightly before the dialogue comes in.

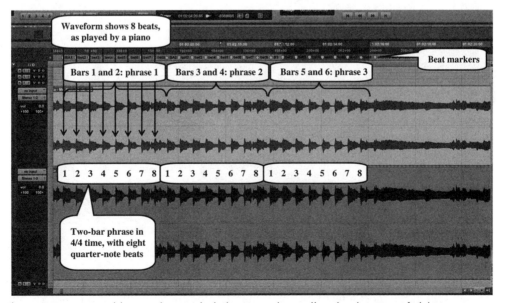

Figure 5.7a A song with a two-bar musical phrase—a descending chord pattern of eight quarter notes—repeated three times. Two bars can be cut here, but cutting in the middle of two phrases rather simply cutting a whole phrase may give a more natural-sounding result. Here, the original track is shown at the top, and the track to be edited below it.

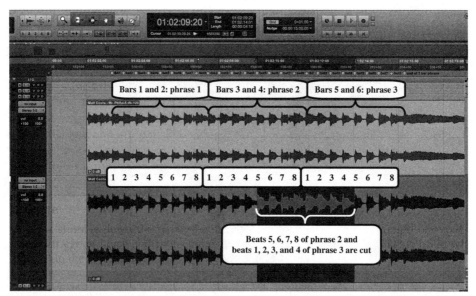

Figure 5.7b The last four beats of the second iteration of the phrase (bar 4) and the first four of the third iteration (bar 5) are edited out. This joins the first and last bars of the same two-bar phrase, from different repetitions.

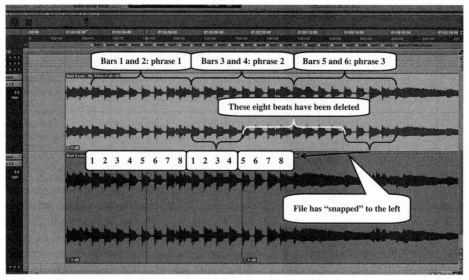

Figure 5.7c The resulting edit shortens the song while maintaining the natural sound of the original.

This technique of sharing sections of musical phrases which are the same or similar is often the most effective way of maintaining the integrity of the melody and phrasing. Particular care is needed, though, if vocal parts are also involved (as they were in the example shown in Figures 5.5 & 5.6), since maintaining the sense and integrity of the lyrics can be challenging. It is also possible to edit in uneven beats or bars, if the musicality of the phrase allows for it.

Tip: In Points and Out Points "On the Fly" Using Pro Tools

Back in the day, when editors used flatbeds and Moviolas, we marked the "in" and "out" points of a section of music by tapping the musics' tempo with a grease pencil on the mag tape as it passed over the play head. Today I use an updated version of this technique in Pro Tools all the time, to establish "cut-to-cut" sections or edit points. This is useful for all kinds of music but particularly handy for rhythmic pieces, with common or even polyrhythmic meters; it's particularly useful for deleting or editing similar sections—for example a repeated part in an introduction, solo bridge or ending, or a repeated chorus.

Audio editors often work by viewing digital waveforms in DAWs and listening to tracks. This technique goes a step further, editing or marking in and out points on tracks "on the fly," while the music plays. The technique is not new to Pro Tools users—in fact it appears in the early instructional books on Pro Tools—and it is easy to implement, practical, and effective. It doesn't trump other possible techniques, though, many of which can be equally effective—rather, it's another "trick in the bag" that you might like to try out, and may find helpful.

Here are some step-by-step guidelines:

1. Set a pre-roll a few seconds—at least two to four bars—ahead of the location in the song you think you want to edit for a deletion or move. You can place markers or memory locations as needed.
2. In the Pro Tools Preferences, on the Operation tab, make sure that "Edit Insertion Follows Scrub/Shuttle" is checked, and that "Timeline Insertion/Play Start Marker Follows Playback" is *not* checked. (When selected, this latter option also appears as a blue button on the main edit window, directly below the pencil tool. Make sure it's not selected—that is, the button should not appear blue.)
3. Play the track and tap the beat (usually quarter or eighth notes) on the "down" arrow key on your computer keyboard—keep a loose wrist and hit the down arrow with one finger, kind of like you are slapping the key; the trick here is to get into the "groove" or rhythm of the beat. Continue tapping the down arrow until you get to the point you want to make your edit "in", making it your last "down slap."
4. Keeping the song playing, resume tapping the beat but now on the "up" arrow key, making your last "up slap" at the point you want to make your edit "out."
5. Once you have played and marked the in and out points, stop playback. Your selection will be highlighted on the track. (If the highlighted area disappears when you stop, check the preference settings; see step 2.)
6. Play back your selection to check it—you can use loop playback to repeat the whole selection or selectivity play through the in point then out point to check their rhythmic accuracy. If you've made a mistake or missed the beat you want—it takes a while to get the feel of this—you can do the whole process over, or (if the in point is correct and you just want to reset the out point) play the selection from the in point and just tap on the up key, to update the out point.
7. To delete the selection, hit the Delete key on your computer keyboard. To move it, use Cut and Paste in the Edit menu. (Note this technique uses Slip mode rather than Shuffle. This is not to suggest Shuffle mode isn't useful—just not necessary in this case.)
8. When you hit Delete or Cut, the edit cursor will remain at the initial in point. Hold down the Control key (Mac) or Start key (Windows) and grab the right side selection. It will snap to the clip boundary at the in point.

Obviously your selection may not have been positioned perfectly on the beat—I am usually slightly late on the draw—but you can tell if the edit will work by following these further steps:

9. Make an empty stereo track directly below the one you are editing on (it can be tricky to make accurate edits if your selections are on the same track). Using the grabber tool, select the "B" side of the edit—to the right of your earlier selection—and, holding down Control (Mac) or Start (Windows) to prevent it moving out of sync, grab and drag it onto the new track.

10. With the trim tool, reveal a bar or two to the right of the "A" side section and the same to the left of the "B" side (now on the track below).

11. Slide the "B" side left or right, as needed, to match the sound and the waveforms of the "A" side. I often look for the higher transient peaks of drums, musical strums, or accents to match up.

12. Play back both tracks simultaneously to listen for the match. Once the two parts of the music, with their revealed sections, play together in time and rhythm, you have successfully matched them. Grab-highlight the "B" side and, again holding down Control (Mac) or Start (Windows) to maintain its position, drag it up to cover the overlapping section on the "A" side.

13. The final step is to choose where the best edit "line" is—it's important to note that your original in point is not necessarily the best place. Use the trim tool to move the edit, revealing more of either the A side or the B side, to find a position where the song sounds smooth and natural, and there's no "bump" associated with the edit. A cross-fade can make an edit sound smooth, but if you find the "zero-crossing" point you can make a perfect edit without any need for cross-fading.

5.5.4 Using Cross-fades

Making effective use of cross-fades is crucial, and editors need to be skilled in using the variety of options in Pro Tools. Many different "flavors" can be created by using either the preset shapes in the cross-fade dialog or the user-configurable shapes. In music editing in general and song editing in particular, a common starting point is to use an equal power cross-fade with the second preset curve shape. This raises the volume in the center of the cross-fade and so avoids any "dip" at the crossing point. The edit is "smoothed out," which is the effect we're looking for when cutting between sections of material which are musically compatible, similar, or exactly the same (and, as described in the previous subsection, this is often the case with song editing). A common approach is to draw the cross-fade equally across the "A" and "B" sides of the edit, which can be done easily with the smart tool. Another is to vary the length of the overlap and the volume distribution of the edit. You should not hesitate to make the fade unequal, to emphasize one side more than the other. This approach can produce a better effect, for example when there are vocals on one side but not the other. It's really all about what sounds best.

While technically the cross-fade tools are designed to be used to blend two clips at an edit point on the same track, you can also cross two or more musical elements on different tracks. "Two tracking" or "splitting off" onto multiple tracks can be a useful editing technique in a number of situations, and can mean the cross-fade blending the two sections will sound better.

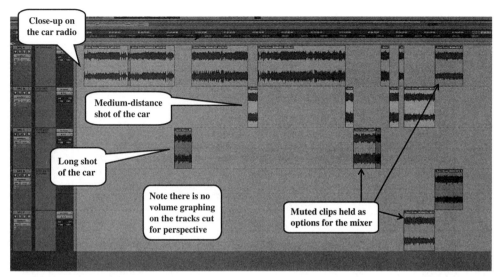

Figure 5.8 A song used as source music cut for perspective. Each different point of view (POV) is represented on a different track.

5.5.5 Perspective Cutting

Depending on how a film is cut, there may be a need for "perspective cutting" of songs that are used as source pieces. This is similar to the change in background sound effects as a scene changes, and cuts, for example, from the inside of a building to outside. The relevant "perspective" here is the POV (point of view) of the camera, and so the audience. As an example, someone driving might be seen first inside the car, then through the front windshield, then stopped with the side window rolled down, all while the car's radio plays. The sound of the radio needs to change to match each different POV—it will (most likely) be loudest inside the car, and more muffled and indistinct when heard from outside, with the car's windows closed. Depending on the particular scene, any number of perspective cuts may be needed.

Using the proper technique for cutting perspectives, the music editor places a song in position and makes a separation edit at each scene change cut in the film, so that the song occupies multiple tracks. Importantly, each different track represents a different POV. Figure 5.8 shows a song edited to play as source music for a scene with a car radio, shot from three different POVs. The POV from the front seat of the car, being the closest to the radio, is on the top track. The next two tracks are for POVs progressively further from the radio, while the fourth track in this instance is a continuation of the song as "scource": we see the car but no one is in it and the radio is off. Here the director is using artistic license and playing the song for dramatic impact.

The purpose of splitting the song across the different perspectives is to allow the re-recording mixer to control the song's sound "position." He or she can treat each track with EQ, volume, and other processing appropriate to the particular perspective. Following a traditional workflow, and giving the mixer complete control of the sound from "fresh," unaltered master music tracks, the music editor should not make sound

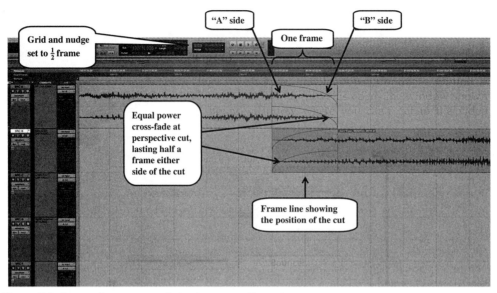

Figure 5.9 An equal power cross-fade at a perspective cut.

adjustments for perspective (note there is no volume graphing or clip gaining in Figure 5.8, for example). In recent years, though, it has also become common for the music editor to provide an alternate set of tracks, prepared with perspective sound adjustments, to allow the mixer the choice of which to use. This is usually because of time constraints on the mix.

Each perspective change dictates where the song should be cut, so that the change in sound is matched to the exact frame the corresponding visual change takes place. After cutting the song and positioning the different sections across the required number of tracks, it is important that the music editor places a small cross-fade at each cut. Without this, there could be an audible "pop" or "bump" at the change, especially since the mixer will be altering volume and often EQs between one perspective and another. Figure 5.9 shows one such edit. Usually Pro Tools is set to grid mode at 1 frame to make the perspective cut and a half-frame nudge to make the cross-fade. An equal amount of audio from each side of the edit is revealed—the amount can vary, depending on the sound, but I usually use an overlap of half to one frame. An equal power cross-fade can then be used to blend the two perspective sounds seamlessly, with the reduction in volume on the "A" side of the cut being matched by the increase on the "B" side. It should sound like there is no cut at all.

The equal power cross-fade half a frame either side of the cut is a good first step, but it's entirely possible that other cross-fades will work as well, and possibly even better. Many factors affect which is optimal. Figure 5.10 shows an "X"-type (or straight-line) cross-fade spanning a full two frames, one frame length either side of the cut. Usually a cross-fade of this type will cause the volume to dip in the middle but in some cases it is an improvement on an equal power cross-fade, and some mixers prefer it. Choosing which fades work best is largely a matter of experiment, determined on a case-by-case basis by listening to each transition at different volume settings.

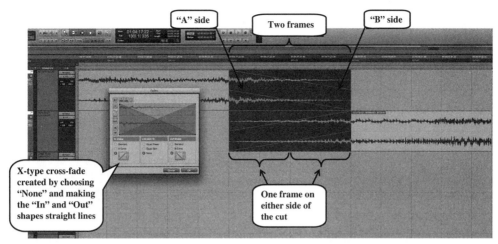

Figure 5.10 An X-type cross-fade.

Most often the picture cuts occur where there are no existing song edits, and the song plays through "as recorded." Occasionally, however, an existing edit falls exactly on a perspective cut and creates a "bump." It's also possible for a sharp sound at the edit point—such as a drum beat or percussive vocal effect—to end up sounding like a bump or rough edit. In this situation it is wise to consider moving the song's overall position, to avoid the particularly jarring effect of a "bad edit" at a perspective change. On the other hand, if the song has been heavily edited this may only create problems at other perspective cuts; you need to make a creative judgment call. If you do decide that moving the song is the best option, a Pro Tools shortcut can be used to do this without losing edits, as described in the next Tip.

Tip

Shortcut: Select the whole edited song, including the clip boundaries. Holding down the Control key (Mac) or Start key (Windows), press either the "+" key to "advance" the song, so that it starts earlier, or the "-" key to "retard" it, so that it starts later. (Note that Pro Tools uses exclusively the "+" and "-" keys on the numeric keypad here, and not the instances of these symbols on the "typewriter keys" of the keyboard.) Each keystroke will advance or retard the song by the "nudge" amount set.

Unless you are moving the song without perspective cross-fades, be careful to avoid using "clip grouping" for the selection, as this often means the fades will not adjust correctly. Additionally, how far you can move the song in this way is limited to the available parent file media behind the clip boundaries.

It is usual to create copies of the tracks and make a few different position shifts to determine which is optimal, always keeping a copy in the original position to revert back to if need be. Of course, you need to listen carefully to check the song after any moves or new edits, particularly at the perspective cuts.

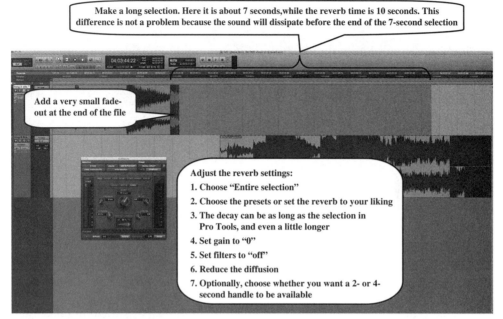

Figure 5.11a To create a reverb ending or transition, make a long selection and process it using AudioSuite reverb. A number of reverb plugins are available—here Avid's "D-Verb" is used.

5.5.6 Adding Reverb

Processing a tone or chord with reverb is a good way of smoothing over either an edit or a song's ending. When a cross-fade between the "A" and "B" sides of an edit sounds too abrupt, you can split the music onto two or more tracks and use AudioSuite reverb for the "A" side, which then rings across the edit and blends into to the "B" side. Reverb at the end of a song, meanwhile, may sound good on just one track, so there may be no need for two-tracking in this way.

However, reverb should be treated with great caution—the different musical elements need to be balanced carefully. In fact, while a music editor may have excellent reverb plugins, at times it's best just to leave reverb to the re-recording mixer. This is, then, another reason to split the music onto separate tracks at the edit point.

If going ahead to implement a reverb, Figures 5.11a–c show the process. The steps are as follows:

1. Trim the file to end with the sound you want to "ring out."
2. Place a very small curve fade-out at this end position so as to allow the abrupt sound to end without hearing a "pop" or bump.
3. Select from a little before the end point to 7 or 8 seconds past the last sound, into the empty space on the track.
4. In the plugin of your choice, choose your reverb settings. Make sure it will create the reverb file in the correct track and select "continuous clip." (Note the reverb settings in Figure 5.11b.)

Figure 5.11b Reverb, as its name suggests, causes the sound within the selection to "ring," in this case across the gap between tracks.

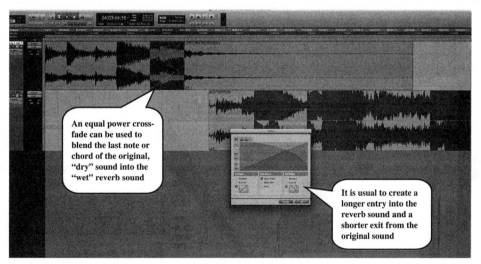

Figure 5.11c The finishing touch is a cross-fade which blends the original sound with the new reverb sound, and helps to create a smooth, natural transition.

5. In Pro Tools 10 and later you can create a handle length that will affect the file beyond your selection. The default is 2 seconds, but this can be changed in "Preferences."
6. Render the reverb sound by selecting "Render."
7. Make a long cross-fade which blends the "dry" original sound (the "A" side) into the "wet" reverb sound (the "B" side). In general, this transition benefits from a longer, gentler curve into the reverb and a harder, shorter shape for exiting the dry sound.

This of course just provides a starting point, and an editor would continue adjusting these parameters until a natural, smooth sound is achieved.

> **Tip**
> Sometimes stretching the note you are going to reverb is very helpful.

5.5.7 Pitch Modulation

Another useful technique involves modulating or changing the pitch of a section in a song in order to introduce a change and so add to the momentum or elevate the emotion of a scene. When pitching a song in digital editing, going up two semitones, or one step, can sound quite natural, as it mimics normal songwriting technique. This type of modulation can be useful when lengthening a song which then might otherwise sound unnaturally long to the audience. It can also give the music an uplifting feel. Another effect—this one especially suited to underscore, for example for a horror film—is to use a semitone increment, which seems to bring more drama to the scene.

While there are numerous processing tools that digitally change pitch, with or without changing the length of the piece, one often used in music editing is Serato's Pitch 'n Time Pro. In addition, Pro Tools' transposing tools and Elastic Time (discussed in the next subsection) can be used to alter the pitch of audio.

Pitch processing should be done carefully and with close attention to the sound of the altered piece, since it can result in undesirable sounds—"digital artifacts"—becoming embedded in the file. These are usually introduced when an inferior plugin is used or by overprocessing the file beyond the manufacturer's recommended range.

> **Tip**
> For optimal results, only pitch up or down by one or two semitones at a time (or half steps): that is, first alter a piece by one semitone, then alter the new, pitched file by another semitone.

Usually pitching is reserved for instrumental sections, since pitching solo vocals typically results in inferior sound quality. It's also tricky to modulate stereo mixes, because *everything* goes up or down, including the drum parts—so suddenly the pitch of the toms and snares, for example, will change. Because (with the possible exception of timpani) drums are "unpitched" instruments, and not meant to change tuning, it is better to try to keep them at their original pitch. However sometimes this cannot be avoided.

5.5.8 Using Elastic Audio

The length of pieces and sections of music often needs to be altered in order to place them exactly, and to "hit" certain moments in the movie. Elastic Audio (or Elastic Time) was added to Pro Tools in version 7.4, and continues to provide a very useful means of "stretching" audio. It is very useful for matching music to dancing, for example, or to on-camera singing or playing (discussed in Chapter 6). As mentioned in the previous subsection, it can also be used to alter pitch. I won't go into all the details of how to use it here—this can be reviewed in the Pro Tools reference guide—but as a general rule for using any plugin or tool that alters length or pitch: use extreme caution. As with overprocessing when pitching music, overstretching can cause digital artifacts and poor sound quality. You may find that time-stretching smaller parts of a file, as a percentage or ratio of the overall selection length, produces better results. Many plugins can stretch audio without changing the pitch. Without changing specific plugin settings, altering pitch will by its nature also change length. While using pitching plugins, be especially careful with stretching vocals or avoid using the stretched vocal parts.

> **Tip**
>
> If you have a choice, stretching smaller percentages on longer or larger selections of audio produces better results.

In Pro Tools, TCE properties can be set to access your installed plugin of choice, via "Processing" in the Preferences menu. The premium Avid plugin for this is X-Form; another option is Serato's Pitch 'n Time. A third-party plugin will usually produce better results than the Time Shift plugin that comes with Pro Tools. Even if you have not purchased X-Form, the Elastic Audio algorithm uses X-Form processing, which is one of the best available for the Pro Tools platform. And if using another, third-party plugin, you can read the real-time stretching information from the Elastic Properties menu as a percentage, and use that figure to process the file in another plugin or program.

> **Tip**
>
> Be aware that if Elastic Audio shows, say, 102 percent TCE, the equivalent to be typed into a third-party plugin may be 98 percent. Different software manufacturers set up parameters differently.

5.5.9 Using Alternates

Editing different versions of takes or perspective cuts and presenting a variety of song selections is common practice with all postproduction audio; it is rare that the ideal choices are made on the first try. The music supervisor is constantly listening to new material and making deals in an attempt to find songs that are just the right fit for the movie's creative direction and budget. The music editor is also editing different songs in different ways, and playing them for the director or producer. As you can imagine, this is very time consuming, and each song provides different challenges.

There are several ways to show alternate tracks in Pro Tools. You can either duplicate tracks or make a new set of tracks and copy-and-paste the selections you want to modify, so keeping the original materials. You can also make multiple playlists. While the first two methods might be preferable, since the different tracks can be easily viewed and hidden, the playlist view in Pro Tools also has its advantages, depending on individual preferences and workflow.

5.6 WORKING WITH THE FILM EDITOR

The film editor often has an early role in the songs and musical direction for a project. They are the first to edit and develop the picture in terms of visual storytelling, sound, and music. While the musical choices in their picture "cut" are often temporary, they can provide an initial guide for the music supervisor and music editor. In Chapter 8, I explore in more detail the creative and technical workflow between the music editor and film editor. Suffice to say here that the dynamic between music editor, film editor, and director is an important, ongoing, and fluid one throughout the postproduction process.

5.7 WORKING WITH THE MUSIC SUPERVISOR

As mentioned at the beginning of this chapter, the music supervisor has a key role to play in creating a successful music soundtrack for any film or television project—in researching and finding the best music, and making deals. The music editor works closely with them to ensure the creative direction is consistent, and that the editorial treatment of the songs matches the movie technically and stylistically.

PAX Quote
"There is great creative skill in finding the best piece of music for that specific scene while also satisfying the director, producers, creative executives, etc. I have heard music supervision compared to hitting three moving targets at the same time."

Check out the next section, where Bob Bowen illustrates the importance and value of the hard work done by a music supervisor.

5.8 INDUSTRY INSIDER INSIGHTS: BOB BOWEN, MUSIC SUPERVISOR, RELATIVITY MEDIA

1. **How would you describe your role as it relates to the overall success of a film or television show? What are some of the key skill sets your job requires?**
   As President of Music for Relativity Media, I am responsible for the overall creative direction, strategic development, and implementation of Relativity's music initiatives. My role as a music supervisor for the studio is to oversee and produce the musical vision for our films. The musical vision must meet the expectations of the filmmakers and the studio, while at the same time being delivered on schedule and within the budget parameters.

The success of a film can be defined by numerous measurements, including: box-office performance, home entertainment/DVD/VOD sales, reviews and/or awards (Oscars, Grammys, and Golden Globes). The relationship with music and the success of a film is difficult to measure because it is not directly correlated. However, a film is usually successful if the audience is invested in its characters and the journeys they go through during the film's story. If an audience is moved by a film and it makes a connection with a mass audience—i.e. large box-office sales—music can be a part of the ingredients that make up that success; along with the costumes, the production design, the actors, the screenplay, the cinematography, the editing, the casting, etc. A film is a collaboration of all of these components coming together to make one great film, and part of my role as a music supervisor is to help make that happen.

I measure the success of music in a film by delivering the most impactful music on time and on budget. However, music can be subjective and as a result it can warrant many different responses based on an individual's tastes and experiences, which can sometimes make it challenging to formulate a collective assessment. In addition, if no one comments about the score or music in a film, then that could also signify that it was a success because it supported the story and characters on screen by not getting in the way. Audiences or critics rarely comment on music in a film, unless it is a musical or a music-driven project. However, film music can be recognized through awards or nominations. For instance a Grammy for best soundtrack, or an Oscar or Golden Globe for best original song or best original score. The other quantitative way to measure the success of music in a film is through soundtrack sales, coupled with the success of the film's box-office and sales performance.

Some key skill sets for my job are the following:

a. Wide breadth of musical knowledge, covering film composers, numerous music genres, songs, songwriters, artists, record labels, music publishers, managers, agents, music attorneys, contractors, recording studios, orchestras, music editors, etc.

b. Brokering deals, music licenses, and relationships effectively—by delivering the optimal creative assets for a film's needs, while being fiscally responsible.

c. Project planning and management.

d. Maintaining and nurturing a robust network within the music community to negotiate deals quickly and leverage that network for favorable deals and access to great artists and talent.

e. Collaborative mindset that keeps focus on the bigger picture, which is creating the best film by supporting it with the best music.

2. **What are some of the similarities and differences between working on low-budget and high-budget films? And between working as a music supervisor in a staff position in a film company and as an independent music supervisor?**

The mission statement for my work with all films—regardless of budget—is to try and make the best film possible that connects with an audience, while delivering unique and original music that meets the expectations of the director and studio. The main difference between a large film budget versus a small film budget is the amount of resources that are available for you to work with. In music budget terms resources can be defined as: time/schedule, song licensing fees, composer fees, music editor fees, and scoring costs (musicians, choir, studio, mixing, etc.). Music budgets for a large-budget film ($75 million plus) are typically around $1 million, whereas a music budget for a lower budget film ($15 million) is typically around $300,000. In addition, the pressure to deliver great music for these films can differ depending on the size of the budget and the expectations of the filmmakers and the studio. For instance, a bigger-budget film will usually have more pressure than a smaller-budget film because large-budget films are expected to perform very well at the box office, because they are targeted for a wider audience ("tent-pole" strategy) and there is higher risk at stake.

In addition, a smaller-budget film tends to involve a different level of filmmakers that can cultivate an atmosphere where trying different avenues to score and create music is expected and a by-product of the budget. As a result, the combination of working with younger filmmakers coupled with a smaller budget forces you to become more creative with your resources. The end result could be hiring an unconventional composer or creating a soundtrack that might not involve very popular artists, which potentially ends up being very unique and original. The film in turn could lead to a more enjoyable experience for the audience because they are introduced to and discover new music or composers.

An independent music supervisor versus staff music supervisor requires similar skill sets, as mentioned above. However, the big difference is that a staff music supervisor at a studio has to manage a larger range of expectations and also perform more administrative functions associated with a media company. Furthermore, a staff music executive has to work closely with key departments within the company like marketing, distribution, and home entertainment, where an outside supervisor would not.

3. **How do you see the music editor's role as it pertains to the overall involvement of music production? Particularly in terms of how it relates to your job, with regard to their technical, musical or interpersonal skills, or any other qualities?**

A music editor's role in the overall involvement of music production can vary depending on a film project's needs. If it is a musical or a film that requires on-camera music playbacks, then their involvement can start before production and go all the way through postproduction. A majority of a music editor's role takes place during postproduction. A music editor's main function is to help sculpt the tone and direction of the music by cutting songs and score to picture under the guidance of the music supervisor, the composer, the director, the picture editor, the producers, and the studio. A music editor's role can sometimes involve just editing and cutting music to picture, because the filmmakers and music supervisor have a deep understanding of music's role in the film; therefore, they do not require a lot of creative input. The opposite of this can happen as well—where the music editor needs to have more creative input in addition to funneling and editing music into the picture.

In order to be effective, a music editor needs to be a great collaborator and have the technical skills to edit music. This requires a deep understanding of music, rhythm, emotion, pacing, and knowing when and where to spot music in a film. An effective music editor requires not only the technical skills but also the emotional intelligence needed to navigate through the multiple creative personalities that come with the creative filmmaking process. In short, personal skills are just as important because when you are working under intense deadlines and you are collaborating with many different creative people (composer, editors, studio executives, directors, producers), you want to have your team prepared and able to adapt to multiple personalities and changes that are presented.

4. **How do you envision your role in postproduction evolving in future, particularly in terms of budgets and expectations?**

During my career film music budgets have trended downwards, whereas the pressure to deliver high-quality music on time and on budget has increased. As a result, I have to manage music budgets very carefully, which means I am more involved in the postproduction process—overseeing schedules, workflow, scoring dates, and delivery dates. I see this part of the job becoming even more important as the industry continues to evolve due to the enhancements in technology—where the expectation and mindset is that changes can be made quickly because we have the technology to do it. However, what music editing and composers do require creative resources that do not always come out of a computer; therefore I have to preserve and manage these resources to insure the process of delivering high-quality music that meets the director's and studio's needs.

5. **Is there a situation in the postproduction industry where it's appropriate or even advantageous for the composer to mix and produce his or her own music, perhaps without the help of a music mixer, orchestrator, programmer, music editor, or other team members?**

As film music budgets continue to be reduced, it becomes more important for a composer to be able to perform numerous functions other than just writing a great score. If a composer can mix, produce, perform, orchestrate, and program his or her music, then they potentially could be considered for more film projects. Since budgets are being reduced more composer deals are constructed as "all-in" or package deals. If a composer can perform numerous duties, then he or she can have more money in their pocket at the end of a project. The film-scoring landscape has changed and the big-budget creative fees are becoming fewer, and the composer for this new age has to be able to adapt and perform numerous duties in order to survive and sustain a career. As a result, a composer today has to be able to wear many different hats than in the past.

Chapter 6
Musicals and On-Camera Songs

6.1 SYNC IS EVERYTHING

Synchronizing the visual performance of a song with the music is more of a challenge than meets the eye. Whenever an actor or performer is seen playing music or singing on camera, it is the music editor's responsibility to make sure the song is in sync with the picture and the music tracks are prepared correctly for the re-recording mixer. Today's high-quality digital cameras can shoot picture at superior resolutions, and they can also capture "production sound" (that is, the sound recorded during shooting) digitally from the set—including for a shot of a band playing or someone singing. However, even on a low-budget film with a single camera capturing all the sound in this way, the camera's sync sound recording may not be usable for the final mix—unless perhaps it is a simple case of an actor humming or one person playing an instrument. On most films and television shows a separate location sound recordist captures the dialogue on set using a digital audio recorder. If there is any on camera music, it will be the music editor's responsibility to replace the production music track, prepare, synchronize, fix, and sometimes replace the music, as needed.

> **PAX Quote**
> "Acting and singing are performance arts that can't always conform to the mathematical constraints of sync. The music editor's job is to clean up after the performance ... to fool the audience into believing the visuals."

6.2 USING PRE-RECORDS

Ever since the Hollywood musical blossomed and the tradition of the Warner Bros., MGM, or Disney live-action film with on-camera singing and dancing was created, the music has been pre-recorded and played back on set for the actors to lip-sync to. This remains the proper and preferable way to synchronize music with visuals; recent examples include *Nine*, *Moulin Rouge!* and *Chicago*. The songs for these films were written and recorded before shooting, then played on set for the actors, singers, and dancers to hear. These "pre-records" might be the same stereo master tracks that are played on the radio, or "split-stem" recordings made specifically for the film (more on these in the next section).

If no dialogue is being recorded at the same time as a song performance, the actors can sing out. This helps to make the performance look real and convincing to the audience—for example the muscles in a singer's neck and face will move and respond realistically. If the scene has dialogue during and around the song, however, the actors can listen to the playback through hidden in-ear monitors that look similar to hearing aids. As the song is played back they must lip sync or "play" silently, to avoid interfering with the dialogue recording. Even in the best of circumstances this latter method is a challenge for all concerned. The starting point for the song's playback (which is usually controlled manually) is likely to differ from take to take, leaving the film editor with the problem of editing shots together to create a finished scene with a flow and pacing that make sense, and in which musical continuity is preserved. Ultimately, though, it is the music editor's job to re-edit the music so that it both matches the edited scene and sounds natural.

There are rare exceptions to the "rule" of pre-recorded music and lip-synced visuals. For a recent film production of *Les Misérables* the director recorded the actors singing on set, with a pianist's accompaniment relayed to them live via induction loop. (Induction loops are typically installed in public buildings to assist hearing-aid users; a signal transmitted by a wire loop can be received by each earpiece in the immediate area.) This gave the actors complete artistic freedom to perform "in the moment" while their voices were recorded "live," as they would be if they were delivering only dialogue. In postproduction the piano accompaniment was replaced by a 70-piece orchestra. While this worked well for the operatic style of this film, projects aiming for more of a film-musical style may benefit from using the traditional "sync" approach. In addition, recording on set, with "live" accompaniment and "live" singers, is much more technically complex. For most productions the level of challenge and cost involved is likely to be prohibitive.

Playback tracks should be managed by a music editor, though for lower-budget films or scenes for which playback does not require as much attention the location recordist may do this. It is important to note that the digital playback recorder needs to be set to match the speed and frame rate of the camera—24 or 23.976 FPS for a film camera or an HD video camera, respectively—and be resolved using the same clock source as the camera, location recorder, and player. In this way, the music playback will be synced with the picture throughout editorial and mixing, even if it needs to be pulled down or up, or converted. The music editor needs to be familiar with the likely technical and postproduction requirements related to audio and video.

6.3 MULTIPLE STEM TRACKS

Many different types of files and track layouts can be used for on-camera sync music. Most often the pre-recorded song played back on the set is in a stereo format. It can be helpful, however, to have "split-stem" tracks, at the very least separating instruments and vocals. For a big "production" piece, having separate tracks allows the person managing playback on set to send each performer a different balance of the musical elements, according to their particular role. The split-stem tracks used for this purpose may also be later be used as the master tracks in postproduction editorial.

These separate stems are best created when the song is mixed, but if this is not possible it can also be done later, provided you have access to the original multi-track recording. The particular stems used will likely depend on the specific requirements for the film shoot—it may be as simple as having a combined stereo track of the rhythm section or percussion, and separate vocal tracks. A good set of track stems to have available for a band-type song, however, would be:

- Bass (mono)
- Guitars (stereo)
- Keyboards (stereo)
- Lead vocals (mono)
- Lead vocals reverb print (stereo)
- Background vocals (stereo)
- Background vocals reverb print (stereo)
- Drum kit (stereo) (occasionally separate kick and snare tracks)
- Percussion (stereo)

And for an orchestral piece:

- Strings
- Brass
- Woodwind
- Piano
- Harp
- Percussion
- Vocals or choir
- Soloists

Tip

Important: Remember to request that the recording engineer provide pre-recorded stems which all start from the same sample location, to ensure that they play in sync.

One of the most important technical requirements for a music editor to communicate to a mixer or recording engineer regarding stem files is that they should all start from the same sample location (see Figure 6.1; the end point can also match across tracks, though this is less important). This is achieved in Pro Tools by "record arming" all the track stems at the same location and time, and pressing play & record while the selector is on all the tracks. If there is a need for separate passes or takes, the selector should be placed on the relevant track so that it records from exactly the same position as in a previously recorded track, which then becomes the reference track. This is repeated for each take, until all the stems have been recorded either as a unit or separately. In addition, even if a stem only contains music for part of the time, it is important that the recording lasts from beginning to end of the song, in sync with all

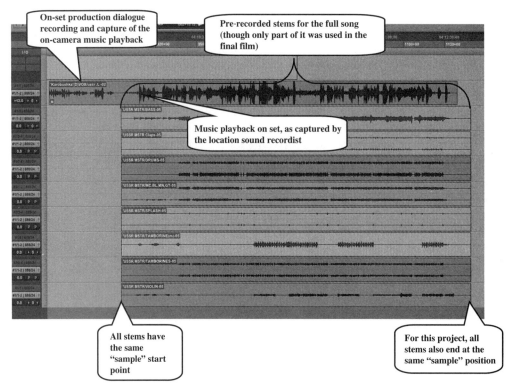

Figure 6.1 An on-set sound roll containing a capture of the play back music (mono track above). Note below, the multiple stem tracks with a common sample-accurate start point.

the other stems. This ensures that the tracks can be aligned by "snapping" them to the leading edge of the clip, so that they then play in time with each other, maintaining phase and sync as the recording engineer intended. An additional check can also be provided if the engineer prints a "sync pop" at the beginning of each file, as a common reference point. (A sync pop in this case is a 1K tone usually for the duration of 1 frame, recorded at the same location in each stem.)

If the recording is complete but the music stems do not start at the same point, you can select the longest to be the reference and then, after audibly matching the rest to it, use the consolidate function in Pro Tools, making the file length the same for all the stems.

It is also a good idea to have a consistent file naming system for stem tracks, so that they are easy to find and organize. There is no standard practice for this, but information typically included is:

- Song title
- Artist, band, or other performance identifier
- Stem number or letter, based on referencing the tracks from top to bottom (the music editor can of course change this order if need be)
- Stem name—typically this describes the parts included on the stem, such as vocals, or percussion
- Descriptor—optional, as needed

So, for example:

- New Song_John Doe Band_01_Bass_master mix stem
- New Song_John Doe Band_02_Drums_master mix stem
- New Song_John Doe Band_03_Lead Vox_master mix stem

6.4 USING THE STEREO MIX AS A REFERENCE TRACK

In postproduction, the original, pre-recorded stereo song mix is imported into the picture editing system, to be synced and edited with the visuals. If the song is a "featured" performance, the film editor must take particular care to cut the synced images and music in a way that maintains a natural musical consistency and a song structure that makes sense to the audience. The constraints imposed by the need to sync the picture and music are obviously much greater than when the song does not need to be directly linked to an on-camera musical performance, when both the film editor and the music editor have more freedom to edit the music to fit and to make sense as a whole.

6.5 BEGINNING TO EDIT

The playback reference tracks (provided they were played back correctly on set and can therefore be used for syncing in postproduction) are sent on to the music editor—that is, from the Avid video editor to Pro Tools—using an appropriate transfer file format, usually AAF file exchange but occasionally the older OMFI.

> **Tip**
>
> Be sure to request that the files be delivered with full-length handles so you can access the full-length master files.

> **Tip**
>
> One common early step in editing an on-camera song is to select the whole imported AAF reference track and use Pro Tools' "heal separation." This deletes any edit lines that the film editor may have made unintentionally by cutting the picture without also intending to cut the audio. Cross-fades in the AAF made by the film editor are undone, the separation revealed and, if not a "true" edit, healed.

Figure 6.1 includes an example of sync sound recorded on set: the top track on the screen is from the production sound roll, and contains not only the dialogue but also captured the song playback for the sync performance—in this case the song was played over speakers. The singer was able actually to sing out as the song played in the background, ensuring a natural-looking performance. As mentioned previously, this approach to syncing is not always possible—this is an instance of a featured musical performance during which no dialogue had to be recorded.

The music editor should also obtain the original stereo master of the song in order to make sure it syncs with the imported AAF reference file. If not, a technical error has occurred at some point in the chain—often the problem will have originated with clock speed selection at the shoot, or with converting or importing the stereo playback reference track. Of course, the reference track received from the picture editor will likely have edits, and so only sections of the original master stereo song will match the AAF reference. When playing the AAF and the original master, the waveforms of both should be matched exactly, peak to peak; this is most easily achieved by nudging the master audio by samples. Tracks synced in this way, by locating them to match an exact or near-exact copy, are referred to as sounding "phase dependent," or just "in phase." Where the waveforms are not perfectly aligned, there is a "phase shift" (or "sync offset") which produces a hollow-sounding "swoosh," caused by some frequencies canceling others out. Eliminating this (which is usually achieved within one or two samples) is an indication that the phase alignment is correct; the sound should become fuller and more natural. Phasing will be more apparent when syncing different mixes—depending on the material you are working with, a small amount of phasing may occur even when the music is in sync.

If you don't have an AAF file from the picture editor, it's also possible to reference the song to the audio track embedded in the QuickTime movie you are working with, by extracting it as a Pro Tools audio file. Matching to this is likely to be a little more challenging than using AAF files, however, since this track will not contain any file separations indicating the film editor's edit points (Figure 6.2).

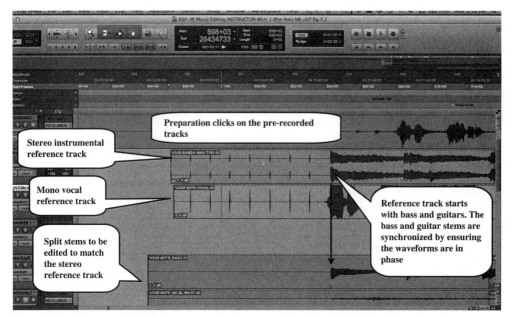

Figure 6.2 Reference tracks for a pre-recorded song and the associated stems for editing by a "group" method. Note the eight "preparation clicks" in each of the pre-recorded reference tracks. In postproduction these can help with syncing stems, and in this case they were also used during the shoot, as a count-in to help the band start miming together—the leader of the band actually stomped his foot in time with the clicks.

6.6 MOVING THE MOVIE

The next step is for the music editor to watch the movie with the reference track to check for any sync issues or potential mixing problems. It is relatively likely that there will be some such issues, related, for example, to the accuracy of the performers' miming or how the picture has been edited. As the music expert, the music editor also needs to make sure that the song's structure and form make sense. If the song as edited by the film editor has sync issues that can't otherwise be resolved, or seems odd or out of step with the songwriter's intentions, it is time to talk with the editor and director about making changes to the film edit. This kind of change is a collaborative and creative effort; it is usually reserved for vocal sync, but it can be made for instruments as well.

> **Tip**
>
> **Important:** The film editor should only be asked to "move the movie" if the issue cannot be resolved by adjusting the music. Most film editors are more than happy to make adjustments that improve the film, but tread lightly in their domain. It's their call.

If going ahead to move the movie, the film editor needs to know which parts to move, and by how much. Carefully make selection edits in the video track in Pro Tools HD, positioning them at either end of the section to be moved (see Figure 6.3). These edits will automatically fall on frame lines; check that they appear in the Pro Tools timeline ruler at or very close to a timecode or feet and frames line (usually

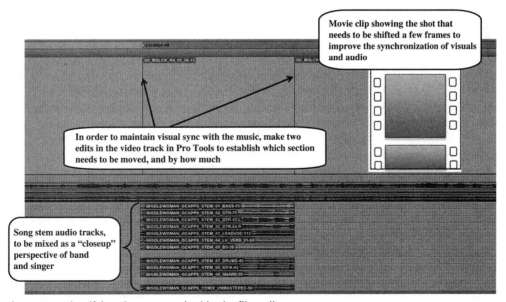

Figure 6.3 Identifying changes required in the film edit.

within a half or quarter frame). Then select and move the clip to the right or left, with the nudge value set to 1 frame. (Video or audio is "advanced" to the left, or earlier in time, and "retarded" to the right, later in time.) When the best fit with the music has been found, make a note of the number of frames and direction the section has been moved. The film editor can then use this measurement to move the shots by making an "internal slip," which avoids changing the picture cut points.

PAX Quote

"Rather than the more technical 'advance' and 'retard' descriptions … we sometimes say 'toward the popcorn' and 'toward the parking lot.'"

6.7 SYNCING STEMS WITH THE REFERENCE TRACK

The music editor can now begin to create the master edited tracks that will eventually go on the final dub, editing the stems to fit the visuals using the reference track as a guide. The first step in this process is to edit and sync the stems to match the reference track, as edited by the film editor, and then to resync them, making any fine adjustments, with the on-camera visuals. I use two main approaches to this: the "group" method and the "stem-by-stem" method. Depending on the song, grouping may be faster, while stem-by-stem tends to give greater individual stem control.

6.7.1 Group Method

This method involves track grouping, which allows each of the stems to be edited and moved as needed while retaining its sync relationship with the other stems in the same group.

After the stems have been imported and placed in the proper tracks, they are first synced with each other. As mentioned previously, it is best to use the same sample start for all stems, so they can simply be "snapped" to each other. To do this in Pro Tools: in "Slip" mode, highlight or tab to the left-hand edge of the stem you want to align to, then hold down Control (Mac) or Start (Windows) with the grabber tool selected, and click in a second stem. It should snap to the first (other options for this operation can be found by right clicking on the second file). Repeat this for each stem, until they are all aligned.

If the stems were not recorded with the same start location but instead have a sync pop, you need to match this sound across the files. Viewing the sync pop at "sample" level (see Figure 6.4) enables you to do this accurately. It's also possible that the individual stems have been previously time stamped, which makes for easy syncing together using spot mode.

Tip

Important: It is not possible to tell by ear whether stems are in sync. If tracks come to you with different sample starts and without a sync pop, it is best to ask the recordist or engineer to reprint the files and include a time stamp or sync pop.

Figure 6.4 Stems with a sync pop, viewed at sample level; the two at the top have been synced by aligning the sync pop.

If the stems are delivered to you playing together properly, but without having the same sample start, you need to make the clips match in the start and length. Stems with a sync pop for alignment may also be different lengths. Select the longest stem and move the selected area to hover over another stem track. With the Edit window "focus key" highlighted, hit P to move the selected area up or ; (semi-colon) to move it down, as needed. With the selected area now hovering over the next stem, choose Edit > Consolidate Clip or press Shift + Option + 3 (Mac) or Start +Alt + 3 (Windows). Consolidating the file in this way allows the resynced stems to be edited, moved, and adjusted as needed, while retaining their sync relationships.

It is a good idea at this point to give the new digital copy of each stem a proper name. One way of doing this is to give the longest track a proper stem title (if it doesn't already have one) and then copy that. Double clicking on the clip brings up a "rename" dialog box. Make sure you are naming the "parent" file and not a subclip— the window should have two radio buttons rather than just one—then copy and paste the filename into the newly consolidated stem. The only difference in the name should be the number of the stem and the instrument. Repeat this until all the stems have been redigitized or consolidated to play together and are properly named.

The stems can now be grouped. Make sure you are track grouping, however, and not clip grouping (clip grouping is handy for moving edited multitrack pieces of music, but means losing some control over the individual stems—track grouping is more appropriate in this case). Having created a track group, you can now go ahead and synchronize the stems with the reference track. Listen to the reference track at the beginning of the song and identify which is the most prominent instrument. Find the track for this instrument in the stems, "solo" it, and move it, along with all the grouped stems, so that it is in sync with the start of the song in the reference track. Remember that the movie may have been edited, in which case the first appearance of the song may correspond to a point partway through the original; in industry terminology, it may play "in progress."

As you synchronize the stems to the reference you should listen very carefully to make sure the transients and waveform modulations in the stems match up with the same waveforms in the reference track. Matching accurately sometimes requires zooming in from the waveform view to the sample level. When the two tracks are played at the same time they should sound in phase; the "phasing" sound described previously—a hollow-sounding background swoosh—should ideally be absent. Even subtle phasing can be heard with a little practice.

You can place a sync mark—"Identify Sync" in the Pro Tools menu—in all the stem tracks in a group by making a cursor selection and keying Command +, (Mac) or Ctrl +, (Windows). There can only be one sync mark in each clip, however. If you need to move it, hover over the bottom of the sync mark with the grabber tool so that it turns into a finger pointer, click and drag the marker to the new position. Then update the grouped stems' position with this new sync mark. Continue until all the edited sections of the stems match the stereo reference track.

The reference track should contain edits which reflect the film editor's intentions in cutting the song in the scene. You need to edit the grouped stems, separating them at the same positions as the picture editor made cuts, so defining each section of the reference as cut by the film editor. At this point, you may want to separate the vocal tracks from the band or instrumental tracks and edit them separately, as they often have different editing requirements with regard to sync. It's also important to recall that the film editor can only edit with frame accuracy, so it's likely that there will be rough one-frame edits at the separation points. At this stage, make a note of the positions of these edits, but don't fix them yet. Ultimately it is your job not only to ensure the music and picture are in sync, but also to make the edits sound smooth and natural. See Figure 6.6.

6.7.2 Stem-by-Stem Method

The stem-by-stem method is an alternative approach to syncing the stems with the reference track. It works in much the same way as the group method, except that one stem is synced first and the remaining stems are edited to match, one by one. Figure 6.6 shows an example of this. The reference track appears at the top of the screen. The bass track, immediately below it, has been used as what I'll call the "guide" stem, and the remaining stems have been matched to it by snapping each section to the equivalent section in the guide track (which will also be included as one of the final music tracks delivered to the dub). With this method, then, the stems must have the same sample start (though, as mentioned previously, it's not necessary that the sample end is also the same).

As with the group method, choose the most prominent part at the beginning of the reference song, and use the stem that represents that sound as your guide stem to

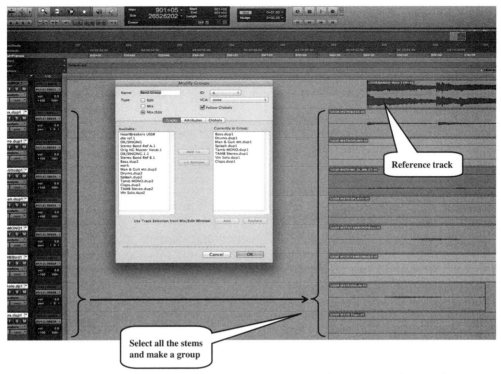

Figure 6.5 The group method: after snapping all the stems to their same respective sample start, make a track group (not a clips group) of all the music stems that match and then sync to the stereo reference track. The reference track is the music that was played back on the set.

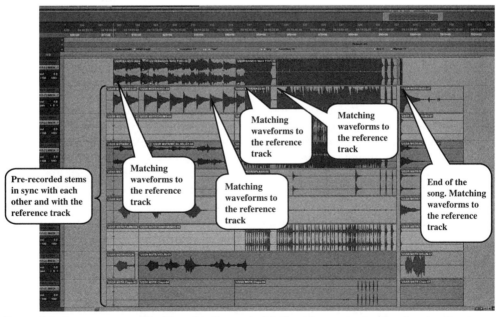

Figure 6.6 Song stems synced with each other and with the reference track using the stem-by-stem method. In this case, the end of the song has been brought forward to match the point at which the band finishes playing on camera (the reference track only shows part of the final chord since the film editor trimmed it; in the stems, we chose to allow the full chord to play out).

sync first. Edit and sync it to all the edited sections of the AAF reference track, paying attention to waveform transients and listening carefully for phasing; cut and slip or nudge the stem sections as needed to match the sound on the reference track.

PAX Quote

"With orchestra stems I have used room noise, chair squeaks, and conductor count-offs prior to the downbeat to find correct sync."

The next step is to add and edit the remaining stems to match the guide stem. This may at first seem like an inefficient and labor-intensive approach compared to the group method, but with practice it can be done quickly and, importantly, it results in very accurate syncing. In fact in the long run it may be easier, since once the guide stem is synced with the reference track the other stems can be snapped into place without the need even to initially listen to them. This method of stem-by-stem construction is also often used to ensure sync within the composer's scored tracks and to correct sync when editing, if stems have accidentally been moved or challenging edits need to be made.

To sync stem by stem, start by making a blank "work" track below the guide stem track. This should be a track of the same type—usually mono or stereo—as the guide stem track. In addition, make sure the furthest left-hand edge of the guide stem track is visible, if necessary using the trim tool to reveal it to its full clip length. The process for each stem is then as follows:

1. Select the first edited section of the guide stem using the grabber tool or by tabbing the cursor to the left sample edge. Choose one of the other full parent file stems from the clip bin list and drag it onto a new track while holding down Control (Mac) or Start (Windows). It should snap to the start of the guide stem.
2. In Slip mode, use the grabber tool to select the next edited section in the guide stem. Hold down Control + Option (Mac) or Start + Alt (Windows) to pull a copy of the selected section onto the blank work track you created earlier. (Holding down Control or Start ensures the clip does not move to the right or left, and so maintains sync, while Option or Alt makes a copy of the clip.) Reveal the start of the copied file by dragging to the left with the trim tool. (See Figure 6.7a.)
3. Hold down Control + Option (Mac) or Start + Alt (Windows) and, using the grabber tool, select the stem added in step 1. This should make a copy of the new stem on the same track, and also snap this copy to match the start of the second edited section of the guide stem. The previously edited section of the new track will remain intact and in place while this copy is synced to the second section of the guide stem. (See Figure 6.7b.)
4. Next, delete the clip on the work track and replace it with the next edited section of the guide stem (as described in step 2). Repeat step 3 for this section.
5. Repeat steps 2–4 for the remaining sections until the new stem is built and synced with the guide stem. (See Figure 6.6.)

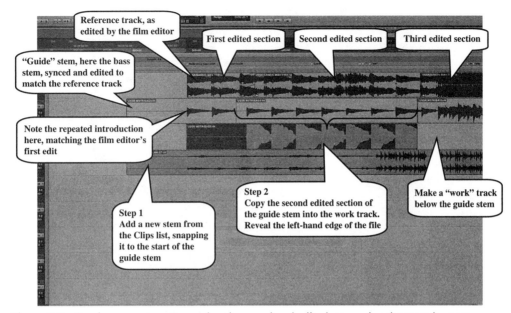

Figure 6.7a Syncing song stems to an already synced and edited stem using the stem-by-stem method: steps 1 and 2.

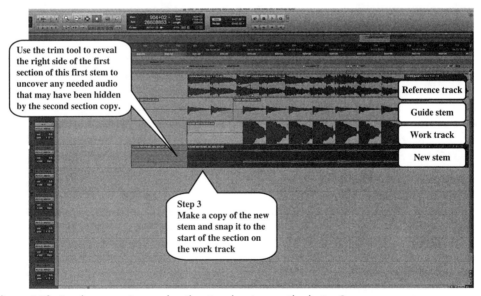

Figure 6.7b Syncing song stems using the stem-by-stem method: step 3.

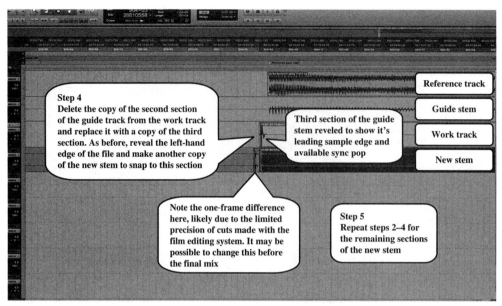

Figure 6.7c Syncing song stems using the stem-by-stem method: steps 4 and 5

If as well as starting at the same point the stems also end at the same point, this can be used to sync the "end" sections of the song. In this case:

1. Use the trim tool to reveal the right-hand clip edge of both the guide stem and the new stem (the stem being edited). Note that if the song has been shortened by the film editor, the new stem file, representing the whole original song, is likely to be much longer than the last section of the guide stem; all but the end section of the new stem can be cut, as unused audio. (See Figure 6.8a.)
2. Place the cursor in the last section of the guide stem's right edge using the tab key; the cursor should flash at this right edge. Do not use the grabber tool in this instance, as this will reference the left-hand edge. Hold Control + Command (Mac) or Start + Control (Windows) and, using the grabber tool, click on the end section of the new stem. This should snap it to the end section of the guide stem. (See Figure 6.8b.)

Continue adding and editing the endings of each stem in this way, until the whole piece of music has been built to match the guide stem (and therefore the reference track).

6.8 EDITING THE SONG

With the stems now edited to match the film editor's reference track, you can begin to clean them up and edit them so that the song sounds natural, and to achieve a precise, nuanced match with the visual performance.

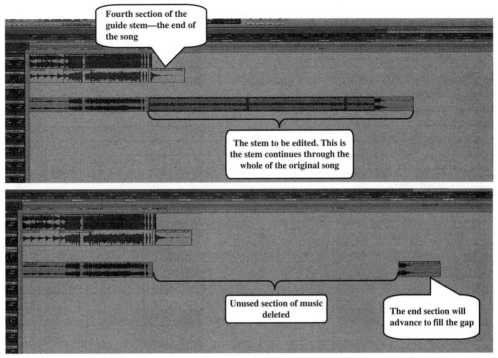

Figure 6.8a Snapping the final section to the end of the song: step 1. This is possible where stems have a shared end sample position.

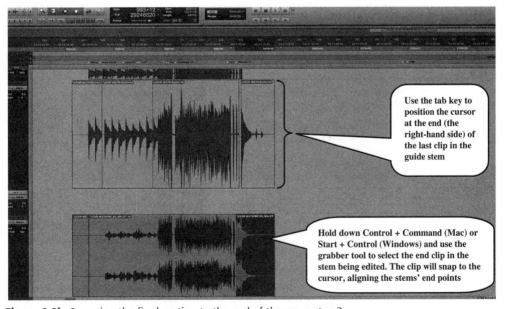

Figure 6.8b Snapping the final section to the end of the song: step 2.

It is crucial, of course, that when you are doing this the picture and audio are in sync. Make sure the Pro Tools timeline ruler and the window burn on the digital picture (the embedded timecode and feet and frames numbering) mark the same position. Note, however, that with a nonlinear digital editing system the digital picture may be out of sync by a few frames, even if the ruler and window burn do not show this. Also, if you are using a third-party video output (such as AJA's Io XT or a Blackmagic Design DeckLink PCIe card), you may need to use an offset in Pro Tools to compensate for the delay in the picture playback on the video hardware. This delay may be in the region of 1 frame or even in seconds, and the offset can be measured in quarter frames or milliseconds; check your hardware and software manuals for the exact figure.

It is also important to note that even if you have synchronized a track to the digital picture on your system, it's possible it will be out of sync on the dub stage. This is because of the greater distance to the screen, and the fact that, due to this distance, the sound takes significantly longer to reach you than the picture (since the speed of light is greater than the speed of sound); the industry term for this distance from the mixing console to the screen is the "throw." This will also affect the audience's perception of the relative sync of the film.

6.8.1 Editing Instruments

Play the movie scene and the song stems to identify any areas that will need special editing. Verify which instruments are shown playing on camera. Where the content of a stem is not directly represented by a player on the screen, you can move or stretch the audio to ensure the edit is smooth and in time with the visual performance. Editing the stems separately here allows any timing errors to be fixed on the rhythm tracks while other instruments—for example guitars, strings, or a solo instrument—play through the edit point, making for a smoother transition. If instruments or vocals are represented on camera at a rough-sounding audio edit point, you can consider "moving" the edit separation to another location in the relevant stems. That is, the different stems do not necessarily have to be cut and crossed at exactly the same location—the editor is free to treat the stems individually in order to create a natural overall sound. Figures 6.9 and 6.10 show some examples.

It's often tempting to use time-stretching tools such as Elastic Audio or Pitch 'n Time to help iron out song editing problems. These are a powerful and excellent solution in many cases ... but they should be used with great caution and in very small doses! They can cause digital artifacts, degrading the quality of certain musical elements. It should also be noted that time stretching is often more successful for instrumental tracks than for vocal tracks—stretching a vocal track greatly increases the risk of it sounding bad.

PAX Quote

"Long lines of any kind are tough because the algorithms don't know where to hide the stretching. Rhythmic tracks are usually better. We are music editors, not music stretchers."

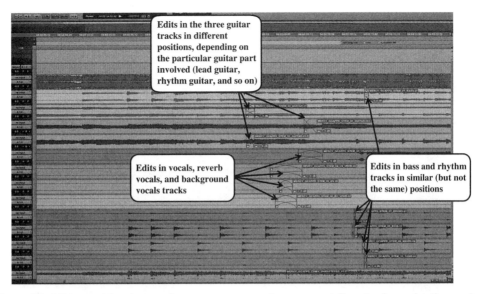

Figure 6.9 Editing multitrack stems for an on-camera performance entails not only syncing the music to the visuals but also editing to ensure smooth and natural-sounding musical transitions. Each music stem should be "soloed" and listened to individually. In this case, there are cross-fades in various positions on the different stems—in fact, no two edit positions are quite the same. Unusually, here the electric guitars have been split from being a stereo file to two distinct mono stems. At the foot of the screen is a muted master mix of the song, to provide a backup way of checking how the split stems are represented in the original mix.

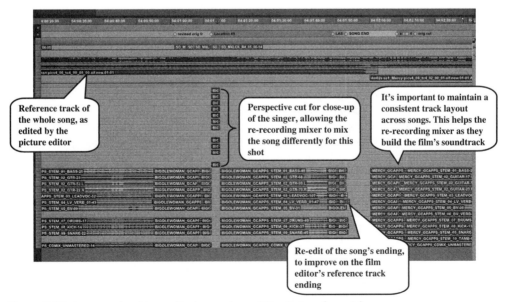

Figure 6.10 An example of two edited songs in multitrack stem format for an on-camera performance by a band in an outside venue. Note: the perspective cut for a close-up shot, the consistent track layout across both songs, and the stereo reference track edited by the picture editor and used here as a guide.

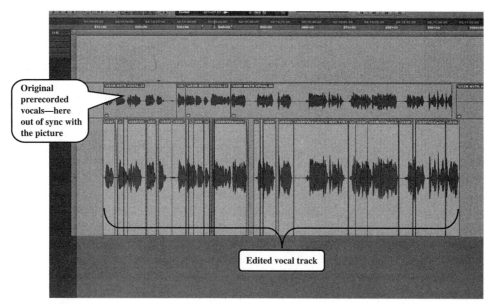

Figure 6.11a Vocal tracks are most often edited separately from instrumental tracks if recorded as separate stems. When the vocalist is not on camera the track should be synced with the band; when they are on camera the audio track needs to be matched to the movement of their lips.

6.8.2 Editing Vocals

It's common for vocals for a band or song-form recording to be a mono track; you may also be editing multi-track choirs in 5.0 or multiple singers, each on their own track. Either the group or the stem-by-stem method can be used for syncing (though it may make more sense to use the group method for a large group of singers). In the examples shown in this subsection, the songs have mono vocal tracks.

It's often best to edit vocal stems separately from instrumental stems, since the performances of the singers and band may not be completely in time with each other (in addition to the difficulty of lip syncing accurately, they may be listening to different play back tracks during recording). If you find there's just too much of a discrepancy between a band's performance and a singer's lip sync to make musical sense, you then need to ask the picture editor to move the movie, as described previously.

If the vocals have been synced using the group method, carefully review the sync between the audio and the images of the singers (when they are not on screen, the vocal stems should be kept in sync with the instrument tracks). Listen and watch for each syllable; depending on the performer's level of experience and on whether they are lip syncing or actually singing, there may be quite a few areas out of sync (see Figure 6.11a).

"Scrubbing" the audio, with the images following, a small section at a time, will allow you to identify precisely where the vocalist's lips form particular consonant and vowel sounds, and so make a detailed check of the audio synchronization. You can place sync marks at corresponding points in the picture and the audio—where the singer's lips are seen forming a particular sound in the picture, and where the same sound is heard in the audio—and "snap" the trimmed audio clip to the edit cursor

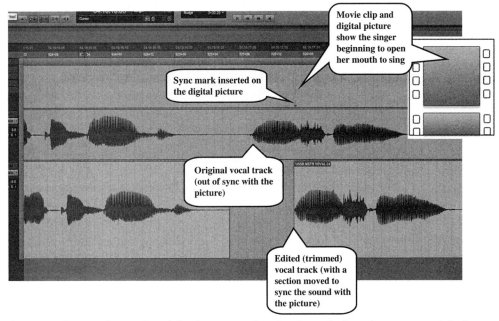

Figure 6.11b Here the vocal track has been synced to the picture by inserting a sync mark in the digital picture, then snapping the matching audio to this location that has been trimmed up to the vocal sound.

positioned at the picture sync mark using Control + grab clip (Mac) or Start + grab clip (Windows) (see Figure 6.11b). An alternate manoeuvre could be used by placing a sync mark in an audio clip at the vocal sound then with the edit cursor at the proper location in the picture track, hold Shift + Control + Grab clip (Mac) or Shift + Start + Grab clip (Windows) to snap the audio clip and it's sync mark to the picture.

An odd or distorted vowel or consonant sound can often be replaced with the same sound from elsewhere in the song, and it is possible to fix sync issues in a similar way. If there are words or phrases that the performer has not matched to the picture, substituting audio from another part of the song—perhaps the same phrase sung a little faster or slower—may solve this. Again, if the performer still has their mouth open when the note has ended, the note may need to be lengthened. If only a very small amount of lengthening is needed, this is one situation in which stretching the audio may work. Conversely, if the vocalist has closed their mouth before the note has finished, you can edit the audio to play shorter (see Figure 6.11c).

Occasionally as you edit, step back and play a longer section of the vocal track while watching the picture, in order to judge whether your adjusted sync is creating an appropriate feeling of reality. For best results, view the picture on a large computer monitor or TV.

Tip

It's a good idea to step away from your editing sometimes, take a short break or do something else, then come back for a fresh look and listen. This is especially true for sync work, but all sound editing can benefit by this practice.

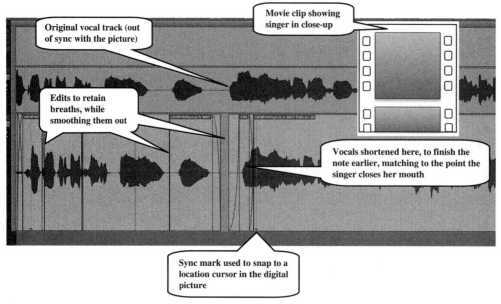

Figure 6.11c Here the vocal track has been moved to match the moment the singer's mouth opens, and also shortened to match to the moment it closes.

In addition to being carefully synced, the vocal stems need to sound smooth and natural. You will want to group the vocal track with any related reverb track for editing—added reverb is often printed (recorded) on a separate track rather than embedded with the vocal track, giving a re-recording mixer control over both the "dry" and the "wet" (that is, reverbed) vocal sound.

A more realistic sound can also be created if breaths and room tone sound natural. ("Room tone", or "mic tone", is the sound that occurs between dialogue or lyrics—the "silence" between words. In some cases the recordist on a movie set, sometimes also in a studio, will make a recording of the room tone specifically so that it can be used in editorial to smooth out the dialogue or vocal tracks.) Pay attention to the breaths the singer takes between phrases, editing and cross-fading them carefully (see Figure 6.11c). Another technique for smoothing out microphone sound and breathing is to "Reverse" audio of the room tone in AudioSuite so that it fills in any drop-out or hole in the track due to film editorial. Filling the track with an alternation from the original room tone to the reversed sound and back creates a smoother transition, and with the help of cross fades avoids a noticeable looping sound or undesirable repetition of the room tone.

6.9 REMOVING OFFENSIVE WORDS

Song lyrics may have words or phrases that the producers don't want included. This is particularly likely for television shows or a movie to be played, say, on airplanes.

Whether the vocals are on a separate stem or you only have one stereo track of the whole song mix, you may need to make edits to remove these words and phrases. In this situation, you can't just edit out the section containing the offending lyric, as this will mean losing the timing and rhythm of the song.

One common technique is to replace a word, or even just a syllable, with a different one from elsewhere in the song; this often works for a word in a repeated section such as a chorus. If there is a separate stem for the vocals, this is a relatively straightforward task. If you only have a whole-band mix, however, you need to listen carefully to the instruments playing behind the vocals, focusing on one instrument at a time—for example, listen to the bass, then keyboard, rhythm guitar, and so on—to check the continuity through the edited area. Sometimes it's best, in this situation, to replace a longer section; it's easy to convince yourself that an edit sounds right, when in fact there are elements that sound odd or incongruous.

Another technique for altering a single word or syllable is to reverse the audio for only that word or syllable. For example, reversing the "f" sound in "f#*^" means that, technically, the word is no longer the same, offensive word. As for room tone, this can be done with "Reverse" in AudioSuite. Again, though, you need to keep in mind that if you are working with a stereo master, the vocals are married to the band, and reversing the vocals will also reverse the band—this may still work if the sound behind the offending lyric is a simple held single chord or a percussion transient that can be adjusted to match the rhythm of the song. If not, sometimes replacing the word, a syllable within it, or a section of the song with an instrumental section is an option.

6.10 SONGS FOR ON-CAMERA DANCING

A movie or television show may include scenes in a club or other venue with a live band or DJ. There are endless possibilities for combining visuals, music, and dancing in this situation. Whether and how these possibilities are realized is likely to depend on how long the dancing scene is, whether it comes at a significant point in the movie, and whether it includes dialogue. If the scene is important, having the foresight and budget to prepare the music in advance will pay off in the final mix. In particular, if possible, the film company and music supervisor should choose and clear the rights of the song or songs to be played during the scene before the shoot. This will help establish the tempo and feel for the music in the scene, and so facilitate the film and music editing.

6.10.1 Making a Thumper Track

When songs have already been chosen for a dance scene, it is common for the music editor—provided one has been hired at this point in the production—to make a "thumper track" to be used when the scene is shot. If the actual songs were played on set, the sound would "bleed" with any dialogue recording, making it unusable: music in the background of the dialogue track would undoubtedly interfere with the re-recording mixer's work, and tying music to the picture in this way would also take away a lot of the film editor's freedom. The thumper track provides a low-frequency pulse for the actors and performers to dance in time to. Ideally the tempo of this pulse should match that of the song to be used (which, as mentioned, should if possible have already been licensed). The frequency of the pulse (40 Hz or below) is below the range of most dialogue mics, meaning the dialogue is recorded but not the thumper track. The location sound recordist may also be able to "roll off" a mic's range below 80 Hz, thereby ensuring the thumper will not be captured with the dialogue.

To make a thumper track:

1. Import the stereo master of the chosen song into Pro Tools. Make sure Pro Tools' settings match the camera to be used (for HD video 23.976 FPS timecode, 48 kHz and 24 bit, and for 35 mm film 24 FPS timecode, 48 kHz, and 24 bit; verify this with the cinematographer, camera operator, or location sound recordist). Also make sure your Pro Tools system (or DAW of choice) is resolved to a word clock or SD/HD video reference. The video reference is always at video speed, but as the signal is passed through resolving hardware (such as an Avid SYNC HD or SYNC I/O) it can be converted to film speed, at 24 FPS. If the film is at the European HD standard of 25 FPS the Pro Tools system should be set to the same frame rate using a matching video reference.

2. The song can either be placed at the proper location in the film, where the edited movie reel is available, or in a fresh session, anywhere after the first few seconds from the start.

3. Add a click track: either select "Click track" from the Track menu or add an auxiliary or audio track (mono or stereo) and place a click plugin on an insert path on that track.

4. Get the feel of the song and determine its meter. Note that it's possible it may be polymetric, combining, say, 2/4 and 3/4 time, or 6/8, 5/4, 11/8—essentially any combination is possible, though club-type dance music is typically 4/4 or 2/4 time.

5. Begin the process of mapping out the tempo of the song by placing the "song start" marker at the first transient of the first full bar's downbeat. (There may be pick-up beats, usually quarter or eighth notes, before the downbeat of the first full bar. You would include clicks for these beats, but, regardless, the song start is the first bar 1 downbeat.) In Pro Tools, the "song start" marker is by default at the beginning of the session. To move it, you can click the red diamond shape and hold-drag it to a new location or place your cursor at the audio transient that identifies the downbeat for bar 1 and choose Event > Time operations > Move song start. The location you selected should appear in the "Move start to" box, and the bar number usually defaults to bar 1. (See Figure 6.12.)

6. Next, listen to the song to get a feel for the tempo and bpm (beats per minute). You can, if you want to, use the Transport window's MIDI controls section to determine the basic tempo by tapping the "T" key on your computer's keyboard in time with the beat. To do this, make sure the Conductor track is *not* selected and click on the bpm number in the Tempo field to highlight it in green (see Figure 6.13). Tap out the beat, and the bpm number will change to match your "tapped" tempo.

7. Next, enable the Conductor track in the transport window so that variations in tempo will be represented in the tempo ruler. Optionally, you can open the

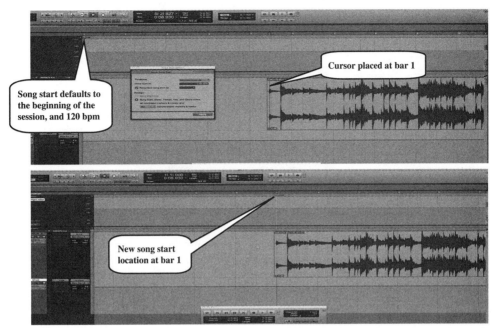

Figure 6.12 Set the song start marker to appear at the first transient of the first bar 1 downbeat. The red song start marker is always on in Pro Tools. It also indicates the start tempo; the default is 120 bpm (beats per minute). This can be changed by double-clicking on the red marker and changing the number.

Figure 6.13 To set tempo, click on the bpm number in the Tempo field and tap the "T" key on your keyboard in time with the beat.

tempo ruler by clicking the triangle in the corner of the window, so you can see each change in tempo and its location relative to the transients in the song.

At bar 1, set the song start to the tempo you feel is correct, then with the selection remaining in the edit window choose Event > Identify Beat to open the Add Bar/Beat Markers dialog box. Make a selection from bar 1 to the downbeat of bar 2 and enter the range (bar 1/1/000 to bar 2/1/000) in the fields in the dialog box (see Figure 6.14). To define a range from a bars' first down beat to another bars' downbeat you need only to type the bar number you want, the following beat number and ticks will automatically be set to beat '1' and '000' ticks, indicating the location of the respective downbeats.

This allows the computer to calculate the tempo for the selection. The tempo in the tempo ruler and bar and beat lines are updated accordingly. Using Command + Click (Mac) or Control + Click (Windows) while pointing to the 'Tempo Change" '+' sign in the tempo ruler, you can change the view of the

Figure 6.14 Listen to the song with the click track and identify each beat that seems not to match the "grid" of quarter or eighth notes in the click track. Listen to and locate the downbeat transient of each bar and where it is different from the tempo map information reset the correct bar and beat in the Event > Identify beat dialog. (Note that when you type a number in either the bar or beat field the numbers to the right "zero out"; so here, typing "3" in the bar field resets the beat location to 3.1.000.)

tempo ruler from only tempo changes to seeing the bar and beat tempo change stalks.

8. Now listening to the song, adjust tempo, bar by bar, to the end of the song, by re-identifying each bar or beat of the song that is different from the tempo of the previous updated beat. As the song plays and matches the click track of the tempo map, there is no need to make an alteration. However where there is a miss match between the audio tempo and the tempo map, you need to adjust the tempo map to match the tempo of the song. Place your selector at the miss matched bar and beat locations in the track, and hit Command + I (Mac) or Control + I (Windows) to insert a new bar or beat marker. (See Figure 6.15.) For example, if you place the cursor on the transient representing bar 25 beat 3 and the bar and beat ruler indicates this falls at bar 25 beat 3.129 (the ".129" indicates ticks or divisions after the beat; there are 960 ticks for each beat or quarter note, in Pro Tools), you can use the "Identify beat" command to correct the location to bar 25 beat 3. The tempo will change from this point, in this case speeding up, to match the actual beat in the song. Continue in this way until you have completed a tempo map of the whole song by identifying each tempo change as it actually occurs.

9. Play through the whole song with the click track, to check that the clicks match the tempo of the song. It is important to correct variations of even a few beats per minute. (An alternative approach to the manual, bar-by-bar method of identifying bars and beats described here is to use "Beat Detective," located in the Event menu in Pro Tools, which marks tempo change locations automatically. However, the manual method is sometimes almost as fast and it is usually more accurate. It can be difficult to achieve good results with Beat Detective—it's best used on a clearly rhythmic song, and you still need to check it bar by bar.)

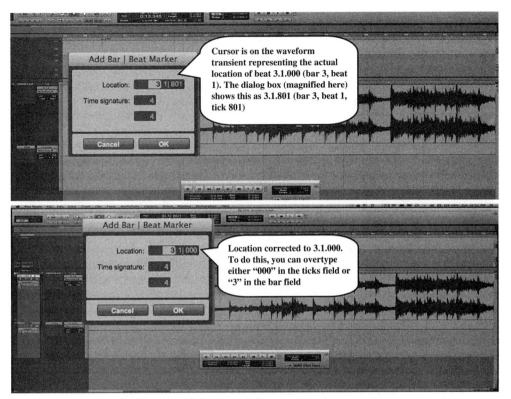

Figure 6.15 Record an audio track of the MIDI click to use as a thumper trigger.

10. Once the MIDI click has been established, record it as an audio file. This is done by outputting the click track through a bus (mono is fine) and making a new audio track to record the click. The new audio track's input path should match the output path of the click track.

    It is important to ensure the click audio file matches the length of the master song file exactly. Select the whole song track, arm the click track to record, and press play and record in the Pro Tools Transport window. (See Figure 6.16.)

    You can add clicks as a count-off before bar 1, either when recording the file, by setting the record cursor to bar "0/1/000" for a one-bar count off, or afterward, by editing in "pre-clicks" and consolidating the click track. To start the count off click two bars before bar 1, type "-1/1/000" in the main counter bars and beats fields.

On set, the click track is played through a converter, providing a trigger for a pulsed "thump" sound on low-frequency speakers for the performers to dance to. Sometimes the thumper sound can be passed through a Pro Tools plug-in or through external hardware. The thumper track will most likely be played from various different points in the song, but in postproduction editorial the song track can be matched to the click track because they have the same lengths, and start and end points (see Figures 6.16 & 6.17).

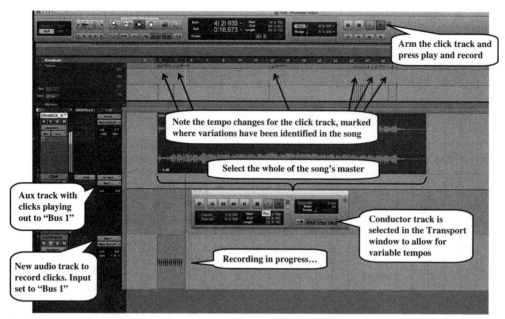

Figure 6.16 Each tempo change is reflected in the tempo map as well as the recorded click track, allowing the song to be matched to the click track in postproduction.

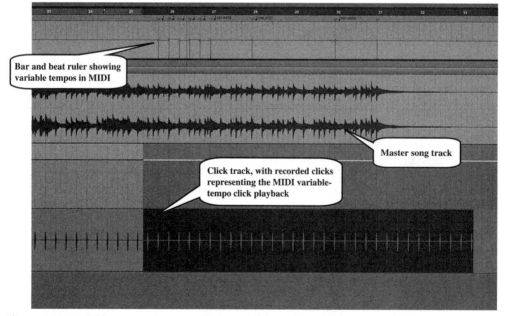

Figure 6.17 Variable tempo map created as MIDI clicks and recorded as an audio click track.

While a thumper track is the best option, often performers simply have to follow the tempo of a song as best they can: it is played over speakers as they start dancing, allowing them to get a sense of the tempo, then turned off as filming starts. Inevitably the dancers slow down, meaning that in postproduction the song needs to be edited to match this slower tempo. Naturally, however, dancers do not move perfectly to the beat all the time, so the music editor can use key visual cues, such as dancers hitting downbeats or the song's backbeat, and the consistency between different dancers' movements, to create a convincing match between the music and dancing.

6.11 MEETING THE REAL-WORLD CREATIVE CHALLENGES: SLOW-MOTION VIDEO TO REAL-MOTION MUSIC

Synchronizing music and visuals can be difficult enough under normal circumstances, but some creative requests can make the task more challenging still. Occasionally, for example, movies or TV shows (and more commonly music videos) include a scene where the director or producer wants the on-camera performers moving in slow motion, but with their lip sync and movements matching the music played at normal speed. With the advent of digital audio, this kind of manipulation is now possible—but not without a music editor's knowledge and skills. Essentially, slow motion visuals with normal-speed sound is achieved by playing the music at high speed for the performers to mime and lip sync to. Then the visuals are slowed down, with the result that the sped-up music plays at normal speed and without any pitch change, and is synchronized with the performers' slow-motion movements. An excellent example of this technique appears in an episode of the TV show *Grey's Anatomy*. In the following box, associate music editor Carli Barber shares her recollections of meeting this challenge.

Grey's Anatomy #718: The Song Beneath the Song

Early on the season when I was told we'd be doing a musical episode, my first reaction was excitement, because we have a cast that includes a Tony Award–winning singer, Sara Ramirez, and other great musical talent like Chandra Wilson and Loretta Devine. As the episode came closer and the meetings began, that's when the panic set in! I hope you enjoy this account of the episode from the music editors' perspective!

We had our first meeting in February, with the music producer, director, multiple producers, the film editor, recording sound mixer, sound supervisor, and re-recording sound mixer. Collectively we wanted to cover our bases to ensure that preproduction, production, and editorial would all run as smoothly as possible. We discussed many things, including whether to pull the songs up before production, or pull them down after, in post. We decided to pull the tracks up for the set playback so there would be less processing of our prerecorded tracks later. We also discussed whether the actors would wear earwigs or music would be played back on set, over the PA. We thought it necessary for the actors to sing out during production so their body language would be right later when we cut the songs into position, so we decided to go with earwigs. There was also the matter, before production, of creating bridges in the songs that would be perfectly timed out so the actors could deliver lines in between singing. Although at the time we did not have a script, nor did we have a final list of songs to prerecord, we knew sitting down with the entire music and sound team to begin a dialog would help alleviate any potential problems that could arise down the line.

It was at this first meeting the director mentioned he wanted to shoot one particular song in camera overcrank (two or four times normal speed). He wanted to achieve the effect that the actress was singing in real time, while the actors around her were moving in slow motion. (When in reality she would be singing at two or four times real speed, and they would be moving around her like normal.) They decided to do a camera test on that bit to make sure we could nail it. We sped up the song to 200 percent for one test and to 400 percent for another. At 400 percent the song sounded like a chipmunk extravaganza. Our mouths couldn't move fast enough to sing along with the track, so we figured they would go with the 200 percent. Well the joke was on us, because even though the track at 400 percent didn't line up after the camera test, since it looked better on film that's what they went with. We knew this would haunt us later, and it did!

As the dailies came in, I would get sneak peeks of scenes and dance numbers, and get excited to get my hands on the material. One particular morning, the editor, Susan, showed me the over-cranked song, "Grace." As we expected from the screen test, it was not syncing up no matter what she did. I asked her to give us the scene so we could work on it before the picture locked. Remember, the actress was mouthing the words at four times speed, which sounded like chipmunks during production, and we had to fit the straight-time lyrics into her mouth.

What a challenge it became. We time shifted and moved words and syllables into place, but doing this threw off the music track. We decided to work them independently. When we were happy with the lip sync, we then had to adjust each downbeat of the music to where it should hit with the lyrics. And then we did it again when we got the final mix of the track and final picture.

Of the ten songs that were in our musical episode, "Grace" was definitely the most difficult to cut, both the lip sync and the music. The rest of the songs had their own issues with lip sync, but the hours and manpower spent on "Grace" were exponentially more. This is not to say the other songs were easy—since there were so many cast members singing, and some dance numbers, they all presented their own set of challenges.

Thankfully we were given most of the musical elements in advance so we could prepare our sessions before spotting and receiving the locked cut. We decided the best plan of attack would be to split the songs up between Carli, Jessica, and me. We each worked on our songs individually over the first few days. Once we were happy with our work, we all met in my office to do our own playback of the songs. It was at this point that we merged our sessions and got down to the nitty gritty, making detailed fixes to each other's work. We would take turns in "the chair" while the others took notes on areas we thought could be improved. There was a lot of extra work involved in prepping for this episode, and we were all very proud of the work we had done and couldn't wait to get to the stage to mix.

The mix was one week after the spotting session, and it was scheduled for three days as opposed to our usual two. Because a lot of the on-camera singing was tied to the story of the episode, the edited lyrics and matching reverb tracks were loaded into the dialogue system, and the music itself stayed on the music system. One other notable difference in preparation for the mix was that we decided to consolidate all of our edited tracks before delivering to the stage. We were concerned with the possibility of some of our fade files being corrupted in the transfer, or having some of the regions moved by accident. On occasion this happens and usually you can simply redraw or recalculate the fades or easily move the regions back into place, but since there were so many edits and specialized fades in some of the tracks, we felt it necessary to take the extra step to consolidate. We kept our original work tracks intact in our work session in case a fix was needed. These changes to our normal routine made any fixes challenging, but we were prepared.

The big payoff came during our final playback, when executive producer Shonda Rhimes and director Tony Phelan arrived. The only note that they had in the whole episode was about a breath—no music notes at all! With that we all breathed a sigh of relief, and went out to celebrate!

Jenny Barak, CarliBarber, and Jessica Harrison

6.12 CONCLUDING THOUGHTS

This chapter has given some practical guidance on how to meet the particular challenges of working on music which is, even more than usual, an integral part of a TV show or movie. On-camera music represents one of the sternest tests of a music editor's skill—and their resilience. If a director or music supervisor, or perhaps the production studio, decides to change a picture edit or even a whole a song, it can put the music editor right back where they started, and they have to begin the whole laborious, exacting process of matching music with movement all over again. However, as Carli Barber's description shows, it can also be a highly creative and rewarding process, and one which puts the music right at the heart of the postproduction action.

6.13 INDUSTRY INSIDER: CARLI BARBER, MUSIC EDITOR

1. **How would you describe your role as a music editor, when working with on-camera songs?**

   We are the link between production and editorial, if it's done right. Depending on the situation, we will have to edit the music as requested, and sometimes alter the speed to ensure that sync is maintained in the editing process. A lot of times, we will also add click tracks to help the actors keep in time, and for practicing.

2. **What are some of the similarities and differences between working on low-budget and high-budget films?**

   Eventually, they both realize that they should've had the music editor in the mix a lot sooner than they did. The more money a film has, the sooner we are brought onto the project. It seems that the lower-budget films try to get away without a music editor as long as possible. Choice of songs definitely can be a big difference. In a lower-budget film a lot of times we will have to help in replacing songs that are sound-a-likes for ones they really want.

3. **What value can your music editorial work add to a film or television project, specifically in relation to songs used as source and any on-camera musical performances?**

   Huge value. And I guess I'm a little biased … but having a good, creative music editor can play a huge role in using songs to their fullest potential when they are cut specifically for the scene. Whether it's simply playing as straight source in the background, or used as a support in a montage, having the music starting, playing the scene, and ending can make a big difference in telling a story.

4. **Where songs are written and created specifically for the film or TV show, how do you approach your work with the songwriter's team—the producer, arranger, music mixer, assistants, and others? What can you do to help a songwriter when he or she already has people that provide music editorial services?**

   We can be helpful in many ways, most notably with timing or spotting notes. Providing correct lengths, specific scene description, and sometimes producers' notes will help a lot in ensuring that the tempo and orchestration is right, and the song will fit correctly into the scene.

5. **From your experience working with many directors and music supervisors, what are the specific skill sets that are crucial for a music editor to have, to successfully maintain these relationships?**

People skills. The more available you are, the more times you'll be called back. But more than that, being able to bring a smile into the room and provide fast answers and solutions really keep them coming back. Of course, being fast at Pro Tools and knowledgeable about your session and the music that you are providing also make for many return clients.

6. **Are there specific music editing or Pro Tools techniques that you find most useful in facilitating song playback on the set, editing, maintaining sync, and preparing on-camera song material for a final dub?**

Organization is key. Keeping your session clean and easy to maneuver makes for the best transition from prepping to the stage. With songs being prepped at different speeds, and with different edits, knowing where all of your bones are buried is super-important.

7. **In what specific situations do you receive or request separate stems for a song, or at least separate vocal and band instrument tracks? If there are perspective considerations, do you split for perspective for the re-recording mixer?**

With source music, I almost always give split perspectives as well as the full track with no perspective splits, so the mixer can use whichever is easiest, depending on how the song needs to be mixed. A lot of time, I'll give the mixer a call in advance of the mix to discuss track layout, perspective splits, amount of available tracks, and general setup and specs.

As far as separate stems or instrumentals, if there is a lot of heavily important dialogue happening in the scene, many times we will need to "cut around" this dialogue with the instrumental part of the song. Any time an instrumental version is available I like to have it just in case, as it's nice to have for editing if there are lots of lyrics.

8. **Can you describe some of the most successful and rewarding music editing experiences you've had during your long career, and perhaps some of the more difficult or disappointing ones?**

The awards that I've won and have been nominated for obviously stand out in my mind. Both of my wins were such amazing accomplishments and were so much work! They are definitely two of my proudest moments.

As music editors, in my experience, we are put to the toughest test on the stage. It can be more than stressful having a bunch of bigwigs standing beside you waiting for you to make a fix. My favorite days are these ones, where it seems that you are asked the impossible, and somehow you make it work.

Every spring I have either a moment of disappointment or a very rewarding one. It's called pilot season. It's a time when you work your butt off, and hopefully your show gets picked up for the next season. And just because the show you've worked on gets picked up, it doesn't necessarily mean you'll be the editor on it. But when you get to see the show go from a script to a pilot to a successful series, that is a great feeling!

Chapter 7
Working with a Composer

7.1 SCORING

Composing, or "scoring," for film is a unique, challenging, rewarding, and sometimes frustrating task. If you are working as a music editor or serious about working in the field you need to know about the craft of film scoring; in this book I assume you are aware of (or able to familiarize yourself with) how composers work, whether through first-hand experience or study.

There are a handful of excellent books written about the film composer's techniques, processes, and workflows, and I draw on some of these in this chapter—specifically *On the Track* by Fred Karlin and Rayburn Wright (second edition 2004, Routledge), *From Score to Screen* by Sonny Kompanek (2004, Schirmer Trade Books) and the *Complete Guide to Film Scoring* by Richard Davis (first edition 1999, second edition 2010, Berklee Press). The chapters on music editing in *On the Track*, in particular, provide a wealth of information pertinent to the work of a music editor. In addition to some excellent historical and technical background, they offer a good understanding of how the music editor supports the composer in their work.

In this chapter, rather than simply restating the information found in these books, I instead uncover some key challenges that face the music editor working with a composer, and in doing so I hope to provide some insights rarely found elsewhere.

7.2 THE COMPOSER–MUSIC EDITOR RELATIONSHIP

The music editor's relationship with a composer involves creative, emotional, and technical support. It may have its origins in an early friendship which continues as you pursue parallel career paths, or in mutual professional connections and referrals, for example by way of a preexisting relationship with a director or post supervisor—or you may meet for the first time at the spotting session for a new project. Often the relationship between composer and music editor lasts many years, and both careers can benefit—even flourish—as a result.

A composer may also be working with more than one music editor at a time, because of overlapping projects (this is also true, of course, for other members of the composer's team, including the orchestrator, arranger, engineer, programmer, contractor, and mixer).

7.2.1 Who Pays the Music Editor?

The composer often gets the music editor "for free," but this arrangement shouldn't be taken for granted. The postproduction budget usually includes a line item relating to payment of a music editor; the Motion Picture Editors Guild by-laws also state that a music editor's fees should not be paid from the composer's budget. This important fact is also a little-known one, however, and as a consequence a music editor may not be hired, simply becasue the composer feels unable to afford their services assuming they have to pay them out of their music budget. It is also possible, particularly on low-budget or non-union films, that the composer's budget will have to include music editing fees. I'm aware of occasions where editors have worked for composers knowing that this is the case, and in these situations we often work for as little as possible in order to support the composer's situation and career development. Sometimes the composer is able to convince the production company to share the costs, however the composer (or their agent) should make every effort to keep the music editor's fees in the postproduction budget. In any event, the value of a music editor should not be underestimated. And while as a music editor you want to support the composer, you should be careful of the scenario in which the production company controls your hours but you are paid by the composer. This could be a recipe for disaster!

7.3 THE COMPOSING PROCESS

7.3.1 The Temp Score

The main purpose of the temp score is usually to provide music for a film's preview, but it is also often the beginning of the creative process for the composer (the involvement of the music editor with the temp tracks is discussed in Chapter 4). Some composers may feel listening to them blocks their creativity, but temp scores are here to stay. For the composer, the particular value of a well-constructed temp score lies in the information it provides about tempo, instrumentation and orchestra size, and the emotional shape of the cues—how they are edited to fit the emotional arc of a scene and how, for example, the musical key relationships shape the emotional shifts within a cue, as well as transitions between songs and other cues.

> **PAX Quote**
>
> "Composers may speak philosophically about the evils of the temp but they ignore it at their peril. In this fast-paced industry it is often the director's most valued tool for conveying musical thoughts and ideas to the composer. Don't fight it—join it. The composer I do most of my work with gets as many demos as possible into the first preview. Let them 'fall in love' with your new music instead of someone else's old stuff!"

7.3.2 From MIDI to Master

Before computers, composers would write music out by hand, starting with a sketch on music paper and working on a piano or other instrument as they wrote. This traditional approach is still a very viable way to compose; indeed, for some film composers it can provide a more insightful, organic score. It is not very often used today, though—typically a composer will develop thematic ideas and start to create cues using a MIDI sequencer program. Commonly used programs include Digital Performer, Logic Pro, Ableton Live, Cubase/Nuendo, Sibelius, and Finale, as well as Pro Tools.

When a composer creates themes and music on a MIDI sequencer, they often use sampled orchestral instruments which are then combined and mixed to sound as full and lifelike as possible; mid- and high-level composers can sometimes afford assistants, engineers, and programmers who can take the raw MIDI scores and create an excellent music mix. When it comes to recording the music, the MIDI file also contains much of the necessary information for the final orchestral score—the musical notation that the conductor and players use on the scoring stage—including tempo (and variable tempos), key, meter, and instrumentation. Usually a score will be compiled by the orchestrator in an "engraving" program such as Sibelius or Finale, in which necessary changes or additions can be made—but some composers' MIDI sketches are so accurate that the players' parts can simply be printed out, and the piece is ready to record.

For low-budget films where the composer's fee might not allow for hiring musicians, the final score is often created directly from the MIDI score, on computer. Many MIDI programs incorporate state-of-the-art samplers that sound almost as good as the real thing—and the samples are in fact recordings of actual instruments, replayed and triggered via the sequencer. In my opinion, though, a sampler will never be able to impart the same inflection and emotional nuance as a human musician. Along with many composers, I'd say there is an advantage, even on a low-budget project, in using real performances. These can be mixed with MIDI sampled tracks with a result that to most audiences is indistinguishable from a completely "human" performance, giving the budget-minded composer the best of both worlds—and in fact this approach has become a commonplace, almost expected workflow for film composers at all levels.

7.3.3 Demos or Mock-Ups

As the composer writes the score cues, their ideas are presented to the director, either by the composer or by the music editor, in the form of demo or mock-up recordings. If a face-to-face meeting between composer and director is possible, for example if the director can visit the composer's studio, there is great value in the personal interaction and instant communication this allows. If not, and the music editor is closer at hand—for example if they are working in the same suite of rooms as the film editor and director as they cut the film—then presenting the music demos can be as simple as having the director come to the music editor's room. It is at this time that the music editor can gain insight to share with the composer regarding the director's important first reactions.

However, with today's tight production schedules, overlapping editing and reshooting, and other postproduction time constraints, the director is often unavailable. In this case, the files can be sent to him or her for review. This "remote playing" of demos is becoming increasingly common—even if the director is literally in the next room, music editors often deliver music cue files electronically or hand-deliver them to the assistant editor to place in the picture editor's project.

7.3.4 Communication with the Composer and Director

From the early stages of a film project and throughout its editing, it is very important that communications between the music editor, composer, and director are good. At the demo stage, in particular—when there may be extensive exchange of ideas, revisions, and more ideas—the music editor can often help the composer and director to reach a common understanding, their communication skills being used to support the sometimes emotional creative process. As noted in Chapter 4, they often have experience of a director's likes and dislikes, and intimate knowledge of their responses to the temp score and to the composer's work. This insight can often be relayed to the composer to help guide their creativity, for example helping to shape the demos or mock-ups the composer presents.

> **PAX Quote**
>
> "We often stumble down the wrong path at first, and we can help the composer avoid it. Leave your ego at home and protect your composer from the same mistake: tell him what you tried (in the temp score) and why they didn't like it."

There are many possible issues, some quite subtle, which mean a cue may not be compatible with the director's vision or taste—perhaps the instrumentation, the shape of the melody in relation to the dialogue, or the emotional impact is not quite right; or perhaps the director feels the tempo or shape of the music isn't providing the right pacing. Richard Davis suggests another aspect to this:

> on [a] rough version of the cue, the director might hear only the electronic-sounding synth strings and not-quite-real-sounding French horn sample and think it is terrible […] . Because he then focuses on the fake-sounding instruments instead of the actual musical ideas, he can mistakenly think that the cue itself doesn't work when all that is wrong is the use of electronic instruments substituting for real ones. It then becomes the composer's job to explain, or even "pitch" the music he conceived, and convince the director that it will work. Or he must change the cue and go in a different direction in order to please the director. Clear communication, and the ability to listen to a director and incorporate his ideas, is necessary.

(Complete Guide to Film Scoring, page 86)

In a situation like this, the music editor can help prevent a whole piece of music being thrown out by suggesting a solution. Some simple techniques—editing, or speeding up or slowing down the piece—might resolve the issue. As a further example, if a director feels that the tone of a score cue demo is too "positive," too "optimistic," this might indicate that the piece sounds too "major". The music editor might suggest to the composer a simple shift of the chord structure from major to minor, or perhaps adding a dissonant-sounding pad or instruments to create a "darker," more conflicted feel.

> **PAX Quote**
>
> "The music editor often has insight into how to mix the demo around sensitive areas, especially if he has made notes—actual or mental—about his own temp music for the same scenes."

The music editor's goal here is to help the composition of the score to proceed quickly and in a positive creative direction. Sitting between the director and composer, they can act as a bridge between film language and musical language. The complexities of music can be difficult to communicate—this is one of the reasons why it is important for a music editor to study compositional techniques for film scoring.

7.4 MANAGING MOCK-UPS

The composer's mock-ups do not arrive all at once, but rather one by one or a few at a time over a period, usually in the form of MP3, AIFF, or WAV stereo interleaved audio files. The director may listen to these files as audio only, but generally it is easier to listen to and make decisions about music if it is played in the context of the film, with the mock-up cues included in video clips of the scenes in which they will play. This is particularly useful if the director is not also editing the film at the same time (and may, for example, be traveling). While music mock-ups or demos could be provided by either the composer or the music editor, it is usually optimal for the music editor to handle their preparation and delivery.

PAX Quote

"For *Bee Movie*, we sent scenes for approval to a yacht in the Mediterranean via satellite."

Files may be delivered via email or an online file-hosting service such as Hightail; other options include posting the files to an FTP site, the composer's web site, or a secure server that can be accessed by the appropriate people; this may be set up by the music editor, the film studio, or the composer's team. File security is likely to be an important consideration here, and the music editor should gain approval from the film company for all distribution methods used.

7.4.1 Bouncing to Video

The usual way to prepare a video clip to include a composer's mock-up for the director's review is as follows:

1. Import the music file into the appropriate Pro Tools session (which may be a "per-reel" session or a "super session" prepared either for the temp process or for the final mix).
2. Sync the leading edge of the file to the timecode label (as shown in Figure 7.1).
3. If the file is not labeled with a timecode, verify with the composer the file edge start timecode number and spot in Pro Tools at that location. You can then

---

Tip

An additional synchronization technique is for the composer's music track can include a bit of dialogue for the music editor to sync to.

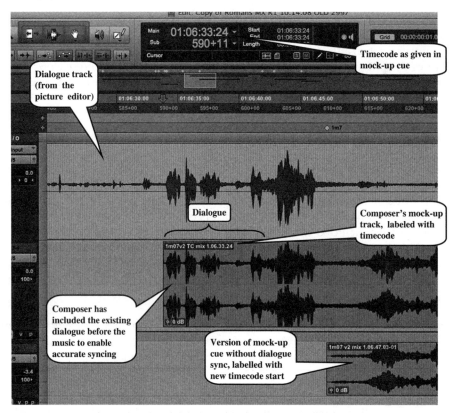

Figure 7.1 A composer's mock-up track labeled with timecode to tell the music editor where to place the cue. On-set dialogue has also been included on the track to help with accurate syncing.

include this information in the file's metadata by adding a "user" time stamp: select the file in the Clips list and hit Command + Shift + M (Mac) or Control + Shift + M (Windows) to open the User Time Stamp window; click on the "up" triangle to insert the current location in the user time stamp field (Figure 7.2).

4. Solo the dialogue and sound effects (DX/SFX) track (or tracks) and the music track (or tracks) containing the mock-up cue (Figure 7.3).

5. Make a selection starting a few seconds before the scene the music is for, and continuing a few seconds after it (Figure 7.3).

6. Play the selection and adjust the volume levels of the DX/SFX track and the music track; you can "write" automation on the music track to "record" these volume moves. Note that the music track should be slightly louder than usual for a movie mix—this is a rough mix of music, DX, and SFX to allow the director to hear the composer's ideas, and not a final mix.

7. Once the sound has been adjusted, open the Bounce window by choosing File > Bounce to > QuickTime Movie… .

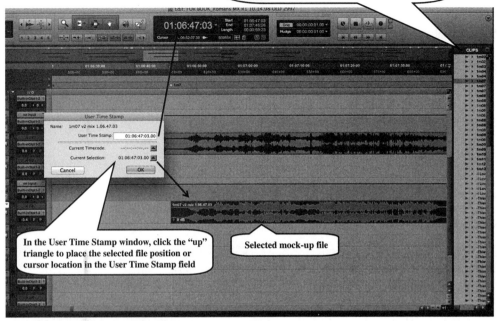

In the Clips list, ensure the correct file is selected and hit Command + Shift + M (Mac) or Control + Shift + M (Windows) to open the User Time Stamp window

In the User Time Stamp window, click the "up" triangle to place the selected file position or cursor location in the User Time Stamp field

Selected mock-up file

Figure 7.2 Adding a user time stamp to a music cue.

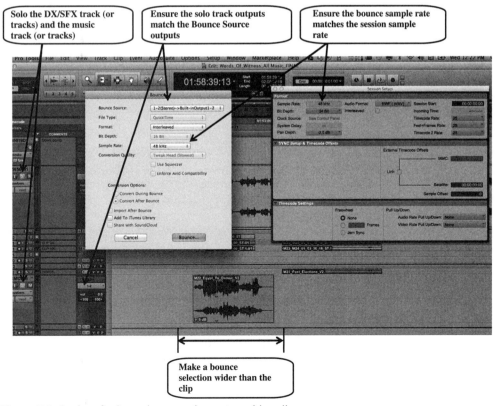

Solo the DX/SFX track (or tracks) and the music track (or tracks)

Ensure the solo track outputs match the Bounce Source outputs

Ensure the bounce sample rate matches the session sample rate

Make a bounce selection wider than the clip

Figure 7.3 Settings for bouncing a music cue to a video clip.

Tip

The usual wisdom is that you can only bounce QuickTime movies to the existing format. Here, though, is a little trick in Pro Tools 10:

- As you click Bounce to > QuickTime Movie..., hold down Control + Option + Command (Mac) or Control + Start + Alt (Windows). This opens the window shown here (instead of the "normal" bounce window where you can't get to the video properties):

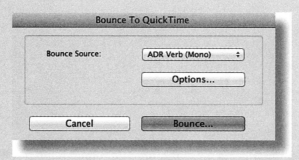

- Click Options... to open another window that will allow you to choose specific settings for video as well as audio:

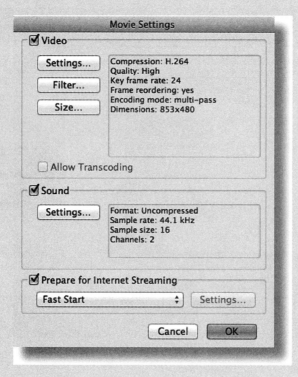

In Pro Tools version 10 and earlier, be sure to select a common output for all of the tracks (dialogue, sound effects, and music). In Pro Tools 11, one can select multiple outputs from the session to be included in the bounce—this is useful for creating stem mixes of music (for example separate mixes of strings, brass, woodwind, and percussion). In Pro Tools 10 and earlier I usually make sure the sample rate in the bounce menu matches the sample rate of the Pro Tools session—in newer versions of Pro Tools this may not be an issue, since you can convert to another sample rate on a bounce. Other features of Pro Tools 11 include the ability to convert to various video codecs (Figure 7.4).

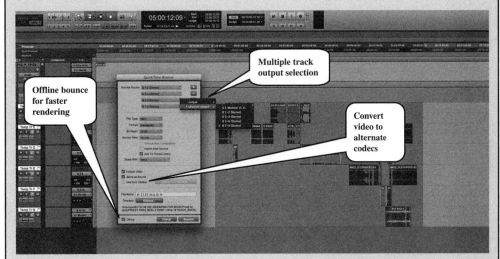

Figure 7.4 Pro Tools 11 features enabling faster "offline" bouncing to video and audio, as well as multiple output selection and the ability to convert to various video codecs, all from the QuickTime bounce window.

8. Choose or make a destination folder on the project hard drive (usually you'd make one folder to save all the video or audio clips that you are planning to send), check the bounce settings are correct, and hit the OK button. The audio (though not the video) will play back in real time during the bounce, allowing you to listen to the mix. (Unless you are working in Pro Tools 11 and have selected an offline bounce, in which case the bounce will be faster than real-time speed and so will happen without audio or video monitoring.) If you detect any problems while bouncing, you can hit Command + . (period) (Mac) or Control + . (Windows) to abort the bounce.

9. Once the bounce is complete, the video clip with embedded audio will be saved to the destination folder. Double click on the file to play the clip in the computer's default player (usually QuickTime Player on a Mac and Windows Media Player on a PC). Check that the dialogue track is in sync with the images and that the balance between dialogue, music, and sound effects is acceptable.

10. The video file is likely to be quite large. Programs like QuickTime Pro 7 (a paid-for option) iTunes, or HandBrake can be used to convert it to a compressed codec such as H.264 or MPEG-4. In addition to making distribution more manageable, smaller files are more convenient for the director, being easier to play on a laptop or mobile device such as an iPad, and easier to share with producers, music supervisors, and others.

Tip

You can use iTunes to convert a QuickTime bounce to an iPhone movie. The picture suffers slightly but the sound quality is very good.

On occasion, you may be asked to compile various clips on a DVD. In this case, be particularly careful to identify and index each clip clearly, so the director can find it easily.

7.5 RECORDING: USING CLICK TRACKS AND FREE TIMING

Once the director has approved all of the composed music from the demos, the next stage typically involves recording. The amount and type of recording varies greatly from project to project, with many factors involved. It should be borne in mind, though, that recording is very often a function of budget—to put this in some context, the traditional guideline for recording with a large professional orchestra is that one hour on the scoring stage ideally produces around five minutes of music.

For the music editor, preparing a cue for recording usually involves building a click track and adding visual timing indicators (known as "streamers" and "punches") to video clips to allow for "free timing". A click track contains a repeated click or beat—a sharp sound—designed to match the music's MIDI file "tempo map" (or "conductor track"). Its main purpose is to guide the conductor, orchestra, or other performers, so that they can keep the music in time with the picture. This is particularly important for making sure that key musical moments, such as "hits," melodies, or beginnings and endings of cues, happen at exactly the right times. A click is also used to ensure music is recorded at a consistent tempo, allowing multiple takes from the scoring stage to be edited together with musical consistency; for this reason, it's important that a click is used throughout recording.

Free timing, on the other hand, is when music is recorded without a click track. This is usually reserved for slower and more emotionally expressive cues, to allow the musicians a freer interpretation in the absence of a rigidly imposed metronome, or where softer playing might cause a click running in the musicians' headphones to bleed into the recording (though sometimes the engineer can avoid this simply by turning down the click track). In this situation, timing is set by the conductor; a conductor working without clicks is said to be conducting "on the stick" (that is, using a baton rather than a click). It's still important that the music remains in sync with the picture, however. The conductor must match the music to the picture at specific sync points (as indicated by the punches and streamers)—as a consequence, free timing relies on having a very skilled conductor who is also experienced in the film scoring process. (For a good description of using clicks and free timing techniques, see Fred Karlin and Rayburn Wright's *On the Track*.)

> **Tip**
>
> Though it's more usual for a cue to be recorded either with clicks or with free timing, it is perfectly possible for a single cue to include sections of each.

7.6 BUILDING A CLICK TRACK

7.6.1 Using a Standard MIDI File

The click track can be created using a tempo map exported from the composer's sequencer file as MIDI information (though it's also possible to build a tempo map from scratch in Pro Tools—see 7.6.3). Usually the composer sends the MIDI tempo map to the music editor, but they may simply send their full sequencer files for the music editor to extract the tempo information as well as the MIDI instrument tracks. In this case, it is best if the music editor has access to the same sequencer program the composer is using. If not, though, most programs allow the MIDI information for a cue to be exported as a "Standard MIDI File" (or "SMF" on some menus). Figure 7.5 shows the use of the "Save As…" option in Digital Performer to export an SMF.

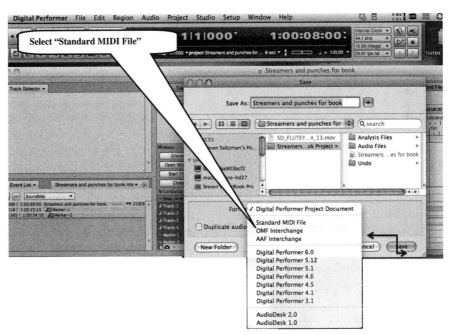

Figure 7.5 Exporting a MIDI file containing cue information in Digital Performer by choosing File > Save As… > Standard MIDI File.

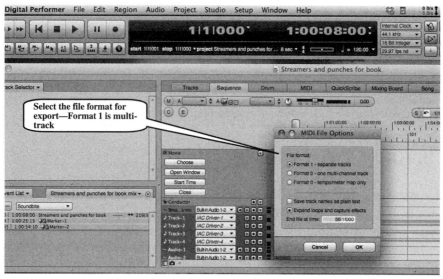

Figure 7.6 MIDI file export options in Digital Performer.

There are various options regarding the information exported in the Standard MIDI File—whether data for the notes themselves, along with associated information such as key signature, is included, or whether only the "conductor track," giving tempo and meter, is exported. The standard formats are 0, which restricts the MIDI information to one output track (or to the tempo map only), or 1, which exports the information on multiple tracks (Figure 7.6). As a minimum, the file should include the tempo map.

7.6.2 Setting Up a Pro Tools Session

It is usual to have one Pro Tools session for each music cue, in which the cue will be recorded, and in which, before that, the click track can be built. When preparing for recording, the first step is therefore to build this Pro Tools session, including the stereo demo for the cue and a track for the click, ready to receive and sync the MIDI tempo map. Also included are the movie reel, along with the rough dialogue and sound effects tracks supplied by the picture editor. If the imported MIDI file includes the information on the music itself—the notes to be played—these can be used to help check the sync between the tempo map and demo. Figure 7.7 shows a Pro Tools session with MIDI instrument tracks and tempo map imported from the composer's MIDI files, and a MIDI click track providing a four-beat count off before the beginning of the music.

You need to pay attention to the setup of the Pro Tools session, making sure the settings are correct for the music recording. Sample rate pulls (up or down) are rare, but if these are required for either audio or video be cautious and make sure your session will work for the recording. Prior to building your Pro Tools sessions, you should contact the composer's mixer (or whoever will be recording the music) to verify

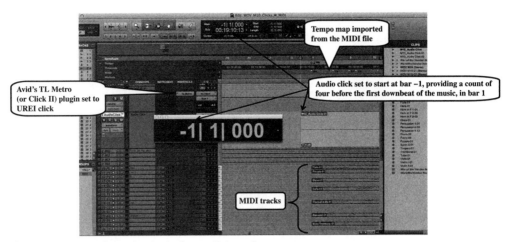

Figure 7.7 Pro Tools session including a click track.

parameters such as sample rate, bit rate, and frame rate, as well as whether any special track layout is preferred.

Make sure the timecode hour of the session matches the reel number of the movie. You should also check the cue's timecode to ensure that the correct start and end times are set. In general, music editors use timecode rather than feet and frames for these sessions. This is because timecode is more commonly used in sequencer programs and most music mixing consoles will sync to automated moves triggered by timecode. (With regard to automation, it is important to note that if the timecode positions in the MIDI music cue are changed for any reason, for example to conform to picture changes, and if the mixer has already recorded a pass with automation, then the mixing board's automation will need to be adjusted to match the new timecode. Sometimes it's possible for the mixer to conform the automated moves to the new picture cut, but this is often too involved to be worth it. Instead, it's usually best to re-automate the moves with the new recording pass.)

7.6.3 Importing the MIDI Information

Note that the figures in this subsection show final music stems already in the Pro Tools session into which the tempo map is being imported—this is in order to show the tempo map's relationship to the recorded score piece. When preparing for recording, the MIDI information would be imported into an empty Pro Tools session.

The Standard MIDI File is relatively small, and has the extension ".mid" (a common format for file interchange among MIDI programs; see Figure 7.8a).

To import the MIDI data into your Pro Tools session, choose File > Import > MIDI. This opens the MIDI Import Options dialog box (Figure 7.8b). Selecting "New Track" provides four options for aligning the MIDI information to the timescale rulers: Session Start, Song Start, Selection, or Spot. "Selection" places the data at the position of the selector in Pro Tools—this is the choice made in Figure 7.8b, where the selector has been positioned at the start—the first note—of the music.

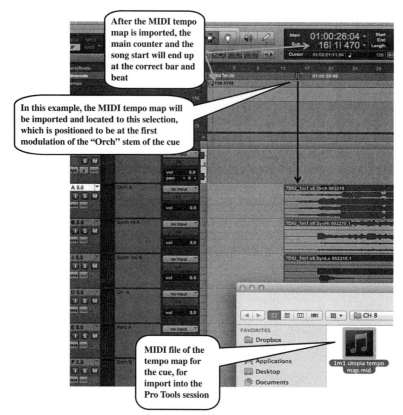

Figure 7.8a A MIDI file containing a tempo map, ready for import into a Pro Tools session.

Usually it's best, however, to "Spot" to the timecode which corresponds to the start of the music, using the timecode start designated by the composer (bearing in mind that this will likely be different from the timecode file edge start of the demo cue). Imported MIDI tracks and their associated tempo map will align to the timecode entered and then assign bar 1 to the cue start (see Figure 7.8c). It is important, here, to make sure of the exact timecode for the first downbeat in the cue (remembering that the music may start not on the downbeat but on an upbeat, as a "pick-up" to the first complete bar). In addition, a composer may have the first downbeat in bar 2 or 3, leaving a count-off in bars 1, or 1 and 2. Even if the composer has set up a standard workflow—for example so that all cues have a file start two bars before the first note—the music editor should double or even triple check the timecode position of the first downbeat in each cue; optimally, they should have a copy (for example a PDF file) of the composer's score, or at least a sketch, to allow them to do this—an example of a score including tempo, meter, bar and timecode information appears in Figure 7.9.

If, once imported to a Pro Tools session, a MIDI file has aligned to the wrong position (for example to the beginning of the session) you can still realign it, using the Song Start menu. To set the bars and beats to the correct timecode position, choose

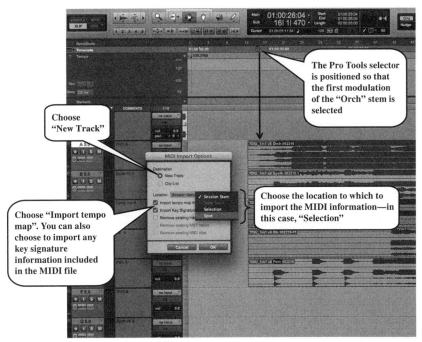

Figure 7.8b The MIDI Import Options dialog box. Select "New Track", "Import tempo map" and the location to which to import the tempo map—in this example the choice is "Selection", so that the tempo map will line up with the start of the music on the "Orch" stem. You can also choose to import key signature information (if the MIDI file doesn't contain this data, this isn't a problem—it simply won't show up in the import).

Figure 7.8c The tempo map in Pro Tools, after MIDI import.

Figure 7.9 Tempo, meter, timecode and bar information in a composer's score.

> **Tip**
>
> After you hit OK in the MIDI Import Options dialog box, your selections cannot be undone. If you make a mistake and haven't saved the Pro Tools session since importing the MIDI file information, you may want to choose File > Revert to Saved and start again. You can reimport the MIDI data with the correct selections, but bear in mind that this may not be "clean," and some information from the original import may remain in the session.

Event > Time Operations > Move Song Start… . In the dialog box, select the field to move the song start to the specific timecode position indicated on the score. Once the song start location is entered, the MIDI tracks and their associated tempo map will locate to the correct bar 1 in the music, and the imported tempo map will jump to the correct timecode. You can then change the song start to reflect a new bar position, or a pick-up or count-off bar, as needed. If you have the stereo demo from the composer, play it, and match up the first note with the correct bar of music in the score, and the correct bar and timecode location in Pro Tools (see subsection 7.6.4 for more detail).

If you have received a full MIDI music sequence from the composer and want to hear the MIDI music or instruments in Pro Tools, it is usually easier to assign or move the imported MIDI music data to an instrument track, and use the Pro Tools sample/ synthesizer plugins. Activate most or all of the MIDI instrument tracks and assign them basic instrument sounds. General MIDI instrument assignments will provide an accurate enough sound.

***

Tip

If a cue begins quietly, assign the MIDI track to an instrument with a clear, percussive sound, such as a piano, to help make the start point easier to hear (even though this may not match the instrument used by the composer—the point is to hear the notes clearly for syncing).

***

Next, import the stereo demo of the cue, the dialogue and effects tracks, and the movie reel. Spot the demo to the timecode location of the file edge, as provided by the composer. If the timecode is not given in the filename, it's best to rename the file to include it. If you don't have separate dialogue and effects tracks, you can import the audio mix embedded in the movie file—choose this option in the dialog box which appears when you import it. Before doing so, though, check in the video properties that the dialogue and effects audio has been panned to the left channel, or Track 1, and the temp music to the right channel, or Track 2.

The click must be perfectly in sync with the demo, the MIDI instruments, and the bars and beats of the score, so, finally, check that the demo track plays in sync with the activated MIDI tracks, and with the MIDI tempo and meter maps. Both of these maps can be displayed in the Pro Tools rulers (as in Figure 7.8c). Ensure that the first sound and the first downbeat of Bar 1 are in the correct position according to the score, with regard both to bar placement and timecode. If they do not match, then there is an error in either the cue start location or the tempo map. It is also important to verify that the frame rate and speed of the session are correct, and that they match the composer's sequencer settings. If the settings are different then the music could drift out of sync as it plays.

Sometimes the demo ends up sounding delayed on playback. This is due to how some programs generate sound from the MIDI tracks—if too many play at once it can create "latency," as the MIDI is recorded to a stereo audio file. If this happens, you need to move the stereo track to play a little earlier, or, in postproduction terms, to "advance" it. Once you find the proper advance amount (by matching the first sound to the tempo map start and bar number in the written score), it can usually then be applied to all the demos sent by the composer. The movement needed can be as little as a few frames (as in Figure 7.10). To make the demo music stretch and adjust to modifications of the tempo map, make a copy of the demo track, enabling Elastic Audio's Polyphonic setting and being sure to set the timebase selector to "ticks"—this means the audio will stretch to match tempo adjustments. It is important to note that adjusting the demo track start to match the tempo map start must be done before any further tempo adjustments can be made.

So far this section has assumed you are using an imported MIDI tempo map. If you don't have this, though, you can create one from scratch in Pro Tools, using the composer's written score and the stereo demo along with the techniques for making tempo adjustments described in the next subsection. Taking this one step further, you

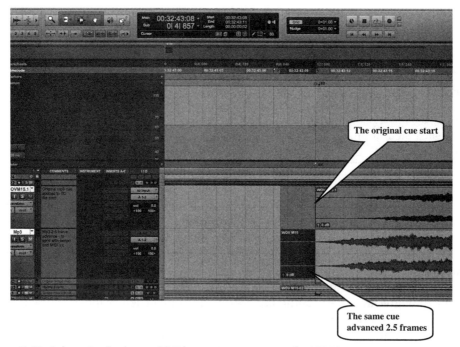

The original cue start

The same cue
advanced 2.5 frames

Figure 7.10 A demo track advanced 2.5 frames to compensate for MIDI latency

can even create a tempo map and click with only the written score and the tempo, meter, and timecode information it provides.

If creating the tempo map from scratch in Pro Tools rather than importing it, the initial song start location should be at the bar and tempo mark indicated on the score. Go through the printed score and map out any tempo and meter changes using the Pro Tools "Identify Beat" function (Event > Identify Beat... , or Command + I (for Mac) or Control + I (for Windows)), noting the timecode positions. Follow along in the written score and make any necessary tempo adjustments, as described in the next subsection.

7.6.4 Making Tempo Adjustments

When creating a tempo map from scratch or when, as sometimes happens, the tempo map doesn't quite match the timecode locations the composer intends (which are usually marked in the score; see Figure 7.9), the tempo map in Pro Tools can be adjusted to generate a click track in which the beats fall as intended. This in turn enables the cue recorded with the click track to "hit" in the right places in the movie.

Create the tempo changes with the appropriate option in Event > Tempo Operations, using the score as a guide (see Figure 7.11). The copied demo file can then be played back to check the changes—the playback won't sound good, since stretching the track will cause some digital aliasing and unpleasant audio artifacts, but this

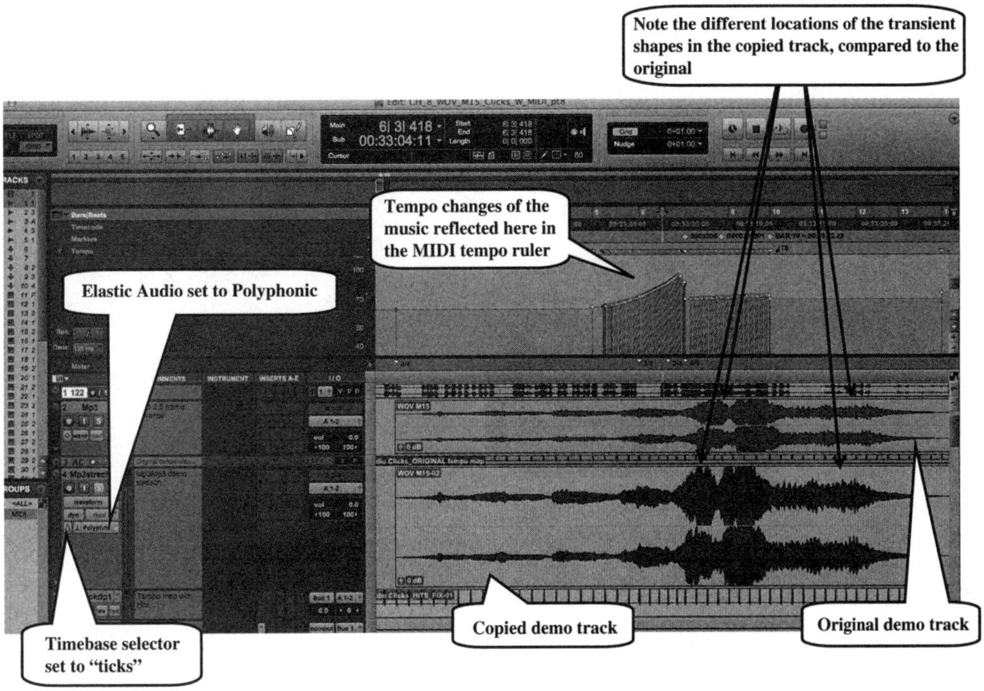

Figure 7.11 Using Elastic Audio to make tempo change adjustments in the music demo.

track is only for the purpose of tempo matching the music to the written score and the movie. (See subsection 7.6.3.)

As an example, an accelerando (increase in tempo) like the one in Figure 7.12 can be implemented as follows:

1. Select Event > Tempo Operations > Linear…
2. Set the Pro Tools Main Counter selector to bars and beats, read the score to determine the duration of the accelerando and then make a selection on a track or in the ruler to indicate the bars and beats at which the accelerando should start and end. Check that the transport window showing the MIDI window has the conductor activated.
3. Click the "Advanced" button in the Tempo Operations dialog.
4. Set the Calculate field to "end tempo." The Selection fields should match your timeline or edit selection, in bars and beats.
5. Set the Sub Counter selector to timecode. The Timecode field in the Tempo Operations dialog (below the Selection fields) will match the Sub Counter.
6. Note that the Start and End fields match the ruler selection.
7. Click in the End Timecode field and enter the timecode position where the last bar and beat of your selection should hit. This is found by looking at the timecode numbers associated with specific bars and beats in the written score.

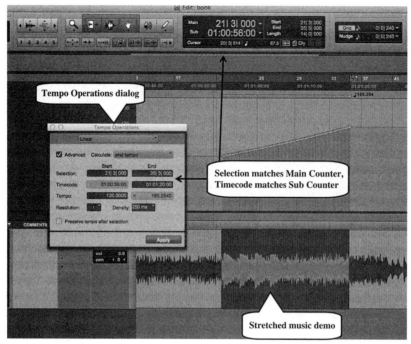

Figure 7.12 Creating a "linear" accelerando using the Tempo Operations dialog.

8. In the lower left of the dialog, select the radio button to preserve the tempo reached at the end of the tempo change, or deselect it to return to the previous tempo—note it's usual to select this, to keep the new tempo reached.
9. Check the settings are correct and click "Apply."

The expanded view of the tempo ruler should now show a gradual change in tempo across the selection; an accelerando is indicated by the tempo stalks getting gradually taller. As indicated in Figures 7.12 and 7.13, the speed and shape of tempo changes can be varied—this is achieved by selecting from the choices in the Tempo Operations dialog, which include "linear," "constant," "parabolic," "s-curve," "scale," and "stretch." In the case of an accelerando, the tallest tempo stalk should occur at the desired end timecode location. As an alternative to making a selection in the ruler or track, you can use the options in the Calculate menu and type in the timecode for the end tempo. You can also make fine adjustments by grabbing, trimming, and moving single or multiple tempo stalks.

7.6.5 Setting Up the Click Sound

To set a click sound, you can either choose Track > Create Click Track, or add a Pro Tools instrument, Aux, or audio track and manually insert a click plugin. Basic click plugins available within Pro Tools include the free-with-purchase Click (Pro Tools 10) or Click II (Pro Tools 11), and TL Metro. These can be found as plugin inserts in the

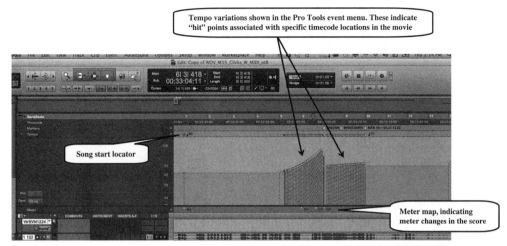

Figure 7.13 A "curve" accelerando, made to ensure the click track provides for "hits" in the correct timecode locations, shown in the tempo and meter maps in the Pro Tools rulers.

instrument menu. Each has certain advantages and disadvantages. The original Avid Click is very basic in its operation, and is limited to only an accented and an unaccented beat volume.

TL Metro and Click II are slightly more advanced, as they can click submeters within the basic meter. For example, if the basic meter is 4/4, you can (in the plugin window) include an eighth-note subclick; you can also choose to have only the eighth-note click. One issue with TL Metro is that it cannot subdivide a 6/8 meter into eighth notes in a 2 + 2 + 2 pattern. If this click pattern is needed, the eighth note clicks need to be set and recorded as a separate click, then combined into the master click track and consolidated.

Most click plugins can trigger a click sound either from a presets library or from any MIDI sound module attached to the Pro Tools system—common click sounds from an external source are drumsticks and wood block. The most commonly used click sound, however, is the UREI click. This is available both in TL Metro and Click II; if using the Pro Tools 10 Click plugin, the click sound MPC provides the closest match to UREI. It is also more common to use unaccented clicks only—although the composer or the booth orchestrator should be asked which they prefer the players to hear.

7.6.6 Making the Audio Click Track

The next step is to print or record the MIDI click as an audio track. Set the output selector of the click track to any mono or stereo bus—usually mono will suffice. Then create an audio track, labeling it "Audio Click" or similar. Set its input path to "receive" the MIDI click output bus.

Set the cursor to start recording the correct number of beats before the first downbeat, as a count-off before bar 1 of the cue—this gives "free bars" in the same tempo and meter as the start of the cue ("How many bars for free?" and "How many clicks for free?" are regular questions when recording). The number of free beats or

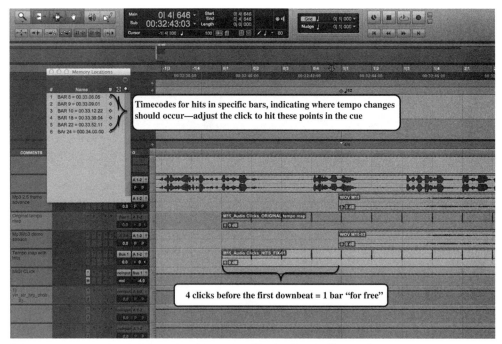

Figure 7.14 A completed click track, with one bar "for free" and a listing of tempo changes

clicks is most often determined by the composer and written on the first page of the score. If left up to the music editor to decide, the rule of thumb is that a slow tempo (usually less than 80 bpm) takes one bar for free and anything faster takes two. The MIDI bar counter will show negative bar numbers before bar 1—to set the click to start one full bar before bar 1, set the cursor to bar 0, and for two free bars choose bar −1 (Figure 7.14). As an example, if the cue begins in 3/4 meter at a tempo of 75 bpm, you would usually set the click track to begin one bar before the downbeat, placing the cursor to record at bar 0. This would provide three clicks at 75 bpm, to prepare the players to begin at this tempo and in 3/4.

7.7 FREE TIMING: STREAMERS AND PUNCHES

Free timing, where the conductor is "on their own," is generally used for slower music cues which require more free-flowing emotional expression (though a slow, emotional cue can also be recorded with a click track). A cue recorded with free timing must still "hit" in the right places, however. The relevant sync points are marked in the score as "streamers" and "punches" (see Figure 7.15), with a streamer indicating preparation for a specific bar and beat and a punch a particular moment in the music or the movie; a streamer often starts or ends with a punch. There is also a variation on the punch called a "flutter punch," which is a series of three, five, or seven punches in

Figure 7.15 Streamers and punches in a score—note the punches at regular 2-bar intervals, to help the conductor maintain tempo, and at the end of the streamer.

quick succession. The "flutter punch" is often used to mark a significant point in the movie the conductor needs to pay attention to.

The exact placement of streamers and punches is commonly determined by the composer, conductor, or orchestrator; it is also possible that the music editor will be in charge of this. These indicators can serve a variety of purposes—they might be used to maintain tempo, or they may help with syncing particular moments in a cue with specific moments on screen. For maintaining tempo, a punch can be inserted at regular intervals, for example every two or four bars. This can allow the conductor to interpret tempo more freely, while still giving them an overall guide.

Once their positions have been decided on, it is the music editor's responsibility to include streamers and punches in visual form as part of a video clip of the relevant scene, which will then play during recording, on a large screen behind the musicians. This means the conductor can watch the movie at the same time as recording, and provides them with a (literal) "guiding light": a streamer is seen as a vertical bar of light which moves steadily across the screen from left to right, while a punch appears as a flash.

The origin of these conventional visual markers lies in the not-so-distant past, when 35 mm film was still widely used: a streamer was created by scraping the emulsion off the film in a straight line, usually for a length of 3 feet, while a punch involved physically punching a hole in the film. When the film was played, the light from the projector's bulb would show through, creating the effects described. Today, streamers and punches are digitally embedded in the video.

A conductor can time and pace a cue following these indicators—seeing the flash of a punch from the corner of their eye every two, four, or more bars, they can match their conducting to the written tempo of the music; they may or may not be timing each bar perfectly to begin with, but as the flashes continue they can adjust their tempo. Streamers can be used to indicate important upcoming "hits," or critical points that need to match the movie. A skillful film music conductor can be accurate to within 8 frames, or one third of a second. The goal is to gain a free-flowing tempo, interpreting the composer's music while also being able to match specific hit points.

A conductor may also have a click track running in their headphones—and some still make use of a large stopclock with a second hand, which they use to match the music to real clock timings noted in the score. (Once a requirement for all scoring stages, today these clocks are increasingly rare items; though Sony Pictures still have one.) Streamers and punches can also provide timing guides for the other performers, of course, as well as the composer and the ADR editor or mixer.

7.7.1 Making Streamers and Punches

Streamers can vary in color and length—typically they are 2 seconds long, but 2.5 and 3 seconds are also common, and many other variations may be used, depending on tempo. Similarly, punches can vary in color and size.

PAX Quote

"We color-coded streamers with fat pens: green for start, red for stop, and so on. The variation in length is all about the conductor's preference. A colleague once used a 4-foot streamer for a conductor who was used to 3-footers. The conductor stood staring at the screen with his hand on his forehead trying to decide what had just happened: Wrong film speed? Stroke? Time warp? He slowly turned and looked at the editor, as if to say, 'Did you see that? Have fun explaining that to a 90-piece orchestra!'"

Various external "boxes" or interfaces can be used to generate streamers and punches, including the Click Stream Machine, CueLine and Video Streamer, though software also now allows us to embed streamers without the need for any external hardware. The Figure 53 company, for example, makes a streamer and punch program (downloadable from its web site, figure53.com) that works as a standalone generator or with an external interface using MIDI timecode and/or MMC (MIDI Machine Control).

7.7.2 The Auricle

One of the original click "machines" with streamer and punch capability is "Auricle: The Film Composer's Time Processor," popularly known as The Auricle. Introduced in 1984, this program is specifically designed to aid the development and performance of music for film, and is still used by most of the top working composers and music editors worldwide, including John Williams, James Newton Howard, Randy Newman, Danny Elfman, Alan Menken, and James Horner. Auricle is revered, particularly on the scoring stage, for the total control it provides over the metric and temporal characteristics of orchestral film music.

The details of Auricle's many operations and functions are beyond the scope of this book, but many articles published on the subject over the years are collected on Auricle's web site (www.auricle.com/presskit.html) and, for the most curious and courageous, the Auricle user guide is also available for download (www.auricle.com/downloads/pdf/CD Manual 3-3.zip).

7.7.3 Digital Performer

The music sequencer program Digital Performer—better known as "DP"—made by Mark of the Unicorn (MOTU), can also be used to create streamers and punches. To do this in DP version 8:

1. In the Project menu, choose Movie, then select the relevant movie clip on the hard drive. Currently, DP can access QuickTime frame rates of 23.976 (23.98), 24, 25, 29.97 (drop and non-drop), and 30, and most of the common QuickTime movie codecs. Be sure to match the frame rate of the movie and the frame rate in DP. Don't forget to set the project sequence chunk start time to match the movie's timecode window burn.

2. Go to Preferences and, in the Digital Performer menu, select Film Scoring Events. Check the boxes for the four Generate... events and one or all four Default Visual Events output options. For this example, set to QuickTime movie overlay. Set the default marker event and default streamer event as required. You can click New Markers Have a Streamer, for convenience (this presets markers as streamers, so you won't need to take the extra step of making them into streamers). There are also choices for streamer color, streamer length, punch color, and punch size. (Note that the Visual Effects output choices include CueLine and ClickStreamMachine, the external machines mentioned previously.)

3. Set the movie start time, in the submenu to the right of the movie clip, to show the timecode for the first frame of action. For a film, this will usually be 1:00:08:00 (the 1 indicating reel 1). For television, the first frame of action might be at 1:00:00:00. If the sequence chunk time was set to match the movie's academy leader start on the timecode hour mark (for example hour 5:00:00:00 for reel 5), it will likely already be set. You can set the movie to start at a different location, where a cue is not at the start of a reel.

   Choose whether the same movie will be used for all sequences. You can make multiple sequences, each with a different start time, in one DP project. For example, if the music is for a show that will always have one movie starting at 1:00:00:00 (rather than separate reels each starting at a different timecode), then you can enable this option for all the music cues. Each "sequence chunk" can be a separate cue and have a different timecode start reflecting the cue start.

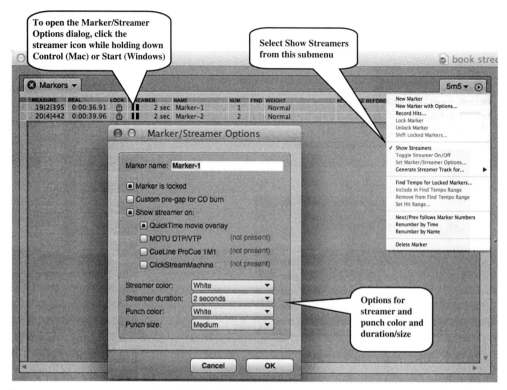

Figure 7.16 Streamer options in Digital Performer using Markers.

4. Under the main Setup menu select Time Formats, to set the time format for markers and other events and selections, then select timecode. In the Project menu go to the Markers tab, then to the mini-menu under the sequence name tab, and select New Marker. (Note that the streamer information can be accessed from this tab as well, by checking "Show Streamers menu.") Use DP's main transport controls to cue the play head to the bar and beat location or time-code at which you want the streamer to end. Select New Marker in the mini-window to insert a marker at this location—this will set a MIDI trigger to start the streamer going, back-timed to hit the right edge of the frame at the location you have selected. In the Markers tab, the frame column fields will contain the timecode location of the end of the streamer. If this field is blank, click inside the empty field next to the relevant marker and a streamer length menu will appear. Select your choice of streamer (the most common is a 2-second streamer).

For more detailed control, hold Control (Mac) or Start (Windows) and click on the streamer icon (the little black bars in the streamer menu) to open a dialog which allows you to set Marker/Streamer Options (see Figure 7.16). You can also change the location of a streamer by moving the marker in Conductor Track or editing its location in the Markers list. To deactivate a streamer, click on the streamer icon so it disappears.

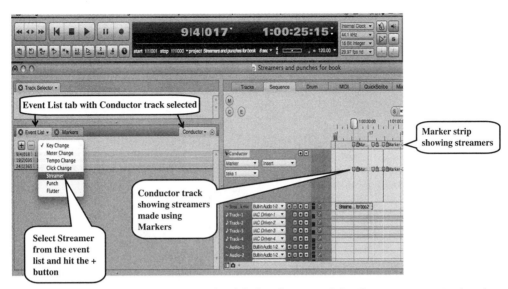

Figure 7.17 Creating streamers as events in Digital Performer and showing streamers as Markers in the conductor track.

The MIDI events which trigger streamers and punches are very accurate—many orders of magnitude more accurate than 24 or 30 frames-per-second film. While this timing will vary depending on the tempo of the music, it will most certainly be close enough, in terms of time and sync, to catch and trigger a streamer for a movie.

If a streamer is used to mark a particular point in the movie, it will be important to lock it to the particular timecode position (which means it won't change position in relation to the picture, even if the tempo changes). The lock field is immediately to the left of the streamer field on the Markers tab. However, if a streamer is being used as a tempo indicator, and is relevant only within the music, then its location should be left unlocked to vary with the tempo.

Streamers and punches set as markers show up in the Conductor ruler, and can be grabbed and moved around as needed. However, if markers are also used for other kinds of information (for example to describe hits), this can become cluttered and confusing. Another method of inserting streamers and punches in DP, one which avoids this potential for confusion, is to make them "events": unlike markers, events do not show up in the Conductor track. This method can be more efficient, and has the additional advantage that a MIDI track of streamer and punch events is created, which can then be exported to another computer or device as needed.

The steps to follow are (see Figure 7.17):

1. With the main sequence tab and conductor track open, select the Event List tab from the list at the right-hand side.
2. Insert a streamer or punch by clicking on the field to the right of the + button (at the top left of the tab) and choosing Streamer, Punch, or (for a flutter punch) Flutter, then +.

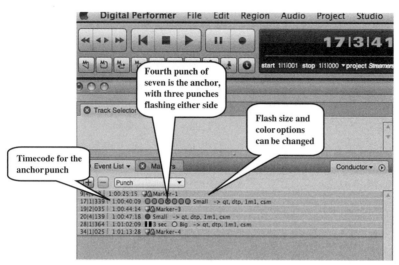

Figure 7.18 Flutter punch, punch, streamer, and other markers all viewed as events under Digital Performer's Conductor menu track.

A streamer created in this way has the same setting options as one created using a marker, with the additional choice of including a punch at the end, and more control over length and color.

Each punch is shown as a circle. For a flutter punch, holding Control (Mac) or Start (Windows) and clicking on the punch icon opens a dialog which allows you to select the number of flutters; one is selected as an anchor punch, and appears as a circle with a cross inside (see Figure 7.18).

You can set a location for your streamer or punch by typing in a timecode number or scrubbing the movie or sequence track—although as punches are often defined using bars and beats, you may need go back to Time Formats on the main Setup menu and add bars and beats to the Events section, so that the Events tab includes bars and beats.

The last step is to export the movie, with streamers and punches embedded in the digital picture, for use in Pro Tools or another DAW. To do this (see Figure 7.19):

1. In the timeline ruler for the sequence, make a selection to cover the complete music cue, the area containing streamers and punches, and a little beyond.
2. Choose Audio > Bounce to Disk, and in the Bounce to Disk dialog box that opens choose as the File Format QuickTime Export: Movie, and also a destination folder. Click OK.
3. The QuickTime Export Options dialog then appears. Check the boxes to Include Video and, within this, to Duplicate the original video data and Include film scoring events track. Click OK.

The movie will be bounced and rendered to disk with the embedded streamers and punches. You can then import it into your Pro Tools session with the score demo, MIDI clicks, and audio clicks to be played in the scoring session. (Even when the intention is to record a cue with free timing, using streamers and punches, it is always a good idea to build a click track, just in case.) Be sure to sync the new video clip to

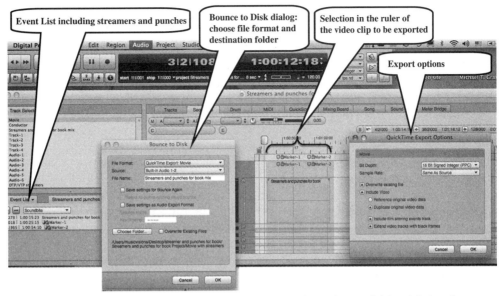

Figure 7.19 Bouncing a video with embedded streamers and punches to disk in Digital Performer.

the correct timecode position, as in the window burn-in (the visual digital overlay of timecode and feet and frame numbers onto a movie reel or clip).

> **Tip**
> You can also play back MIDI and audio stems and the movie output, with streamers, directly from Digital Performer.

7.8 THE SCORING SESSION

A scoring session is an exhilarating, exciting, and nerve-racking experience for all involved—many interpersonal dynamics, including those involving the studio, producers and director, come into play—and the composer may even still be concerned about whether the director likes their music. The music mixer and crew need to be as prepared as possible. The music editor has to have the cue recording order, click tracks, movie clips, mock-up tracks, and dialogue and sound effects tracks ready. He or she also needs to be ready to change click timings and fix sync issues, in case cues are changed or rearranged during the session. A major consideration in score recording is whether the score is to be mixed down into stems after the instruments are recorded, or whether the recording session should be treated also as a mix down directly into stems for the film dub, as this affects the recording mixer's setup. As you would expect, the first of these options will be more expensive, as it takes more time; however, it usually yields a better mix.

The recording order is usually decided by the composer, however the music editor may be asked to do this. There are numerous factors to consider, but usually the priorities will look something like this:

1. The cues which require the largest orchestra—the "A" orchestra.
2. Cues using the "A" orchestra that are orchestrated in a similar way (and which often involve playing the same thematic material).
3. The "A" orchestra's longest cues … now they've warmed up a little!
4. The "B" orchestra's longest cues.
5. The "B" orchestra cues with similar thematic material.
6. "Doubling" (overdubbing) of instrumental groups or solo instruments, such as a doubling of a string section. (Overdubbing is used to layer more instruments for a "thicker," richer sound, or for added instruments that need to be recorded in isolation so their sound can be mixed independently with the main ensemble.)
7. Solo pieces and other "wild," non-sync recordings, and miscellaneous overdub performances. ("Wild" recording is usually of percussion, piano, or special instrumental effects not recorded to picture, which can be used by the music editor on the dub stage, as needed.)

Tip

Be careful when overdubbing an orchestra. Consult with the contractor (who is in charge of hiring the musicians and making the payscale deals) or you might end up paying more money than expected!

Whether ten or a hundred musicians are involved, there are usually multiple takes for each cue. The music editor has the responsibility of combining the best takes, known as "comping," using their unique skill set to edit together a complete cue. This is similar to the commercial music industry practice of combining the best takes from vocal or instrumental performances for a song. The digital recordist or recording engineer's Pro Tools assistant may do the preliminary comping during the scoring session, handling the Pro Tools recording rig and track layout, and keeping track of the takes, however it's important for the music editor also to be able to do this job, if needed. The on-the-fly comping from the scoring session will then be verified and refined by the music editor, creating a completed cue to be presented at the dub.

The music editor must also keep track of score cue recordings during the scoring session, making accurate notes of cue and take numbers and the details of each "record" take. These details might include, for example, the start and end bars, the instrumentation (where there is an "overdub" or "doubling" of instruments), and whether the take is a "pick-up" or a whole new take. Each take is either "kept" or "thrown out," with each kept recording being assigned a number. Reasons for throwing out a take include a playing error, a false start, or a poor entrance, though very often even takes that are false starts or that include mistakes are kept, even though they will not be used, to avoid creating any confusion over take numbers. In general, there are two approaches to take numbers. They can be numbered continuously from the first through to the last recording in all sessions; take 1 to, say, take 250 or 300.

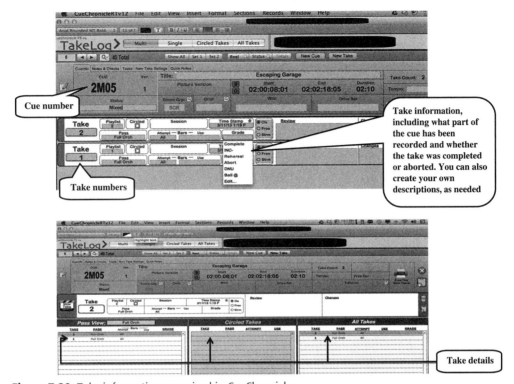

Figure 7.20 Take information organized in CueChronicle.

Alternatively, takes are numbered by individual cue—for example, takes for cue 3m01 might be 3m01_tk01, 3m01_tk02, 3m01_tk03_PU from bar 25 ("PU" here meaning "pick-up"), 3m01_tk04_PU from bar 25, starting a new cue for example with 5m01_tk01, 5m01_tk02, and so on.

The program CueChronicle (discussed in Chapter 3) can be used to keep track of take information (see Figure 7.20).

The decision to record another take or pick-up may be made by the composer, conductor, engineer, music editor or director. Reasons include:

- recording a particularly long cue in sections
- an overdub is needed
- an alternate section, whether planned or from a rewrite made on the stage
- a mistake in performance, or where the composer or conductor feels another take might yield a better performance.

While some of these decisions are made in the recording session, the need for further recording may only be discovered later, after all the players have left, when listening back to the various takes.

The key guidelines for recording a cue in Pro Tools are as follows:

- In the cue's existing Pro Tools session, set the tracks for all the instruments as one group, and make sure all the track labels are highlighted.

- Before the first take, label the track nameplate with the cue number, instrument names and take number "..._01." There are third-party programs that keep track and update the labeling as the recording session progresses; one such program is QuicKeys. The recorded data is automatically labeled with the track name information and automatically time stamped.
- The mixer or digital recordist places a marker or memory locator at a position for recording to start a few seconds before the one- or two-bar click count-off. This location will be the same for each take that begins at the start of the cue. If there are pick-ups or new takes from within the cue the recording starts before the requested bar record location.
- Keep Pro Tools' cursor in the same location for each take; that is, each successive take should have the same sample start location. Likewise, for a pick-up or take starting at a different, later bar in the same cue, each further take starting at the same bar should have the same sample start location. While it is recommended that each take maintain their own same sample start position, it is important to note that each recording in pro tool is automatically time stamped. If a cue or take is listened to out of it's original Pro Tools session, that piece can be time stamp spotted into it's original recorded sync position in a different Pro Tools session.
- When the orchestra and conductor are ready to record, the digital recordist or the mixer arms all the tracks and hits record.
- A request for any new take would usually come from the orchestrator or score reader in the booth, who reviews the score as each piece is recorded. (The conductor, composer, mixer, and music editor can all suggest a new take, but typically a recording moves along very quickly with just one person calling this, without any big discussion.)
- With the tracks still grouped, make a new playlist for the second take; it will be labeled "..._02" by default.
- If a pick-up is recorded, this might be labeled, say, "...03_PU from bar 25." The cursor would then be located before the start of (in this example) bar 25, in order to make sure the start of the pick-up is recorded. It is useful to use a consistent pre-roll of 1 or 2 bars.
- As each cue is recorded and completed with multiple takes, a consensus is reached as to which are the best takes; these are "circled" as the ones to use for the final mix. It's very possible that there will be more than one circled take for a cue, which means a "comp" is needed. The music editor or digital recordist copies the circled takes into a fresh, blank playlist, then pastes sections of the selected takes into a "comp" track. This creates a rough version, used in the recording session to give an idea of how the final cue will sound. It can be changed on request, by going back to any previous playlist, copying material, and pasting it into the comp track. At the end of the day circled takes are listened to and compared to verify the best recording.
- The final step—ideally reserved until after the mix, when there is more time available—is for the music editor to refine the comping, making sure that edits are positioned and cross-faded so that the cue sounds seamless and complete, and the overall sound is as intended. During recording, all parties should be aware that this "perfecting" stage is still to come.

Sometimes it is necessary to make changes to cues during the scoring session. Whether the reason for the change is creative or technical, this is often where the music editor's expertise is called on. Sonny Kompanek offers an example:

> On one session, a climax point was moved a couple of seconds later than planned for a 70-piece orchestra. We had to start at the same place but get to bar 21 two beats later than expected (this happens fairly frequently, especially in the jingle business). So our very capable music editor simply chose to make bar 20 a six-four bar instead of four-four and we had the orchestra extend their figures in bar 20 for two beats. The climax then occurred at the right place. When you do this, remember to subtract the number of beats you added somewhere later in the cue, so that the total number of beats remains constant.
>
> *From Score to Screen*

For this example, note that any click track running would also have to be adjusted to compensate for the two beats of music added in one section and deleted from another. In Pro Tools you can delete and insert silence to adjust the tempo map.

Some of the many issues requiring the music editor's attention that can arise at the scoring session include: altering or fixing click tracks as music is changed on the stage, making suggestions for last-minute musical changes due to picture changes or to match the director's desires, and making music edits in newly recorded material to demonstrate how a problem might be fixed editorially, rather having to reorchestrate, rewrite, or rerecord. The role of music editor is ever-changing, and wholly new situations and demands can arise at any time. Part of the specialist skill set of a good music editor is being able and ready to deal with this continuous evolution, applying their musical and technical knowledge to solve problems and adapt.

7.9 FROM THE COMPOSER'S STUDIO

The combined effect of composers' fees becoming smaller and the tremendous developments in music production technology has been to change the landscape for film scoring. A relatively recent development, one which particularly lends itself to low-budget and independent film and television projects, is the ability to use a score recorded in a composer's studio.

A low-budget project puts tremendous pressure on the composer and their team. Ideally the production company would pay for the services of a music editor, but budget constraints often mean an "all-in" fee structure in which the composer is asked to hire who they need and pay for it from their budgeted fee. A current rule of thumb is that a budget for an "all-in" composed score is about 1 to 2 percent of the film's total budget. As a result there is often very little money for an orchestrator, copyist, recording studio, music mixer, or music editor, and the composer may work largely alone, using a sequencer program. While this may seem to place unreasonable limits on a composer's ability to produce a high-quality score, this is successfully achieved every day, all over the world. If they can use a few real players and combine live recordings with their MIDI files, all the better. Compared to the "live recording" approach described previously, the technical requirements are here very different. In these situations a music editor may only work on the music delivery and the final dub, and on cue sheets and music delivery requirements for the movie.

Figure 7.21 Score cues as stems.

7.10 MAKING STEMS

Once the score has been recorded—whether with live performers or in the composer's studio—the next stage involves getting it ready to be handed over to the music editor for the dub. The score is usually created using "split-out" stems. This is important for two reasons: first, the mixer is able to adjust volume, EQ (equalization), or surround placement for certain parts; second, the music editor has more control where editing is needed to meet the director's needs or to conform to picture changes. Which elements are split out is up to the composer, though the music editor may advise. Typical stems include solo instruments or other "featured" instruments, and sections of the orchestra such as strings, brass, woodwind, synthesizer pads, choir, or percussion. Sometimes composers want to limit the number of stems in order to "protect" their music from inappropriate changes being made on the dub stage. On the other hand, the music editor can take advantage of more separation to help them "save" a cue through editing on the stage.

Stems are best split to match the tracks in common film sound mixes:

- the six 5.1 channels in a film channel format—1: left, 2: center, 3: right, 4: left surround, 5: right surround, 6: sub or Lfe (the re-recording mixer may also use a SMPTE channel format, such as 1: left, 2: right, 3: center, 4: sub or Lfe, 5: left surround, 6: right surround)
- the five 5.0 channels—the same as 5.1 but without the Lfe

- Quad—1: left, 2: right, 3: left surround, 4: right surround
- LCR—left, center, right
- stereo
- mono

> **Tip**
>
> Mix all your stems in 5.1. Don't mess with LCR or 5.0—they can be placed in a 5.1 stem with a few open tracks. This allows the editor to intercut different stems and share tracks. If you have room in your session, this will save a lot of time and calculating when something needs to be moved quickly. Mixers like it, too.

Although film-style split tracks are more common, on occasion, for example for a low-budget film, a composer may deliver stems in stereo format—that is, each stem on its own stereo track. While this layout will work, the re-recording mixer will most likely have to take extra time to place the stereo track stems into a surround mix environment. This is because stereo tracks only sound from the left and right channels, and when played in a 5.1 film mixing environment the centre is missing or heard as a phantom track (it is perceived as sound coming from between the two speakers). Given that dialogue is played almost exclusively through the centre channel, this means the re-recording mixer needs to take particular care when working with stereo-only material.

> **Tip**
>
> Using only stereo tracks also means you won't have a "hard center" (a 5.1 center channel separately available for the mixer). In some cases this lessens the clarity of the music, and vocals and drum kits are likely to really suffer.

Once the music editor has the composer's stems, they place them in their correct positions in the film reels and in the track format required by the re-recording mixer. Whether the score is recorded on a scoring stage or created in the composer's studio, it is critical that each stem starts at the same sample position (even if it doesn't "play" until later in the cue; see Figure 7.22). This is something the music editor should insist on, since it will be very important for correct placement in the reel and for any music editorial needed.

The score cue files should also be time stamped. A time stamp indicates where in the timeline the file is to be placed, and is embedded in the file as metadata. In many sequencing systems (including Pro Tools), a file is automatically time stamped to the timeline position at which it is recorded. In addition, the user can move the file position and add a "user" time stamp for the new position (see subsection 7.4.1 and Figure 7.2). If the score does not include timecode information for each cue, the music editor needs to obtain a list from the composer—although timecode location will have been included in the spotting notes, the composer may have changed it.

Whether the files are time stamped or not, it is a good idea for the composer to label the files with a timecode start. It is also crucial for the music editor to know whether this file start is the timecode position of the file clip edge, or the first

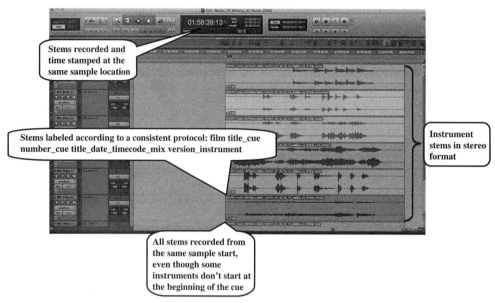

Figure 7.22 Stereo instrument stems with identical sample start position and time stamp, and consistent labeling.

modulation of the music (the "transient" or first sound on the track). If the composer has not either time stamped or labeled the files with the timecode start, it is in the music editor's interest to re-label each file to include this information.

Another way the composer can ensure the music editor is able to accurately sync a cue with the film is to record a small section of dialogue from the film in one of the music tracks, to end before the music starts (see Figure 7.1). Some composers record the whole dialogue track throughout the cue as a mono reference track. This will of course be muted or discarded once the music has been properly synced. Note, though, that the cue tracks should still be recorded with the same timecode start, and time stamped. This helps, in particular, with ensuring cue stems will be placed and synced correctly when they are imported cue by cue into Pro Tools by the re-recording mixer. Cues can still be moved, if required because of picture changes or musical edits.

7.11 LABELING FINAL SCORE CUES

It is important to maintain a consistent file labeling protocol throughout a project. For example, the stem at the foot of the Pro Tools screen shown in Figure 7.22 has the filename

EGYPT_1m25_VOTING LINES_121911_01_58_39_13_AMMix v5_STEM_PIANO

This follows the following labeling protocol:

film title_cue number_cue title_date (optional)_(file start) timecode_mix version (optional)_stem_instrument

The film title should remain consistent throughout the cue demo and scoring processes. Considerations for labeling, dealing with each component in turn, include the following:

- The film title may be an abbreviation or nickname: "EGYPT" in the example in Figure 7.22 came from the composer, and reflects the fact that the movie, the title of which is actually *Words of Witness*, takes place in Egypt. Having been introduced, this title was used throughout the project; an alternative, possibly preferable approach might have been to use the abbreviation "WOW."
- If the cue number is a single digit, include a "0" before it—to give, for example, "1m03"—so that it is automatically ordered correctly in cue listings.
- It may be preferable to abbreviate the cue title.
- The cue's version number is usually used only at demo stage, and not for the final version. On the other hand, carrying the version number through to the final mixed tracks would be appropriate in many circumstances. It is very important to be able to keep track—there may be multiple versions shuttling between composer and director, and you need to know which is which.
- The date is often optional.
- The timecode refers to the position of the cue file edge, not the actual start of the music. (The actual start of the music should reference the timecode start in the spotting notes.) Note that a timecode field in a filename usually includes periods rather than colons as separators, since many computer operating systems and programs won't accept colons in filenames. Alternatively, sometimes there is no separation between the hour, minute, second and frame numbers.
- The mix information is usually optional.
- In the example given, the stem instrument is given as "STEM_PIANO." "STEM" is a bit redundant, but in this case the mixer included it make sure the music editor knew the track was one of a group of stems. Occasionally a stem may feature two or more different instruments, playing at different points within the cue. This most often occurs on percussion tracks where the cue features a variety of percussion instruments. The track label may refer to this by using a catch-all term, such as "PERC" for percussion, but it may also refer only to the main instrument sound—for example our "PIANO" stem might also feature a harp—and therefore be slightly inaccurate.

7.12 COMPOSING BY EDITING: RECREATING MUSIC

One of the most controversial, creative, and important skills of a music editor is the ability to edit music which has already been recorded. This may seem to run contrary to the purpose of having music written for the movie, and indeed to the music editor's primary goal of protecting and preserving intact the composer's music as they originally conceived and created it. However re-editing is a reality for many projects.

There are a variety of possible reasons for changing a composer's score, including:

- The movie has been recut since the score was recorded—that is, a "conform" is needed. (See Chapter 9.)

- The director has added a scene and would like to include music that wasn't spotted for.
- The director wants to reshape some or all of the score elements to redefine the music's emotional or dramatic impact.
- The score is interfering with one or both of the other elements of the soundtrack (dialogue and sound effects).
- The composer may not have had the time or money to complete all the cues, requiring the music editor to create cues from stems recorded for other cues.

It is in the music editor's best interest to let the composer know when there is a likelihood that the score will be edited, for any reason. The music editor should also have established at an early point whether the composer wants to be kept informed of any or all changes to their music; however, since this kind of editing often occurs at the dub, when the music editor is under great pressure, he or she may not be able to inform the composer prior to editing. In most circumstances, the composer will understand the potential for this and will trust the music editor to do their best to maintain the integrity of the music; this kind of trust between composer and music editor is often the result of working together on many projects. .

The technical and musical considerations for this type of creative editing can include the following:

- When shortening or lengthening a piece, maintain the integrity and intention of the music. Pay particular attention to keeping hits or musical shifts in their intended positions in the scene.
- Be careful not to lower or raise volume or digitally process individual stems—the composer mixed their cue in a specific way, and with the emotional arc of the scene in mind. However, these kinds of changes might be done or requested by the re-recording mixer.
- Individual stems and parts of stems may be eliminated in part or as a whole to address the creative or technical needs of the dub mixer or director. They can also be re-edited, copied, or moved to address new picture changes. However, the priority in making these kinds of alterations is avoiding changes that interfere with the overall impetus of the original cue.
- Make every effort to avoid the director's throwing a cue out—the music editor is often asked about this, and so should make their opinion known. On occasion deleting a cue can be in a film's overall best interest. This is particularly true if the composer has been asked to provide what might be considered too much music. In this situation, look for scenes that play better without music.
- Choose your battles wisely! If the director is concerned about multiple cues, pick the most important one to defend or discuss with respect to changes. Reaching a consensus can be challenging. Some of the most important things to consider are thematic melodies, the music's emotional impact, and keeping its structure.

Tip

Only the director and composer trump the music editor when it comes to music placement.

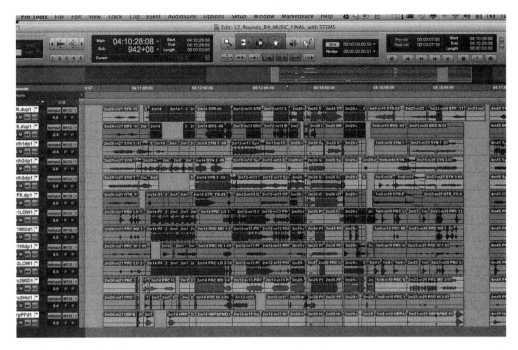

Figure 7.23 An example of cues created by a music editor by finding and re-editing material from other cues. In this case, three cues which were spotted but not recorded (4m42, 4m43, and 4m44) have been replaced by editing the music from six others (2m13, 2m14, 2m22, 2m23, 1m9, and 1m10).

7.13 MORE COMPOSING BY EDITING: CREATING MUSIC

The ultimate creative collaboration between music editor and composer comes about in the rare situation the composer brings the music editor raw recorded materials, and together they create a piece of music from scratch. For the 2009 Batman movie *The Dark Knight*, composer Hans Zimmer recorded and sampled multiple musical elements and brought them to music editor Alex Gibson. A true collaboration followed, with editing and mixing creating a piece of music that composer, music editor, and director were all happy with. This type of creative editing often entails hundreds of tracks of music and audio, and harnesses at the same time the technical and musical expertise of the music editor, and the vision and ideas of the composer (see Figures 7.24 and 7.25).

7.14 CONCLUDING THOUGHTS

The music editor's work with a composer is unique and ever evolving—there are new technical and interpersonal challenges with each new project. A long-lived career in music editing depends on properly valuing and working to maintain this key relationship.

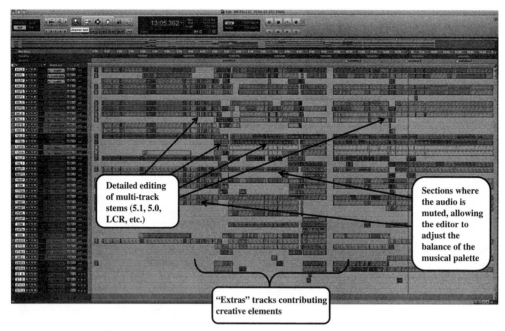

Figure 7.24 A reel from The Dark Knight containing over one hundred tracks, with multiple track layouts (5.1, 5.0, LCR, and so on). Note the extensive editing and blending, with multiple and variable edit locations, as well as the use of muted tracks to "thin out" the musical texture of the cues.

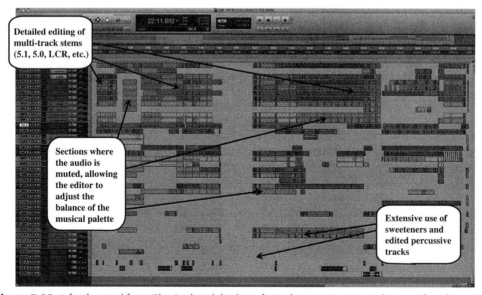

Figure 7.25 A further reel from The Dark Knight, here featuring sweeteners and percussive elements.

7.15 INDUSTRY INSIDER: JOHN DEBNEY, COMPOSER

1. **How would you describe the composer's role, as it relates to the overall success of a film or television show?**

   Having a great theme or "sound" is a really important thing for the overall experience for an audience. If the music is crafted properly, it becomes an integral part of the fabric of the show. The goal of a composer, I believe, is to create a sound that becomes intimately associated with the product. Overall success is certainly not helped or hurt by a score, but having a well-crafted score that can be listened to away from the film is important.

2. **What are some of the similarities and differences between working on low-budget and high-budget films?**

   Low-budget films have their own set of challenges. The biggest is the shackle on the ability to pay top musicians. We are in a bad state of affairs at the moment. Realistic budgeting of film scores has gone out the window, and it becomes more and more difficult for composers to deliver a great score. The composer must adapt and become adept at creating more for less.

3. **How do you envision your role as composer evolving in future, particularly in terms of budgets and expectations?**

   I truly hope that composers become part of the budgeting process. In this way, the composer can help craft the proper budget, after the style and scope of the score have been discussed.

4. **How do you see the music editor's role, as it pertains to the overall involvement of music production? Do you have staff or assistants that provide you with music editorial services?**

   I work with freelance music editors and hire them on a show-by-show basis. Having a great editor is an invaluable asset. With the amount of last-minute changes, it is critically important to have a competent editor. Music editors must also adapt to the new dictates of a lean and mean business.

5. **How does a music editor's work relate to your role? Particularly in terms of their technical, musical, or interpersonal skills, or any other qualities they bring to their work?**

   The music editor must be a good "people person." Oft-times, the music editor must "read the room" and offer helpful advice. The number one job of the music editor is to protect the composer and the music. It is also imperative that the music editor know how to cut music. Cutting ability is crucial.

6. **Can you describe the workflows between you and the director, film editor, and music editor? What are the dos and don'ts, and things to watch out for?**

   There is always a fine line between a music editor who can facilitate helpful discussion, and those that simply want to make points with a director. Job number one is to protect the integrity of the music. Be a cheerleader for the composer. This will help you greatly, and the bond created can span many years.

7. **From your experience of working with many music editors, what are the skill sets that are crucial for their success in this industry?**

   As stated in the previous, it is imperative that the music editor be the most positive person in the room, facilitating creative discussion. Help the composer get to the finish line!

8. **What are some of the technical or communication issues that you as a composer come across with regard to the music? Has a music editor helped resolve any of these?**

Yes, oft-times the editor becomes the filter or interpreter of notes for the composer. Composers must choose wisely as to who they hire as a partner. Be sure of the ethical and temperamental makeup of the person you will be spending many days/hours with.

9. **How do you feel about the temp scoring process, and its positive and negative influences on the composer's creativity and ability to deliver the music score?**

I love a good temp score. It gives me a starting point in my discussions with the director. A bad temp job I simply ignore, if I feel it is not really appropriate for the show.

10. **Do you feel the composer should have a full say in the hiring of the music editor for a project? Or will you defer to the production company, the director, or producer's choice?**

The one thing I'm learning to insist on is the music editor. There is a shorthand and a level of trust that comes with time, and it is critically important for the composer to have "his" or "her" person.

11. **Do you have any insights for those who feel they have the knack for music editing, as to how they might break into the business? Of course, the question needs to be asked: Will there be a need for music editors in the future?**

Music editors must develop a knack for pleasing directors. Being facilitative is imperative. Also, make friends with as many composers as possible. This is a relationship business and thus the editor must get to know as many industry professionals as possible.

12. **Is there a story or two relating to your working relationships with composers, producers, music editors, or directors, whether about positive or difficult situations, which you can share as something we might learn from?**

There are too many stories here (both good and bad). The one thing I'd say is that the editor must become the calmest person in the room. Job number one is to help the composer reach the finish line and give the director the score they want.

7.16 INDUSTRY INSIDER: WILLIAM ROSS, COMPOSER

1. **How would you describe the composer's role, as it relates to the overall success of a film or television show?**

Music has the ability to evoke a wide variety of emotions. The composer's efforts are a critical part of the emotional arc of any musical experience, whether it's the score to a film or television show, a song on the radio, a concert performance of a piece. Music is such a powerful emotional stimulus.

I believe music has the same role in any film, regardless of budget. The budget may or may not affect the quality of the storytelling involved with the film, and in that sense may effect certain musical choices, but the central role that music plays in a film is, I believe, the same regardless of the budget.

2. **What are some of the similarities and differences between working on low-budget and high-budget films?**

The differences may relate more to some of the musical options available to a composer. An example might be the ability to use a large orchestra and choir to record two hours of music for a film with a very substantial budget. That is most likely an option not available to the composer of a film with a $5 million budget. I don't, however, believe that necessarily has to affect the emotional impact of the music for the film. Barber's *Adagio for Strings* first appeared as a string quartet. The emotional impact of those four players, playing that music, is profound.

3. **How do you envision your role as composer evolving in future, particularly in terms of budgets and expectations?**

It seems to me that composers have been asked to take over more and more responsibilities that were once the domain of the studio infrastructure. There was a time when the composer was given a fee to write the score to a film. The support personnel necessary for the composer to do the job—orchestrators, music editors, copyists, musicians, studios, etc.—were, at least at one time, part of the studio music department.

With the ever increasing use of packages, the producers of films have passed on the responsibility for all of the infrastructure to the composer. I don't see that changing. I believe it will only continue in that direction. I think the composer of the future that offers "one-stop shopping" will be a more commercially viable entity. I think it has its pluses and minuses. Regardless of that, however, I think there's a good chance things will continue in that direction.

4. **How do you see the music editor's role, as it pertains to the overall involvement of music production? Do you have staff or assistants that provide you with music editorial services?**

I think a good music editor is always beneficial to the success of a score. The job of the music editor has to be done. Whether that job is done by a music editor hired by the studio to work with the composer, a music editor hired and paid by the composer, or an assistant working for the composer, it's a job that has to be done. Like anything, the more experienced, knowledgeable, and professional a person doing that job is, the better potential for a successful and high-quality outcome. It's really that simple.

5. **How does a music editor's work relate to your role? Particularly in terms of their technical, musical, or interpersonal skills, or any other qualities they bring to their work?**

A music editor is a key member of a composer's team. As I mentioned above, the job a music editor does has to be done. It may be done by an experienced, musically and technically proficient individual with effective people skills … or it may be done by an assistant with far less of all of those attributes. I know who I would want in that position when it's crunch time and the level of stress is in the red zone!

6. **Can you describe the workflows between you and the director, film editor, and music editor? What are the dos and don'ts, and things to watch out for?**

This is an interesting question. One of the areas where music editors can be invaluable is in the temp track process. Many times the music editor is temping a movie before the composer is hired. The music editor may be working closely with the director and have a real say in what music ends up resonating with the director and/or producer(s). I've come onto projects where I felt I was working, at least at first, for the music editor—helping realize the vision for the score that grew out of the relationship between the director and the music editor. It's easy to see how the workflow can be different on every project, depending on the relationship between the director, music editor, and composer.

The "dos and don'ts" that apply to music editors are the same that apply to any collaborative team effort. I believe that film music has become what I call a "team sport." It may be a silly description, but it has a powerful element of truth to it. The things that make for an effective team—well-defined and common purposes, good communication, good listening and people skills, etc.—are all important elements whose presence helps make the team more effective and, hopefully, the efforts of that team powerfully effective in achieving a goal.

As an aside, I suspect that film composition and scoring has always been a "team sport." The difference seems to be that in years past much of the payroll of the team was taken care of by the studios, whereas now it seems that the composer is being asked to be financially responsible for more and more of the members of his or her team. This isn't true in all cases, of course, and it may be that things will head in a different direction in the future. Who knows?

7. From your experience in working with many music editors, what are the skill sets that are crucial for their success in this industry?

I think that for any of us to be successful in the film music business it requires a great deal of patience, ability to manage our thoughts and emotions in ways that help solve problems as opposed to creating or inflaming them. We are all problem solvers. Regardless of our job title, we are hired to work on and solve certain kinds of problems. The skill set to solve those problems varies depending on the job. I believe it's important to understand and embrace the technical aspects of whatever job it is that you take on—in this case music editing. The ability to work *with* people, and everything that that word implies, is another important quality. This is a question that can be endlessly asked and answered. Perhaps the smartest among us are those who are open to self-examination and the desire to continuously improve at what it is they choose to do in life.

8. What are some of the technical or communication issues that you as a composer come across with regard to the music? Has a music editor helped resolve any of these?

I could write for hours on the ways that music editors have helped me in my job! They have helped me focus on the musical direction of a score, helped in finding the right musical arc of a cue, facilitated the relationship between me and the director and/or producer(s) … the list goes on and on! I've worked on projects where I felt like I was working for the music editor! In some cases, primarily when I was orchestrating, it was actually the case: I *was* working for the music editor!

It's an important question and I hope my answer doesn't seem flippant in any way. The question goes to the heart of what a good music editor can bring to a project. I'm deeply indebted to so many of the music editors I've worked with. They have consistently been some of the most important people I've dealt with on a film score.

9. How do you feel about the temp scoring process, and its positive and negative influences on the composer's creativity and ability to deliver the music score?

I think the temp process can be a source of good and, unfortunately, be a real source of difficulty in getting to the end of the scoring process with an effective score. I think a temp can help a director and composer communicate when used as a "guide," and, conversely, be a real impediment to the ability of a composer to do the job they are hired to do. I've seen too many instances where a director has become "married" to a temp cue and no one—I mean no one!—can understand how the director wants *that* music in *that* scene! Maybe one day we will understand that there is a kind of "imprinting" that goes on when we watch a film with music. Just like the cliché of the ducklings who follow along with the first animal they see in a process called "imprinting"—maybe there is something like that going on with music and film.

The clichés about the "good" and "bad" of temp scores are endless. My perspective is that a temp score is like any tool: it can be used in effective ways to solve problems … or used in ineffective ways to solve problems. I've been saddened to see directors become so married to a piece of music in a film that they are unable to see how it's working against the emotional arc of their film. By the same token, I've worked with directors who have used the temp very effectively to end up with a score that seemed to work wonderfully.

10. **Do you feel the composer should have a full say in the hiring of the music editor for a project? Or will you defer to the production company, the director, or producer's choice?**

    If I come onto a film where there is already a music editor who has, for example, been temping the film with the director, then I like to do my best to size up the situation—to see how effective the relationship is between the director and music editor, to see whether there is good "chemistry" there: are they working together to solve problems? Is the music editor someone I feel I could work with? And so on. I have no problem working with a music editor who I haven't worked with before as long as I feel there will be a good and effective working relationship between the music editor, the filmmakers, and the members of my team. I've had some wonderful experiences with that.

11. **Do you have any insights for those who feel they have the knack for music editing, as to how they might break into the business? Of course, the question needs to be asked: Will there be a need for music editors in the future?**

    I think there will always be the need to solve the problems that music editors solve. I don't see that changing. I'm not sure how a person would get started as a music editor. If the kinds of problems that music editors solve are of interest to someone, I think they need to look into who is in need of having those problems solved. It may be interning with other music editors or a large music editor group, interning with a composer … those are just some rather obvious ways. Of course it's much easier said than done. Our business is haunted by the reality that there are far many more people who want to do what we do than there are jobs available for them. It's a reality that has created so much difficulty for so many people. I have a lot of empathy for all of that.

12. **Is there a story or two relating to your working relationships with composers, producers, music editors, or directors, whether about positive or difficult situations, which you can share as something we might learn from?**

    I recently worked on a film, a "broad" comedy! By the time I was asked to do the score, the music editor had temped the film—many times! I didn't know the music editor but felt the relationship between the director and music editor was a good one. I thought the temp was excellent. I met with the music editor and liked the way that meeting went. I chose to keep the music editor on throughout the scoring process. I couldn't have been happier with the results. I look forward to working with him again. Projects like that have introduced me to several music editors for whom I have the greatest respect, not only in how they work to solve the problems of the entire scoring process, but also how they carry themselves as individuals. Many of them have been a tremendous help to me in getting from the start to the end of a project. For that I am incredibly appreciative.

    I think a good music editor is an invaluable part of the scoring process. As I've mentioned above, I believe the problems that they solve are not going away. As long as there are problems—in any area of life—there will be the need for those who are good at solving those problems.

7.17 INDUSTRY INSIDER ANSWERS: JOSEPH S. DEBEASI, MUSIC EDITOR

1. **How would you describe your role, as a music editor working with a composer, especially regarding technical requirements and interpersonal skills?**

Most composers have a tech person working for them, however I find that the more technical knowledge and experience I have the better I am able to assist the composer in his job. My last project I used Pro Tools, Cubase/Nuendo, and Digital Performer to help prepare for our recording session at Air Studios. The composer was writing in Cubase and wanted to mix in Pro Tools. I had to export all of his pre-records with their automation into Pro Tools. Not so simple. First some of the cues were written in off a timeline and starting at a random measure. I corrected the timeline, created a variable click track, and started the cue at an appropriate measure. I then exported the MIDI for the orchestrator and got it lined up in Digital Performer. Finally I created a Pro Tools session with a click track and pre-records with automation for our recording session. Knowing these programs helped me accomplish my task.

2. **If the director or producer makes editing requests at the dub of the movie, do you proceed with those requests without first gaining the composer's approval?**

Yes, all the time. It isn't appropriate to stop the dub to get the permission of the composer to make an edit. The composer knows that this could happen and is usually okay with it, especially if you have worked with the composer before and the trust has been built. During the dub, at the end of every reel, I would let the composer know what, if any, changes were made and why and how I did the edit.

3. **How do you respond if any disagreement arises between the composer and director regarding musical changes, either before or after the score has been recorded? Do you edit the composer's music after it has been recorded, to adjust for picture changes or to meet the director's request for changes to the music?**

This is tricky situation. In the end, you do work for the film and must always strive to please the director, all the while keeping the integrity of the composer's music. If there is a disagreement between the composer and the director, I do my best to let the two of them work it out. It is best if they can come to a solution that I can implement. If they cannot work out a compromise then it's really the director's call as to the direction of the cue. I also tell the composer what I am asked to do. Sometimes the composer is upset with the director's choice, and in those situations I encourage the composer to speak with the director. Generally speaking, it is usually just a cue or two. If it is more than that, then the score has bigger problems.

Chapter 8
Working with a Picture Editor

8.1 THE EDITOR—STEERING THE SHIP!

The picture editor, sometimes referred to as the video editor or film editor, is a key player as the postproduction develops on any film or television project. Whether the project is low-budget or high-budget, the editor is often the main guiding factor both creatively and technically. While the editor is often considered a team player with the director, he or she is the one who shapes the film and helps realize the director's vision and dream of their project. The art of storytelling with picture and sound should never be underestimated, and the musical elements of the soundtrack are intended to support, enhance, and shape the storytelling of the picture. This being said, any good picture editor should have an understanding of how music works or doesn't work with picture, as they work collaboratively with the music editor. It is of the utmost importance for the picture editor and music editor to have mutual respect and a valued working relationship throughout the postproduction process.

PAX Quote

"While we are in charge of all things music in the editing room, the picture editor is the ranking officer over all things editorial, including the music and sound editors. So while he should have a healthy respect for your expertise, he can occasionally give direct orders and will judge your creativity and work much in the way the director does. Often the picture editor plays a role in hiring the music editor and will be invested in your success. If you are not cutting it, he is likely to let you know."

Often a picture editor works with an assistant editor. Even on medium- or low-budget films or television shows this is often the case. It is important to note that many of the technical procedures of music editing go through the assistant picture editor. In fact, the assistant editor can often provide valuable insight as to the inner thoughts and workings of the editor and director. While the assistant is primarily the technical person facilitating and supporting the creative work of the main editor, they also hold a key role, responsible for a smooth workflow between all the sound and visual effects of a movie. On some occasions the assistant can end up cutting music when the picture editor or music editor is not available.

This book will not venture into the many technical settings and workflows of Avid Media Composer, Avid Symphony, Adobe Premiere, or Apple Final Cut Pro; however, I do hope to share some of the key workflows between the music editor and picture editor pertaining to Pro Tools.

8.2 THE CREATIVE

The picture editor's job is very creative, in terms not only of visual storytelling, but also of working with music. The early musical aspects of building a story in tandem with the picture can start even as the dailies are being compiled and cut together with the guiding script. This initial guide to how the various scenes are going to be cut together is called the "continuity." This document is usually written by the assistant editor and shared with all concerned, including the music editor. As noted in previous chapters, the picture editor may start listening and placing temp music in the visual timeline, sometimes even before a music editor is hired. In some cases, when there is not enough money to hire a music editor, the picture editor or their assistant might create an entire temp score.

PAX Quote

"Often it's his assistant feeding the music to the editor. If I can't get on early [to work on the temp score], sometimes I will read the script and then send what I think may be some appropriate scores to the picture assistant to help establish a tone."

This process of the picture editor spotting and cutting in music is relatively new in the overall history of filmmaking. The editor (and possibly the director) will likely have access to other film scores, as well as iTunes and other resources for background underscore music. Some picture editors and directors may have a strong musical background, and often their choices of music and edits with the temp music tracks can work quite well, providing a good guide for the music editor.

Some of the considerations the picture editor should take into account pertaining to the music are the tempo of the music, the instrumentation, and the overall general feel and thematic direction. Keeping these musical elements in mind will greatly benefit the editing of the movie.

The director and editor are usually eager to add music in their initial cutting, although there are those in the industry who feel these early additions of music can inappropriately be used as a crutch against which the film is cut, and believe that a film should be edited and cut to tell its story first, without music. On the other hand,

and as you will notice in the interviews, many picture editors usually appreciate using music to help guide their editing with feel and pacing as they cut the film.

> **PAX Quote**
>
> "I could argue that there are times when pacing can be greatly helped by cutting with music … or music in mind. A montage is a good example. Also, old-school editors would play a piece of classical music in the cutting room so as to put a tempo in their head. Pace is the goal here, however, not emotion."

Music can then be added to emotionally elevate the scene or drive the action in a way that the picture may not quite be able to achieve on its own. The other, equally valid, option is to edit picture to fit the tempo and musical elements of a piece of music. This is generally reserved for rare situations, and is usually done with song material. I believe, for example, that when the temp music for a scene is muted, the film drama or action should stand on its own.

In some cases, there are scenes where perhaps the actors were not delivering at their best on that particular shoot day, which can happen to even the best of them. While in some cases the film company can re-shoot the scene, most often a re-shoot is not possible, and the picture editor is left to cut the scene the best he or she can to deliver the desired emotion. In these cases, it is often believed that music can fix poor scenes. This is a common mistake: Music should not be relied upon to cover up bad acting. If the music is cut or composed well, it can help the scene … but it cannot fix it completely.

> **PAX Quote**
>
> "The best acting in the world can't convey the evil creature waiting around the corner … music, when used correctly, tells the story almost as much as dialogue. But you are right … it can't fix a bad performance."

Often when a composer is hired and has been producing demos or mock-ups of their music, the picture editor usually begins placing these pieces of music into their respective scenes. At this early creative stage of the music composition and film editing, the music is often re-cut to fit or shape the scenes as the picture editor and director continually change the movie. Working in this way with composed music that will be part of the movie is quite different than a picture editor cutting scenes to temp music that will eventually be thrown out.

The picture editor is confronted with additional opportunities for musical creativity when editing songs and on-camera musical performances. As described in Chapter 6, any on-camera editing of the music is often initiated by the picture editor, so the eventual shape of the song is heavily influenced by the picture editor's cutting, just as the picture edit is heavily influenced by the structure of the song.

8.3 THE TECHNICAL—FILE PROTOCOL

As a music editor starts to work on a project, one of the first steps is to understand and communicate the file-naming protocol that the picture editor has set up. While this is not particularly difficult to understand, it is very important to grasp and incorporate into your workflow. Usually this file protocol starts with the digital picture file name. Each picture editor has a preferred way of naming and labeling files, and this naming convention is often implemented by the assistant picture editor. In some cases, the main editor will defer to the assistant, allowing him or her to implement a file-naming convention that they feel makes the most sense. This file-naming is inclusive of each of the sound departments—dialogue, sound effects, and music—so that everyone is using the same shorthand. Usually the naming consists of some abbreviation of the film title, then what department the file is for, followed by a reel #, then some additional information, such as a version number and date. One will often see the film reels labeled as 1AB and 2AB respectively. This is a holdover from the days of actual 35 mm film, when a reel of film for a movie could not be more than 1000 feet, because the projectors in the theaters could not hold a reel any larger than that size. In addition, a 2000-foot reel was overly cumbersome to physically handle and move around.

> **PAX Quote**
>
> "I actually think the 1000-foot reels were as much as a human editor could handle in post-production. Two-thousand-foot sound reels were just too heavy. Studio projectors have had 2000-foot capacities for a long time, but try dragging 30 2000-foot magnetic-stock reels around with you!"

When projectors were eventually built to hold 2000-foot reels, the labeling became Reel 1 A/B, the A referring to the first 1000 feet and B the second 1000 feet. Although we no longer, or rarely, work in actual film, the A/B label has stuck, and some picture editors still like to use that nomenclature. Although the A/B label is not used here, following are a few picture-naming schemes taken from actual film projects and you can see, there are many ways to systematically organize the editing protocol of movie clips in postproduction.

SD_MXLCK_R3_05_08
SD = film title abbreviation (*Straw Dogs*)
MX = music department
LCK = locked
R3 = reel 3
05 = date month (May)
08 = date day (08)

REEL 03_v17 110325 MUSIC
REEL 03 = reel 3
v17 = version 17
11 = year (2011)
03 = month (March)
25 = day (25)
MUSIC = for the music department

REEL 03_v18 110531 MUSIC
REEL 03 = reel 3
v18 = version 18

  11 = year (2011)
  05 = month (May)
  31 = day (31)
  MUSIC = for the music department

R3_Pass_18_1-14 mx qt
  R3 = reel 3
  Pass_18 = pass (or version) 18
  1 = month (January)
  14 = day (14)
  mx = for the music department
  qt = QuickTime movie

BW R1 50 5-9v16
  BW = film title abbreviation *(Bewitched)*
  R1 = reel 1
  50 = cut number
  5 = month (May)
  9 = day (9)
  v16 = version 16

Note that in this last example, the picture editor includes a number that refers to a cut version of the film. The "50" is based on a numbering system the editor likes to work with that starts at 100 and counts backwards. So, the next cut number that might be made after #50 would be #49 (and not #51 as you might expect). However, this editor also likes to define his picture versions by using a "v," or version number, that follows the date. These numbers increase as multiple edits of the film are created.

While these files usually have MX or Music in the titling, if the movie clip was destined for the sound effects department, the label would be FX or SFX instead of MX, because each department (such as dialogue or sound effects) requires a slightly different spec for the movie file they will receive.

PAX Quote

"I will use the Sound FX specs if possible to help the assistant limit outputs, and to be sure that if there is a problem with the files, we all know it."

The movie reels or television show acts are delivered as QuickTime movie files with a variety of codecs such as: Avid DNxHD, DVC PRO, Apple ProRes, H.264, Motion JPEG and many others. While almost all QuickTime codecs with work with Pro Tools, it's best to talk with the assistant picture editor first and perhaps do a test video import. To find the detail specs of the QuickTime movie clip, open the movie reel in QuickTime Player and then choose Window > Show Movie Inspector to view the following information (Figure 8.1).

The imported QuickTime movie in Pro Tools usually contains embedded audio with the movie picture (see Figure 8.2). The audio spec request from the music editor to the assistant picture editor should be channel 1: dialogue + sound effects, and

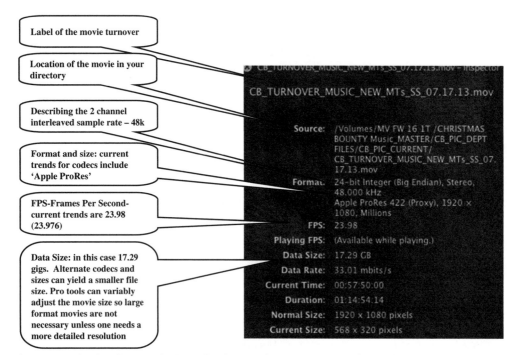

Label of the movie turnover

Location of the movie in your directory

Describing the 2 channel interleaved sample rate – 48k

Format and size: current trends for codecs include 'Apple ProRes'

FPS-Frames Per Second-current trends are 23.98 (23.976)

Data Size: in this case 17.29 gigs. Alternate codecs and sizes can yield a smaller file size. Pro tools can variably adjust the movie size so large format movies are not necessary unless one needs a more detailed resolution

Figure 8.1 Viewing the specs in the QuickTime Movie Inspector to verify the digital picture specs for your project.

Select New Track for the first time importing. Select Main Video Track if you want to over-right than existing video track. This will be necessary in NON-Pro tools HD, as there can only be one video track in Pro tools

Figure 8.2 When importing a QuickTime movie with the embedded audio file, the file will usually be attached as a stereo file, however, the left and right channels may contain different sound elements. This figure shows the initial importing of the movie, selecting the session start as the position, and including the audio files in the import. Note: One can import audio from a movie clip without importing the movie itself by selecting Import Audio from the Pro Tools menu while selecting the movie file or right clicking on the already imported video file in Pro Tools.

channel 2: any and all the music that has been placed in the picture editing system, such as temp music, composer demos, songs, and source music. These two mono audio channels are embedded or interleaved as a stereo track, with the left channel representing channel 1 and the right channel representing channel 2.

Figure 8.3 This example shows the imported stereo track from a QuickTime movie. While in this case it is a stereo audio track, one could have a multi-track embedded audio of more than two channels.

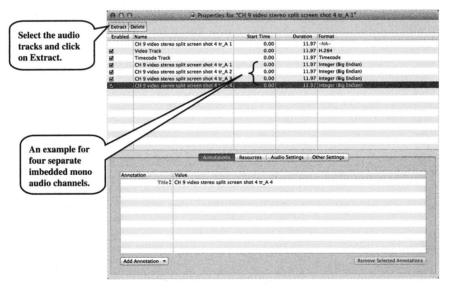

Figure 8.4 It is possible to embed a QuickTime movie with multiple channels such a Quad, 5.1, etc. To view the multiple audio channels from a movie, access the Show Movie Properties window. Select the audio tracks and click on Extract. This will place the embedded files in a location of your choice. Each file may have a .mov extension or .aif. You can simply replace the .mov with an .aif extension so the file will translate into Pro Tools.

8.4 THE TECHNICAL—FILM SPEED AND VIDEO SPEED

Tip

The readers of this book should familiarize themselves with all pertinent technical information dealing with postproduction video. It will also be important for the music editor to fully understand pull-up and pull-down. There are many technical documents online or in books, that explain these two important aspects of postproduction picture and audio in more detail than I will present in this volume.

When the film is shot, the speed that the film runs through the sprocket holes of the camera is the "film speed", 24 fps. Black and white television was originally shot with video at 30 fps. Color standard definition video in North America is shot at 29.97 fps (Non Drop) for long format material, while standard definition broadcast television is shot at 29.97 (Drop Frame). HD video in North America is usually shot at 23.98 fps, although 24 fps (while less common) is sometimes used as well. Outside of North America, 25 fps is commonly used for both standard definition and high definition video projects. Generally the production audio recorder will run at a frame rate and speed matching the camera. Although 24 fps and 30 fps are different frame rates, their respective audio speeds are identical. While the standard 35 mm film speed protocol is 24 frames per second, the recent 2012 film, *The Hobbit*, was shot at 48 frames per second using dual RED Epic cameras on a 3D rig. The digital camera can be set to shoot at various speeds, including 23.976 fps, 24 fps, 25 fps, 29.97 fps, 30 fps, 48 fps, etc. Traditionally, and in the not too distant past, filmmakers shot movies at 24 frames per second, and then when the time came to edit the movie, the video and audio needed to be "pulled-down" (or slowed down) by 0.1%. All editorial work was done using videotape, with a standard definition speed of 29.97 fps, which is 0.1% slower than 30 fps. This transfer process from film speed to video speed is known as telecine. Both 29.97 and 23.98 are generally regarded as running at "video speed" in reference to the days when we used video tape for editorial. These video and audio speeds are in fact identical; only the sub-division of each second is different, as you are dividing each second into essentially 24 parts (frames) or 30 parts (frames). The speed difference between the shooting camera and the videotape was basically due to the fact that in order for the videotape to represent color picture, as opposed to black and white, it needed to be slowed down by 0.1%. Because current postproduction editorial no longer uses videotape, you would think that this slowed-down speed would be irrelevant. Not true: We still use the format of 29.97 fps of slowed-down video and audio. In fact, the most common editorial speed currently is 23.976 fps (also referred to as 23.98 fps), which is 24 fps slowed down by 0.1%. One nice thing about 23.98 video speed is that it divides the second into 24 parts or frames in the same way film speed (35 mm film) divided the second into 24 parts or frames, i.e. 24 frames per second. In Pro Tools we can set both the 23.98 timecode ruler and the 23.98 film ruler in the edit window and the frames will line up. Even with the advent of digital, there is still a protocol of shooting at film speed and essentially pulling-down for postproduction.

The final step after editing the entire picture, all of the audio, mixing and print mastering the film, is re-converting (using a 0.1% pull-up) the audio back to its original film speed of 24 fps, so that it can be properly synchronized to the film print or Digital Cinema Package (DCP). Increasingly, more and more films and television shows are being initially shot digitally at 23.976 fps, remaining at 23.976 fps throughout the entire editorial, mixing and print mastering process, avoiding the need for all but one audio pull-up. This takes place at the very end of the postproduction process, when the final printmaster audio stems are converted back to a 24 fps film speed by applying a 0.1% pull-up, so that the audio synchronizes with the final film print or Digital Cinema Package (DCP) master.

When converting audio between 23.976 fps HD video projects and 29.97 fps standard definition video and broadcast television in the U.S., no audio pulls are necessary, despite the frame-rate difference, which greatly simplifies this process, saving both time and money.

Although there are multiple pull-up and pull-down settings in use on film projects worldwide (such as pull-up by 4% for converting from 24 fps to 25 fps, as would be necessary for PAL, the European standard film speed) most film project workflows have transitioned to utilizing fixed-frame rate settings and sample rates with no audio pulls for the entire postproduction process, in order to avoid the confusion and potential mistakes that had occurred in the past.

To check these audio and video settings, first communicate with the picture department or picture editor, then view the file codec type in the QuickTime software to make sure the settings in Pro Tools are correct, and finally verify that the Pro Tools main timescale display matches the window burn on the digital picture (see Figures 8.5 and 8.6).

Working with film projects that require audio and video pulls can be confusing, and are not the only valid ways of working. The reader should investigate multiple sources in order to become well versed with this technology.

Tip

Some web links to documents discussing pull factors:

http://www.soundonsound.com/sos/jun10/articles/masterclocks.htm
http://en.wikipedia.org/wiki/Telecine
http://en.wikipedia.org/wiki/Three-two_pull_down

8.5 THE TECHNICAL—TURNOVER—AAF AND OMFI FILES

The term for the exchange of data from the picture department to all the sound departments is "turnover." The turnover contains the most current digital picture cut, all associated audio files, and change notes. (Change notes will be covered in the next chapter.) If you are working on a feature film, most often the film is divided into reels, which are typically 20 minutes, or less, in length. For an average film length of 90 minutes, this would total either five or six reels. A 60-minute episodic television show, however, may be delivered as a continuous 43-minute file—because of network formatting and advertising, a 60-minute show has an actual running time of 43 minutes—and a 30-minute sitcom will be about 23 minutes in length. A multi-night television mini-series show may be organized into full-hour elements, with one element of

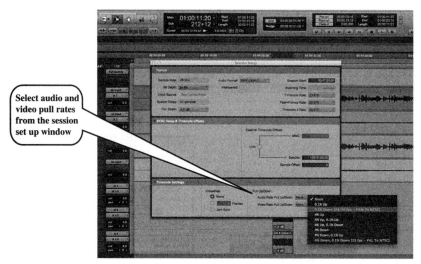

Figure 8.5 The Pro Tools session setup window shows the ability to set the audio and video data to a pull factor. The many choices are 0.1% up or down for audio or video, and 0.4% up or down to convert audio files for PAL speeds.

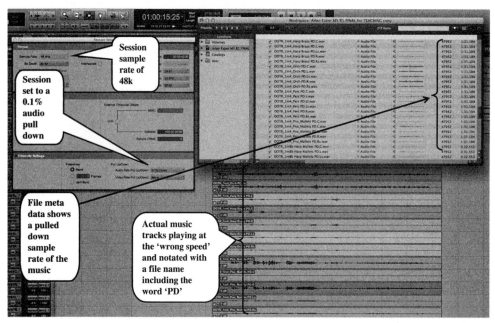

Figure 8.6 This example shows a Pro Tools session in which the audio is being forced to play back at the wrong speed according to the sample rate settings. This is used to compensate for a pulled-down session of 0.1%, and the imported music being recorded at a non-pulled-down speed. One can convert the audio files on export to a pulled-down sample rate of 47.952, and import without converting to the 48k sample rate of the Pro Tool session. The music files in this case will then play at the correct sync speed.

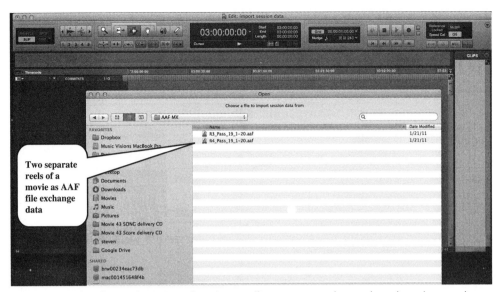

Two separate reels of a movie as AAF file exchange data

Figure 8.7 As the picture department's assistant editor turns over the movie reels to the sound departments, they make the AAF or OMF file-exchange formats to the desired specs. In this example, the AAF file data contains all the necessary pointer information as well as the actual files of audio embedded into this one piece of data. The sound editor can then either import this file as Session Import, or in most situations double-click on this file to open it as a Pro Tools session, with the Import Session Data window open.

film/video and audio unit starting at 1 hour (1:00:00:00), and the next hour unit at 2 hours (2:00:00:00), with each reel referring to the timecode hour.

The common file transfer, using AAF or OMF, essentially hands over all of the selected audio files and tracks that the picture editor is working with (see Figure 8.7). For the music editor, it is most important to receive all the music tracks that the editor is using in their timeline. It is unnecessary to transfer dialogue or sound effects AAF files to the music editor—these AAF files should be sent to the dialogue and sound effects departments. Instead, the music editor will receive the dialogue and sound effects as an embedded single mono or stereo file extracted from the QuickTime movie clip, or as a separate mono or stereo audio file.

Usually the AAF or OMF file will be one single file, as seen on the computer desktop (if it is saved as an embedded export). On occasion, it can be in two file folders, one containing the media and the other the metadata file as the reference document pointing to the media. There are multiple ways to import these files into Pro Tools. With more recent versions of Pro Tools, you can double-click on the AAF document file itself, and Pro Tools will open the AAF as a new Pro Tools session. If you wish to import the AAF file into your current open session, choose File > Import > Session Data from within your open Pro Tools session, then select the AAF document file and hit Open. You can also drag and drop the AAF data file onto your edit window in Pro Tools, which then brings up the Session Data window. With any of these

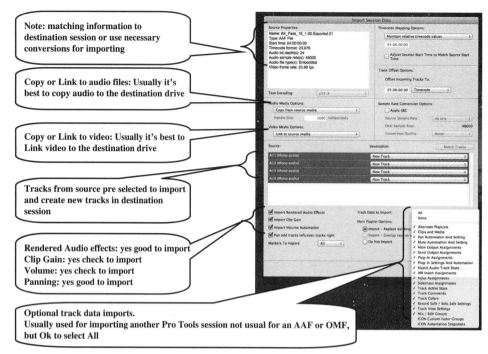

Figure 8.8a Import Session Data window opens when selecting data to import from another Pro Tools session or AAF–OMF exchange media.

import choices, the Import Session Data window opens, where you have some choices and selections to make in order to import the files correctly (see Figure 8.8a).

Note the following selection choices in the Import Session Data window:

- Copy or Link Audio from Source Media
- Copy or Link Video From Source Media
- Note: File Type and Sample Rate—Pull Down or Pull Up (see Figure 8.8b)
- Timecode Offset Options
- Timecode Mapping
- Import Clip Gain
- Import Volume Automation
- Pan odd tracks left/even tracks right
- Track Data to Import
- Sample Rate Conversion Options

Upon making the correct selections, the audio tracks from the AAF file should enter your session as new tracks in their mono track format. The next common step is to make new stereo tracks in the session to hold the AAF music files as a stereo track format rather than separate mono tracks. Since music is usually recorded in stereo, this makes for a better editing workflow in Pro Tools. Note that there can be audio tracks in the AAF export that do not have a corresponding left–right channel track, meaning they are not stereo recordings. These mono track files should be listened to and either left on a mono

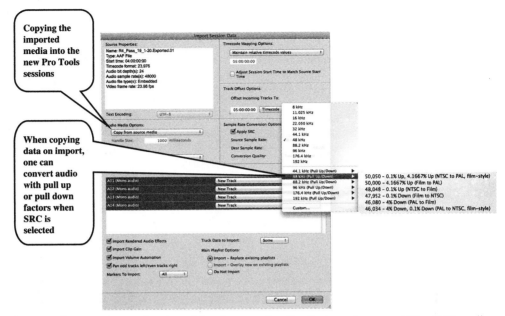

Figure 8.8b Importing session data either from another Pro Tools session or an AFF or OMF media, one can convert the audio files as a pull-down or pull-up sample rate in order to adjust to the destination session.

track, or determined if they are really needed. The picture editor may have inadvertently left a mono sound effect or extra unintended piece of audio on a track. Sometimes they use a mono track to simulate source music in the Avid, and this mono track should remain in your session. The AAF file can be as simple as a 2-mono-track layout, or up to eight or more mono pairs, depending on how the picture editors built their music tracks.

For example, if there were six mono tracks to import, the music editor would make three new stereo pairs for these music elements. To do this, select all six mono tracks from the very beginning of the session, through and over the last piece of audio, then hold down Control + Option (Mac) or Start + Alt (Windows) while Grabbing the selected files and dragging them onto the three empty stereo tracks. This will make a copy of the mono elements into their respective stereo left and right channels. Then select the track nameplates of the six mono tracks, right-click on one of the track nameplates, and choose Hide and Make Inactivate. By doing this, you can always refer back to the original AAF files, and have the convenience of working in stereo pairs.

The next step will be to select all of the audio on the three stereo paired tracks from the beginning of the session through to the end, and then heal any separations. The Mac command is Command + H, or Control + H for Windows. If the picture editor made edits in the video and also sliced through an audio file unintentionally, there will be an edit line in the audio file that is not really an audio edit. In this case, the audio in Pro Tools can be "healed." Note that if any cross-fades were transferred from the picture-editing system, those should be deleted temporarily, one at a time,

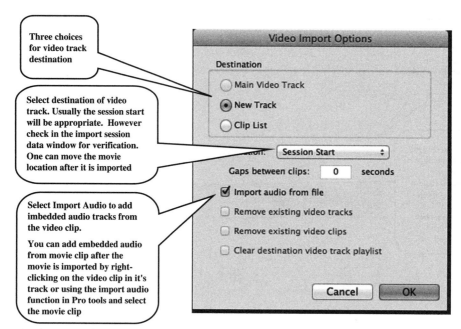

Figure 8.9 Video import makes a new video track in Pro Tools and then imports the embedded audio associated with the video file, as offered in the selection below. If Main Video Track is selected, it will replace an existing main video track upon import. Only Pro Tools HD software supports more than one video track in a session.

in order to determine if a heal separation may be needed. To proceed with this, select each cross-fade individually and delete it, then place your selection across the edit and press Command + H (Mac) or Control + H (Windows); this checks if this edit separation can be healed. If the edit line remains, then select Undo and the cross-fade will be restored.

The next step (if not already completed) is to import the reel of the movie or any video clip that the picture department is delivering with the turnover. Choose File > Import > Video. Locate the video file and make the following selections from the menu:

- **Session Start.** Particularly if the timecode matches the reel.
- **Import Audio from File.** It's possible the assistant editor did not embed audio tracks in the video clip. In this case the associated audio tracks will be part of the turnover, as an audio file for dialogue and sound effects together, with music as a separate file, or perhaps as separate audio for all three elements.
- **Destination—Import as "Main Video Track."** If you are conforming, you may want to import this turnover video as an additional New Track and save and hide previous track versions of the video for reference at a later time.

If you are working in a session containing no preexisting video tracks, the New Track import will be the only available option (see Figure 8.9). Pro Tools (non-HD) software limits you to one video track per session. Also note that in Pro Tools

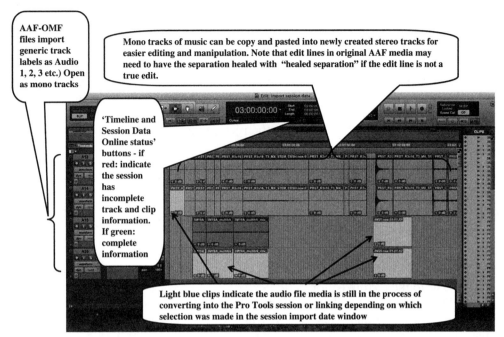

Figure 8.10 AAF or OMF media imported into an existing Pro Tools session.

software, you cannot edit or cut the movie clip, although you can when using Pro Tools HD software. Sometimes, if the movie clip was not prepared to start at the proper left file edge, equal to timecode per reel (1:00:00:00 = reel 1), you can edit or trim the video clip to assist with sync. With the ability to move and cut the movie clips, you can also check the changeovers from one reel to the next and listen to how the music transitions between reels. As previously noted in Chapter 6, this can assist the music editor in locating and calculating necessary picture "slips" to adjust for music sync when working with on-camera songs.

> **PAX Quote**
>
> "I have also made picture edits at the director's request … just to try something out. But be careful not to go experimenting on your own—probably the best way I can think of to make the picture editor something less than your friend!"

Importing multiple movie reels can be important as you conform the reel(s) to compare old edits to new edits. However, you need to make sure the current reel is the active online video in the session you are working in. The imported audio tracks associated with the video clip should be one track of dialogue plus sound effects, and a music track of any temporary music the picture editor has placed in the movie. These tracks, extracted by Pro Tools, will be in a stereo format and line up to the frame edge of the imported digital picture (see Figure 8.10). Once imported onto a stereo track, they should then be split into mono using the track menu function in Pro Tools.

You can either Control + Click (Mac) or Start + Click (Windows), or right-click on the track nameplate and select Split Into Mono. By using the mono tracks of these two elements, you can easily send these tracks to separate outputs, and mute or solo these elements as needed.

This is a good time to listen to and check the music between the AAF elements and the extracted tracks, to make sure that they are in phase or in sync with each other. If you discover that there is something out of sync or missing when comparing these two tracks, it's time to notify the picture editor or their assistant about the problem.

8.6 THE TECHNICAL—THE MUSIC EDITOR SENDING MUSIC TO THE PICTURE EDITOR

As the music editor begins to work within a Pro Tools session, they may need to send edited music to the picture editor.

In Pro Tools, it is possible to select tracks and export them as either an AAF or OMF file-exchange format. This process will allow sending selected audio files of the music back to the picture editor, in the same way that they sent AAF audio tracks to the music editor. Depending on the workflow, this may be the most efficient option to choose, particularly if the music editor has to share a significant amount of music edited on multiple tracks. The menu selections for this export can be found under File > Export > Selected Tracks as New AAF/OMF.

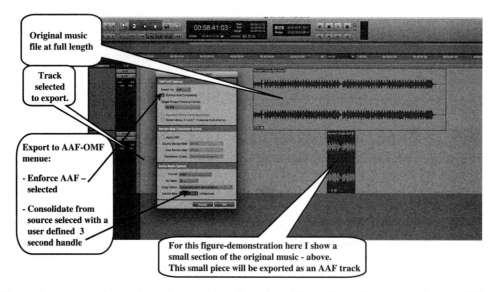

Figure 8.11a Exporting a selected track with audio enforced for Avid (Media Composer) compatibility. Note: a 3000 ms handle on exported track media is the equivalent of 3 seconds.

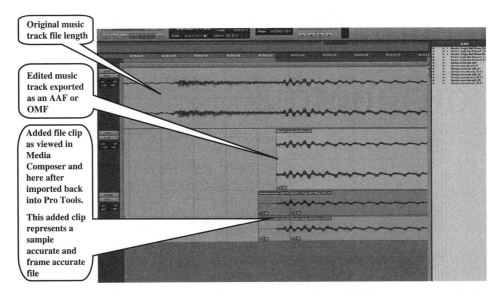

Figure 8.11b After importing Avid-compatible tracks into the picture editing system, the audio files will have an added extra piece of audio attached as a separate clip, bringing the audio file edit to the sample accurate frame edge as required in Avid Media Composer. This added clip does not include music beyond the original track's export definitions, but fills the clip with a flat-line audio with no sound. This added clip is not to be confused with the designated handle length. This figure is an example of an AAF import into Pro Tools, but would look the same if one were viewing it in an Avid Media Composer audio track.

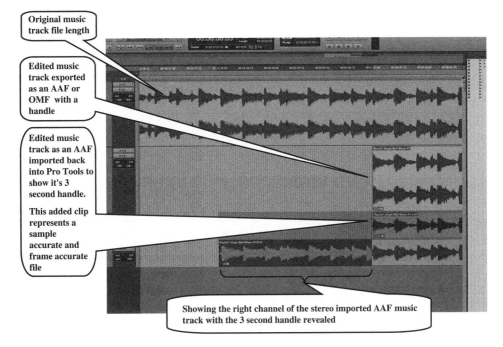

Figure 8.11c Example showing the user-defined 3-second handle.

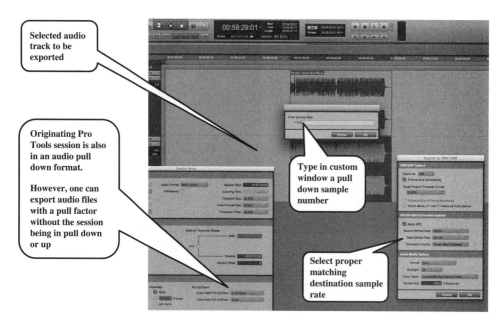

Figure 8.11d Exporting to AAF–OMF allows pull-up and pull-down compatibility in the export to be set. This example shows the export ready to match the sample rate of the Avid destination as 47.952 kHz (a pulled-down 48 kHz). Select Dest Sample Rate and then open the Custom menu to type your desired sample rate.

For more information about exporting AAF or OMF in Pro Tools, consult the Pro Tools 11 Reference Guide.

In addition to exporting audio tracks as AAF–OMF media, the Export Clips As Files export option in the Clips list menu will export a music file/clip (or collection of clips) as individual audio files, with or without using enforced Avid Compatibility mode. Note that this export option allows files to be exported as WAV, MXF, or MXF file types. Similar to Export Selected Tracks as New AAF or OMF, it forces the newly exported audio files to start and end exactly on a frame boundary, by padding the file edges with blank audio media to match the picture editing system's required one-frame grid.

This Export Clips As Files option will only export whole clips or single sub-clips, so if the music editor is going to use this function, they need to make sure that all the clips that make up the edited piece of music are first consolidated into one whole clip file. It is advised that the consolidated files be a copy of the edited sub-clips, and not the only representation of the music editor's work.

Note some of the following radio button selections for an export as AAF file:

- **Enforce Avid Compatibility.** Selecting this will force the clip-file information to fill the edit to the frame edge in the film editing system, because those systems only support frame-edge material.
- **Export As.** Select format AAF or OMF (AAF is recommended).

Figure 8.12a Exporting whole clips as files with Avid compatibility will only work if you select a complete file, or a collection of edited files after they have been consolidated. This process only exports the clip, or series of selected clips, and not their placement in a track. However, if the exported file has a user-time stamp embedded in its metadata, then it can be imported and spotted to its user-time-stamped position.

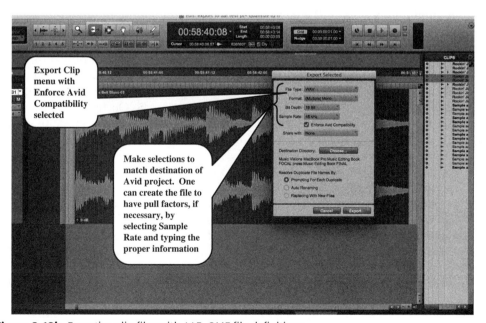

Figure 8.12b Exporting clip files with AAF–OMF file definitions.

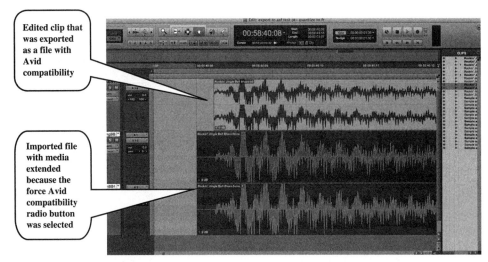

Edited clip that was exported as a file with Avid compatibility

Imported file with media extended because the force Avid compatibility radio button was selected

Figure 8.12c A file imported with forced Avid compatibility into another Pro Tools session, or into Media Composer, creates a file that adds silent media to snap to the required frame boundary. The file's position is "wild" unless there is time-stamp information embedded in the metadata, or the file name has accurate file-sample edge start or placement information.

- **Sample Rate Conversion Options.** Change sample rate and bit rate. If the music editor is working in a specific sample and bit rate, this selection can allow for a conversion of the sample, bit rate, and format of the files or tracks selected. On occasion, it may be important to convert the exported files as a pulled-down or pulled-up sample-rate format. This should be done with great caution and tested in the video editing system for any sync issues. Know that the picture editor or their assistant will need to select Do Not Convert Audio On Import if the intention is for the audio to essentially play back at the wrong speed in the film editing system. This speed difference can be useful to compensate for pull up or pull down setting in editorial.
- **Audio Media Options.** File type and bit rate usually set to match the video editing systems settings.
- **Consolidate from Source Media.** This combines all the edited materials into single audio clips, and the handle size determines how much extra audio will be available to the picture editor outside the edited clip boundaries.

8.7 THE TECHNICAL—THE MUSIC EDITOR SENDING MUSIC TO THE PICTURE EDITOR WITH POPPED FILES

The most common way to export files and give music edits to the picture department is by bouncing your selected edited piece, or whole collection of edits, to a file format compatible with the picture editor's project. By adding a sync reference with a dialogue line, or a pop at the start and end, you can verify that all the Avid import settings are friendly, which for one or two musical edited ideas, is often the fastest and most efficient way to do so. It is important to check the imported audio in the picture editing system, to make sure the files are placed at the same sync location that you have in Pro Tools. When sending files remotely via the Internet, you can easily check this with a phone call or email. The benefit of bouncing audio in this way is that you can select multi-track edited pieces of music that are meant to be played together, and bounce and convert them into a single stereo interleaved audio file that can be easily imported into the picture editing system. Make sure when selecting the multi-track edited music clips that they all are assigned to the same stereo outputs, so that they will all be combined into the bounce file. If you are using Pro Tools 11, you can bounce multiple output paths. In addition, it's important to make your selection go beyond the actual music clips' edges on either side of the audio for at least a frame, and to set the selection on a frame line as designated in grid mode. You can use either time-code frames, or feet and frame if your project is using a 24-frame (23.98) timecode and 24-frame (23.98) film setting. This will help insure that the imported music clip will be able to sync in the picture editor's system with frame accuracy. For further verification of sync, it is a good idea to place a 1 kHz tone at a low volume (usually −20 dBFS) with the duration of exactly one frame, prior to the beginning and after the end of the musical piece you are sending. The one-frame tone can be made simply with the Audio Suite plugin Signal Generator, under the Other sub-menu. Make the following selections on the plugin: Create Continuous File, Playlist, Use in Playlist, Clip by Clip, 0.00 Handles. Make a one-frame selection on a mono or stereo audio track then render a 1000 Hz sinewave tone at −20 dB. Additionally you can place a burst of dialogue or one-frame pops on a frame line a second or so before the music file starts and after it ends.

Tip

If the picture has been cut, or the music clip is pulled into the wrong version of the film, timecode means nothing!

By making your selection match the left file edge of the first sync pop and the right file edge of the tail pop, the bounced selection will then fit on the frame lines in the video editing system. One more reassurance of sync is to label the file that is being sent with a timecode, or for film, the feet and frame location representing the leftmost edge of the file. This way, in addition to the time-stamping metadata that embeds into the audio file and the added sync pop the assistant picture editor can spot and place the music file in the exact location that the file is labeled, and easily verify this location by glancing at the name on the file.

Once the exchange protocol has been set up and proper sync has been verified between both audio and video systems, the music editor should be able to trust this workflow and not have to include pops for future exports (see Figure 8.13c). However, for safety's sake it won't hurt to include this information for all future exchanges.

One thing to note for current and future file-exchange capabilities is the advent of a real-time push-pull media-sharing protocol between Media Composer and Pro Tools. While this has been available in various formats in the recent past, it is becoming, and I suggest will become the new way of implementing a fast and very efficient workflow between picture and sound. Stay tuned!

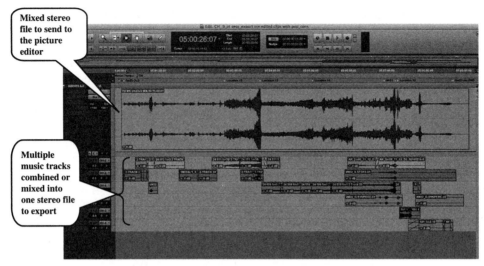

Figure 8.13a Example of multi-track temp music tracks mixed into one file in preparation for sending to the picture editor. Often the mixed file will not land on a frame line, so before you export the file without Enforce Avid Compatibility, it's important to proceed with 8.13b–c.

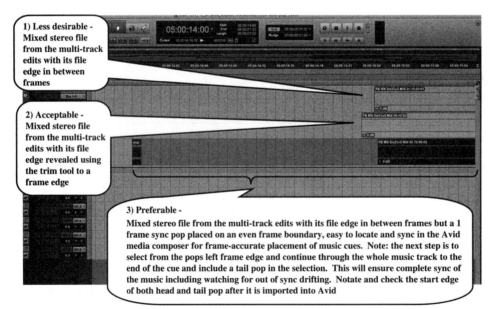

Figure 8.13b Three methods of file formatting, in order to send to Avid with frame- and sample-accurate edges. This will help insure the music tracks that are imported into Avid maintain the original sync as edited by the music editor. These methods are usually easier, and for the picture editor, preferable to an AAF or OMF export.

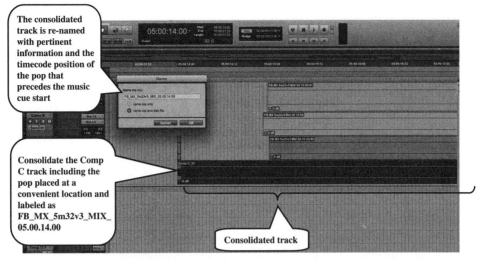

Figure 8.13c The export of a mixed music track for the picture editor as shown above includes a sync pop. The pop is placed in Avid at the specific frame location as designated by the file name. The tail pop (not shown here) should also end in the same position in Avid that it was in the Pro Tools session. Even though these files show no waveforms, the musical material will follow shortly after the silence.

8.8 THE TECHNICAL—TURNOVER

As mentioned earlier, the process of exchanging file information from the picture department to all the sound departments on a film is called "turnover." While this term may be used on feature film projects, it can have other names on a television show, or no name at all on an episode or independent low-budget production. It doesn't matter what it is called, but that this technical and creative exchange of videos and audio files is clear, accurate, and maintains a consistent workflow within the post-production departments.

The actual turnover materials include the latest or perhaps the final-locked cut of the movie, video, or reel, the associated audio files as an AAF–OMF as well as the embedded audio attached to the video clip, and finally a document called the "change notes" or "change list." This last item will be discussed in the next chapter, on conforming. The following are a few examples of the file labels that are included in a turnover (see Figure 8.14). Note that similar to the film-naming nomenclature of a movie or video clip, these labels can vary from picture editor to picture editor.

The turnovers can happen at any time during the film editing process, and often they are used during the temp process, building toward a preview of the movie for an audience or studio executives. The last turnover should contain the final picture and sound reference information before the final mix or dub.

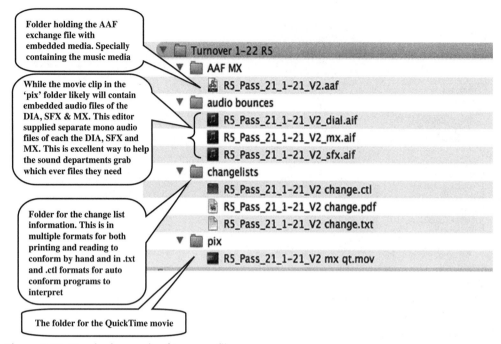

Folder holding the AAF exchange file with embedded media. Specially containing the music media

While the movie clip in the 'pix' folder likely will contain embedded audio files of the DIA, SFX & MX. This editor supplied separate mono audio files of each the DIA, SFX and MX. This is excellent way to help the sound departments grab which ever files they need

Folder for the change list information. This is in multiple formats for both printing and reading to conform by hand and in .txt and .ctl formats for auto conform programs to interpret

The folder for the QuickTime movie

Figure 8.14 Standard example of turnover files.

Tip

The picture editor will decide when it's time to bring his sound and music crews up to speed with a new turnover. He knows when the picture is in a more stable form.

8.9 ON THE MIX STAGE—TEMP DUB

Since the temp dub process can be fast and furious, no pun intended, the technical and creative communications between the music editor and picture editor during these mixes is crucial. Most often, these mixes last one to three days, but can go on for as long as up to six days or more. This leaves very little room for error, and these fast mixes rely heavily on the AAF or OMF files that were created in the picture editor's system (see Figure 8.15). The picture editor and their assistant are often saddled with editing and pre-mixing the sound, including the dialogue, sound effects, and music. Whether audio tracks are pre-mixed in the computer or on a stage, we call this pre-dubbing. Often, these tracks are created within the computer software, and are relied upon as a creative as well as a technical guide for all of the audio departments concerned. Since the music editor uses the AAF supplied by the picture editor as a guide, these tracks are made available to the re-recording mixer at the temp dub mix. In addition, the music editor supplies the mixer with complete music tracks, cut to

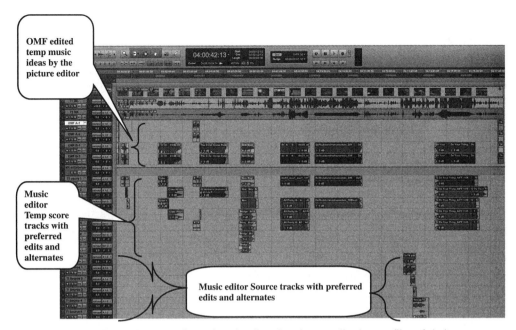

Figure 8.15 This figure shows a mix session that has the picture editor's OMF files of their temp music work, shown here in their mono track pairs, and labeled OMF A 1 and 2 (for left and right channels) and B 1 & 2. The music editor then either fixes problematic areas of music with newly loaded music tracks, or replaces the OMF music with new temp music ideas. Note: The temp music files that are preferred by the director are enabled to play, while alternate edits are file-muted as other options created by the music editor.

match the AAF, as well as alternate cuts or improved cuts of temp score music, perhaps including some composer demos and all of the songs and optional song ideas for this temp, preview mix. The preferred music tracks for the printmaster are ideally made with fresh, newly imported master-quality music elements, edited by the music editor. It is very important to note that often the director may prefer the picture editor's AAF music tracks from the AAF, since the director and editor have often been editing and living with those throughout the film editing process, and have grown attached to them. The music editor should have their master tracks cut to match to the picture editor's waveforms, but may additionally have fixed or cleaned up any awkward edits as exposed in the AAF. The music editor's tracks should be played as the first choice, rather than the AAF. However, the back-and-forth of AAF and music editor's tracks is common in this temp dub workflow.

8.10 ON THE MIX STAGE—FINAL DUB

The final mix or dub of a movie, as it relates to the picture editor and the music editor, shifts in dynamics from the temp mix. At the final dub there will be composed music tracks as well as final songs that need to be mixed into the movie. The picture editor may likely have been working with the composer's music in the form of mock-ups or demos, and may have been playing these, and sometimes even editing them, with the director. If these composed pieces of music intended for the final movie end up being edited by the picture editor, the music editor must know about this and receive the altered composer's demo from the picture editor. This way, the music editor can address the picture editor's and director's ideas and implement them by editing the final full score, or giving the composer the opportunity to fix the music and discuss it with the filmmakers. The final dub of a movie often lasts at least seven to ten days, on the short side, and can run into months for big-budget Hollywood films.

The picture editor is usually present at the final mix, as they have intimate knowledge of every aspect of the film—they know all the angles, cuts, and perspectives pertaining to the music, dialogue, and sound effects. Their participation is a great help during this last process of postproduction—delivering the final product. Since this is the last time it will be possible to fix, move, replace, or correct anything, there is a significant amount of pressure on all concerned. At the same time, however, this stage can be very creative, as all of the final elements of the soundtrack are mixed and blended.

8.11 INTERVIEW: DAVID RENNIE, FILM EDITOR

1. **How would you describe your role as it relates to the overall success of a film or television show? What are some of the key skill sets your job requires?**

    Well, my job is to tell a story as interestingly and potentially as efficiently as possible. "Efficiently" is a bit of a loaded word—it can be dangerous because efficiency isn't necessarily interesting. It's the way to tell a story that is not boring, that doesn't ramble, that doesn't repeat—that is the essence of the story and keeps the audience interested and tries to not get too far ahead of the audience but does not get behind the audience. If it's too far ahead of them then they aren't following—they're bored because they are not following—and if you are behind them then they're ahead of you and it's too predictable and we know what's going to happen and this isn't interesting. They are thinking, "Why should I bother watching this?" My job is to figure out the pacing that is needed to tell the story effectively. I do a lot of comedy and that's another aspect of it—how to tell the joke best. That's why it's dangerous to use the word "efficiency" as it connotes speediness—sometimes the comedy of a joke relies on it *not* being told too quickly. Don't mistake efficiency for effectiveness. So my job is to overall successfully figure out how to tell this story as well as possible. Now, within that is finding the right performances, finding the subtleties and the nuances.

    [...] Much more than finding performances, it's creating them. I think sometimes, like musicians—although I can't pretend to be one—sometimes you're a little surprised at how you don't necessarily realize that *a* plus *b* equals *c*. I don't necessarily see *c* beforehand because it's so much more powerful than just *a* plus *b*. You don't realize sometimes, and that's why it's kind of interesting to me, and that's the skill set I guess you use—being able to figure out what is important, not just from a story standpoint, [though] that's a big part of it, but also what's important from a look. What does that look ... if I put that look in there at that moment, what is that saying? Is that intriguing, is that confusing, is it confusing in a good way, does it tell something? I remember in *All That Jazz*, the music editor—Michael Tronick, by the way, who is a wonderful picture editor now—there was a shot, and I may be remembering the details wrong, but there was a scene where, I think it was when Joe had just demonstrated to them [the song] "Take Off With Us" to the backers—his version of it, which was, you know, scandalizing—and I think it was where it was one of the backers' aides—a minor character, an extra maybe, an actor that didn't even have a line, one of the dancers—but you see him glancing, a medium shot of him glancing and a medium shot of the other guy glancing back, and in just those two quick cuts with these characters that are not part of the story—you never saw them again and yet you saw in those two quick cuts [...] these two were probably going to hook up later. It's in one sense irrelevant and in another hand it brings the richness, the harmonies—it's irrelevant in the same way that a chord is irrelevant because you always have your lead line, but it's so relevant because that's what makes it a full story and that's the kind of thing that I hope that I can find and bring out into a movie ... to enrich it, to make it more than just guy does whatever: grows up, breaks up, so there you go ... .

That's part of what I do and I think maybe it's not coincidental [that] I tend to tell stories. I get to tell ... I wouldn't say parables necessarily, but sometimes it is. To me that's what's powerful about jokes, that's what's powerful about parables: it tells, it communicates. A good storyteller—and I'm not saying that I am one but I try to be—can communicate the story hoping that what they put into their story is what the person's getting out of it, [or] if not specifically what they are getting out of it, maybe the person gets the essence of it and you hope that you get the essence. I think that's why if you read the New Testament when Jesus spoke in parables—instead of saying ... just saying "Love your neighbor," he would tell the story of the Good Samaritan, which rings much, much more. Although it's actually been misunderstood now because we all think a Samaritan is a good thing, but the idea [then] was that Samaritans were bad and everyone hated Samaritans, [and] even [a] Samaritan did this—and that's the kind of thing that you can tell with a story. So I tend to speak in stories, I tend to tell jokes; I tend to use that as a way of communication.

2. **What are some of the similarities and differences between working on low-budget and high-budget films?**

Well, with a high-budget film one can get a little more complacent ... it's more of a directing thing. You have to make do ... hopefully. The problem is, I'd love to say ... on a big-budget film you get everything you want that's easy, but in a low-budget film you're trying to put together ... and it's a mess ... it's jut not the case. It's all about the discipline and talent of the director. It's so hard to say. There are certain benefits—financial—to working on big-budget movies versus low-budget movies; you may or may not end up with a better film. There are an awful lot of really, really expensive movies made every year that are complete messes. More money does not guarantee a better film by any means. I think if a low-budget director is disciplined then he or she can make a great film and if a high-budget director is not disciplined it doesn't matter how talented they are.

Here's a story about a very successful director who makes great movies—a friend of mine told me this. He came in to look at the dailies on this guy's film—it was another director's film that he was producing—and he came in to look at the stuff and said, "It's too dark," you know, and everyone's asking, well, what's going on? He says "I can't see, it's too dark," and so they ran around adjusting the foot lamps on the projector and they tried all these things, and he said, "It's still too dark, it's still too dark." So this went on for a while and he finally said, "You know what—it's okay, it's fine. I'm leaving." So he walked out and he went into the bathroom and when he was finished he washed his hands and he looked up in the mirror and he realized he had his sunglasses on ... and no one had had the courage to tell him. His sunglasses were on, that's probably why it's too dark … and that's what happens. And I think you see that in some of his movies— not all of them because he is incredibly talented—but I think people were afraid to tell him that he had his sunglasses on. It just comes down to, is the director disciplined, if they have—hopefully have—a good idea. But it's not always the director who has a good idea—because you look at *Apocalypse Now* and you look at *Hearts of Darkness* and that was a disaster and they didn't know what the hell they had, and it's a brilliant movie—but it sure makes a much more pleasant experience when the director has an idea.

3. How do you see the music editor's role, as it pertains to the overall involvement of music production? Particularly in terms of their technical, musical or interpersonal skills, or any other qualities they bring to their work?

The music editor, as you know, has two categories that are distinct. One is temping and one is working with the composer, and obviously there are a million others. The stuff working with a composer generally is not as vital to me; it depends on who the composer is. Some of these composers, they don't want anything to do with me, and some composers I have become good friends with. So it all depends on them and then there is sort of this interacting with them and then interacting with their music editor. That's usually not a problem because generally if I'm not invited to the scoring session, I'm going to be on the stage, and I will have final selects—or the director will, but I will certainly be there— to have whatever music was final music recut if it needs to be, to help service the scene— not that it happens very often but to make the case if it had to happen.

One last thing: if I think the comedy wasn't as good as it could have been because the music in one of the cues went just a little longer than I felt it should … [in an example from a dub,] Tanya was there—one of the music editors—and I said you should try this … . She was open to it and it all worked, and Jon liked it. You certainly want someone who is interpersonal. I have only had one really bad experience with a music editor—I won't say who it is—who felt that, well, now we are getting in the temp stuff—which I feel is much more important to my job throughout most of my job—as opposed to the final. This music editor felt that I had no place and it was not my business to talk about music. I talked to a couple of picture editors while I was doing this and I said this is the first time I have come across this—am I out of line here saying that if I don't like the cue I'm not going to put it in or that I think it should be changed? Nobody I know who he has worked with that would have been a picture editor that took that, so that was a little alarming and that was tough because it was just constantly battling and he was the director's guy, so it was just a clash and it was an annoying clash because I had enough to deal with. I'm extremely collaborative, I'm not dictatorial in any way except relatively will say I really think this is it, but I am open to this collaboration and so I want to hear what the music editor has to bring; it doesn't mean I'm going to like it, or the director's going to like it. If the music editor feels strongly about something, unless I really, really feel strongly that it's not right, I will say, "Let's sort this with the director. I will let him decide." I'll present my case why I think it works or doesn't work, but ultimately it's not my place, it's the director's.

You want someone who has—a universal relationship is obviously very important, and personal skills—but you want someone who has a great knowledge of all the different types of music, all the different types of what you're going to need. On *Last Vegas* we were dealing with all kinds of dance music, which I don't know a damn thing about so I needed someone to do this music so they would know how it should be appropriately … it was about clubs … so this was one of the first times that I was really out of my league musically, because this is just not a music I like—it's not a location I go to. So I don't know how it's played there, and all that stuff, so that was a little tricky. That said, it had to ultimately inform the scenes and the story the way I wanted it to, so it was definitely a collaborative effort—very much—with the various music editors. For the temp I want someone who has a great musical library in their hard drive and in their brain—so that's a vital thing.

4. **How do you see the workflow between the film editor and music editor evolving? And are there any particular dos and don'ts, or things to watch out for?**

You know I think … because of the hierarchy, at least the way it is now, the hierarchy is the picture editor runs the room or runs the post or whatever—is sort of the general to the director's commander-in-chief. I think for a lot of picture editors it goes to their head a little bit. I personally feel like it's entirely collaborative—ultimately it has to be one unifying vision. Ultimately that's the director's but penultimately it's the editor's, and so that's the argument I was having with the music editor that I was telling you about: I have an overall story in my mind here, I have to keep so many different elements in play, in harmony to each other. The music is one of them; in the same way you don't want an actor coming into the cutting room giving you advice on their stuff—because they are going to end up seeing their stuff and you have to see the whole. So it's important to defer, ultimately, to the picture editor or director.

I think along the way I feel it's best when it's collaborative. I think you end up with the best movie; I think you end up with the best experience and life, because who wants to work just as a pair of hands and just being told what to do? I want to hear what the music editor's suggestions are. And with the understanding that it doesn't mean I'm going to agree with them but it may mean that I will absolutely agree with them and say, this is wonderful … and you play off of each other's ideas and build with them … . That's the ideal thing, is to remember that this is a collaboration. Unfortunately, however, it's not necessarily going to be the music editor's place to decide whether it's a collaboration, any more than it's the editor's place to decide it's a collaboration with the director—they lead the dance and because of the hierarchy generally the picture editor leads the dance, and you hope that you have a picture editor who doesn't have an ego problem. Well, that's the thing I always tell everybody in my cutting room—that we check our egos, there's no ideas that are good or bad because they are our ideas, they are just good or bad, and that doesn't mean you can still believe in them, and that's still subjective, but I never want it to be because it's my way or the highway—that's just a bad way to be and that's a bad way to create.

5. **What are some of the technical issues that you as an editor come across with regard to the music? Has a music editor helped resolve any of these?**

Well, I can't think of any offhand that are going to stand out. I mean there's always the … it's timing. One of the things which I might have mentioned before was the skill set that you bring as a film editor … I think rhythm is important—part of your job in telling that story is to have a rhythm. I tend to cut musically, there is just a rhythm and sometimes the director will say, "Why are these three frames off?" Or "That works better." Why does that work better? I can't necessarily say, it's just the rhythm was right, and it's not necessarily a musical rhythm, it's not necessarily a set rhythm, but it's the rhythm of life. Being tuned to that. And I don't mean that in a big "circle of life" type of thing, I mean just the way we talk—[how] somebody pauses before they answer a question, or if they interrupt—all these things, they tell a different story. If you add six frames between someone finishing a sentence—whatever the distance is between the time that person finishes the sentence and the next person talks—if you add, say, six frames there, that tells a different story, or it doesn't always but it can—it can say this person is a little slow, or this person is thoughtful, or different, depending mainly on the context of what they are saying. I remember a cut I made in a movie: one character was having an argument with another character, and the first character brought up an incident that had happened 30 years earlier, and the way the actress played it, there was a little bit of a pause—while she thought of it, that she had to remember it—and then she defended herself on it. When I cut it, I cut it so that […] she immediately answered. What that said was she knew what the issue was—she didn't have to remember it and [it] was in her mind too, that she had done this bad thing, and that she immediately knew what this person was talking about. It was a subtle thing, and it's not as though anyone in the audience will turn to the person next to them and say, "Oh yeah, she got that," but it's a subtle, unconscious thing—and that's the kind of thing that's important in the rhythm. You have to have that same sense with the music because the music can shift the tone. It may not be a technical issue, but it's a creative issue in a sense, that you need to help tell … whatever this is … that music … and that's not entirely technical, but it's aesthetically, it's creatively … it's using that to solve the problem. Sometimes the technical problem is this scene isn't working: it's not funny, it's not emotional, it's not … etc., etc. The music, properly applied, can change that.

I have a longstanding friendly argument with a dear picture-editor friend of mine about this very topic. He prefers to show his assembly without any music. My argument is that music is vital—it's so important to the story, you can't say that … . He says, if it works without music then it will work with music. I say, if you look at a beautiful woman, but you take her nose off, she's not going to be beautiful—because the nose is part of it, and the music is just as important to a movie as the nose is to someone being beautiful. So you can't just say, well, that's nice-looking woman but leave off the nose. Now, you look at *Jaws*, and if you look at *Jaws* and take the music out—that first shot is just a bunch of seaweed and there's nothing scary about it—and that's the kind of thing that is vital.

6. **Can you comment on the film editor being asked to temp the music as they are cutting the film?**

Well, I think it's a vital part of the cutting for me. In an ideal world maybe the music editor would have the Avid interface so that the Pro Tools and the Avid could be hooked up and we could be looking at the same thing and I could give him the cut the same way that I could give my assistant a cut. That's to me the biggest drawback with bringing a music editor on, is we have to do an output and it takes the time away from … we lose a machine for that time. Then every time I make a cut—literally a cut, not a change from the entire scene, but a cut—well, now that last cut is no longer relevant, because we just took 10 frames off, and it's like, now it's not working. I would love to have a music editor that could have real time with my cuts and have them on at the same time. Unfortunately technologically we can't do that right now—I don't know why with all the things we can do, but for some reason Avid doesn't do that. So not having that choice, I have no choice but to temp and track the music myself. I would love to bring a music editor on sooner [rather] than later, but because of the workflow, because if we are in the process of cutting and every time we make a cut I have to do a new output, then it just becomes technologically a big bottleneck. I lose my assistant for a big chunk of the day while he is prepping this for the music editor and then outputting it to the music editor, and then by the time he gets it that cut may well be obsolete. That's frustrating … it's more of a political thing. Aesthetically I would love to have a music editor doing this, I don't particularly enjoy going through … I love putting music in there and I love working with music … I don't particularly enjoy spending … when I have so much stuff to do … you could spend hours or a complete day listening to all kinds of different things trying to find something and not find a thing. You feel like, "Oh, I just lost a day," and you can't very well say to the studio or director, "Well, it wasn't that I wasn't working today, I was just that I was trying to find this … and I never found anything." So, that can be frustrating. I'd love having someone there who is just to cut the music—they have the great library, they have the great experience, far more experience than I do in that—but because of technological reasons, it's a problem. So that's a longwinded answer.

It's very important to me whenever I do have a music editor on, to work with someone who understands what I am going for in the scene and that can be difficult. My assistant Keith tracks a lot of my stuff and he knows what I want and I work closely with him. He doesn't just track it and lay it in and that's it—he tracks it, he shows it to me and I say okay, well this is working here and now this is the wrong idea here—so I would want someone who was definitely collaborative—that's even more important. Because by the time the music editor comes on my movies, generally it's been tracked the way I like it and it's more like, okay here's … the start here and see if you can make it better. If you think music is good in this scene, show me what you've got. But a lot of the work's been done and it would be great to have someone come on from the beginning and do that working with me. But again it's because of the technology aspect it's been difficult. Hopefully by the time your book comes out it's no longer the case.

8.12 INTERVIEW: KEVIN TENT, FILM EDITOR

1. **How would you describe your role as it relates to the overall success of a film or television show? What are some of the key skill sets your job requires?**

    Well … everyone likes to think they have some role in the success of a film, editors included. But the truth is it's a miracle if anything works and is successful. There are so many elements involved in making a movie or television show. The cast, the producing, the editing, the marketing … but probably the most important, in my opinion, is the basic premise and script. Almost all of these have to be right or close to right to make something work. It's like cooking or chemistry. You mix all these elements together, bake it for a while, and hope to hell it tastes good. One spice too strong and you can ruin the stew. I guess the editor is the last line of defense for the finished product. If a spice is too strong—let's say a character or actor is stealing the focus of a scene—it's up to the editor to hopefully regulate that and keep a balanced approach to the scene and ultimately the movie overall. I just used an actor as an example but it could be anything. If you have an action movie and it's wall-to-wall action, an audience will become numb, exhausted, and eventually bored. The editor has to keep a balance. He or she has to build peaks and valleys, give breaks and breaths so the audience has an overall satisfying experience.

2. **What are some of the similarities and differences between working on low-budget and high-budget films?**

    I remember when I got my first big studio film. It was *Girl, Interrupted* directed by James Mangold. I think the biggest budget I had ever worked on before that film was like six or seven million. And I thought that was big. I started out at Roger Corman's studio. Most of the films were probably half a million or something. If I remember correctly, *Girl, Interrupted* was in the 25 million range. That was huge to me! I was freaked out! But I remember on my first day as I was carrying a crate of film to the screening room (we still had film dailies back then) when it dawned on me that it's just film … just like all the other film I've cut. It's gone through a camera. It went to the lab. There's a lot of it and

I've got to cut it down just like all the other times. Granted it was more expensive film. There was more of it. It looked better and had great actors … but my process was going to be the same. I found comfort at the time in this realization.

So from an editor's perspective in some ways editing a low-budget or big-budget is the same. The problems an editor experiences on a low-budget production may very well be the exact same things he or she might experience on a big-budget production. Actors miscast or not up for the role, lighting not matching because the sun went down. Scripts not up to snuff. All these things happen at all levels of filmmaking. The good news if you're on a bigger production is you're going to have more time to figure stuff out and make more money. And in that respect there is a big difference. Time equals money I always say. When it comes to low-budget films, less money equals less time. Which makes things more challenging. But doesn't mean you can't be creative. That was one of the great experiences of working for Roger Corman. Especially as an editor—you had to be resourceful, clever, and creative to get those films of his to work in the time you had. It was a great training ground for being an editor.

3. How do you see the music editor's role, as it pertains to the overall involvement of music production? Particularly in terms of their technical, musical or interpersonal skills, or any other qualities they bring to their work?

On the movies I work on now the music editor is critically important. Music, I feel, is one of the most important elements of a movie. The right music makes all the difference in the world. I have had the pleasure of working with some of the best in the business. Richard Ford has been working with Alexander Payne and myself since *Election*. And on the last two films we didn't use a traditional score. We scored the movies with found music. Richard did an absolutely brilliant job on *The Descendants*. Brilliant! Alexander, while shooting, casually mentioned to me "I'm thinking of just using Hawaiian music instead of score." I was, like, "Okay man … don't know how that's going to work." It proved my ignorance, of course, because I really didn't know Hawaiian music very well. I foolishly believed it was all sort of the clichéd campy stuff we usually associate with Hawaii and its music. Well I was way wrong and I took a crash course in learning about what's really going on over there … . But back to Richard: he and our music supervisor Dondi Bastone did an amazing job finding, cutting, and manipulating all these source cues into a brilliant score. Richard did it again on Alexander's upcoming film *Nebraska*. While cutting the assembly I was having a real hard time finding music that worked for the movie. Usually I can find a piece or two to work in a couple of areas—this was a tough one. Once Alexander got to the cutting room we lobbied to get Richard starting right away. And it was a good thing we did. It took a little time but he found the sound that worked with the movie. He pulled mostly from a San Francisco band called Tin Hat Trio. Once we settled onto a couple of big pieces from them we asked Mark Orton (of the band) to tweak some cues and write us some new ones. It's come out beautiful and brilliant.

Back to the original question though … . The music editor's role is critical. They are often the ones who, with their temps, shape what the score will eventually be. Composers are so busy and most don't want to be writing music till a film is close to being finished. It's understandable. However you can't cut a film without music—at least, I can't. So it's often up to the music editor to get the "sound" of the music: the emotion, the tone, the feel of the score. What music an editor presents so often is what winds up being in the final film. It drives some composers crazy, I know. They often hate having the music already figured out before they show up. And most of the time there is temp love, so they feel stymied in their creative process. But from an editorial point of view or the director's point of view, having a chance to live with a score, even if it's a temp one, is an invaluable asset. To be able to tweak it and fine-tune it while screening for audiences is so important. Music can save a movie during the preview process.

4. How do you envision your role in postproduction evolving in future, particularly in terms of budgets and expectations?

Budgets are getting smaller, things are getting tighter all the time—they are making less movies, at least as far as film goes. They're making less smaller movies, and television of course is doing great stuff and there's lots of television and they're being very creative. It has been good. I mostly work in features, but I think features are a lot like the American economy in some ways—it's like the middle class is going away, you just have very low budget films and big budget films and there's not very much in between any more. *Nebraska*, for instance, was a fairly low-budget movie; it was around twelve, twelve-and-a-half [million], something like that. For a guy that just won an Academy Award and had numerous Academy Awards, it was actually a tough film to get off the ground, even for him. It's tough out there for sure. And, me personally, yeah, if the movie's a low budget, the editor's going to be paid less than they would on a big-budget film, so you kind of go all over the map—sometimes you work on something that has a decent budget and other times you're working on something that has no money—but, it can be tough.

5. Can you describe the workflow between the film editor and music editor? Do you have any particular dos and don'ts, or things to watch out for?

I personally work very closely with music editors. There's a lot of back-and-forth. I have a pretty good knowledge of music but their knowledge of music is generally much deeper and stronger … at least it better be. On Alexander Payne's films there's lots of detailed interaction between Richard Ford and us. We have general meetings as we start working on the temp, and as we hone in on the "sound" of the film our meetings become more specific and detailed. Richard will keep narrowing down what it is that we like and keep building on that sound or feeling. Obviously while editing we shorten and lengthen scenes. We often hit up Richard and say, "Hey, we have to shorten this scene—can you make all your music hits work again?" On the other hand he's been known to call me up and ask, "I need 18 frames for this music to land in this nice spot. Can we do it?" And we see what we can do. If we can make it work and keep it elegant, we do it. There is a lot of back-and-forth. We cut scenes or reels, Mindy our assistant will prep them for him, and we send them off. A few hours later we'll get a call from Richard and he'll be sending us cues. Alexander Payne loves working with Richard Ford. It's a really important relationship to him.

6. From your experience of working with many music editors, what are the skill sets that are crucial for their success in this industry?

a. They have to know music. That's a no-brainer. They should have a really deep knowledge of music. And even more importantly a deep love of music. If they are temping a film, they should have a library of movie and television scores in the back of their mind, ready to drop into a scene. The best music editors I've worked with love music on a deeply profound level. I've worked with a lot of great ones and many are musicians, but more than that they are connoisseurs of music. That comes out in their work.

b. They have to be open and flexible to outside ideas. Whether from the director, editor, or producer … anybody. They should be willing to try things—if the director has an idea, even if it seems bad, he/she should try to make it work. There should be no resistance to trying a different approach or moving a start or stop time. Most editors who are really at the top of their game may be hesitant about an idea but they'll say, "Let's try it!" I think it's really important to be willing to shake up what you think you know and try different approaches. That goes for not only music editors but film editors as well.

c. They have to be a good people person, be willing to work with people. Sometimes with people who are under a lot of pressure, who may or may not have the greatest bedside manner. A basic understanding and sensitivity to other people is a good quality to have. Especially as there are so many artists in the field. The film business is such a great business and there are so many interesting and talented people within it. The process of working on a picture should be an enjoyable one. There are always deadlines, stress, and conflicts, but I'm a big believer that they should take a breath, look around, and enjoy what they're doing.

d. They have to be willing to work hard. When they're tired and frustrated and they don't want to go back and re-edit a track the seven hundredth time, they have to reach down and find it in themselves to do just that. It's been my personal experience that hard work always pays off.

7. What are some of the technical issues that you as an editor come across with regard to the music? Has a music editor helped resolve any of these?

Here's a good one: it's really interesting when you're cutting old music that wasn't recorded with a click track—like an old song from the fifties or sixties—a live drummer or bass player was never exact with their beats and rhythms, so cutting older tracks can be tricky. It's also tricky cutting music without separated tracks, which happens a lot when you're using old songs. Of course, nowadays the problems with timings can be fixed by dumping the tracks into Pro Tools and speeding up or slowing down a track to make the beats right. It's interesting how today's music is so measured and perfect.

8. Can you comment on the film editor being asked to temp the music as they are cutting the film? Do you see this as a positive industry standard workflow or perhaps a distraction from the film editorial process, better left to the music editor?

Music is a critically important element of a film or television show. When you're an editor and you're working on a scene, temp music can make all the difference on whether it plays or not: it can give you the emotion that is perhaps not coming from the actors; it can totally alter the meaning or intent of a scene—it's really remarkable. So for you as an editor, you want to do anything you *can* do to make your scene work, and by extension to make a whole movie work. I'm not commenting on whether it's positive or negative on an industry level, I just know personally I cut music so I can make my scenes play.

When I first started out I never even had a music editor to work with, so I would cut the temp music myself. Now, I'll often pull tracks that I know are not completely right but they might hint at the direction of the music and how it's supposed to color a scene. A great relief is knowing that your choice may not be perfect but your music editor is coming on board and he/she will build on what you've started or top it with something completely different and better.

Now, back to the original question: whether it's expected from the industry. I don't know if it's expected, I haven't experienced that yet. I expect it from myself not because some producer or someone asks or forces me to cut music. I love working with music. But if the intent of the producer or studio is to save money by not hiring a professional music editor then, yes, that is lame. And shortsighted. A lot of picture editors don't like cutting music or they're not good at it. And as I said before finding the right music and cutting it can take forever—so yes, it can be a distraction. But if I were a music editor I wouldn't be concerned that picture editors all over the world will be taking their profession away. There will always be a need for good professional music editors.

9. **Has this always been the case? Was it ever expected?**

Well, I have been around quite a while. I've been film editing for the last 25 years. I started out on moviolas and KEMs: one track for dialog and, if you had a six-plate, one track for music and sound effects. Even back then I cut music to make scenes work. So that hasn't changed. However technology has now allowed us to do so much more and make things look and sound so much better. A lot of that is falling into the picture editor's lap. Hell … you can even preview a major motion picture for an audience straight out of the Avid. It's incredible. So I guess basically the answer is yes and no: it's always been the case that editors have cut music but now there are more options and it's more time consuming. I guess there is more that's expected of you.

10. **Is there a story or two relating to your working relationships with composers, producers, music editors, or directors, whether about positive or difficult situations, which you can share as something we might learn from?**

On *The Descendants*, Richard Ford really delivered the goods. He did an incredible job and put all his heart and soul into the music of the movie. During production Alexander had a vague notion of using only found Hawaiian music. He wasn't sure the idea was going to work and I for sure wasn't sure it was going to work. Rolfe Kent had done all of Alexander's previous films so abandoning a traditional score was quite a leap. Thank goodness we had Richard, who with the help of Dondi Bastone our music supervisor found the perfect "sound" for the film. They combed through thousands of hours of Hawaiian music and filtered hundreds of pieces to us in the cutting room. Once we started honing in on a sound for the film Richard really went to town with editing the songs. He did a brilliant job in the choices he presented to us and a brilliant job in his editing of the cues. Overall the music just gave this great feel to the movie. One of the reasons it did so well, I believe.

Chapter 9
Conforming

9.1 EVERYTHING CHANGES

One of the primary reasons that filmmaking is so creative is that there is always more than one way to tell the story. Filmmakers are constantly lengthening and shortening shots and moving scenes around. For the music editor, this means that the minute you think you have completed a task, it has the potential to be disassembled and put back on the "to do" list. With luck, you won't have to start your work all over again.

Welcome to conforming! Postproduction audio conforming is the process of re-editing or altering the audio sync of a movie when picture changes have occurred. For instance, if a preview of a show or movie leads to changes in the picture, conforming will be required to repair and or improve the soundtrack. While this seems simple enough, as we have seen in much of this book, nothing is quite as it seems on the surface, and isn't necessarily simple to implement. In this chapter, I will show you how to conform audio tracks in Pro Tools. Most of these techniques can be used for all postproduction sound, including music, dialogue, and sound effects.

Movies, television shows, made-for-TV movies, or any visual media that combine sound and picture to create a finished product, most likely will need to be conformed. Conforming is both an arduous, detail-oriented job, and a creative one that involves re-editing music to work to the new picture structure. This conforming process is one of the most crucial parts of any sound processes of the movie. Any sound editor needs to know how to conform their audio: If the audio is out of sync, it is a major issue. The technical part of conforming is quite mechanical and was once left for the assistants to do, but as budgets shrink and producers are trying to get more out of their main editors (both in picture and audio), assistants are not always available.

There are many ways to conform audio. I will discuss a few of them, and talk about auto-conform software programs, including the pros and cons of using them with music.

9.2 CHANGE NOTES

The initial conforming process starts with the picture department generating change notes. If there are no change notes to guide the sound departments, then the alternative is to compare the old and new video and audio tracks. Change notes are a computer-generated list of all the picture edits that have taken place from the previous turnover to the present "new" turnover (Figures 9.1a and 9.1b). It is important to note that this list does not show changes in the audio, only the picture. The change note list is not an EDL (Edit Decision List).

Change notes most often contain the following information:

- **The Header information.** The New and Old ID labels of the picture and the reel that is changing. Also included are the type and number of events in the change list.
- **Moves.** The number representing each move (sometimes referred to as an event) or change the picture editor has made. This can also refer to a "re-balance."
- **At This Footage.** An instruction listed in feet and frames, which can be also be in timecode.
- **For This Length.** Defines the length of the picture section that has changed.
- **Do This.** The editing action that the picture editor took.
- **Clip Name.** The label of the movie and production sound clip that is being used for each event.
- **At this Record TC/Start TC.** This is the timecode as embedded metadata for the sound roll that was recorded on the set.
- **Key Frames.** An identifying mark embedded in each frame of the film in feet and frames as well as an identifier of the company that made the film stock. For example, Kodak.
- **Sc/Tk.** This notates the audio sound roll name/label in the form of the scene and take that was recorded on the set and used in association with the video clip.
- **Total Change.** Notates a cumulative change in feet and frames or timecode that is occurring as the movie changes from the beginning of the reel or act—for television, through to the end of the changes.

9.2.1 Header Information

While change notes or change lists may vary in how they look, depending on different software programs, the top of the page refers to the version of the movie you are conforming, and some overview of the notes that are to follow, such as how many events there are, number of deletions, and the number of inserts and moves. As discussed in the last chapter, it is up to the discretion of the picture editor (or perhaps the assistant editor) to present these picture-version labels with clarity and consistency. The important information here is what reel or act you are looking at, and what version of the picture you are going from and changing to. These are referred to as New and Old versions. It's also possible to have change notes refer to non-consecutive changes, and this is known as a "skip pass." This happens when the editor's most recent cut might be, for example, version 8, several versions away from the last turnover. Although the previous version of the movie cut would be version 7, the change notes could be referring to the Old cut as being version 5 and the New one as version 8, therefore skipping versions 6 and 7. The music editor or other sound editors should pay attention to this and make sure they conform their audio reels from the Old version 5 to the New version 8. However, this scenario is not so common, and may be a special request from a sound or music editor.

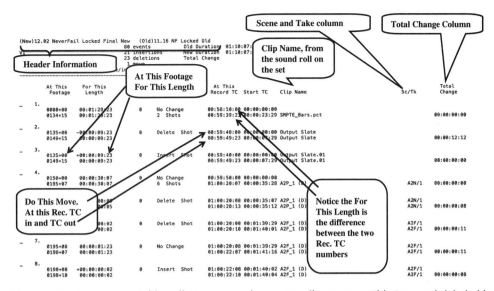

Figure 9.1a Items on an Avid Media Composer change note list. Note: At This Footage is labeled in feet and frames, while For This Length is in timecode. While it is not standard practice to have these two columns as a different frame type, in this case it can be done because the timecode frame rate of 24 frames per second is the same as the feet and frames rate of 24 frames per second.

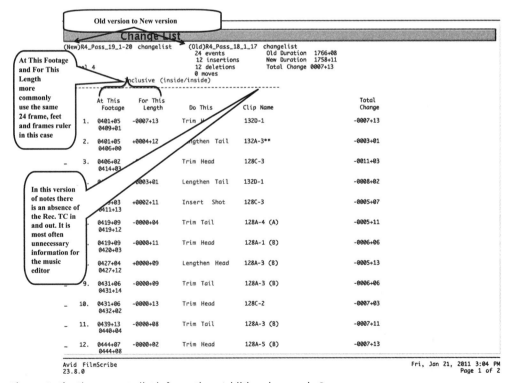

Figure 9.1b Change note list information, Additional example 2.

9.2.2 Moves

Moves are simply the total number of deletions, inserts, trims, lengthens and re-balance moving of scenes or shots that the picture editor did from the previous version of the reel to the present turnover. Even if two or more moves essentially cancel each other out, they are still included in this number list. A cancelation of moves for audio conforming might be, for example, a shot that was deleted, for let's say 10 feet and 14 frames, with another shot inserted in the same place for the length of 10 feet and 14 frames. Essentially, although the picture has changed, there is no change in length. This does not mean that the sound departments do not need to address the different shot, however: They do.

9.2.3 At This Footage

The At This Footage column lists the point where the picture editor made some kind of change in the picture. While this example (see Figure 9.1a) shows the number in feet and frames, it could also be represented as timecode numbers. It is important to note that there are two numbers represented: a top number, and a bottom number directly beneath. For our purposes right now, you should ignore the bottom number, as it will be described in Section 9.4, on conforming manually

9.2.4 For This Length

The For This Length column lists how much material the picture editor either deleted from or inserted into the movie, starting at the indicated At This Footage. Note: There is usually a small "minus" or "plus" sign directly before the For This Length number. This refers to the next column …

9.2.5 Do This

The Do This column lists the instruction after you have made a selection in your audio, in order to follow exactly what the picture editor did for the current event. An editor can do one of three things:

- Trim Tail, Trim Head, or Delete Shot, indicated by a " − " sign.
- Lengthen Tail, Lengthen Head, or Insert Shot, indicated by a " + "sign.
- Move, i.e. placing a part of the movie (audio) to another position, as a delete and insert.

Sometimes, a cancellation occurs and this is often an indicator that one shot was simply switched out for another, and does not affect the length of the movie. This could be done for many reasons, such as the quality of acting in different shots, or for a different camera angle.

> **Tip**
> Because visual effects for movies develop over time during the editorial process, they often result in conform changes that are simply swapping out shots in a scene.

It is important to note that this may not require a change in the underlying audio, because the event durations are the same, and the " − " is equal to the " + ," thus canceling each other out. However, the switching of shots or scenes may actually require changes in dialogue or sound effects, or even music, in that section.

9.2.6 Clip Name

The Clip Name column refers to the metadata label of the video clip used in this shot, specifically the scene, take numbers, and camera angle letter. For example: sc56K tk2 A would be scene 56K take 2 camera A.

9.2.7 At This Record TC

Record Time Code In and Out is a reference to the original timecode for each clip that was filmed. Timecode numbers, names, and the lengths being used are relatively less important for change notes, but they're a good reference point to the audio portion of the video clip that was used in the conform list.

9.2.8 Key Frames

Key frames are essentially a unique identifier that refers to the exact start and end frames of the clip to either be taken out, inserted, or moved, according to the changes. These key frames can be seen on each frame of the whole movie. Although film stock is becoming rarer, a film company will buy lots of it to shoot an entire film, and one production might use over 8000 feet of film stock. These are sometimes left out of the change list, although on occasion it can be valuable for the sound editor who is comparing video frames of specific shots.

9.2.9 Sc/Tk

This column represents the scene and take of the audio clip that was recorded on the set. This information should match with the scene and take information from the video clip portion. This is not so important for conforming notes, but it's a good reference point. However, if you are using a sound source of music that is specifically recorded on the set (for instance, somebody humming, singing, or playing a handheld instrument), you can refer to the audio clip that references the video portion. This can be important when you are trying to clear a piece of music that was actually recorded on the set. In some instances, the sound roll from the actual picture take of the musical performance might be inferior to the sound of an alternative take. The music editor can then either use the alternative take, or perhaps combine takes to improve the performance and/or audio quality of the music.

9.2.10 Total Change

The last column is a cumulative list of how many feet and frames or timecode lengths have been deleted or inserted after each event on the list. This is critical for the music editor, because music doesn't usually occur continuously throughout the whole reel, as for example background sound effects do. Therefore, musical cues can be moved as a single unit or grouping of audio, according to the total change. While this is not always the case, when possible, it is a major time saver.

9.3 MOVES AND RE-BALANCING

Moving parts of the movie can entail moving a scene, or even frames, to another location in the same reel or in a different reel. (see Figures 9.2a–9.2d. The music editor must then cut the audio that is in sync with the deleted scene and paste it into its new location. If this location is in another reel, for example, the change note for reel 1 will say "delete this from reel 1 and move to reel 2," and the change note for reel 2 will say "insert from reel 1" at that specific location. When you are using Pro Tools and you cut or copy something in one session, the software does not remember that information in the computer's clipboard in order to close the present session, open a new one, and successfully paste the audio tracks or files into the new session. Instead, for this operation you could make a clip group out of the selected audio and paste a copy to a set of duplicate tracks, or perhaps just copy and paste your music section in those new tracks. Then, close the current session and open the session of the reel the music is going to be moved to, and select File > Import Session Data. Import into the session the selected new duplicated tracks made in the previous session containing the music you need to import or move. Even if your present session is at a different timecode

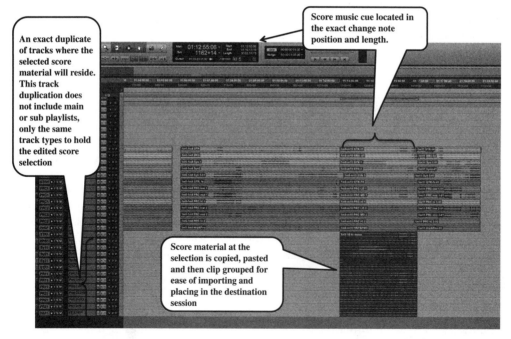

Figure 9.2a Conforming music stems to a change note instruction in reel 1 to "move" the scene from 01:12:55:06–01:16:13:19 (or in F&F 1162 + 14–1460 + 11) to a new location in reel 2, inserting this scene's music—to 02:14:14:19 in reel 2 (see Figure 9.2b).

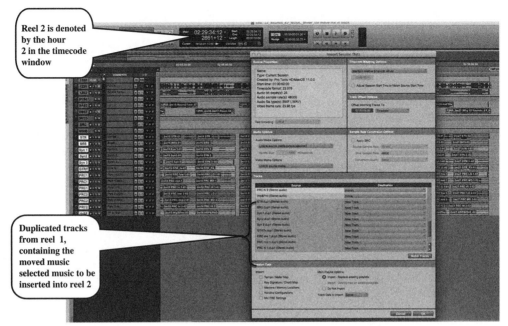

Reel 2 is denoted by the hour 2 in the timecode window

Duplicated tracks from reel 1, containing the moved music selected music to be inserted into reel 2

Figure 9.2b Conforming move to reel 2. Import session data from reel 1 and select the duplicated tracks to a new track destination. One can ignore timecode offsets because of the reel's TC start times. Note: The imported tracks will only have the selected section of music from reel 1 as designated by the change notes.

Imported music cue from reel 1, which will be placed into its new position according to the change notes for reel 2

Figure 9.2c Preparing reel 1 music selection to move to change note in reel 2.

Figure 9.2d Prepare to insert the reel 1 music material into the proper position as instructed in the change note at 02:14:14:19. Note: The timecode position is both selected and separated on the original reel 2 score tracks. One can either Spot the reel 1 audio to the proper insert position, or as noted in the next figure (Figure 9.2e), use Shuffle mode to place the new music into the proper position, while at the same time moving all the music to the right by that same amount.

session start, it doesn't matter because you will be placing it at an altogether different position in this reel. You can then cut or copy and paste it, or spot it to the exact frame location that the change notes for reel 2 indicates. If you are working in a super session, where the whole movie is in one Pro Tools session, then moving around audio and conforming can be easier. However, as we will see in the following sections, one type of conforming operation uses Shuffle mode (see Figure 9.2e), which is tricky in a super session. There are, of course, various workarounds to manage this.

Conforming for a re-balance involves a similar moving of audio. Re-balancing is the moving the of the beginning or end of one reel to another—to make them more "balanced" in terms of their length and weight. It historically refers to the shifting of the "weight" of the reels of film, stemming back to the old 2000-foot movie reels, as previously discussed, each reel being about 20 minutes long. So, if reel 4 is 18:30 minutes long, and reel 5 is for example 14:45, it's possible the editor may cut about 2 minutes from the end of reel 4 and place it at the head or beginning of reel 5, making each reel a more manageable length of about 16 minutes.

Even though we are working in the digital medium, this re-balancing can be useful for other reasons. Films were edited from film stock into 5 or 6 reels in total, making the average length of a movie 90 minutes. In order for an audience to see the continuous movie, each reel had to be edited with careful consideration of the visual and sound at the reel breaks or transition points from one reel to the next. When a movie theater played multiple reels in this way, it used a double projector system. If edited and mixed

While in Shuffle mode, grab and move the reel 1 music file previously below onto the separated files in the reel 2 music tracks

The music after the insertion point moves later in the time line by the designated amount, as indicated on the change list

Figure 9.2e Using Shuffle mode, insert the reel 1 music into the proper frame position in reel 2, moving all music remaining on the same track later in time by the insert amount. After this move/insert, the music editor can un-"clip group" the section of music, then continue to edit and conform the material by following the remaining instructions on the change list.

together well, when the projector played the end of reel 4 going into the start of reel 5, the audience would not notice that there was a reel change, or what we call a "change-over." Some older theaters still use this double-projector system, where the projectionist has to manually switch from projector A playing reel 4, to projector B playing reel 5. One-projector systems in theaters are much more common today, where the projection-ist, before playing the movie, has to literally tie or splice the reels together so they play as one long unit. A large round platter in the projection booth holds the film unit. In either of these cases, the joins between reels must be edited and mixed so the transition point between reels is smooth, and can happen without a visual or a sound glitch. One way to assure for a smooth transition between reels is to not have music play over the reel change, or the audience might hear a bump, a jump, or gap in the music as it plays across the join. Music editors and dubbing mixers take great care to limit the likelihood of this happening. When the film is "plattered," as above, it is almost never an issue; however, if the projectionist has to manually switch between projectors, it may likely be a problem. In order to prevent this, there may be the need for a re-balance.

PAX Quote

"When reels are delivered to a theater to be plattered, they have a piece of film wrapped around them with a label on it. This is the head leader. Projectionists have been known to leave a couple of frames of picture attached to the leader when they separate them from the reels, to aid in re-assembly when the film's run is complete. As you can imagine, arbitrarily losing frames on the join will cause the sound to 'bump' when played in the theater. Don't assume your plattered changeovers are safe."

With many of today's movie theaters transitioning over to a digital file-based method of playback and projection using the theatrical film standard, DCP (Digital Cinema Package), these issues of reels and re-balancing are becoming less important. However, the old ways are still common practice, even as we work with modern-day digital film and audio.

9.4 CONFORM IT—THE MANUAL WAY

The primary and foolproof way to conform audio using change notes is by hand (manually) in Pro Tools. This is not exclusive to music: All the sound departments can use this technique to conform audio. While there are some automatic conforming software programs available, for music it's best to use either this manual conforming technique, or one of the following alternative techniques, depending on the situation you are working in. While I recommend not using automatic software for conforming music, there are some useful programs that do conform audio in Pro Tools. I might use these to help move the music as a starting point or as a reference, and then follow by working through the details of editing the music properly. Some of these automatic programs include Reconformer, Virtual Katy, Syncro Arts' Titan, and Maggot Software's Conformalizer, to name a few.

    The following are the steps one would take to conform a Pro Tools session with a change list in hand.

> Caution: The following steps are designed to be used in a Pro Tools session with only one reel to be conformed, and are not for use in a super session (see step 10 and Section 9.6).

1. Open your current Pro Tools session, and then Save As with a new name containing some information about the session, such as Reel 3_conform_ Temp 2, or something similar.
2. Prepare your session to include the Old and New files from the picture department. You may want to label in the "comments" column the proper version of these audio tracks and video reels to help with organization. By having both the old and new media in the session, you can conform using a variety of alternative techniques. Import the new turnover data that was supplied to you by the picture department, including the new QuickTime movie with either or both the embedded audio and/or the separate DX/FX/MX audio files (Figure 9.3).
3. Select all of the audio track nameplates containing the music that will be conformed, including the score, either temp or master composer tracks, and songs and source music. Make a track group labeled something like "original tracks" or "old tracks," then with the track nameplates still highlighted, on any of the tracks' nameplates click Control + click (Mac), Right + click or Start + click (Windows), and under the sub menu, select Duplicate and include the active playlist. This will make an exact copy of all your music tracks in the session, allowing you to go back and reference the old music, or compare the old music tracks with the newly edited tracks.

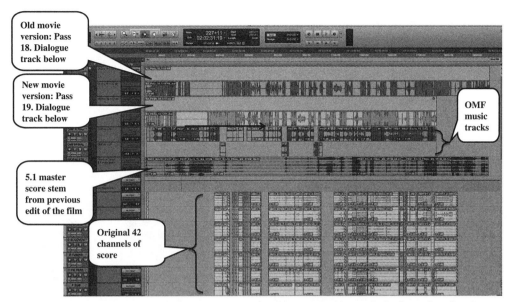

Figure 9.3 The example above is from versions 18 to 19, or sometimes called a "pass." Notice there already was a 5.1 mix of this movie, but now they want to change the movie's editing, which is why the 5.1 master stem tracks and the score tracks are included, and are already edited. The OMF A & B tracks represent the editor's re-configuring of the movie's music stereo track as he changes the movie's picture edits. The music editor needs to move and sync the 5.1 stems as well as the master score tracks to match the OMF music. This is achieved through conforming.

Figure 9.4a Before conforming, it can be a good idea to select all the music tracks that are to be conformed and duplicate them, then hide them from view. This allows the editor to go back to the original cue positions any time for verification of sync or editing.

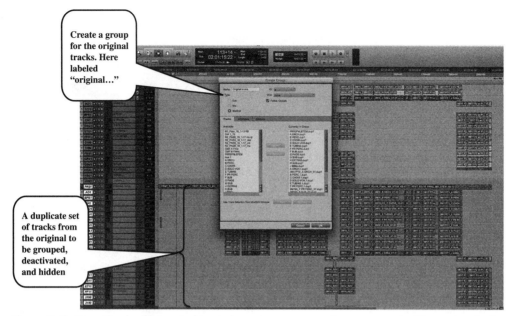

Create a group for the original tracks. Here labeled "original..."

A duplicate set of tracks from the original to be grouped, deactivated, and hidden

Figure 9.4b Once the duplicate set of tracks is made, one can make a group out of them, deactivate them, and hide for future reference as needed.

With the all the duplicated tracks selected, choose Hide and Make Inactive, by going to any tracks' sub-menu. This will take those tracks off the timeline and allow you the freedom to conform the set of remaining music tracks (Figures 9.4a and 9.4b).

4. Make a new audio track group that includes all the music tracks, and be sure to include the old dialogue/sound effects reference track from the turnover. This new group might be called "conform master" or something similar (see Figure 9.5).

5. Enable both Shuffle and Grid modes. This is done by holding Shift while clicking on either of the Second buttons. Both should light up: Shuffle = red, Grid = blue. Place your grid and nudge values to match the frame type that the change notes reflect. In film it will usually be feet and frames, while for television this is most likely to be timecode. Set the nudge and grid value to "1 Frame."

6. Make sure your selector tool is placed in your session and the flashing edit cursor is present on all of the music tracks (including the old DX/FX [or DX only] track).

7. Go to the Start End Length window in Pro Tools (located to the right of the main counter) and type the first event's feet and frame number in the start field. A short cut to go to this window is the slash key on the numeric keypad of a full-size keyboard. If you are using a laptop without a numeric keypad available (or a full extended keyboard attached), some functions in Pro Tools either will not be possible via a key stroke, or might require an additional modifier key.

8. While in the Start End Length window, either hit the slash key twice to get to the length field, or just click on the length field and type in the feet and frame number for event #1 that is shown in the column For This Length. After this move, you should have a selection in your Pro Tools session that goes through all the music tracks and the old DX/FX track (Figure 9.6).

Figure 9.5 Once the original music tracks are grouped and hidden, the tracks to be conformed should be selected, along with the old dialogue track extracted from the movie reel. It is important to note that conforming can take place for temp scores, in addition to recorded scores. In this view, the score actually continues through the lower tracks.

9. Take care to note differences between Avid, or other non-linear video editing systems, and Pro Tools, as shown in the figures (9.6 and 9.7). Picture editing systems notate the change list number directly below the top At The Footage number as what you would expect to be the last or end frame of the event. However, this number, underneath the top at the Footage number, will be one frame different than Pro Tools if it is typed in the End field of the Pro Tools Start End Length menu fields. The reason for this is that Avid Media Composer calculates the frame after the frame has been completed. In other words, the right side of the frame edge is the bottom number on the At This Footage change note list. Pro Tools, on the other hand, always places the cursor or location of a frame line at the left side, or the start of the frame. Therefore if you use the end number (underneath the top number) from the change note list, the conforming will be one frame off. Additionally, the one-frame difference will not occur just the once, but the conforming notes are cumulative, and if you make all the change moves in this fashion, you will continue to add the one-frame error through the whole list, making the entire session or reel potentially extremely out of sync.

As described in #7 and 8, the proper numbers to insert in Pro Tools are the "start" and "length" numbers only.

10a. Now you are ready to make your first deletion or trim-tail event from the list. While the selector tool edit cursor in Pro Tools is positioned through all of the correct tracks, and Shuffle mode is enabled, with all of the files unlocked, hit the Delete button (Mac) or Backspace key (Windows). All

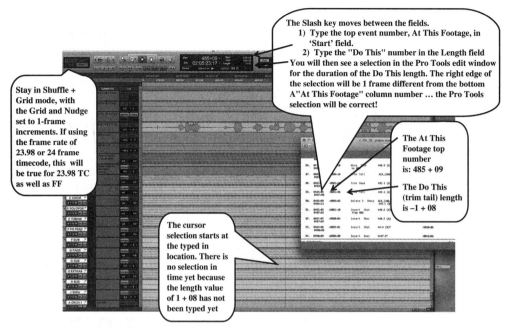

Figure 9.6 The first step in this type of manual conforming is to select the start, end, and length of the selection of music to be either deleted or inserted. In this example the figure shows us a conforming instruction at event #89. It is important that when starting the conforming process, one must start at the first event and continue in order through to the last event listed on the note list. Use the slash key on the number pad to move from field to field. First type the top number from the first event from the At This Footage column in the Start field, and then type in the number from the For This Length column into the Length field. It is important to *not* type in the End field. If you type in the bottom number from At The Footage in the event list, it will be wrong and cause your conform to be out of sync.

of the files after the deleted selection should move to the left by the exact amount indicated in the Length field. (*Caution: This move is for use in a session that contains only one reel of the movie to be conformed. If you are trying this in a super session, make sure you lock all the files in reels you are not conforming. There is also an additional Edit menu option in Pro Tools called Shift. While using this function in Pro Tools will essentially do the same kind of conforming operations, it is not as effective and may cause sync issues if it is used for audio conforming in postproduction. The Shift menu option is designed more for working with MIDI, bars, and beats.*)

10b. To make an insertion or add length, make the proper selection (as described earlier in steps #1 -9) in the tracks via the Start End Length window, and then choose Edit > Insert Silence. The shortcut is Shift + Command + E (Mac) or Shift + Control + E (Windows). The event duration for this kind of move should place a hole in the Pro Tools session where the event took place, and move all the track material to the right by the length amount.

10c. If there is a requirement to move a section of audio to a new location in the reel, instead of hitting the Delete key for a scene deletion, hit the Cut key. This

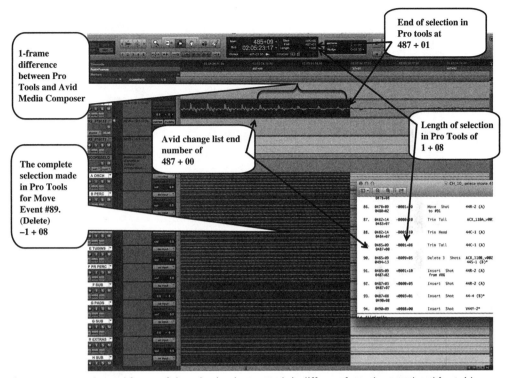

Figure 9.7 Note the end frame of the selection in Pro Tools is different from the stated end for Avid Media Composer's change notes. The end Pro Tools frame is 487 + 01, and Avid's change note says it should be 487 + 00. The frame difference is due to how Avid calculates the frame. Its counter for the length includes the frame through to the right clip edge, whereas Pro Tools measures the frame from the left starting frame edge. While this may seem like it would cause a problem with sync, it does not. Follow the instruction to ignore the end field number in Pro Tools, and type in the length as the change list notes.

will still delete the audio in the Pro Tools Edit window, and will adjust the audio following the cut, with the added benefit of allowing you to paste the cut audio to a later position in the timeline.

10d. To move a cut piece of audio to a place in the same reel listed in the change notes as the next event number, place your curser at the frame location where the moved files will be inserted, make an edit selection in Pro Tools, and while the cut audio is on the computer's clipboard and you are still in Shuffle mode, hit Paste. This will insert the appropriate audio, and move the music material to the right by the same amount, therefore correctly making the Do This action as noted in the change notes.

10e. If the moved files are to be placed in a location (or a new reel location if you are in a super session) indicated by an event later in the change notes list, then you must paste (to hold) the audio you just cut to a position outside of the present movie length, in the exact same set of blank audio tracks. Then when you get to the event asking you to insert the previously cut section, copy the audio (just in case you make a mistake), and while still in Shuffle mode, make

Figure 9.8 Once the selection for move #89 has been made in Pro Tools, hit the Delete button on the computer. Because the session is in Shuffle + Grid, selections snap to the one-frame grid, and all audio on the grouped tracks will move in the same fashion that the picture editing systems operate. A deletion is earlier in time to the left in Pro Tools, or also known as an Advance. Conform move #89 is now complete and you are ready to go to the next event on the change list. Note the next event, #90, starts with the same feet and frames number as #89. This is because the deletion in move #89 placed the cursor position right back to the same location

an edit selection in Pro Tools at the proper time line location, and paste it in the proper location, representing the inserted or moved event.

An important reminder to note: Because these change notes are cumulative, you need to start with the first event and continue conforming in the sequential order as they occur in the list, and not skip an event. Even if there is no music at an event location, you still need to make the proper move in all the audio tracks. Part of the reason that we select the old dialogue and SFX track, is that when we make an event move, we can verify in those audio files where the edit was made.

While I just stated that you should go through each and every event move in order, there could be hundreds of events to do. Following are techniques to help manage multiple events with one edit in Pro Tools and can make the conforming process more efficient.

The amount of silent time inserted is 1 + 10 (Feet & Frames) as noted on the change note by Insert Shot, event #91

Figure 9.9 Move #91 requires a insertion of time, because the picture editor inserted or added frames in this section of the film. Event #91 is selected in Pro Tools the same way as #89, except that when the selection is ready in Pro Tools, the user hits Insert Silence instead of Delete. While still in Shuffle + Grid mode, Insert Silence moves all the selected audio to the right in Pro Tools. This move is also known as a "Retard."

Check if the change list has any consecutive events that all start at the same frame number. Each of these events might be a deletion or an insert, but they all return to the same frame position after the event is implemented. In these cases, you can calculate each event and their respective instructions by subtracting and adding all the consecutive events together. After doing the math, you come up with one deletion or an insertion, considering all of those events. You can then make one move reflecting the collective events (see Figure 9.10). It may be possible for Avid change notes to be set up to eliminate automatically any shots that are an even swap with inserted shots, but this is not common.

If there are many of these types of events in the change list, to do this math manually might be more time consuming than just making all the moves in Pro Tools. However, there are a number of frame and timecode calculators on the market, and even some free apps available that can help this speed this process along.

The last and more challenging operation after you complete all of the event changes on the change list is to then edit, fix, or alter all of the music that is affected by the event moves. If a piece of music has been moved in its entirety, without any edit separations or inserted holes in the music files, then there is nothing to be done by the music editor for that piece of music.

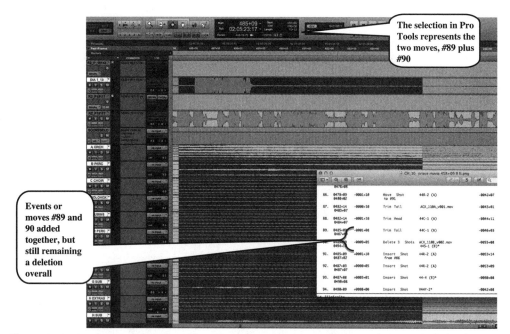

The selection in Pro Tools represents the two moves, #89 plus #90

Events or moves #89 and 90 added together, but still remaining a deletion overall

Figure 9.10 On change notes where there are two or more events in a row (consecutive) that have the same start or top feet and frame number, one can combine the deletions and the insertions to essentially make one move. In this example move #89 can be combined with move #90 to make a total deletion of 10 feet and 13 frames. Because one is adding deletions, the total will still be a deletion. So − 1 + 08 plus − 9 + 05 = − 10 + 13. The selection shown represents the total deletion, and can be deleted in Shuffle mode to address two events at the same time.

9.5 CONFORM IT—ALTERNATIVE TECHNIQUE: MOVING AND MATCHING

Another technique for conforming that works quite well is a combination of using the change notes as a guide and moving each piece of music individually. Rather than negotiating many hundreds of event moves, the music editor can conform using a hybrid technique. This process involves reviewing the change notes and noticing the Total Change column, and at what frame a collective range of events happened. If the first range of changing feet and frame events occurs, for example, between the positions of 150 + 01 and 325 + 10, and the Total Change number at the end of this selected area cumulatively equals a deletion of 28 + 04, and any music falling within this range can be moved earlier in time by 28 + 04.

> **PAX Quote**
>
> "The tricky part is that this is music that 'should' be falling in that area, and not necessarily the un-conformed music that is already sitting there. It takes a combination of knowing the movie and using the editors stem crash downs to determine this. It's tricky, but *very* fast."

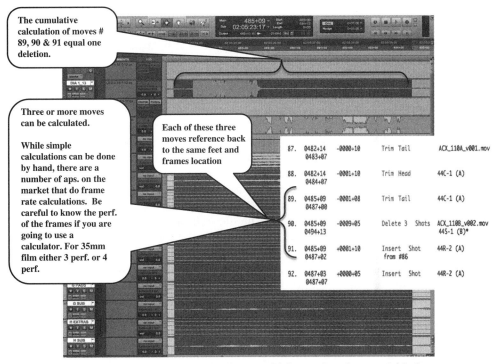

The cumulative calculation of moves # 89, 90 & 91 equal one deletion.

Three or more moves can be calculated.

While simple calculations can be done by hand, there are a number of aps. on the market that do frame rate calculations. Be careful to know the perf. of the frames if you are going to use a calculator. For 35mm film either 3 perf. or 4 perf.

Each of these three moves reference back to the same feet and frames location

87.	0482+14 0483+07	-0000+10	Trim Tail	ACX_110A_v001.mov
88.	0482+14 0484+07	-0001+10	Trim Head	44C-1 (A)
89.	0485+09 0487+00	-0001+08	Trim Tail	44C-1 (A)
90.	0485+09 0494+13	-0009+05	Delete 3 Shots	ACX_110B_v002.mov 44S-1 (B)*
91.	0485+09 0487+02	+0001+10	Insert Shot from #86	44R-2 (A)
92.	0487+03 0487+07	+0000+05	Insert Shot	44R-2 (A)

Figure 9.11 In the case of change notes that have multiple numbers in a row with the same start frame, one can combine those events or moves by adding and subtracting the deletions and the insertions. In this example, moves #89 plus #90 equal − 10 + 13. If one continues to add the next event, #91, one has to calculate the cumulative deletion of − 10 + 13 with an insertion of 1 + 10. Remember that there are 16 frames in a foot. So a − 10 + 13 plus 1 + 10 equals a − 9 + 03 move. Note the selection length is 9 feet 3 frames. The editor can delete this whole section, therefore implementing three moves at one time.

It's possible that a grouping of a few pieces of score and songs can be affected by this range of insertions and deletion events. If this is the case, you can grab all of the music in this area and move it. If a small portion of the music plays over the ending event of 325 + 10, then that portion of the music should be kept in the audio tracks and reviewed with regards to editing appropriately. When using either of these techniques, it is often helpful to include the old dialogue track and move with your selected music tracks. This can then be used to check if the operation is actually in sync with the new dialogue, therefore verifying the conforming events.

To proceed with this technique, stay in shuffle mode with grid mode and set to 1 frame grid and nudge. In order to make sure the piece or pieces of music move by the proper amount, the editor can use two techniques to quickly place the music in its proper conformed position:

1. Determine if the collected move amount on the change notes is a retard, later in time, noted as an insert or " + ," or an advance, earlier in time, noted by a

deletion or " − ." While in Grid mode, place your cursor start location on an exact frame line, as indicated by the change notes. The left side of the selection must start at a grid line, but it doesn't have to be exactly on the edge of the music clips. The actual clip may not fall on a frame line, but it will still be in a relative frame position according to the timeline. Continue your selection across all of the music to the right so that all the music you intend to move is selected, making sure you have selected over the clip boundaries on either side of the audio files. Using both the nudge and the following spot technique, remember to also separate the dialogue clip at your selection by using the short cut focus key, letter 'b' or 'e'. Into the Nudge Value field type the total change amount listed from the conform notes affecting the area covering the pertinent music cues. With the selection covering the music, ready to activate as the Nudge move, hit return on the computer keyboard then hit the minus key on the numeric keypad to implement a deletion move. The file or files should advance by that exact amount. (For an insert to Retard a selection, for the last step hit the plus sign.)

2. Another way to move music files by one amount of time is to use the Spot mode function. In a similar fashion as the previous Nudge version, make sure you know the amount of time and direction you need to move the music. You also need to make the selection on a grid or proper frame line to maintain accurate sync. Select Spot mode, and then click on the selected area with the grabber tool. The Spot mode dialog box opens. In the Start field, type first either a minus or a plus sign, depending on the direction or instruction in the change notes, before you type the total change number. Once the correct number is entered, click OK or press the Enter key. Note that there is no warning dialog box, the music files just snap or move to their proper position. This type of spotting audio can be a bit finicky, and fortunately you can undo this move if necessary. In this case, be sure to check that your files actually are located in the correct track position. If not, repeat this operation again.

If using either of these procedures to move audio, it is an excellent idea to verify the sync and phase accuracy of the music from the new video, as placed by the picture editor. This verification is very important, and can be checked by playing your newly moved music tracks against the extracted audio music tracks, the AAF music tracks, or sometimes a music stem crashdown, if the film was previously mixed. This valuable listening may reveal some changes in the musical ideas that have come from the director or picture editor, and may not be represented yet in your temp music score, songs, or composed score. In addition, you should always listen to their conformed music tracks with the picture editor's music, because it's possible there could have been exclusive changes in the music without changing the picture. Hopefully all communications pertaining to altering musical material from the director and or editor will be have been relayed prior to a conform.

9.6 CONFORM IT—WORKING WITH SUPER SESSIONS.

Conforming audio with a single session per each reel or act of a show, or a with super session, works well with either of the two previous examples. However, using the manual method in a super session with Shuffle mode will create many problems unless some precautions are taken. Following are two workflow suggestions.

One way would be to lock all the audio tracks that are on either side of the current reel you are conforming. However, if there are audio files to the right of your editing area, each time you make an event move, there will be a dialog box asking you if you want to temporarily unlock files and go ahead with the move.

An alternative way to manage Shuffle mode while conforming in a super session, is to make a duplicate set of tracks, by selecting a grouped track's namplate while holding Control (Mac) or Start (Windows), or right clicking and selecting Duplicate from the sub menu. You may not want to select the option to include active playlists. This will make the same set of tracks as your chosen group, but without the audio files. Then in Slip mode, you can grab one whole reel at a time that you are about to conform, selecting past the clip boundaries, hold Control + Option (Mac) or Start + Alt (Windows) with the grabber tool, and drag the music into the duplicated set of empty tracks. In this way you will be able to work in Shuffle mode to conform the audio without disturbing the other reels in the super session. Once that reel is conformed, de-select Shuffle mode and you can either delete the un-conformed reel or cover over and replace the un-conformed reel by placing it back into the tracks holding all the reels of the super session.

> **Tip**
> Be very careful using Shuffle mode … be sure you understand the implications, particularly while conforming.

This workflow will also allow you to easily move sections of the music to another location in the same reel, or another reel, and is good for re-balancing.

9.7 CONFORM IT—MATCHING MUSIC TRACKS

The previous examples utilized the change notes to guide the conforming of the audio material with frame accurate information. It's possible, however, that this printed sheet could be inaccurate. It's also possible that the editor may not have generated a change list, for multiple reasons. In the case of a low-budget project, the change list may seem unnecessary or technically not possible to create. In these situations, the music editor or other editorial staff can conform their audio material by working in a less formal way than previously described.

If the music in the movie before the conform has been accurately represented in the AAF and the embedded audio in the video clip, then the music editor can rely on moving and matching by ear the non-conformed music tracks to the AAF music elements.

Using this technique, you must be very careful to be phase-accurate in waveform matching and listening for any changes that might have occurred in the music tracks from the picture editor's work. The picture editor could have done any number of changes in the music, which should show up in the AAF, including re-editing the music, making cross-fades and volume changes, as well as moving or copying small sections to different locations in the movie for dramatic effect.

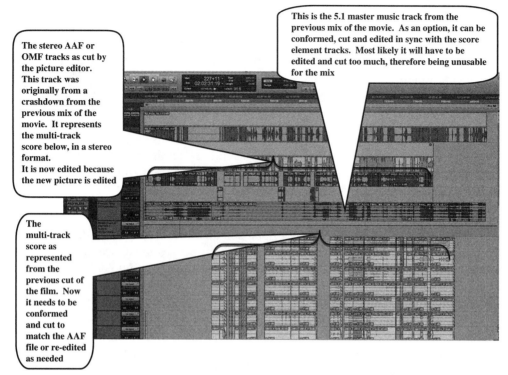

Figure 9.12a If there are no conform notes available, or if the music editor does not wish to move music files strictly by the change notes, it is possible to slide the musical score, songs, or temp music to sonically match the stereo AAF or OMF file, which represents how the picture editor moved the music as the picture changed from one version to the next. It is important to note that the film editor can only move audio in frames, so you as the music editor may want to set Pro Tools in a 1-frame grid so as to emulate the picture editor's restriction.

When moving the music to conform in this way it is usually good to work in grid mode until the reel is conformed then switch to slip mode to proceed with editing. Anything can happen, and it is important for the music editor to rely on their eyes, ears, and musical sensibilities, and to ask questions.

9.8 CONFORM IT—MATCHING VIDEO

Comparing videos is an additional conforming method that could be used in situations where there are no notes or conforming information, except for a new and old picture. It is much the same as the dialogue referencing technique in the following section, although you will not be using the Shuffle + Grid mode. With Pro Tools HD software, you can actually edit the movies and place them in the same position in the timeline on two separate video tracks. Knowing that there is a difference in the two movies, you can go through the reel or the act and find where the picture has changed. This is time consuming, but can work in certain situations. In these cases,

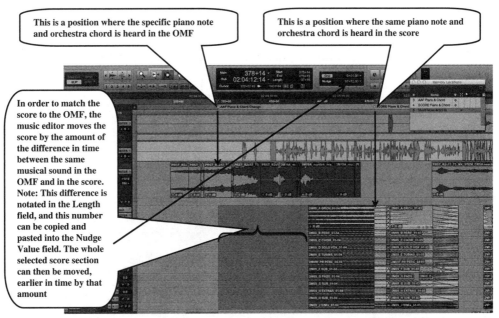

This is a position where the specific piano note and orchestra chord is heard in the OMF

This is a position where the same piano note and orchestra chord is heard in the score

In order to match the score to the OMF, the music editor moves the score by the amount of the difference in time between the same musical sound in the OMF and in the score. Note: This difference is notated in the Length field, and this number can be copied and pasted into the Nudge Value field. The whole selected score section can then be moved, earlier in time by that amount

Figure 9.12b When matching the score or other music tracks to the AAF/OMF, the music editor should listen for same musical notes, chords, or passages in the score that are represented in the AAF/OMF. The editor can either slide, nudge or spot the track, or all the tracks of music, so the AAF/OMF and score sound at exactly same time. Note: The film editor may have actually re-edited the music, and the exact position may no longer be found in the same place as in the master music tracks. This indicates that the music editor needs to re-edit the score in an appropriate way to address the picture editor's musical concept.

you are essentially trying to discover where the editor made cuts and changes in the movie, in a way working like the picture editor, but in reverse. It will be very tedious to find the frames in the movie that have changed between old and new versions, but can be done by continually switching the two video tracks back and forth between "online" and "offline" (because two movies cannot be viewed at the same time in Pro Tools), clicking on the associated video track's online button. When you find a changed scene from the old version to the new picture cut, it is likely that there was a deletion for the new cut, and that scene is simply gone or perhaps moved to a new location. After selecting the area of picture change, measure the duration from the frame in the old version to that same frame in the new movie cut. This selection can be saved in the Memory Locations window by choosing the Selection button in that window. In this way, the selected duration can then be assigned across all the grouped music tracks, and can be conformed by deleting, inserting silence or moving audio, whichever is needed to match the new movie position.

You can use this process to get the tracks in their correct conform positions either with or without Shuffle mode. You have to make this judgment call on a per project basis, because if you use shuffle mode, moving all of the audio following the event move, based on the picture edit, may be inaccurate. Using this method you can also

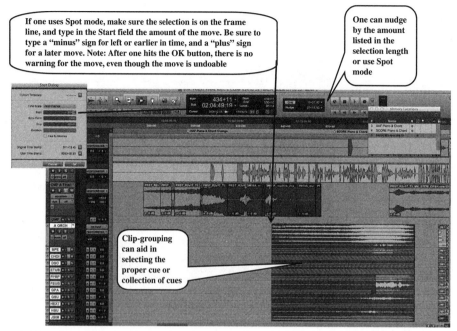

Figure 9.12c After measuring the conforming move distance and placing it in the Nudge Value field, the music editor may want to clip-group the music cue or cues to encapsulate all the fades and edits before the cue is moved. Note: An additional way to move a cue is by using Spot mode. Although one does not have to clip-group the music, it may make the move selection easier.

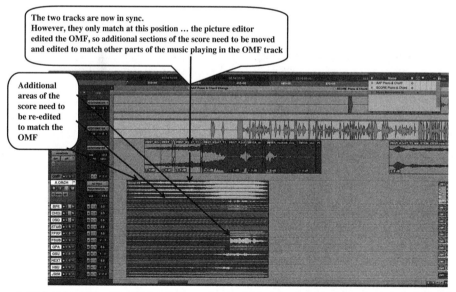

Figure 9.12d Using either the Nudge Value or Spot mode, the selected piece of music is shifted into the proper position, which should match the OMF music track. Be sure to listen and zoom in on the two files to hear and see the waveforms—they should sound the same. While the music cue *may* be in sync with the OMF with only a small portion of the music, it's very possible that additional editing will be needed.

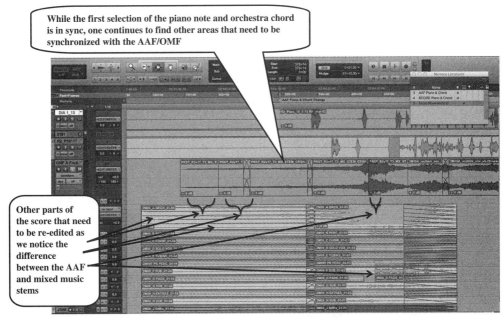

While the first selection of the piano note and orchestra chord is in sync, one continues to find other areas that need to be synchronized with the AAF/OMF

Other parts of the score that need to be re-edited as we notice the difference between the AAF and mixed music stems

Figure 9.12e As the music editor continues to conform, by moving music cues into their new synchronized positions, they become aware of the many areas of music that may need re-editing.

One section of the music moved because the picture has been moved

The score needs to be deleted here and edited to match the OMF

Figure 9.12f One example of a section of the score that needs to be re-edited and moved to match the OMF. Note: In many situations the edit in the OMF is *not* a good music edit. The music editor in this case makes the score sound as natural and smooth as possible while addressing the composer's, picture editor's and director's musical concepts.

Figure 9.12g An additional example of a section in the music that needs to be deleted to address the OMF music tracks position.

utilize dialogue-matching between old and new dialogue tracks to help verify the picture edits.

> **Tip**
>
> **Caution:** Be afraid of sloppy film editors! See Section 9.8: How to line up new and old picture together in the session and calculate a *real* offset at any given point. Fast and *completely* accurate. And remember: Picture is king … never audio. This technique is every bit as accurate as a change note. Matching waveforms is not.

9.9 CONFORM IT—MATCHING DIALOGUE TRACKS

Similarly to the previous conforming methods, but less accurate than comparing old and new picture, and less formal than using change notes, you can also use the position of the old dialogue track compared to the new one in order to move the music tracks into a new conformed position (see Figures 9.13a–9.13g).

Make sure you group and select all of the audio (including the old dialogue track), making edits and selecting through and beyond the clip boundaries of each piece of music. When the video editor replaces parts of a scene without actually moving the audio a conforming edit in the music would likely not be necessary. Also, it's trickier and more time consuming to search and find dialogue that may have been deleted in one place, only to find it in another reel. The question you have to answer

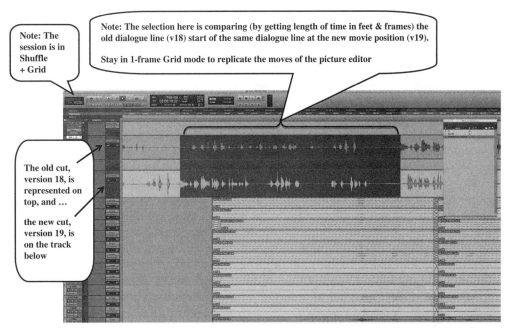

Figure 9.13a Using the dialogue track to compare the position of the music tracks from the old version to the new version is a viable conforming technique. However, as you will notice over the next few screenshots, it is not always the most accurate or desirable way to conform music.

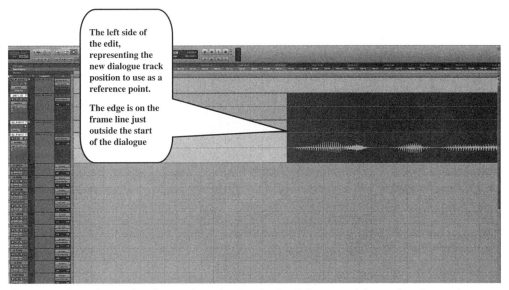

Figure 9.13b As the music editor makes selections in the dialogue track for conforming, make note that the 1-frame grid must be used on both sides of the selection, and in the same relative position to the sounding dialogue section. In addition, the selection starts on the lower new track and includes the old track above.

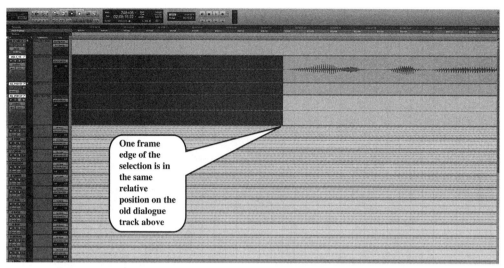

Figure 9.13c This screenshot represents the right side of the selection made in the two dialogue tracks. Note that this side of the selection is in the exact 1-frame position relative to the same dialogue line that is in the new dialogue track.

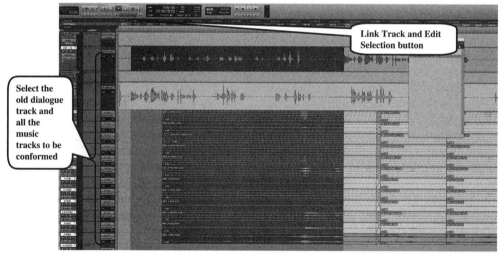

Figure 9.13d The selection made in the old and new dialogue tracks can be saved in the Memory Locations window. Once saved, you can place their selector cursor in the score tracks to be edited, and in the old dialogue track. All of these tracks will be deleted or moved by the length found in the selection made. Note: One must be in Shuffle + Grid mode in order for the conforming process to continue affecting all the music and old dialogue track of the editing area. The music editor can use the memorized selection starting in either the dialogue track or the score/music tracks, and while holding Shift, and then selecting the nameplate of the tracks you want to include in your selection, move the selection up or down with the keys "p" or ";" respectively. You may want to keep enabled the blue Link Track and Edit Selection button. If the old dialogue track and the music tracks are not grouped, you can temporarily make a selection in either one or any track, and then have the same selection occur in any other additional tracks you choose.

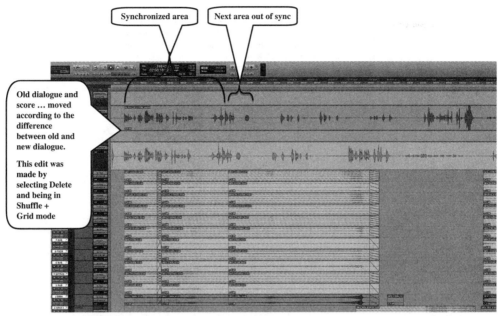

Figure 9.13e As you continue to compare the dialogue tracks, you will notice very soon after the conformed edited area is done that the dialogue is out of sync again. This is due to the continuous change that occurs as you play the two tracks, hearing where the dialogue is out of sync with the old and new versions. When you find a new out-of-sync position, an edit must be made.

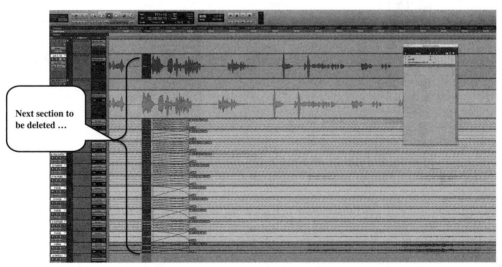

Figure 9.13f The following section in the dialogue track is only a 4-frame conform or insertion in this case. The old dialogue track was earlier than the new one, which means the picture editor inserted 4 frames of picture here. Although the music is moving appropriately, as the conform notes indicate, the music editor must consider the overall sound and musical effect of the edited score of cutting the music in this position.

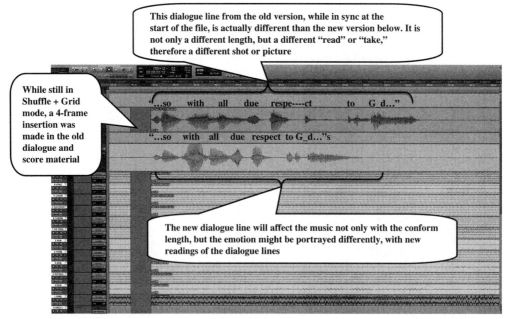

Figure 9.13g In this example, the dialogue is a actor's different line, between old and new version of picture, yet only in a different position by a few frames. While this needs to be addressed, it might make the music edit awkward if the original music was closely cut or composed around the old dialogue line. The music editor should consider the whole emotional arch of the scene, and what the composer's previous musical intent was, before the music is cut. It might be more appropriate to do a music edit in another position in the score, rather than where the dialogue is cut.

is how to edit the music in the new position, or with a replaced scene. Although it's possible to work in this way, it's not optimum. However, using any of these conforming methods, you can use the dialogue track as a verification of the conforming moves, bearing in mind, though, that it may not be a reliable source for a final conform decision.

9.10 LFOA SHEET

In addition to the assistant picture editor providing the sound departments with change notes, another important document is the LFOA, or Last Frame Of Action, which calculates in frames and timecode the duration of each reel as it changes, and eventually can be used to calculate the final length of the movie (Figures 9.14a and 9.14b). Sometimes it's known as the LFOP, or Last Frame Of Picture, or for television, LFOA (Last Frame Of Act). The nomenclature can also be used to label the first frame of picture (FFOP or FFOA).

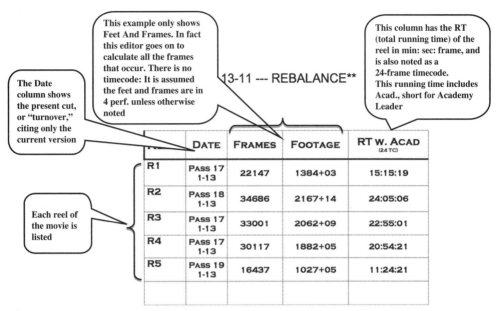

This example only shows Feet And Frames. In fact this editor goes on to calculate all the frames that occur. There is no timecode: It is assumed the feet and frames are in 4 perf. unless otherwise noted

The Date column shows the present cut, or "turnover," citing only the current version

This column has the RT (total running time) of the reel in min: sec: frame, and is also noted as a 24-frame timecode. This running time includes Acad., short for Academy Leader

13-11 --- REBALANCE**

Each reel of the movie is listed

	DATE	FRAMES	FOOTAGE	RT W. ACAD (24 TC)
R1	PASS 17 1-13	22147	1384+03	15:15:19
R2	PASS 18 1-13	34686	2167+14	24:05:06
R3	PASS 17 1-13	33001	2062+09	22:55:01
R4	PASS 17 1-13	30117	1882+05	20:54:21
R5	PASS 19 1-13	16437	1027+05	11:24:21

Figure 9.14a Even though this LOFA list says it's a re-balance, it is essentially the same as a turnover. The editor is clarifying that there likely will be no changes within the reel, but only that the reels have changed size/length by moving their lengths and starts. While simpler than the next figure, it contains all the required information.

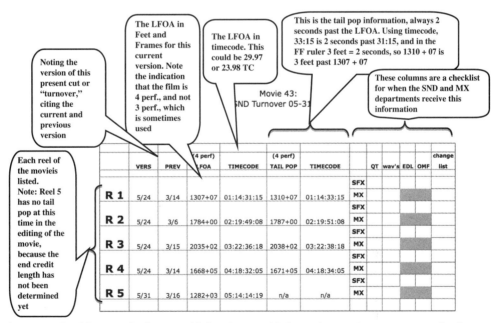

The LFOA in Feet and Frames for this current version. Note the indication that the film is 4 perf., and not 3 perf., which is sometimes used

Noting the version of this present cut or "turnover," citing the current and previous version

The LFOA in timecode. This could be 29.97 or 23.98 TC

This is the tail pop information, always 2 seconds past the LFOA. Using timecode, 33:15 is 2 seconds past 31:15, and in the FF ruler 3 feet = 2 seconds, so 1310 + 07 is 3 feet past 1307 + 07

These columns are a checklist for when the SND and MX departments receive this information

Movie 43: SND Turnover 05-31

Each reel of the movie is listed. Note: Reel 5 has no tail pop at this time in the editing of the movie, because the end credit length has not been determined yet

	VERS	PREV	(4 perf) LFOA	TIMECODE	(4 perf) TAIL POP	TIMECODE		QT	wav's	EDL	OMF	change list
R 1	5/24	3/14	1307+07	01:14:31:15	1310+07	01:14:33:15	SFX MX					
R 2	5/24	3/6	1784+00	02:19:49:08	1787+00	02:19:51:08	SFX MX					
R 3	5/24	3/15	2035+02	03:22:36:18	2038+02	03:22:38:18	SFX MX					
R 4	5/24	3/14	1668+05	04:18:32:05	1671+05	04:18:34:05	SFX MX					
R 5	5/31	3/16	1282+03	05:14:14:19	n/a	n/a	SFX MX					

Figure 9.14b This example shows multiple columns of information pertinent to communication from the picture department to the sound departments. There are many variations of the LFOA document. The one shown here is designed similarly to a checklist for the picture assistant, while also containing important information for the sound and music departments, verifying the reels and their respective lengths and sync pops.

9.11 CONCLUSION

After the conforming is done ... the creative work has just started. While I have presented multiple scenarios for the conforming process, there are many ways an editor can achieve a conforming workflow to re-sync their audio tracks. Conforming operations are crucial, but the hard work remains after all of the moving of audio is completed. The skilled music editor will need to re-cut the music in a similar way to the previous version of the movie, but now to a different picture cut. It may involve adding material, having a discussion with the director, or using different segues and key transitions, to name a few of the considerations. It's also possible that the music from the old position may not work at all in its new position, no matter how it is edited. These are some of the ultimate creative challenges for the music editor. You need to edit, re-edit, fix, create, re-create, and re-sync all of the affected music.

Chapter 10
The Final Film
Sound Mix

10.1 THE MIX, AN OVERVIEW

The final sound mix also referred to as dubbing of the movie, TV show, or documentary, is the time when the director, producers, sound people, and anyone else who has a vested interest in the outcome of the film, come together to finalize and balance the sound of the movie. While it is becoming more common to change or re-cut picture and audio at the last minute (and sometimes throughout the final mix), the sound departments should enter the dub stage with all of their respective elements of the movie soundtrack prepared correctly. There are long-standing methods of how to prepare tracks, audio, and picture for the dub, and each department has workflows that have been used and built upon since the early days of recording on MAG through to today's digital age. (MAG is film stock that is coated with magnetic oxide, usually covering the complete width of the film, and enabling the analogue recording and playback of audio, and which can be locked, sprocket hole by sprocket hole, to the motion picture images.) In this chapter, I will present the basis of preparing music for the mix, as well as a workflow for re-editing and fixing music tracks. The reader should know that while there are tried-and-tested ways of preparing music, digital formats have become more varied and flexible, depending on the specific needs of a mix and on requests from the re-recording mixers.

Traditionally three mixers were assigned to dub the movie, who were, and still are, known as the re-recording mixers or re-recording engineers. Each of these three persons would be responsible for one of the three main elements of the soundtrack of a movie: dialogue, sound effects, and music. About ten to fifteen years ago, producers started wanting to save money, and figured they could make do with only two mixers, thinking, how hard could it be to mix music, right? With the advent of digital picture and audio, it was assumed this was reasonable, given that the non-linear nature of digital audio workstations (DAW) meant one could work faster and better, and the use of two mixers instead of three has been the common working situation for many years now. However, despite the flexibility of digital systems for both editing and mixing, the art of mixing a movie remains the same whether you are working digitally or on a linear, tape- based system.

The division of power between the two re-recording mixers usually means that one mixer takes care of the sound effects, and the other the dialogue and music. Taking this workflow scenario one step further, mixes occasionally use just one re-recording mixer, although a one-person mix is very rare, and is generally only found on low-budget films, documentaries, short films, webisodes, games, perhaps a temporary mix, a quick print master, or an M & E (M & E stands for music and effects, referring to the mixing delivery configurations specific for foreign-language markets). Often the sound effects supervisor will mix with the re-recording engineer.

10.2 MIXING WORKFLOW

The traditional style and workflow of mixing is to have all the sound elements that have been prepared by DX, FX, and MX play in real time while the two mixers blend the three elements together, balancing the volume, panning, EQ, and other sound treatments on their respective material. Sometimes the dialogue is mixed first, and then the other elements are added around it on separate passes. Dialogue takes priority over the other elements, since it tells the story most directly, and utilizes more of the overall soundtrack's volume. The remaining is left for sound effects and music.

> **PAX Quote**
> "An Oscar-winning sound engineer told me that music, in his mind, is the second most critical element, in that it can tell the story in a way that other sound elements often do not."

Usually, mixers play through one scene at a time, including the transition points from the previous scene to the current scene. In the early days of re-recording for film, without the benefit of automated mixing the process was much more difficult. The mixers had to record through a reel of the movie continuously from beginning to end, and if they made a mistake or wanted something to be different, they would have to go back to the beginning and re-mix the whole reel again, trying to remember the previous volume settings and changes. As technology improved, engineers could play and record in shorter sections of the reel, and were able to punch in and out of Record manually. Now, computer-controlled automation makes matching, punching, and re-creating passes infinitely easier.

A current style of mixing has developed from this traditional workflow, where small sections of the film expressing an emotional arc are mixed by going back and forth over that group of scenes, until it sounds just right. It is common for a mixer to balance the audio by manipulating volume levels, processing audio with digital plugins, and setting panning assignments using the computer software, mouse, and an optional hardware mixing controller. This process is commonly referred to as "mixing in the box." However, what is even more common is for the mixers to make basic settings of volume and audio processing in the computer, as well as adjusting mix parameters in real time. Part of the benefit of mixing in real time is to hear what the other soundtrack elements are doing. None of the three elements should be mixed in isolation, without hearing the combination of the other two soundtrack elements. As the mixers progress through the reels of the movie, in small sections, they are then able to review at any time the mixing moves that they have performed. Reviewing each mixed reel upon completion is known as "playback," and is usually listened to by all those present at the mix, and sometimes studio personnel who may come in to hear the results. From these playbacks notes are taken, and then the mixers re-mix, addressing the changes or fixes.

10.3 PRE-DUBS

On big-budget movies or television shows, the mixers sometimes prepare pre-dubs. These are a large number of tracks mixed down to a stem or a smaller track count unit, to then mix into the movie, and are often requested by mixers working on films with many separate tracks of sound effects, music, or perhaps complicated dialogue scenes. For example, the sound effects for the *Transformer* movies commonly had hundreds of audio sound effects tracks. It would be very time consuming for the sound effects mixer to manage, find, and sort through all those track elements. They would therefore make a pre-dub of those elements in grouped stems, to help the mix go smoother and faster. The stem layout is usually a few sets of 5.1 or LCRs, stereos or quads. This would be determined on a per project basis. These pre-dub stems would be taken from the element tracks and recorded as their own audio files in sync at the proper location in the movie. Pre-dubs can include either musical elements or sound elements. Occasionally a large multi-track score, or sometimes a multiple-stem song of an on-camera performance, requires this pre-dubbing. Any time there are more source tracks than inputs to the dub stage, a pre-dub may be called for.

10.4 SOUND EDITORS AS MIXERS

It is the re-recording mixer's job to prepare pre-dub audio tracks. Some films purposely use less-expensive pre-dub mixers at smaller facilities to save money, and then spend more money for the final dub stage mix. Current practice involves the sound editor balancing levels, panning and EQing their sound elements in Pro Tools before it is sent to the re-recording mixer. It is becoming common for the sound editor or sound designer and in certain situations the music editor to deliver a pre-dubbed Pro Tools session to the temp mix and occasionally to the final mix often by-passing the need for a re-recording mixer to create these pre-dubs. Although this is not the traditional way to operate, and sometimes frowned upon within the traditional sound community, in the interest of shortened schedules and tight production budgets, it has unfortunately become a non-publicized expectation. However, there is often good reason for the music editor to create multi-track temp music, pre-mixed as one piece of music, as mentioned in the chapter on temp scoring. Pre-dubbing is not only about pleasing the boss, with regards to efficiency, but also about the primary goal for all those in sound and movie making: Wanting to do the best job possible for the good of the film, and representing their craft at the highest possible standard.

10.5 DELIVERING MUSIC TO THE DUB

The music editor is responsible for compiling, syncing, formatting, and editing all of the music for the final mix or dub. It's possible for there to be multiple or even no music editors on a project, but as I stated earlier, I believe it's essential that there should be at least one or more music editors at the final dub, to carry out the final preparation and presentation of material for the mixer.

Track layout for the re-recording mixer is very important, and while there are certain guidelines for this procedure, it's best to confer with the mixer about how they prefer the score and source music layout to be constructed—ideally, this should be communicated before the music mixer prepares the stems. The composer may likely build tracks in a specific order and present them to the music editor, but the music editor may then re-order them and set up the dub session according to the various guidelines and preferences of the re-recording mixer.

Prior to a dub, the music editor will usually:

• Verify whether the dub will be mixing with a super session or in separate reels. Also ask if the re-recording mixer will expect a separate Pro Tools rig on the stage to play the music in real time or simply be able to add the music session to the stages' Pro Tools system for mixing.
• Confirm the sample rate, bit rate, and audio connectivity of the mixer's console. This will be necessary if the audio workstations are to feed the console audio in real time, or if the mixers are working exclusively with Pro Tools and using a Pro Tools controller-console. Common types of these consoles are the Avid S6, Avid System 5, D-Control, D-Command, or some other compatible worksurfaces that offer tactile control of Pro Tools.
• Verify with the mixer or the machine-room operator the number of channels that they expect will be available exclusively for music. Often these track counts are in even banks, such as 8, 16, or 24 tracks. It is important to note that while the mixing stage may have a limitation as far as the track count availability for music, renting or purchasing of additional equipment is sometimes an option to be discussed with all parties concerned: composer, music mixer, and re-recording mixer.

10.5.1 Track Preparation

While this is not a rule, a music editor may prepare the music tracks according to the following order:

1. The orchestra or score tracks start at the top of a Pro Tools session, and run vertically to the last track, totalling the number of tracks that the largest or highest track-count piece of music contains.
2. Source music, and its respective perspective cuts.
3. Source and song music tracks that might have split vocals and instrumental parts.
4. Tracks of on-camera singing and playing music, with their respective stems.

Note: I follow this template as a starting point, and retain its layout consistency throughout each Pro Tools session presented to the re-recording mixer. Another music editor may use a different track layout, but it is important to maintain consistency.

> **Tip**
> Talk with the re-recording mixers to get the track layout just right for your mix.

The track layout one chooses should give the mixer an un-cluttered view and consistent materials to work with throughout the entire film mix. If the tracks were to differ from one reel to the next, the mixer's I/O (input/output) settings and EQ presets would alter the performance of the music and contribute to a slower, less efficient dub.

Figures 10.1a, 10.1b, and 10.1c give an example of a master session created by the music editor and brought to the mixing stage to work with and manage edits and changes. The top section includes the previous movie and the current movie, for any comparisons needed, the OMF tracks, muted, and the composer's demos for reference. Note: These top tracks would not be given to the re-recording mixer, as he or she would not need them. The following sets of score tracks in this case are set in their mono track configurations, as would be requested by the re-recording mixer to the music editor. Usually the music editor prefers working in single multi-track formats as opposed to splitting the music into all mono tracks. This would be one of the differences between a music editors 'edit' session on the dub stage and the delivered session for the mixer.

In Figure 10.2 the super session for the mix shows all the music stems as 5.0 tracks; the tracks below the score are stereo tracks for the stereo source material. Note that there are two sets of score tracks, listed as A and B, e.g., Orch A, Synth Hi A,

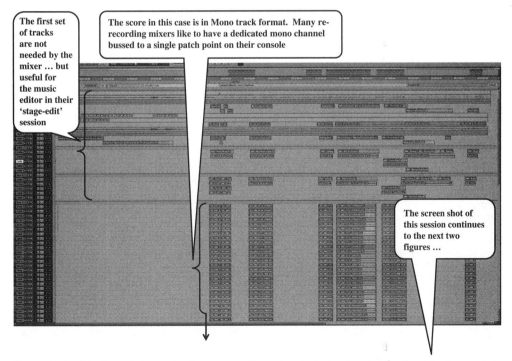

Figure 10.1a Music track layout for the re-recording mixer but also showing tracks at the top useful for the music editors 'stage edit' session.

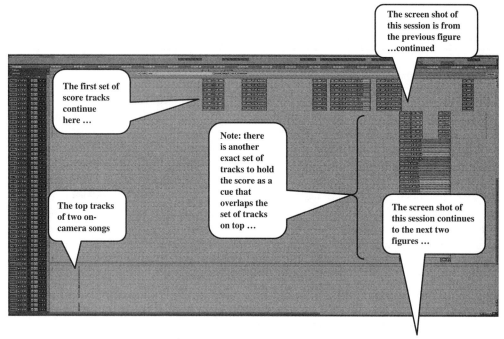

Figure 10.1b This figure shows the previous figure's session, continued to view its lower set of tracks. One can also see the start of a song that is split into separate stems, as well as split for perspective. The source and songs are at the bottom of the entire session.

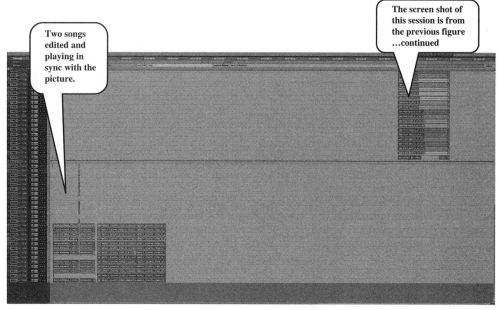

Figure 10.1c This last figure in the set of three shows the bottom of the session, with the songs and source cut in sync with the movie. This on-camera song utilizes splits to include voice tracks and instrumental tracks. In addition there is a small sliver of the song placed on a separate track that is a cut for perspective.

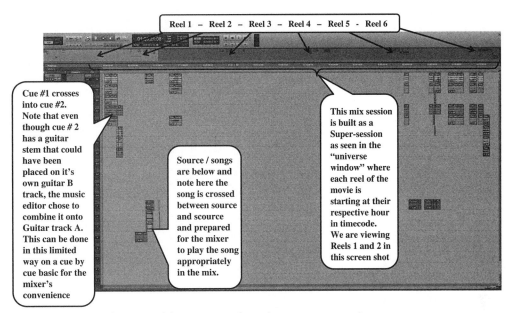

Figure 10.2 All music prepared for a re-recording mixer as a super session.

Synth Low A, Grt A, and Perc A, and following underneath, a set for the same type of stems but labeled B. This is designed for overlapping cues. Note also that the second cue overlaps the first cue on the same labeled tracks, utilizing Pro Tools cross-fades to achieve a smooth transition, although they share the guitar track. It's also very possible and sometimes better to leave the crossing between two pieces of music to the re-recording mixer to handle in real time and not place a Pro Tools fade-out or -in on the files.

10.5.2 Score Track Layout

In most dramatic movies, the score, either as final music tracks or as temp score tracks, takes precedence over the other music elements. If the movie is more song driven, however, the instrumental score may likely take a back seat.

In the case of a temp score, the music you are mixing will most likely be stereo tracks placed in sync with the film. If these stereo elements sound smooth between cues and transitions, the music editor can conceivably make the whole score play on one stereo track. While this is certainly not the main goal, it might prove to be easier for the mixer. More common, though, is a checkerboard layout, with an A track and underneath it a B track. The actual number of Pro Tools tracks is less important than the mix outputs or inputs available for music. Any number for Pro Tools tracks can be output to the same sub-master or master fader track.

When building a multi-track composed score, the music editor can choose to line up the orchestral music stems in a certain order. If this has already been pre-determined by the music mixer and composer, it's best to maintain the same order that the

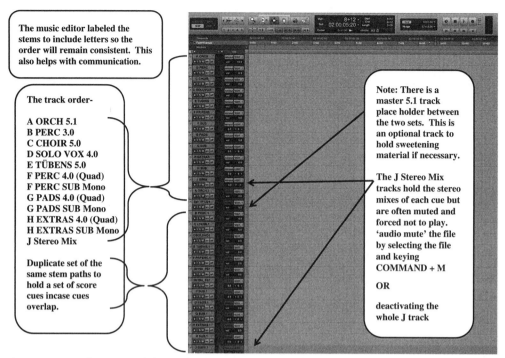

The music editor labeled the stems to include letters so the order will remain consistent. This also helps with communication.

The track order-

A ORCH 5.1
B PERC 3.0
C CHOIR 5.0
D SOLO VOX 4.0
E TÜBENS 5.0
F PERC 4.0 (Quad)
F PERC SUB Mono
G PADS 4.0 (Quad)
G PADS SUB Mono
H EXTRAS 4.0 (Quad)
H EXTRAS SUB Mono
J Stereo Mix

Duplicate set of the same stem paths to hold a set of score cues incase cues overlap.

Note: There is a master 5.1 track place holder between the two sets. This is an optional track to hold sweetening material if necessary.

The J Stereo Mix tracks hold the stereo mixes of each cue but are often muted and forced not to play. 'audio mute' the file by selecting the file and keying COMMAND + M

OR

deactivating the whole J track

Figure 10.3 Basic score track layout for the re-recording mixer looks like this example. Starting from top to bottom, the tracks descend from the most prevalent music stem to the lowest track, represented by a stem that might be the least used on the overall score. Note: This ordering is always changeable, and often determined by the composer's mixer or the music editor.

music stems were in when they were delivered to the music editor. If left to my choosing, the following is a basic guide I like to use. From top to bottom:

- Orchestra or strings
- Woodwind
- Brass
- Percussion
- Piano
- Choir or vocals
- Solo instruments

There is a good reason for consistently ordering score, source, and songs, bearing in mind that the music–dialogue mixer sits in the center of the console, and the sound effects mixer sits to the right. (Of course, this can be reversed, or there could be only one mixer, as alluded to before.) The logic follows that when these tracks and on-camera music are laid out on the mixing board, the low-number tracks, or top tracks in Pro Tools, will map to the very far left of the mixer's seat position at the console, and the higher-numbered tracks closer to their left side, within arm's reach (Figure 10.3). When dealing with ten, twenty, or fifty stems, in order for the mixer to reach and adjust the orchestra section music-track faders, he or she will have to roll their chair to the far left. However, the score should have been mixed by the music mixer and composed to play in a balanced fashion against dialogue and sound effects. Except for an overall lower volume from unity or certain extreme circumstances, the music score should be able to be left on its own to play, without the re-recording mixer having to move across to the left and adjust the individual levels of separate stems. With this situation in mind, the score can therefore be set to play on the far left, and the remaining music elements play from the console, as the layout gets closer to the re-recording mixer's sitting position, therefore keeping him or her closer to the center of the screen of the movie. In a session that might contain score, songs, and multi-track on-camera songs, the music tracks closest to the mixer's left side will be the on-camera song vocals and instrumental tracks, making it an easy reach for the him or her to balance this most complicated and challenging musical element at that moment in the film.

This track layout design will serve in most all situations. Even if a music editor doesn't prepare their track layout in this way, there are mixing techniques that can deal with wide track layouts. If a mixer is using a Pro Tools console-controller, they can bank and select groups of music to place the fader controls physically closer to their left side, preventing the need to roll their chair long distances. In addition, the mixer usually makes a sub-fader that can control multi-track groups with one fader. This also facilitates the functionality of the mixing process.

In the score session in Figure 10.4, some cues are presented in mono tracks one for each channel—5.1, LCR, Tracks, etc.—and stereo mixed stems are set in stereo output tracks. This is usually because the mixer has requested that any music stem in a 5.1, 5.0, LCR, or Quad format be split into its mono complements. However, stereo music material should reside on a stereo track. This score has music cues that were mixed in an orchestra format with the following stem types: Orch—5.0, Harp/Mallets/Brass—5.0, Piano—5.0, and Percussion—5.1. The stereo-only cues were of a different style of music and included: Bass, Piano, Vibes, Windchimes, Sample Strings, Kenon, and Bansur. Although this mixture of track types is common and can be built for ease of mixing.

Figure 10.5 shows a one-hour movie built in a single Pro Tools session. At the mixer's request, even though score cues overlap, the music editor placed all the multi-track score music on one set of tracks. To address cues crossing from one to another, the use of Pro Tools cross-fades was necessary. Note that the small cross-fade window box and the individual incoming and outgoing fade pre-sets windows show a picture of an upside-down and backwards L shape, which when applied to the crossing of the two audio files allows for the sound from the incoming music to occur immediately, with no gradual volume increase or decrease—appropriate for this figure and its purpose: to cross fade from the outgoing musics' smooth fade out to a clean, full entrance of the next piece!

Figure 10.6a shows a set of score tracks prepared for the mixer in panels of A and B. Alternating the score cues allows the music to clearly overlap or segue from and into each other. Not only is this a clear visual representation of the music playing, but a practical one, because the music cues were written and designed to cross seamlessly. It is important to note that while this is an acceptable method for the music editor to prepare tracks for the dub, some re-recording mixers prefer the music be combined and placed on one set of tracks. If it is possible for the music editor to do this using

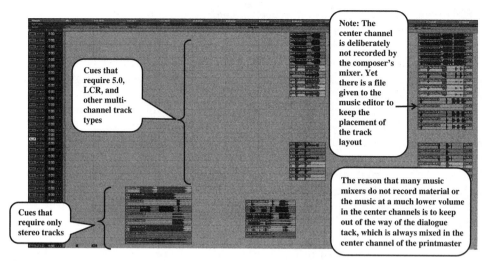

Figure 10.4 Typical multi-channel tracks as a mono and stereo track layout.

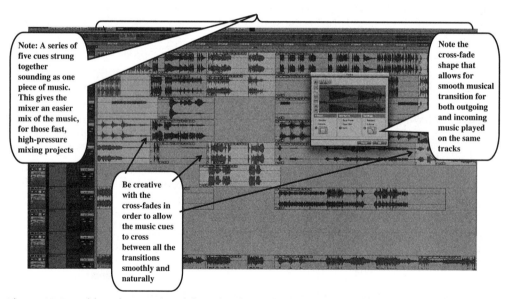

Figure 10.5 Multi-track score material overlapping and played on the same tracks, as per request by the re-recording mixer.

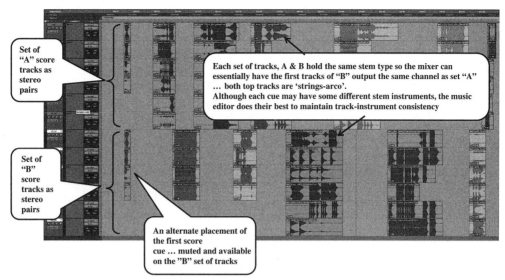

Figure 10.6a Multi-track score material overlapping and played on separate A and B sets of tracks.

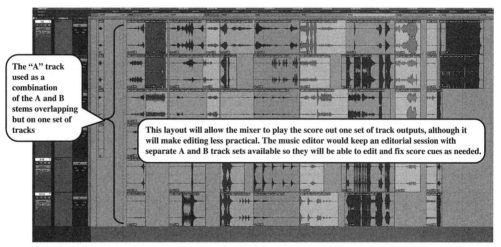

Figure 10.6b Here is an actual session view of the previous figures' score cues combined onto one panel as requested by the re-recording mixer. This would entail the music editor moving the previous B set of tracks up into the top A set of tracks. It is important for the music editor to hold Control after grabbing the files to move up, in order that they stay in the correct position. Another way would be to copy and paste while maintaining the selection (if these files have been time-locked, they can be moved up or down while maintaining sync without using additional modifiers). The music editor would then need to create any cross fades necessary to assure the music plays seamlessly.

cross-fades, and making sure all the music sounds and outputs correctly, this is a perfectly feasible way to build the session, as noted in both Figure 10.5 and Figure 10.6b.

10.5.3 Source Track Layout

Songs as source tracks are usually cut from stereo pairs, and therefore use stereo tracks in your Pro Tools session. Their track output, however, is most often set to separate I/O (input/output) channels. Depending on the complexity and quantity of source songs, it is optimum for song, score, or source material to have a track layout that reflects the individual song's sonic position in the movie. For example, all songs that will be playing from a re-occurring source, such as a car radio or someone's iPod, should be on the same tracks/channels. This will allow the mixer to set a certain consistent level and EQ for the specific re-occurring music track, as the audience hears it more than once. This being said, the mixer will expect to adjust the music sound coming from this re-occurring device, depending on the specific song's production value and other specific variables such as perspective cuts.

The other consideration regarding the placement of source music tracks is the presentation of alternative choices for the mixer. As discussed earlier in this book, the final decisions regarding songs in a movie can often be left until the final mix, in which case the music editor may have prepared various choices to play at the dub for the director and/or music supervisor. In order to be very clear about which song is to be played first, the music editor should "clip" mute the alternative choices that are cut and yet still available in the Pro Tools edit window. The mixer can then choose other cuts to play by muting and un-muting the alternatives, using Command + M (Mac) or Control + M (Windows) while the selecting the full clip(s) edge to edge. The mixer or music editor may want to pre-set these song alternatives to play out of the same channel outputs, in case the mixer has prepared the sound qualities to address the specific usage in the scene.

In a situation of perspective cutting, as described in Chapter 5, the music editor can prepare a separate set of tracks that retain the different camera perspectives reflected in the splitting of the song on those POV changes. Any number of stereo pairs as needed can be prepared this way. Another challenge to music editing with perspectives and alternatives comes when the director or music supervisor wants to hear an alternative positioning, or internal edits of any song choice.

The remaining track layouts for a mixer are songs with split vocal and instrumental tracks, and on-camera song stems. While working with either of these types of song preparations, it is essential to maintain sync and track consistency. Even though the mixer will likely bus these stems to sub-master faders, and will be viewing the waveforms in the Pro Tools Edit window, labeling and consistency is still very important.

To help the mixer blend a song from its use in the movie from "scource" to "source" or vice-versa, the music editor should place the exact same song edit on two adjacent tracks. The mixer then prepares each track to sound differently in the mix, and gradually cross-fades between the two. Pictured, in Figure 10.8, is a similar situation, but in this case the stereo track that starts the scene is playing on a radio, then shifts to being played as "scource." The music editor gives the mixer control over the sound for the scource performance by providing split tracks, one stereo voice track and one stereo instrumental track. These will blend in sync from the out-going stereo master track playing as the radio source.

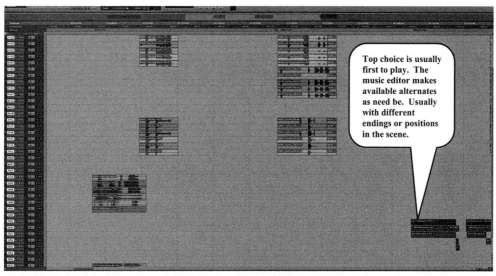

Figure 10.7 The source track positioned below the score material shows alternative cuts available for the mixer and the director to choose from. The music editor's preferred track is usually placed on top, with the alternative choices below. Note that here there are alternative endings available. One could also have alternative song titles to choose from. Often it is preferable to use "clip" muting rather than track muting, so that there is no question for the mixer as to what music should be played, and what is available as an alternative.

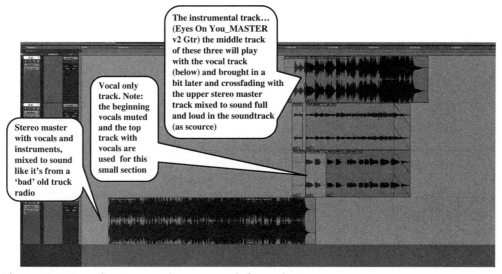

Figure 10.8 Preparing source and scource music for a mixer.

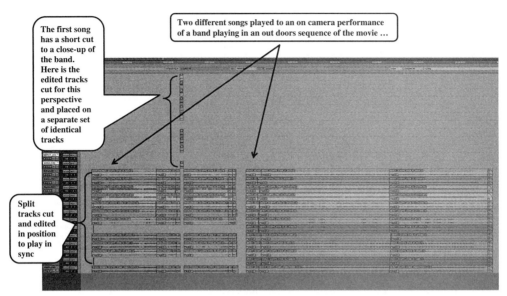

Figure 10.9 The music editor should acquire multi-track splits stems of a song to prepare for the dub of a featured on-camera performance. In this example, the artist delivered to the music editor the following tracks of their song: Bass, Guitars, Lead Vocal, Lead Vocal Reverb, Background Vocals, Drum Kit, and separate Kick and Snare tracks. In addition, a reference master mixer track is at the bottom, edited appropriately but muted.

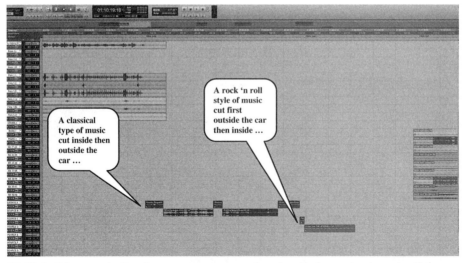

Figure 10.10 In this example, the stereo source cues are placed on their own tracks and split for perspective. At first the song plays from the camera's POV, or the audience's, hearing the song inside a car, then outside the car and so on. This is reflected on alternating tracks. The second song is cut from outside the car to inside the car. Note it has its own set of separate tracks, because it is a totally different type of music than the first piece, and will be treated differently by the mixer, even though the music is coming from the same car and the same source!

10.6 STEMS ORDER AND LABELING

Along with track layout, the proper labeling of tracks and audio files is valuable to the mixer. The music editor should pay attention to the score tracks' nameplates and keep them consistent. In addition, some tracks' music information can be placed in the Comments field for each track. This field is sometimes more visible to the mixer on their console, and will help them verify what instruments they are hearing on any one specific track or stem. With regards to multi-track score stems, the actual sound of the audio may not always exactly match the label of the stem. For example, a low percussion stem might not necessarily be a drum sound, but a low synthesizer with percussive elements. The music editor can make note of these situations and either label the comments with more detail, or inform the mixer another way about the slight variation between the label and the sound.

Regarding songs as source music, tracks are usually labeled in the most simple and consistent way, i.e., stereo source tracks could be labeled simply as SRC A, SRC B etc. The details of what occurs on each of those tracks can be understood by its track position, comment information, and perhaps descriptions written in the audio file's clip name: for example, master, vocals, instrumental, or drums, etc.

10.7 ETIQUETTE ON THE MIX STAGE

Once the music editor has prepared the music stems, songs, and any other music for the project, there can be requests for music changes or fixes during the dub. While ideally the music would be pre-approved by the director, there can be situations where the director, producer, music supervisor, or composer wants to change or edit the music. As noted in previous chapters, this can happen at any time for any reason. Aside from the picture changing and the need to conform the music, any part of the music might receive a request for further editing.

In these situations the age-old adage comes into play: "Choose your battles wisely." As the representative and protector of the music, the music editor must at this point evaluate the request for a music edit and make the necessary judgment and technical decisions, and in an ideal situation, there would be plenty of time for this before they had to present a conceptual idea or an actual audio edit. Here are some of the considerations and questions that may occur to the music editor when faced with an editing request:

- Is the edit request reasonable in terms of not altering the composer's dramatic intention of the piece of music?
- Will an edit force an altering of the music in a non-musical way?
- Can the edit request be implemented quickly and with musicality?
- Can the reason for the edit be implemented by a mixer's volume change perhaps, within the music stem itself, therefore avoiding an edit?
- Review the offending area in the movie and consider who is making the request for a change. If the suggestions seem too radical, talk with the sound department or mixer to see if there are other elements of the soundtrack (voice-over dialogue or effects) that can perhaps be added or taken away to help realize a solution.

PAX Quote

"I always look at it in military terms: If the person requesting the edit has more stripes than you, but fewer than the director or composer, you should recommend that they all have a chat."

- Is the piece of music to be edited a major thematic part of the drama in the movie, such as for the main title, emotional climax of the film, end title, or finale? If so, can the director be convinced to re-consider the edit idea?
- Can adding, deleting, mixing lower or higher one or part of the music stems achieve the desired effect, without adversely affecting the musical integrity of the music?
- Can the editor modify only one or a few stems within the piece without affecting the overall emphasis of the cue?

The goal of the music editor on the final mix stage is to respect and retain the composer's musical intentions at all times. Prior to the final mix, the music editor should have a discussion with the composer regarding their opinion of the director's request to music edits or changes on the final mix stage. Most composers are happy to relinquish their emotional ties to their music to make the director happy.

PAX Quote

"But beware making a change for a film editor or executive without direct approval from a commanding general!"

However, this goes hand in hand with the trusting nature of the music editor and composer's relationship. The music editor should always be very familiar with the composer's music, including the style of their writing, orchestrating, and the direction of the movie's score.

PAX Quote

"This is so true. You could write a whole chapter on trust between music editor and composer. If you even once violate this trust, your working relationship will never be the same. You can make editorial mistakes, but always be the composer's best and most trusted ally. I actually think great friendships are formed here. A nice perk."

10.8 FIXES ON THE MIX STAGE

One of the most critical jobs for a music editor is editing music while on the stage at the final dub of a movie. Sometimes this situation can be unnerving and pressurised, such as when the mixer has stopped the mix and is waiting for you to fix the music and send it to them, although the mixer will usually move ahead in the mix, giving you some time to do your edit, audition for the director, and deliver to them. At this juncture, you must do your best to avoid delaying the mixing process and work quickly, efficiently, and carefully.

While I will go on to describe in detail two ways to send audio fixes to a mixer (in Sections 10.8.1 and 10.8.2), there are of course multiple ways to transfer audio materials across computer systems on a mix stage. It should suffice here to simply mention some of the other possibilities, rather than go into the details, assuming that you the reader will either be familiar with these procedures, or investigate and practice them on your own.

- **Export clips as files.** This is a fast way to save and send one or more clips as separate files. If you have a multiple edited piece of music, you can save a copy of the edited work and then consolidate the edits to export the clip as a single file. Remember to time-stamp the file and even embed the file timecode location in the file name.
- **Export clip definition.** This is less common, as it requires a re-linking on the part of the Pro Tools system receiving the file edit information.
- **Bounce selected soloed track(s) to make a consolidated audio file.** Use Bounce to Disk to achieve this by soloing the tracks with audio that you want to bounce. If you have not made a specific selection, your curser can be placed anywhere in the track timeline, and the whole track's audio will be bounced up to the longest file in the edit window.*
- **Bounce selections from a consolidated audio file.** After you have consolidated your edited music clips, use Bounce to Disk after selecting the specific audio file(s) you want to bounce.*
- **Export tracks as AAF or OMFI file transfer data.**

---

*Tip

New to Pro Tools 11 you can use "offline" bounce. This Bounce to Disk is considerably faster and more efficient than previous versions of Pro Tools, and includes the option to bounce an MP3 file format at the same time as your main file-type selection.

On the technical side of working on the mix stage, there are a number of work-flows the music editor should be familiar with.

In many mixes on medium- or high-budget films or TV shows, the music editor will have a Pro Tools rig on the mix stage, with the final music sessions ready to play back in sync with the movie controlled by the music re-recording mixer usually through SMPTE time code lock. Current practice also utilizes the Satellite synchronization protocol by Avid. This music editor's Pro Tools system needs to be locked or resolved to the "house" sync, which the mix stage sends to all Pro Tools systems and dubbers playing back for the mix. The resolved clock is usually an SD or HD video reference, or a word clock. In order to work this way, the music editor's system needs a Sync HD (or Sync I/O) or similar third party interface that can receive the clock and resolve the playback of the Pro Tools session (Pro Tools 11 requires the latest model of the Sync HD). You need to make sure the session's sample rate, and bit rate, matches the mixer's other Pro Tools sessions and digital setting of the mixing console. This is of particular importance if the mixing console is not a Pro Tools controller, and will be receiving the sound information from the music editor's rig via an analogue or digital protocol. If using digital, and the sample rate and bit rate do not match, there is a great likelihood that the sound files will come across to the mixer with digital pops, digital distortion, or at the wrong playback speed. Once the music playback system is connected and configured properly, the mixer can easily play and re-play all of the music in real time, along with the other soundtrack elements (dialogue and sound effects).

While the music is being played through this system, the music editor needs to be able to make changes to the music as required, and perhaps be able to prepare upcoming music for the mixer. The music editor can either edit on the playback system or have a second Pro Tools rig available for this purpose. A second available system is ideal, because if there is a need to make extensive edits, the mixer can keep mixing forward in the reel while you work. Current computer technology allows the use of laptops as a second Pro Tools system for this situation, since they now possess enough power and controllability. To have everyone waiting for you on the stage while you make an editorial change is not only harrowing, it is very expensive.

While this double system workflow is a good way for the music editor to manage the music for the mix, current trends allow for an alternative workflow. Most re-recording mixers view and access multiple Pro Tools systems, feeding sound to the mixing stage's console directly from the machine room (a room separate and isolated from the mixing area or mixing stage, that holds the audio playback, recording systems, and video projection). The mixer will either work in one super session, or sessions per reel, and can be set up to switch between separate locked Pro Tools rigs, or have all the sound material loaded into one master Pro Tools system that is integrated into the stage. The music editor makes a complete prepared music session that they then hand over to the machine room for the re-recording mixer to import into their Pro Tools mix rig. In either of these cases, the music editor will be free to use one Pro Tools system on the stage for preparation and/or editing. Ideally the music editor would have a small room on or near the mixing stage, where they can still make themselves available to the director and re-recording mixer while having a private space. More commonly, the music editor is required to be on the mix stage with their editing rig, and in this case, they use headphones to hear what they are editing, trying not to be sonically interrupted as the mix plays through the enormous theater speakers. If working in a side room, it is important for the music editor to have both speakers set up, as well as headphones. Whether you are on the stage itself or in a side room, most of your fixes on the stage will be sent to the mixer through one or more of the following ways.

These are only two examples of a workflow. As noted previously, there may be many ways to deliver music to the re-recording mixer.

10.8.1 Delivering Edited Materials to the Re-recording Mixer—Example 1

If you are using any version of Pro Tools:

1. You should be editing in a session that matches the session you gave to the re-recording mixer via the machine room's Pro Tools system. In this working edit session, make an empty set of matching duplicated music tracks where the edit is to take place.

2. Select the music cue over its clip boundaries and hold Control + Option (Mac) or Start + Alt (Windows) and drag a copy of the music cue to be edited onto the new blank tracks in the same layout as the music stems. You can of course select the cue, and copy and paste it below, being careful to keep it in its exact sync position.

3. It is often helpful to label the tracks that will hold the edited music as "fix" tracks, or perhaps the cue number and something like "fix-A." This will help make sure you send the correct edit to the mixer. Another way to distinguish between the separate tracks that will hold the music edit is to create two AUX tracks: one placed above and the other placed below the duplicated tracks that contain the edited material. These are used for visual purposes only, as they clearly look different in relation to the standard audio track. These two AUX tracks are only for internal bussing, therefore they do not use any additional Pro Tools audio voices. Often I will label the first of these AUX tracks "2m3_fix_A_below," meaning the tracks below this AUX track begin the edited material, and the second AUX track "2m3_fix_A_above," indicating the end of the selected edited tracks.

4. Edit the musical passage as deemed necessary and requested. Feel free to create alternative edits as your musical interpretation dictates. Edit and cross-fade stems, listening to them as separate elements, and do not rely on only one cross-fade through all the stems tracks. Make all the edits, deletions, duplication, and crossfading of music material sound natural and smooth, as if the composer had written and recorded it that way.

5. Invite the director to listen to and approve your newly edited material. While some directors will just tell you to hand your work over to the mixer to play on the big speakers in the main room, without hearing it first, it is better to have them listen to your material in your separate room or even on headphones if you are situated on the mix stage. If the edited material plays in the big room and doesn't meet with the director's approval this will add inefficient additional time to the mix and you still need to go back and re-do the edit again.

   If possible, play your edited musical material over speakers and not headphones, and be sure to play it with the dialogue and effects track in a basic level balance with the music. Do your best to edit with the director's exact request in mind. If you have edited the material with alternatives or options, you can take this opportunity to "sell" your favorite option for the fix, particularly if it might be slightly different from what the director asked for in the first place, and explain why you feel it is the best one to use.

6. When the edited materials are approved, you can send the tracks to the mixer. Make a new Pro Tools session with the same set-up parameters as the mixer's session, then choose File > Import > Session Data. Locate the working session where your edited materials reside, and select only those tracks where you have the fixed music cue. This is why, in large sessions, it is helpful to have the AUX tracks labeled "below" and "above," so you import the correct edited material. You can select Link Audio instead of Copy Audio, because in Step 8 you'll prepare the tracks for the mixer, and will be copying the audio.

7. Make a folder in your project directory called Stage Fixes, or something similar. This will hold the sessions that will be sent to the mixer.

8. Save this session as a Save Copy In session called "2m6_Fix_A ..." with perhaps a scene descriptor in the session title to indicate more information. At this time, enable the option to include All Audio Files. This will copy all of the audio for the music, including the edits you made, placing them into the Stage Fixes folder you made. An alternative way to do this is to make a new blank Pro Tools session as in step 6, and import session data while copying the audio tracks you select. This makes a new session with new audio files of your edited materials.

9. After you have made a session with the music edits and a copy of the audio (remember the advice here is to give the mixer newly copied audio files instead of forcing them to re-link to their original files), locate the folder that links (usually via a LAN network) to the re-recording music mixer's computer and upload your "fix" session, including the audio files folder to the mixer's computer directory.

   After this is complete, the mixer can import the session data of your fixed music piece, in sync, into their master mixing session.

> **Tip**
>
> The advice to give the mixer new audio files, even though they may already have the original audio in their session, insures that the edited music gets to the mixer's tracks without them having to take the time to re-link (sometimes the edited audio session information will not re-link properly). It is important that at the completion of the dub, the mixer's Pro Tools session of the music that has been mixed in the movie should be saved, using Save Copy In, including audio, to protect against re-linked audio files that may end up missing if this is not done.

It is important to note that you may want to remind the mixer to set their Pro Tools session to *not* import automation from the files you are sending.There is a rectangular button on the edit window of Pro Tools called Automation Follows Edit. It is a toggle on–off button that turns blue when enabled and orange when disabled (when using Pro Tools 11.x software). Your fix session should not have any volume, panning, EQ, or plug-in automation you feel they are absolutely necessary and critical for the mixer to use. When your fixed music is brought into the already existing music cue tracks of the mixer's session with Automation Follows Edits enabled, any automation moves the mixer has already made (including volumes, panning, plugins, or EQ) will be deleted and overwritten by the imported fix files, therefore making the fixed section of music void of the mixer's previous automation. Instead of delivering one small fix section, you can give the mixer the whole music cue, containing the one small edited area. This way you allow them to choose to overwrite or replace the entire original piece containing the new edit, with Automation Follows Edit disabled thus maintaining their automation and perhaps allowing for an easier way to re-mix the cue with the fix.

If the mixer decides to import the fix music edited piece by linking to the audio from the fix music session, the file will point to the Fix File audio folder. If the mixer copies the audio files from the fix session and imports into the mix session, Pro Tools stamps each file a new unique identifier, even though the name may be the same. Both procedures can work for the mixer, but to insure that the musical edit gets to the mixer without any technical errors, a re-copying of the audio is less risky than allowing Pro Tools to re-link to the original audio files. If the mixer linked the files to their original ones in the mixer's session, they should then be able to heal the separated edit at the point where the edited piece overlaid the inside original piece. Note that there is a difference when using the copy function from the Import Session Data window and the Import Audio window.

10.8.2 Delivering Edited Materials to the Re-recording Mixer—Example 2

If you are using Pro Tools 10 or later:

Replacing steps 6 through 9. Instead of making a new Pro Tools session to hold your edited material, Pro Tools 10 and above has the menu option to select tracks to export as a session. While still in your main editing session, highlight the nameplates that fall between the AUX lines labeled as "below" and "above," then choose File > Export > Selected Tracks As New Session. Include the option to include All Audio Files and then hit OK. Re-name the session with a label that describes the fix, something like "2m6_fix_A_car chase_for mixer." Locate the LAN (local area network) folder on the mix stage that allows the mixer to access the files and click OK. A new Pro Tools session will be made holding the new audio of your edited piece of music. This process is fast and accurate, saving considerable time in the music editor's and mixer's workflow.

It is practical to utilize the new features in Pro Tools 10 and 11 that enable exporting selected tracks as a new Pro Tools session. In this example (Figure 10.11a) the music editor made a set of tracks below the main session track playlists. These tracks will hold any fixes or edits needed to be sent to the re-recording mixer, who will then input the new or revised music into the master dubbing session. Figure 10.11a shows a newly created piece of music, edited by the music editor from the composer's score. This added transition cue was a request from the director. The edits are made in the fix tracks, then the track nameplates are selected before choosing from the menu: File > Export > Selected Tracks as New Session. Because there is nothing else on these exported tracks,

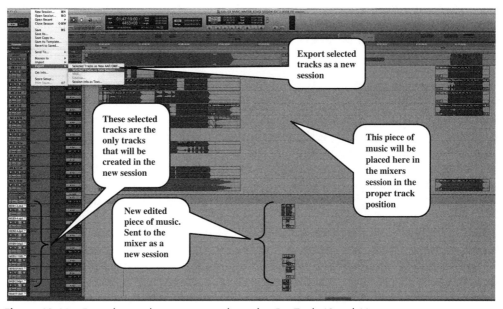

Figure 10.11a Exporting tracks as a new session using Pro Tools 10 and 11.

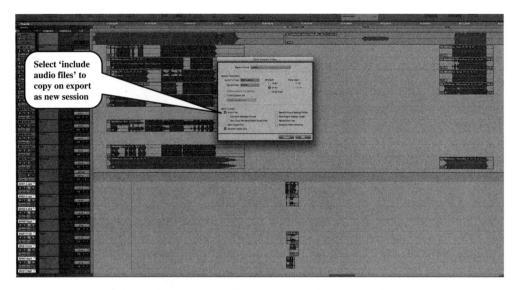

Figure 10.11b Exporting tracks as a new session using Pro Tools 10 and 11 (continued).

the mixer will receive this newly created piece of music as a single session, including new audio files, and already in sync, ready to place into the master mix session.

The next automatic step Pro Tools takes you to is the Save Session Copy In window, giving you the option, in selecting Items To Copy, to include audio or not. It is recommended that you select Include Audio, since the mixer's session may or may not have the audio files you are sending in the new session. If you do not include the newly copied audio, the mixer's Pro Tools session will then need to search and link to the imported files. While this may not be a problem, time is of the essence in preparing and sending fixes to the stage mixer, and any time saved is important. Therefore it is optimum for the music editor to create new audio from the files they are sending. Fixes are often minimal in size, so the space on drives is usually not an issue.

10.9 KEEP CALM

Keep calm. Be quiet. Unless there is something to say about what the mixer is doing or how they are mixing the music, don't say anything. If there is small talk amongst the director or producer, you can comment or join in, but most often, I don't start an unnecessary conversation. Talking in the room is the prerogative of the director or producer. Talking that goes on behind the mixers is very distracting, although most mixers will do their best to listen through any talking they hear behind them.

There can be many reasons to get nervous or upset on a mix stage and I have experienced many different pressures there. It's not easy editing music directly at the mixing console while everyone is waiting for you and listening to the editing process. This is nerve wracking no matter how you cut it. No pun intended. How you handle yourself on that stage shows all your peers and bosses and future colleagues how professional you are. Working through the pressure takes practice and time, and every mix is a new challenging experience. These challenges, as well as the positive experiences, are what keep this work interesting and fun. Conflicts can arise out of the egos of people feeling that another person is purposely trying to place them in a bad light—you've heard the term "thrown under the bus." The best way to handle internal personal dynamics on a mix stage, however, is to stay calm, don't get emotional, and know that most likely it's not about you, it's about the other person's ego and insecurities in relation to the job at hand.

The mixing of a movie soundtrack is a fluid, ever-changing process. It is fast-paced, high-pressure work—even more reason for the sound departments, including music, to be prepared, organized, and ready for any requests or technical issues that might come to their attention—and the ability to communicate in a straightforward and not overly dictatorial manner is an acquired but necessary skill. Note the following interview containing some real-life experiences at the final mix.

10.10 INDUSTRY INSIDER: GARY BOURGEOIS, RE-RECORDING MIXER

1. **How would you describe your role as it relates to the overall success of a film or television show? What are some of the key skill sets your job requires?**

   The key role of the re-recording mixer is to blend the three main elements of sound for a show (dialogue, music, effects) in a way that communicates to an audience what it is that the director intends to say. Working closely with the music editor, picture editor, and sound supervisor, one hopes to achieve the desired effect as a team. If successful, then the craft of sound is quite often to support and bring a "patina" to the final product that the audience simply blends into the overall experience. If the requirement is to be bold and bombastic then it must still be within the framework of not taking over the visual. In mixing, a great sense of rhythm is needed. Not just in the interpretation of the flow of the sound but also of the picture editing and sensibility of the tone of the film itself. A mixer must know how to present an overall volume that makes it easy to hear the dialogue without it hurting the ears when too loud and yet not so low as to miss what is being said. The effects should create the atmosphere around us so as to put us in that place and also be effective in massaging us in emotional ways also. The music, played properly, can have the ability to say so much and either lead us or support the action where necessary. Playing the music just right can make the audience cry, but alternatively, when played incorrectly, can leave the scene flat. Quite often it is the mixer's role to find just that right balance to be effective.

2. **What are some of the similarities and differences between working on low-budget and high-budget films?**

   The greatest difference between a high- or low-budget show is in the preparation. The target result is the same. Inevitably the quality of preparation that comes to me on a high-budget picture is from professionals, having been given the time and resources needed. A lower budget picture usually is short of that same care and energy, and yet we are supposed to solve all the problems with no time and no money. Greater challenges sometimes are rewarding but only if the efforts have been appreciated!

3. **How do you see the music editor's role, as it pertains to the overall involvement of music production? Particularly in terms of their technical, musical or interpersonal skills, or any other qualities they bring to their work?**

The music editor's role varies quite a bit according to numerous elements involved. Ideally one is hired at the same time as the composer and brought into the process at the onset. In the director/composer spotting session, the music editor can have great input as to the pacing of the overall score, and adds opinions on starts and endings, etc. An experienced composer with a longtime editing partner has shorthand about these things but a newer composer or director can learn a lot from an experienced editor. At the subsequent scoring session the editor is like mother hen, and keeps all the information and flow of the session together. On the mix stage the music is prepared for the mixer in ways that make the process flow well also. When changes are necessary because of picture edits or simply a change of attitude towards a scene, then the music editor knows best how to do that and what resources are available to him/her. The music editor, throughout the process, must understand all the technical requirements of the scoring engineer and also the re-recording mixers, and be able to liaise with each effectively. Most music editors (not all) are musicians or have studied music composition, and apply that knowledge when editing so as to create a seamless flow. On the mix stage, that is one of the most important roles. The music editor, like the sound supervisor and mixer, must have the ability to interpret what it is that the director wants and put it into action with expediency.

4. **How do you envision your role in postproduction evolving in future, particularly in terms of budgets and expectations?**

Tough question, requiring a crystal ball … . I have been mixing for over 40 years and have seen many changes, technological as well as philosophical, and many attitude shifts. Some changes are due to the technology and some because of filmmaking style. Although I have constantly embraced many new ways of doing something, the end result seems to be the constant. Roles of various crafts are being redefined and I find that some people have a hard time accepting that. Change is inevitable and one has to see the bigger picture in order to continue to be involved. Sometimes change is not appreciated at first and the feeling is that the craft is being subverted. Yet I have been through so many changes and I always find myself doing high quality work and having fun doing so. Keeping an open mind as to how we define ourselves is a key factor in survival.

5. **Is there a situation in the postproduction industry where it's appropriate or even advantageous for the composer to mix and produce his or her own music, perhaps without the help of a music mixer, orchestrator, programmer, music editor, or other team members?**

I am one who believes in a team effort and consequently feel that a collaboration of professionals will generally have superior results. It is very difficult for one person to know all the elements involved in each person's craft. Most experienced composers know what is needed and inevitably conclude that hiring suitable help is preferred. Those who choose to do everything solo inevitably short-change themselves, and others down the line in the process.

6. **From your experience of working with many music editors, what are the skill sets that are crucial for their success in this industry?**

Most craft people in the industry vary in their abilities and strengths. Relationships are built on need: if a director or picture editor needs someone to simply be a "set of hands" then the relationship is usually short lived; on the other hand, mutual respect for one's talents, and what one brings to the table, usually ensures a longer-term relationship. Identifying that need is crucial for the talent. If you are a "problem solver" and not a "problem maker", then your value is realized. Diplomacy, an ability to communicate well, being able to stand up for your opinion as well as being able to bend are all characteristics that will be appreciated. High standards and being ethical go a long way also … .

Chapter 11
Delivery Requirements

11.1 HAND IT OVER

As postproduction winds down, it is customary for the music editor to compile all of the pertinent data and musical materials from the film, including the music cue sheet (see section 11.5). These are part of the delivery requirements, and the responsibility of the music editor. The Pro Tools final mix session should be acquired by the music editor from the mixer, with all the audio copied intact, unless the film was mixed from music that came exclusively from the music editor's rig, in which case you already have it.

11.2 DATA DELIVERY OF MEDIA

In most all projects, the film or television production company will require some kind of delivery of the music media. If the film is being sold, the buyer may require certain deliverables, and if the film or TV show is being broadcast or created as a Video on Demand (VOD), those requirements may be different. Any or all of the following items may need to be compiled by the music editor for delivery:

- Stereo master files of the music score cues as originally written and recorded by the composer.
- Stereo master files of the musical score cues as edited in the film, but without volume moves made by the mixer.
- Stereo master files of all of the songs and source music in their full-length unedited versions.
- The complete printed manuscripts of the conductor's score music (excluding the separate musical parts and condensed score).
- The composer's stem mixes of the musical score.
- The full archived Pro Tools sessions, including all the master score music, all the songs and source music, as well as the music printmaster that was made on the dub stage. This is usually in the form of a 5.1 or 7.1 music stem.
- The Preliminary Music Cue Sheet, sometimes delivered and saved in multiple document formats and as a Data file.

11.3 CREATING STEREO MASTERS FOR DELIVERY

After the music editor imports the printmaster music stems and calculates the cue sheet times (see 11.5), they will then create the stereo music tracks for delivery. While the composer will have printed (recorded) stereo mixes of the score along with the score stems, the music editor may also make crashdowns or fold-downs of the multi-track score cues.

Figure 11.1 below shows a super session prepared for delivery. Note that this session includes the printmaster 5.1 music stems to verify and measure the lengths of the music cues. Printmaster is the final balanced soundtrack of the film containing at least three separate 5.1 stems, one each for dialogue, sound effects, and music. When these three stems all play together the resulting sound is what gets printed as the optical track or in the DCP for delivery of the finished film. Also, the multi-track stems of each 5.1, 5.0, LCR, and Quad track are "split into mono" by holding Control (Mac), or right-click, or Start (Windows) while selecting sub menu on the multi-track name plates. Use the mono tracks to set individual fold-down levels and proper panning, to make stereo bounces of the master edited stems of the score and songs.

It's possible that the music editor's session, or the one that the mixer was working from, has the music cue stems already split into mono tracks. This would have been determined prior to the first day of the mix. However, if the stems are in multi-track format, split them into mono (but keep the stereo track in stereo) and then delete the multi-track stem tracks (see Figure 11.1). To make the audio delivery of stereo music

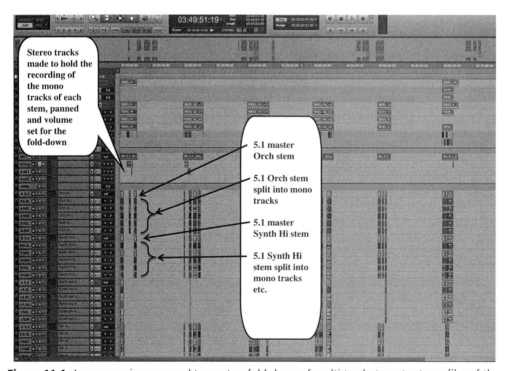

Figure 11.1 A super session prepared to create a fold-down of multi-track stems to stereo files of the score.

files, the multi-track formatted music stems of a cue will need to be outputted into a stereo field. It is particularly important for 5.1, 5.0, 7.1, and LCR stems to have each of their channels treated as a fold-down. Folding down a multichannel stem to a stereo one entails lowering the volume of certain channels to compensate for the transfer to a stereo sound field from a surround-sound or LCR track. It is common practice among engineers to have properly balanced 5.1 materials to work as a fold-down to stereo. Note that the music editor's session will not usually have volume changes in the music; however, if it does, then lower the volumes for a fold-down by using the Trim mode. To proceed with a fold-down, manually lower each channel of the music stems as follows:

> **For a 5.1 standard film mix:** (Note that there are different 5.1 channel assignments available for different mix situations. In which case follow the left, center, right, etc. labels. For 5.0 use the 5.1 example without the Channel 6.)
> **Ch 1** Left—Keep at "0" VU
> **Ch 2** Center—Lower to −3 dB
> **Ch 3** Right—Keep at "0" VU
> **Ch 4** Left Surround—Lower to −6 dB
> **Ch 5** Right Surround—Lower to −6 dB
> **Ch 6** Lfe—Lower to −6 dB (some mixers will exclude or mute the Lfe for the fold-down)
>
> **For an LCR:**
> **Ch 1** Left—Keep at "0" VU
> **Ch 2** Center—Lower to −3 dB
> **Ch 3** Right—Keep at "0" VU
>
> **For a Quad:**
> **Ch 1** Left—Keep at "0" VU
> **Ch 2** Right—Keep at "0" VU
> **Ch 3** Left Surround—Lower to −6 dB
> **Ch 4** Right Surround—Lower to −6 dB

While this process is often done manually track by track, there are third-party plugins available that claim to do automatic fold-downs to stereo. Two companies that supply these are Maggot, with its Spanner software, and Waves. While these plugins may work well, fold-down for postproduction does not have the extensive requirements as it might have for mastering, but simply to achieve a quality stereo track from an edited cue for archiving or making a music CD. Since a music editor usually implements a fold-down only a few times a year, the cost of such software is probably not justified.

Tip

"DownMixer" is a free Avid AAX Native plugin included with all Pro Tools HD systems, which works quite well and is designed for fold-down from 5.1 to stereo. It even includes pre-sets, or you can save your own settings.

If there are no edits in the score music stems, then the music editor can use the composer's stereo mix of the cue, which should have been delivered along with the stems from the music mixer. To maintain continuity, the music editor may wish to duplicate those stereo files and re-name them using the naming system, usually including the cue number and cue title.

This first set of stereo files represents the edited cues as they exist in the film, but at full volume (not from the printmaster music stems which contain volume changes balanced around dialogue and sound effects).

> **Tip**
>
> Carry the composer's stereo tracks in sync and grouped with your multi-track score, but keep them muted. Over the course of the dub, if you have to cut the multi-track music, these muted tracks will be cut with them. At the end of the project, you will have edited stereo tracks that match what is in the movie. Often there will be no need for a fold-down.

The second set of stereo files created is a representation of the composer's music as it was created for the film in its unedited state. These unedited stereo files may exist as part of the music sent to the music editor from the composer's mixer, and if this is the case, these stereo files can be used to directly archive this media for storage or making a CD. These tracks can also be used for a soundtrack CD for sale or marketing, although the composer may want to re-mix their music for this purpose.

Of course not all the music in a movie is edited, so there will be music cues that will be identical both in the "edited" set and "un-edited" set. In this case, both sets should still contain all the score cues, for consistency. Both sets of stereo music need a common, listenable medium, such as a CD, to verify any copyright issues that may arise with regards to the music licensed to the film. For CD compatibility, the music editor needs to convert the stereo files to AIFF (16-bit/44.1 kHz sample rate, interleaved), although most CD-burning software (such as Roxio Toast or Apple's iTunes) will take most any file format, bit rate, or sample rate, and convert the files to the CD standard during the burning process. If the music editor can convert to Red Book specification as a standard CD format, it is preferred, but not usually necessary.

After the multi-channel cues are set to the correct fold-down volume settings, it's time to bounce to disk. There are two basic ways to do this:

1. **Bounce tracks by recording**
   - Select a score cue to bounce, and output each of the channels to one stereo bus with correct volume and panning as described above and in the next section, 2a.
   - Solo only the stems you will be bouncing.
   - Create a new stereo track with its input path matching the same stereo bus output of the stems, arm it to record and solo it. In Pro Tools HD you can select input monitoring to listen through the stereo track before you record.
   - Select an area in the timeline covering the music cue, overlapping the beginning and end of the music duration by a second or two, then press Play and Record to record the cue onto the stereo track.

- Once the recording is complete, re-name the stereo music cue that was recorded using labeling similar to the following: "PR_01M02_EDIT_ST_ The capture." The name should include the following basic information: abbreviated film title, cue number, an indication that the music has or hasn't been edited (even if the cue has no edits in it, for consistency), number of channels, such as ST for stereo, and the cue title. The reason I usually write "edited" in the file name, even though that cue may not have actually been edited, is to show it should match the music in the finished film, after the printmaster is made, whether it was edited or not.

2a. Bounce to disk (Pro Tools 10 and lower versions)

- Select the score cue to bounce, and output each of the channels (including the mono tracks) to one stereo output. Check that the mono and stereo tracks of the score have the proper volume levels and have been panned correctly—Left for channel 1, Center for channel 2, Right for channel 3, etc.—for the proper fold-down from 5.1 and other surround formats.
- Solo only the stems you will be bouncing, then select an area in the timeline covering the music cue, overlapping the beginning and end of the music by a second or two.
- Choose File > Bounce To > Disk, and in the Bounce Source field, select the same output that all the music stems are set to, making the files the same sample rate and bit rate as the session. Usually your Pro Tools session will be set to 48 K and 24 bit, a higher quality than the 44.1/16 bit used for a CD. These files can be interleaved or multiple mono, but note that earlier versions of Pro Tools cannot import interleaved files directly. Create a new folder and location where the bounce will reside outside the main audio files folder of the session, and enable Import After Bounce.
- For a direct bounce for CD compatibility: Choose File > Bounce To > Disk, and make the Format choice: interleaved stereo, with the bit depth 16 bit, and the Sample Rate 44.1. This will make files compatible with listening or burning to a CD.

2b. Bounce to disk (Pro Tools 11)

- Select the score cue to bounce, and output each of the tracks to the same stereo output pair or use multiple outputs for printing stems (multiple output paths are supported in Pro Tools 11.x and higher). As in 2.a, make the selection a little outside the clip boundaries.
- Following the previous Bounce to Disk procedure, in Pro Tools 11 you can select "offline" bounce. The offline bounce function allows Pro Tools to bounce audio up to five times faster than real-time bounce (sometimes even faster, based on the complexity of the session and the available CPU processing resources). As in previous versions, you can also select the bounced file to be imported directly back into the Pro Tools session. If not checked, the offline bounce can be imported back into the session manually.
- For additional convenience, using Pro Tools 10 and 11 you can select Import After Bounce and Add to iTunes Library, and send to SoundCloud and Gobbler directly.

After the score stereo files are created and imported back into Pro Tools, select the songs and source music that were edited in the movie. If this music is already in an edited track, you should copy it and place it on an empty track, or locate a section of the song edit found in the clip bin and move it to an empty track. In either case the source/songs must be revealed using the trim tool to show their full-file original length for archiving. Even when revealed as a full audio file they can be consolidated or audio suite duplicated, then re-labeled in a similar way as the score, and stored in the archiving folder designated as Source and Songs, which is often separate from the score materials. Once you have all the music compiled in a stereo format, you can then burn a CD (or CDs) that contains all music in the film, in which case the songs can be included in an All MX CD, although each CD is limited to around 700 MB, or about 74 minutes of music.

11.4 ARCHIVING FOR DELIVERY

After the stereo music files are created and placed in their own data folder and/or as CDs, then the entirety of the final music Pro Tools sessions (if made from individual reels or as a super session) should be re-copied and made available as an archive. The best way to do this is to first select all music in the session that was not used in the final mix, which would include all score and song alternatives. Then make sure the music contains all the edit fixes that were done and make them playable from within the proper stems of each edited cue. From the Clips list menu, choose Select > Unused Audio Except Whole Files and clear the selected clips, which will clear from the Edit window and Clip list only the unused clip definitions, leaving all of the used clips and any whole audio files in the session. Another option is to clear unused audio only—this will clear from the session even whole files that are not used. It's actually pretty safe to clear all unused audio, because the goal is to archive only what was used in the final mix, but one still should be careful, and err on the cautious side. Choose File > Save Copy In... and in the Items to Copy section, select Audio Files and Movie/Video Files to include in the archived Pro Tools session. Incidentally, if you keep the session format as "latest" and you are using Pro Tools versions 10 or 11, if someone attempts to open your archived session with a previous version of Pro Tools, they will not be able to. To make the session compatible with older versions of Pro Tools, you can do a separate Save Copy In... but this time select the session format Pro Tools 7–9. While saving the session this way makes two full copies of the session file and its associated audio/video media, it is the safest way to archive the materials. If storage space is an issue, you can Save Copy In... using Pro Tools 10 and 11, and an additional Pro Tools Save Copy In... using Pro Tools 7–9, but in the case of the 7–9 save, do not select the audio or movie/video options. If Pro Tools version 10 or 11 included these files, then version 7–9 should be able to link to those files. This will save duplicating digital information unnecessarily.

An additional option for archiving the Pro Tools session is called "compacting." This has been a Pro Tools feature for many years, and was designed to clear and delete any unused audio in the session that is to be archived. Even the whole files that clips refer or point to will be deleted in part, according to the handle length the user designates in the Compact window. The handle length defaults to 1000 milliseconds, which translates to a 1-second handle on either side of each clip boundary within the whole file. The user can change this length as they wish. Before you use compacting, it is advisable to clear any audio clips that are not being used in the session, as described previously. While compacting sound files is possible, it is less commonly used today, as cloud-based backup solutions and new means of storage have increased capacity, and have also become less expensive.

11.5 MUSIC CUE SHEETS AND ROYALTIES

The last document that the music editor is responsible for is the music cue sheet, which is a document listing of all of the music in the film or TV show. Once completed, it is how composers, artists, songwriters, and music libraries receive performance royalties for the broadcast, cablecast, or Internet VOD programming, etc., of their music. Note that in North America, theatrical (movie theater) performances and exhibitions of a movie's soundtrack do not pay these kinds of royalties.

First, it is important to note that because these cue sheets become legal documents, the music editor should title the music cue sheet as Preliminary Music Cue Sheet—the music editor is not an attorney and should not be responsible for claiming the information in the cue sheet as legally binding. The music editor simply gives their information to the legal department, which in turn compiles the legal music cue sheet. This is then distributed to all the pertinent performance rights organizations (PROs), such as BMI, ASCAP, SESAC, and many others around the world. Many of these organizations have a web presence describing their individual style of collections, payments, and cue sheet information. The cue sheet can be delivered to the film's post-production company and directed specifically to their attorney or legal affairs agent. Common document formats are created as Microsoft Word or Excel documents, or possibly a PDF file. Each film company may have its own template that it requests the music editor fill in with pertinent information. It is a good idea for the music editor to retain copies of the music cue sheets, in both paper form and digitally, for any future questions. In addition, it is a good idea to keep the master Pro Tools sessions.

As discussed in the previous chapter, on the final dub, the music re-recording mixer often fades in and fades out music, occasionally editing as needed in the movie. In this case, the music editor acquires the mixer's final session with the music, and uses that material, comparing it to the final printmaster stems to determine the correct information for the music cue sheet. If the music editor cannot gain access to the mixer's session, they must still use the final music printmaster stems, along with their music "stage" session, to determine individual cue information, such as accurate length, usage, and timing of all the music. The music editor is actually one of the few and sometimes the only person with access to the Pro Tools session containing the final usages and lengths of the music cues, these being the two major parts of the cue sheet that determine the amount of money paid to the composers and publishers.

11.5.1 Header Information

Basic header information on the preliminary music cue sheet contains the TV series or film title, any AKA if applicable, television series title and episode, broadcast or air date if there is one, the production company, total length of the film or program, total minutes and seconds of music, and sometimes the name of the preparer of the document, such as the music editor. On occasion, there will be a legend containing the industry standard shorthand abbreviations for the various types of music usages.

11.5.2 Cue Title and Number

The listing of the cue number and title is in direct relationship to the music spotting notes and the cue title as listed on the score. The title on the score takes priority over the spotting notes, because those may not have been updated through to the time the cue sheet is compiled.

Tip

Cue titles and numbers must match the final printed scores wherever possible. If there is ever a legal issue with the original music, you can be assured the cue sheet and paper scores will be the first things referred to.

Although the spotting notes and cue timings should be updated by the time the final mix is completed, you should still review the mixer's final Pro Tools session to get the correct music information. If a cue is deleted from the final mix , it may cause a question from those who notice it is missing on the cue sheet; therefore, it is preferable to keep the cue number in the listing on the cue sheet and label it as Omit or Deleted. Write in the total time column :00 minutes and :00 seconds. Any information should be clearly stated, without any room for questions. The titles of the cues again are often chosen by the music editor at the spotting session, but before the preliminary music cue sheet is made, the music editor must confirm that the cue titles printed on the score and the cues on the cue sheet will be one and the same.

11.5.3 Entitled Parties

Entitled Parties refers to the names of all of the composers or writers and publishers who will be receiving royalties for the music. The publisher owns the music, and the writer owns the intellectual property rights, which pertain to the performance of the music. The shorthand label on the cue sheet is usually the letter C or W for composer/writer and P for publisher. However, I have also seen the letter E, standing for publisher or entitled party. When a composer writes the score for a movie or television show, they usually assign the ownership or publisher of the music to the film company under a Work For Hire contract. Therefore, the film company that hired the composer owns the music, similarly to a publisher. Experienced film production companies know that obtaining a music publishing entity can allow them to gain future income from the performance of music in their movie. It's possible for a composer to negotiate a contract that allows them to retain their own publishing rights, and therefore gain future publishing income and the right to re-use their music in other projects. While this is less common, it can occur for low-budget projects, as a way to compensate for the composer's low pay. As mentioned earlier, movies that play in theaters in North America do not gain any music performance royalties, but if the movie plays theatrically abroad (for example in Europe or Asia), royalties will be paid. Payments in North America are designed for broadcast, cablecast, and, increasingly, Internet play for webisodes and VOD productions.

In the case of songs, some large film entities, such as Sony and Warner Bros., have huge song catalogs, and they will encourage filmmakers to use their songs in their movies. However, there is no guarantee that these pieces will service the film as well as ones commissioned from outside sources. All songs' entitled parties and their detailed information is supplied to the music editor from the music supervisor. It's also possible for the music supervisor to directly input song information into the music cue sheet. Sometimes part of the music supervisor's delivery requirements can include sending the lyrics of the songs to the film company. Often, each composer of a song has his or her own publishing company, and the license or contract to use songs is arranged on a case-by-case basis by the music supervisor. On some occasions, the film company will hire a songwriter to compose and perhaps perform a song specifically for their movie, in which case it's possible that the contract or license deal can reflect the film company as owner or partial owner/publisher of the music.

The composer or writer is listed using their full name as stated in their respective PRO (Performance Rights Organization) contract. There can be more than one composer on a piece of score music and it is common to have multiple songwriters or composers as entitled parties in the listing of songs. (It is important to note that the artists/performers are not necessarily the songwriters.) Sometimes these cue sheet credit lists are confused with the screen credit rolls at the end of a movie that list the movie's music and their respective permissions. Screen credits are indeed based on a contract the music supervisor makes with the publishers, but are not necessarily the same as a song's composer and publisher listings in the music cue sheet.

As with composers and songwriters, it is also possible for multiple publishers to be listed. Because there are both songs and underscore pieces of music in the cue sheet, the publisher information is different for each. In the case of a film or television show, the production company will have its own publishing contracts from multiple PROs, such as BMI, ASCAP, SESAC, and many others, insuring they will be able to share in the royalties of a composer's music by matching the composer's PRO. If the composer's and publisher's PRO do not match for a particular piece of music, there is a risk that either will lose out on collecting royalties but if the cue sheet is delivered to both PRO's it's not usually a problem.

An administrating publisher oversees and collects for another publishing entity. For example, Sony Publishing may be the administrator for a composer's own publishing company, and be assigned by composers to collect on their publishing companies' behalf.

11.5.4 Performance Rights Organizations

There are many Performance Rights Organizations (PRO) throughout the world, usually for-profit companies that collect royalties for their clients. Some of these are as follows:

- ASCAP (USA) The American Society of Composers, Authors, and Publishers is the oldest performing rights organization in the United States.

- BMI (USA)
- SESAC (USA) SESAC is the second-oldest performing rights organization in the United States.
- AKM (Austria)
- SOCAN (Canada) Society of Composers ,Authors, and Music Publishers of Canada
- KODA (Denmark)
- EAU (Estonia)
- TEOSTO (Finland) Bureau International du Droit d'Auteur des Compositeurs Finlandais
- SACEM (France) Societe des Auteurs Compositeurs et Editeurs de Musique
- GEMA (Germany) Gesellschaft für Musikalische Auffuhrungs und Mechanische
- IMRO (Ireland) Irish Music Rights Organization
- SIAE (Italy) Societa Italiana degli Autori ed Editori
- BUMA (Netherlands)
- TONO (Norway)
- RAO (Russia) Russian Authors' Society
- SGAE (Spain) Sociedad General de Autores y Editores
- STIM (Sweden) Svenska Tonsattares Internationella Musikbyra

While it can be most useful for a composer or publishing entity to engage under contract with one or more of these companies, it is not necessary, and composers can collect their royalties on their own behalf if they choose. Independent collectors can also be contracted by clients to acquire monies due to them. Individuals trying to collect money on a regular basis from multiple worldwide PRO entities may find it is not worth the effort and small amount of money they might save by not contracting with one of the common PROs, such as BMI or ASCAP.

11.5.5 Percentages

When breaking down a song's entitled parties, it is common for a songwriter/composer to split the royalty share with the publisher 50/50. This represents 100% of the composer's share of the royalty amount and 100% of the publisher's share. If the songwriter/composer has their own publishing company, the composer would gain the full share of the money (the composer's share and the publisher's share combined), paid by their collecting PRO. For example, if a song is written and published by the same person, and the PRO pays $100 for the one performance of the song in the movie, then the writer gets $50 and the publisher gets $50. In this situation, they are the same person, so the total income to the composer/publisher is $100.

It is common to have multiple writers and publishers for songs and sometimes underscore music. In this case each writer listed on the cue sheet will get a contracted percentage of the shares as a writer (which might vary according to their personal agreement between the other writers), and if those same writers have their own publishing companies, they will receive their same percentage of the publisher's share. Their agents or attorneys usually handle this kind of agreement—and in this case, the music editor needs to pay attention to the multiple writers of a score cue and their respective PROs, so that the film's publishing PRO can match the writers'.

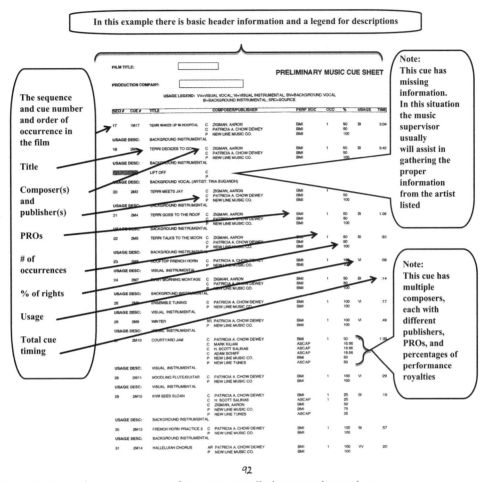

Figure 11.2a Various components of a common preliminary music cue sheet.

If a composer has been contracted as a Work For Hire, the film's production company will usually list their own music publishing company as the publisher. They will also make sure that their publishing entity is the same PRO as the composer's. The publishing companies usually match the same percentage of the royalty as the writer's share, as noted in Figure 11.2a, although these can sometimes be different percentages, and even shared or split amongst multiple publishers.

The administrating publisher is listed in the cue sheet with the letter A, in the identification column, indicating that they are the administrator of the client's funds, and will collect and distribute the royalties accordingly.

11.5.6 Usages

The usage column refers to how each piece of music was used in the film, and the various identifiers are one factor determining how much money will be paid for the piece of music. Needless to say, as everyone is interested in making as much money as

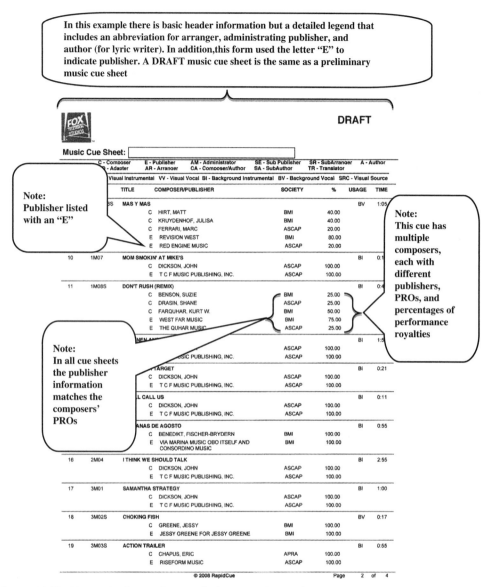

Figure 11.2b Alternative format for a preliminary music cue sheet.

possible from their creative work, the proper usage labeling is an important aspect of the music editor's job. As a rule, a piece of music featured and played as an on-camera source music with vocals will pay the writers and publishers the most money. Theme / main title music for television shows also pays at a good rate, the reoccurrence on each week's episode bringing regular performance income. Background instrumental music usually pays the least amount but then there is usually quite a bit of background music in a project therefore it adds up, contributing to the royalties collected. Note in figure 11.2a the column for occ. or occurrences. This information on the cue sheet is usually optional. The following are standard representations of how music can be used in a show:

BI—Background Instrumental

This is any music that does not have a vocal in it and is heard in the background of the movie. Usually it is underscore, but it can also be a source piece of music. If a song with vocals in it is used as a source piece, and the editor places or edits the music where the audience does not hear vocals, it will be listed as a background instrumental. This is also true if instrumental tracks of songs are used, even if they originally had vocals.

BV—Background Vocal

This indicates music played in the background, either as score or source, containing vocals in the music. The vocals must be heard in the film. Even if the piece of music is composed and scored with perhaps with a choir or vocalist as part of the composed music, it is labeled as BV. I have recently heard from a colleague that some PROs are requiring that any vocals heard must contain discernible lyrics and not just sounds such as 'ooh' or 'aah' as found in perhaps a choir singing in an underscore piece. The PRO claims that if the vocals do not have lyrics they will not pay at this higher rate.

VI—Visual Instrumental

Visual instrumental music refers to music where the audience can see the musicians playing on-camera, but they do not hear any vocals. It's possible there might be a vocalist seen by the audience as part of the band, but if they are not actually singing, the piece is labeled as a VI. If perhaps the vocalist is seen and only hums a little part of the song or is seen for a moment not singing but then is heard off camera, it would then become a VV (as an implied visual vocal).

VV—Visual Vocal

If the song is performed on-camera, with vocals heard by the audience, it is labeled VV. This performance does not have to be a featured performance to be listed as such. A featured performance refers to a scene in a movie when the focus of the audience's attention is on the song and the performers on-camera, or when the song's performance is an important part of the storytelling behind the movie. A VV performance could be incidental but yet seen on camera, even for a short time, for example in a bar or club scene.

TO—Theme Open, or MT—Main Title

The Theme Open is also known as the Main Title. This pays the composer and publisher at a higher rate than background music, particularly if it's in a television series and broadcast many times. For a piece of music to be considered an opening theme or main title, it must be heard while the audience sees the title of the TV show or film, or at least part of the title on the screen.

TC—Theme Close, or ET—End Title

Similar to the Main Title, the Theme Close, or End Title, music plays under the title of the film as it shows on the end credits, or at least under the main cards of the movie or TV show. There are often two areas of credits in a movie: the card title section, and the scroll or rolling credits. This labeling is not the same as music that plays under the rolling credits; that music would be labelled BI.

EE—Logo

The logo area is usually at the opening of a movie and is a short visual of the film production company (usually 8 to 15 seconds long). There could be multiple production companies and logos, and each one could have its own associated music cue. When you see the famous Twentieth-Century Fox logo, the music that plays under it has its own writer and publisher. It is possible that a logo does not have music written for it, or even if it does, it can be the creative choice of the director or producer to not play the logo music, but have the composer of the movie write music that continues through the movie in the introduction before the action, therefore under the logo.

It is important to understand that the music editor may be faced with many situations that do not conform specifically to these usage definitions. Take for example the VI term—imagine a scene where there is a hologram of a performer playing music in a scene of the movie, or perhaps a toy robot that is "performing" a piece of music. Would these be labeled as VI or BI according to the descriptions above? These kinds of puzzles can be a challenge. A music editor has to interpret each situation on a case-by-case basis, and make a note to the legal department, stating their opinion of the proper label.

11.5.7 Times

The timing of each cue is listed in this last column of the cue sheet. Each cue's length is arrived at by the music editor listening to and measuring the length of each cue (in Pro Tools) as heard on the printmaster stem audio files—these times should be accurate to within a second. The printmaster will usually be a 5.1 master mix of the music only. On lower-budget films, the these tracks might be Lt/Rt tracks (Left total and Right total), or even a stereo. It is important to include in the calculation any reverb that may extend the sound of a cue, giving the composer the maximum length of each cue's time for their royalty calculations. Occasionally, a piece of music may have a silent section in the middle of it, when the instruments are not playing, which is a deliberate writing technique called a "grand pause." It is usually not long enough to make it necessary for the cue to be split into two parts, but short enough to keep the recording going and continue the piece after this silent tacet. In this case, the length of the music cue should be calculated to include the grand pause.

When all the cue times are added up, the total amount is placed in the header information under total music. You can also include separate information by calculating the total time of composed score and total songs.

11.6 CUE SHEET DELIVERY

Upon completion of the music cue sheet, the music editor sends this document to the composer for review, so that they can verify cue titles, lengths and usages. When the composer has approved it, the music editor sends it to the film's production company. If there is a legal-affairs department, or a person on the staff who handles the legal contracts for the film, they will take the cue sheet information and collect any missing information (usually songwriters/composers and their publishers). With the help of the music supervisor, they can then fill in the missing information. It's possible that the film company has a document template that they may prefer to use, in which case insert the information in their document template, then send it along with your own document. The legal department should then send copies of the cue sheets to all the PROs listed. It is important to note that under some composer contracts, there may be a stipulation that until the music cue sheet is delivered to the production company or the film company, they may withhold any remaining payments to the composer. So it is in the best interests of all parties that the cue sheet be completed in a timely fashion. (In the case where a film company hires a separate production company to make a movie, if that film company is also a publishing entity, it's possible that they might control the composer and payment distributions.)

For a low-budget film or TV show where there is no separate production entity, they can submit the cue sheet directly to the PROs, and if the composer wants to submit to their PRO they can do so, although this is not common practice and is frowned upon. In these situations the music editor may be helpful, but the issue again stems from the music editor not being an attorney. It should really come from a non-interested party, or better yet the production company's legal department. In the case of an independent film, particularly if the composer has negotiated that they will retain the publishing rights to their music, it can be a help to the filmmaker if the music editor or the composer sends in the music cue sheet. In fact, this is an assurance that the information gets registered correctly, so that the composer will see royalties in a timely fashion.

The music cue sheet document becomes part of the delivery requirements for a film when it is sold or distributed; in fact, it cannot be sold until all the contracts and legal documents are in order, again demonstrating the importance of this document.

11.7 ARCHIVING

Once all of the data files and CDs are made, and the preliminary music cue sheets are compiled, the music editor delivers everything to the production office. If the audio Pro Tools sessions are small enough to fit on a data DVD (4.7 GB for each single-layer DVD, or 8.5 GB for a dual-layer DVD), you may archive onto this type of media. Otherwise, the production company should supply you with a hard drive to store all of the archived materials. Some larger film studios have servers for data storage, where they can take your archived materials and make a copy to their storage drives. This usually entails you either going to the studio location, sending a hard drive to them, or sending the files over a secure Internet-based server from your location to the studio.

11.8 MUSIC EDITING FOR TELEVISION

Music editing as a learned and acquired skill is transferable to many types of visual mediums with music attached to them. Even though television incorporates many types of projects, any of the editing information in this book can apply. There are, however, some differences between the formats of broadcast media as compared to films for theatrical performances, some of which are as follows.

In television the workflow pace can be much faster with regards to turnaround or turnover. This is particularly true with episodic television, where traditionally there will be a mix for a show every two weeks, or in some cases each week. This process places pressure on the music editor to produce and deliver spotting notes very fast to the composer, and in turn the composer must write, produce, and record the music very quickly. Traditionally, television production season started in September and went through May, but this is less true today, because shows are produced any time in the year, and not necessarily mixed and completed in regular intervals of one or two weeks. A music editor could be hired to work on a recurring show for a week, then be on hiatus for three weeks, then back on for a week or two for the following episodes!

While a television show, once in production, will rarely have temp music, a television pilot will. The television pilot is a full edited and produced show, made to sell the show to a network or studio. Because these pilots are only for presenting as a sales pitch, the music editing is much the same as a temp score for a film, except delivered at a much faster pace. Of course there is usually less temp music needed. On occasion, a TV pilot will have a composer attached, and the music might be a combination of composed music, temp music, and source and songs.

Other types of television projects include sitcoms, reality television, cartoons, movies, documentaries, webisodes, and miniseries. Generally these projects will use timecode and not feet and frames as the main timescale. While the standard time-code for (SD) television delivery is 29.97 Drop Frame (for standard-definition television in the U.S.), Currently many television shows are being shot and edited in high-definition (HD) digital, similar to films at a frame rate of 23.98 (23.976). Although television shows in the US use 23.976 fps for high def, and 29.97 fps for standard def, there is no difference in the speed or running times between these two formats, so the exact same mix can be used for both SD and HD broadcasts with no speed changes necessary. Virtually all of these projects will need music and therefore have music-editing challenges. I have laid editing challenges out in this book with film in mind, but all the techniques can be applied to the problems and puzzles that occur in television.

11.9 MUSIC EDITING FOR GAMES

The game audio world has progressed leaps and bounds from being a simple 8-bit sound file format, to music being composed by big Hollywood composers and full orchestras. As these game productions grow, the need for music editorial has also gained momentum, but in a slightly different way from traditional Hollywood postproduction. The composed music for games carries a unique challenge—because the advanced games give the player the opportunity to choose multiple plots, dramas and actions in real time, the music needs to follow those user choices and twists and turns. When the scenes change upon a viewer's whim, the music for those scenes should be composed in such a way that they can shift to a new scene and not sound awkward or unnatural.

The basic approach for this kind of variable composition technique is usually described as writing in "layers." Many games currently seek out to hire a composer to write and often record with live musicians for main themes and important musical pieces. These become musical elements that then may be 'composed' or layered by the game sound editorial team. The game world can have different requirements for a music editor regarding spotting notes, and delivery formats, although the traditional support work from the music editor for the composer, including spotting notes, timing notes, presenting demos, and final score recording, might apply here as well. Please read Appendix A, an excellent interview from the game-sound designer and programmer, Scott Gershin.

11.10 MUSIC EDITING FOR DOCUMENTARIES

The documentary filmmaking process is sometimes low budget, as compared to feature films, and there might be only a handful of persons working with the postproduction audio and video. If it's a higher-budget project, however, the postproduction will closely resemble the workflow of a feature film. It's common to have the writer as the director, and sometimes the picture editor of their movie, although they will still likely need a recordist for the dialogue and postproduction sound work. There is most often a composer hired, and perhaps some songs and source music licensed. A music editor indeed can be useful, perhaps writing spotting notes, guiding the composer, gathering their final music mixes, preparing for the dub, and delivering the final cue sheet. While there can be numerous deadlines and pressures, in much the same way as full-blown feature films or television shows, the documentary style and processes are usually overall less stressful. This does not mean that these films have less of a need for excellent sound and music work. They truly deserve and require the best from all parties involved. I have worked on numerous documentaries, and they have been enjoyable to work on and provided a wonderful experience.

11.11 WHEN THINGS GO WRONG AND KEEPING IT RIGHT

Aside from all the numerous technical issues that can arise in postproduction, the types of things that can go wrong while working on a project often involve human error or oversights. There's usually a great deal of stress for all concerned in a film or TV show, and when you have people working together under stress, there is a high risk of miscommunication, misunderstandings, errors in judgment, and almost any other human interactive situation one can imagine. Add to this situation the many egos involved, combined with the innate career insecurities of working in the entertainment industry, and you have a recipe for potential disaster! Most of this volume has been about the technical and creative challenges with regards to music editing, but while I am not a psychologist, my many years in the industry, both as a composer and music editor, have left me with some insight into the dynamics of preventing things from going wrong. By no means do I claim to have all of the answers, but I continually learn how to keep this even keel, so to speak, in each new project; mistakes can happen, and I've found it's best to not to allow those eat away at our success or be carried from project to project. It seems worth mentioning here some common sense reflections: keep a professional work ethic, strive for perfection but more realistically do your best work possible for every project that comes your way—no matter the pay scale, everyone you meet and work with has the potential for being or connecting you to your next job and ultimately for building a successful career. It may seem like I'm painting a negative picture of the industry; on the contrary, most interactions I have had over my 30 years in this business have been positive, fun, and rewarding.

11.12 FINDING WORK AS A MUSIC EDITOR

If you are interested, patient, and truly passionate about music editing as a career, there are some current trends to follow for success. In the past, there were recognized entrées into the postproduction industry for aspiring editors and mixers. Times have changed, though, and apprentice and assistant positions have become exceedingly rare. As you may reflect on entering this career path keep in mind that it is essentially a freelance self employed career with all the ups and downs of continually looking for work in between those fortunate times of employment. Even the most seasoned editor can be experiencing this roller coaster ride. The potentially harsh influences on what might be considered a 'normal' life is all part of the ride.

There are a few long-standing music-editing companies, which may be a viable place to try to start. However, those few small companies usually do not have training or assistant programs, and will expect that an editor come to them with already established contacts and relationships with composers and directors. Therefore, it would follow that one way to start a career is to build those relationships with composers, directors, producers, music supervisors, and postproduction supervisors.

It is common for someone at the beginning of their career to get to know established music editors and learn alongside them, although in this financial climate, there is rarely more than one music editor required on a project. Some of the bigger-budget movies may have two or more editors, and while this seems like an excellent opportunity for a new music editor to get experience, it is difficult even for an assistant to gain entrance into a real project, as there is significant pressure with these types of films. The expectation is that the editors already know what they are doing, and there is no mechanism for training an inexperienced editor. So, you are up against the all too familiar Catch 22—you can't gain entrance into a field to get experience without first having experience. To gain some experience, there are however a growing number of postproduction audio programs and coursework around the country. While I will suggest that none of these will prepare you as an expert, they can help give you a leg-up with a knowledge base in this competitive field. Sometimes these postproduction audio programs focus mostly on re-recording, dialogue, and sound effects missing out on what may sometimes feel as the invisible music editing element of postproduction. Another developing direction to consider are online courses.

There are a couple of workarounds for this door-slamming reality, however. On occasion, an established music editor may be asked to work on a low-budget project, and when the money is less than they would like, they might bring in a trainee editor to do the work, while mentoring or overseeing them. (It would be hoped that the senior music editor would make some kind of financial arrangement and not expect the trainee to work for free.) This serves a dual purpose. The established editor can accept a job perhaps with clients with whom he or she wants to maintain good relations, at the same time bring in new eager talent whom they can custom train, with a view to a future working relationship. In this scenario, the new editor might gain enough experience to be officially hired as an assistant, and later as a full editor either out on their own or when their mentoring editor has a job that can support two editors.

Considering that the more experienced editor may likely be in the Motion Picture Sound Editors Guild (the trade union), this may also allow the new assistant to gain entrance into the union, an important point for anyone serious about all types of sound editing, re-recording mixing, and picture editing. While the union is no longer very active in helping editors get work, it does have excellent benefits, and provides a base salary for union jobs. In order to gain entrance, the new editor needs to fulfill a certain amount of hours of work experience according to the union rules, so working as an assistant with another editor on non-union jobs can be a great boost toward your career goals.

Another direction for a new editor is to assist composers in multiple facets of their work. While this is a less direct route towards the music-editing world, it can be of great value. The duties of an assistant to an active composer can include synth programing, office work, technical troubleshooting, engineering, orchestrating, arranging, answering emails or the phone, office clean-up and organization, as well as preparation and supporting recording and mixing of their music. Some composers who have been successful enough to have built a small support team could require some help with music editing tasks such as spotting notes, stem management, collecting cue sheet information, and some delivery requirements. As you can see, this kind of job, while it will not pay a high salary, requires the assistant to be skilled in many areas, including the operations of Pro Tools, Digital Performer and/or Logic Audio Pro, as well as many "third-party" hardware and software technologies.

While I have cited two directions a new editor might take, nothing, however, can replace hard work, learning about the craft of music editing, composing, postproduction, and most importantly meeting people. I have always felt that the strongest networking for success in this or any industry is to get to know people as friends. While the meaning of this word may have been diluted in recent history through Facebook and other social Internet media, nothing will ever replace or be more important than meeting people face to face in a friendly environment. The development of true friendships enables you to establish invaluable connections that you can comfortably call upon as your career develops.

11.13 WORDS OF WISDOM

As a finishing touch to this book, I have asked my music-editing colleague J.J. George to share some of his dos and don'ts, which he contributes here with eloquence, humor, and insight. I could not have said it better.

- Be honest, but don't be afraid to withhold comments and opinions for the appropriate time. It's easier to keep your foot out of your mouth when you keep it closed.
- Be direct, particularly around any technical issues you might be having.
- Avoid placing blame. We are all part of the same team, with the same goal which is to make the best film possible.
- If you have a problem with a teammate, go directly to them and speak privately. Leave the yelling and screaming to the big dogs … unfortunately that is their prerogative. You will have some good stories to tell later about their lack of composure, but don't be the story.
- Don't prejudge or underestimate anybody—we are an eclectic and highly talented group.

> **PAX Quote**
>
> "I worked for a company where a casual young director (soon to be well known) with long hair came in for a meeting, and the receptionist announced over the intercom: 'Jeff, there is a courier at the front desk for you.'"

- Honor your word if you pledge to keep quiet about something. The industry is fueled by drama, and you should try to avoid it.
- Call on your personal ethics and integrity regarding the job, and always respect the creative vision of the filmmaker.
- Do your best to fix the music by editing it, rather than call to the composer to re-write it. Of course, let him know if you are being asked to alter his original intent, but otherwise he will probably be happy for you to keep it off his plate.
- If at all possible, on the mixing stage you should reserve your comments and critiques for your element—music. The sound and dialogue crew should grant you the same courtesy. There are a few exceptions, most notably a sound that is adversely affecting the music. A boat horn that's in the wrong key can sound like a drunken tuba player. If you hear a problem with the sound or dialogue that is not being addressed, you should carefully pick a private moment to discuss it with the sound supervisor. He or she is likely to appreciate your discretion and will be more open to addressing the problem, if they're not already working on it. Remember that if you drop a bomb on them, they might throw two more your way.

Appendix

Interview: Scott Martin Gershin, Sound Designer—Games

1. **How would you describe the game sound designer's role, as it relates to the overall success of a game?**

   I think, in relation to what role a sound designer plays in the gaming industry, first of all sound design in gaming is not really postproduction, it's more part of the production process, in that the assets are created during production which will later be edited and mixed into the game. A sound designer's major role is to create sound-designed assets that allow the player to have an interactive experience that sonically allows them to audibly submerge themselves into the illusion of the game.

   There's a process in gaming called "audio integration" which is closer to that being done in film and TV audio postproduction. I'd say the equivalent to audio production in gaming is similar to the postproduction process of an animated film. Like animation, there are similar schedule dynamics, as well as a technological component to it. In an animated film it's not just like you can go out and reshoot a new scene, it just doesn't work that way.

   The difference in sound design specifically is that any sound that you create, by the nature of the gamer playing a level over and over, has the potential to be very repetitive, which is different than linear formats where something goes by once and it's gone. So there has to be a randomization to the sounds, which are utilized in such a way as to not feel repetitive, advancing the illusion of a simulated environment. If you had to create a soundtrack for a movie using a sampler, how would you do it? That's exactly the way the gaming is done. Game consoles and computers are really samplers. You need to be able to trigger sounds or events based on how the user plays, so there is a randomization to that.

2. **What are some of the similarities and differences between working on low-budget and high-budget projects?**

   I think gaming is a little different than film. In films you've got low-budget films and high-budget films. Most of the film audio post industry is freelance and somewhat centrally located; in gaming most of the audio teams are in-house and spread around the world. Because they are in-house they have more time than people who would be working on film. A lot of times audio teams will be on a game for years. I know of a game where the crew's been on it for almost five years—for one game. Little by little they are always updating, always working the technology. They are in lock step with the animators, designing sounds as the animated elements are completed or sometimes before there is any animation at all.

As far as low-budget to high-budget goes, I think the equivalent would be console games and mobile games. Console games have a certain depth, because they have more memory, more CPU and DSP (Digital Signal Processing) power. In addition to triggering sounds in RAM, consoles have the ability to stream multiple tracks of audio and support multispeaker formats, include advanced real-time DSP, and do some really in-depth audio integration. When you're playing a game on a mobile device you have a limited amount of CPU and memory—it almost goes back to the Nintendo/Sega days when you only had a little bit of memory and low sample rates. In mobile games you've got to stretch the little you have a lot further because of needing to be able to download all the content wirelessly. It's not really between high-budget and low-budget projects like film, it's more about console games versus casual or mobile games.

3. **What is the sound and music workflow for creating a game? In what ways is it similar to or different from the workflows in film and television?**

I think that the way music and sound design interact with each other in gaming is similar and also different. Let me give you a good instance: in video games there are different gameplay perspectives—some are trying to be immersive, where you *are* that person in that environment, whether it's a sport, where you're a football player or a soccer player, or a soldier in a WWII battle, or driving a car, flying an aircraft or manning a spaceship. Some games aim to create an ultrarealistic simulated scenario in which music would not play a dominant role, because in those situations, as in real life … there is no music underscoring our daily lives. So it depends what the game is trying to create. If a game is trying to create another world, another story, or another emotion, then music becomes a much more cinematic experience and then you have to decide how the music gets played, when it gets played, and how it's helping to enhance the gameplay. You have to ask the question, if you are in an all-out fight, how does the music play? How do the weapons play? Each game has a different perspective on how it wants those different components or different art forms to be utilized—whether they want them more realistic or not.

The big difference, I think, on the music side, between movies, TV and games, is that in a movie and in TV the action is predictable because it's scripted, it's a linear form—you know when you're going to create tension and release based on the drama that's occurring in that linear format. During gameplay there is no linear format, everything has to be interactive, so the music has to be built in so that the computer can raise the tension or lower the tension—it's not pre-scripted, it's based on gameplay. Now, leaving this all aside, in many games there is both interactive gameplay and cinematics; while there are titles with no cinematics, many titles have numerous hours of linear cinematics. Cinematics are used to help create the folklore of the actual game, to give the player a backstory, to set the scene in which the player will interact.

4. **Is temp scoring part of the process of developing a game's sound?**

Not really, some people might use temp music for the cinematics, or they may use temp music to give the feel [or] the vibe of a section of gameplay that the animators can put on their headphones to animate to—we have had those situations. But there is no temp dub.

There is a process called "vertical slice", where they show off a small section of the game to get players' feedback or use as promotion for the game. But the vertical slice is taken from a small portion of the actual game that has been completed or nearly completed. Usually the composer is writing cues and they are on and off the project throughout the production. There really is no editing in gaming. The editing is actually done by the computer based on the dynamics of gameplay. There are some games that trigger music that just loops cues. In those instances it is being utilized to create a sense of timing, of how they want the gameplay to feel, whether it's fast paced or slow paced. In more sophisticated music tracks, music is used to create an underscore, similar to film and TV, where they are supporting the gameplay to create tension, release, and imagery. The composer usually writes a theme early on—and again music is not postproduction, you don't have to edit the film first before the composer gets involved. Many times the composer will write music never seeing a whole lot of picture at all, unless they're doing the cinematics, and even then some of the music they write is edited to fit the cinematics which again... the cinematic portion is very similar to movies.

5. **How do you envision the sound designer's role in games evolving in future, particularly in terms of budgets and expectations?**

Some games are not story driven. They are more twitch or puzzle games. However, I think that as games have evolved they have learned and taken a lot of their knowledge from the film industry. What I see happening is developers and studios are trying to cross-franchise IPs [intellectual properties] across multiple mediums, whether they are movies, anime, spinoffs of TV shows, or comic books, they are trying to create franchises. That's where the money and the success is. Marvel and George Lucas have shown the power of cross-platforming, as well as the mega-company Disney, who just recently acquired them both. It's the chicken-and-egg scenario—does a film become a game or a game a movie? A good example of this is *The Chronicles of Riddick*. A game was created, simultaneously with the film, called *The Chronicles of Riddick: Escape from Butcher Bay*. It became a successful hit in the gaming world. Movies have drawn themselves from comic books and books—I believe that movies are going to be drawing themselves from the IPs of games. Games are going to create continuations of stories from movies and they are going to be very intertwined. I know a lot of people are trying to figure out how they can put the two together and in a very high-quality way. I believe that entertainment is no longer going to be where you just go into a theater or just watch a show when it airs on your TV. Right now you can watch TV shows on your iPad, or use a computer or mobile device to get updated about the show's mythology and a behind-the-scenes story about the actors online. They want to be able to drag you into a show's world, finding joy submerging yourself in their mythologies.

In the past a lot of this has been centered in Hollywood, New York, and San Francisco. I think that's ready to bust wide open because gaming is not centrally located anywhere: there are many technological hubs all over the world with a lot of creative people in those areas. So will Hollywood still be the center hub? It is yet to be seen, but the people that are creating content technologically are spread coast to coast and all through the world. So I think the future is going to have very interesting dynamics. Being able to communicate all over the world has become quite easy—we are no longer stuck with having drivers move around tapes or drives. We have the ability to communicate successfully over the Internet. Many of our clients don't live anywhere near LA, so we have been doing that for almost a decade already.

6. **How do you see the music editor's role, as it pertains to the overall involvement of music production for games? Do you have staff or assistants providing music editorial services?**

I think every industry and every technology has their own terms for different tasks and jobs that need to be accomplished. Many people try and describe a job in one industry and to see how it correlates to another. The term "editor" is an interesting term in gaming because there's not a lot of editing outside of cinematics. There is something called "music integration", which is how the music is going to be put together within the game. The music that was in a linear format in other mediums is no longer in a linear format during gameplay, so because of that there is no, quote–unquote, "editing" to be done. For interactive music to occur, whether it's the composer spending time doing this or another person, aka a music editor or music designer, it's almost going back to the days where we used sequencers. Sequencers now are just very linear based, like tape machines. In the day there used to be little bits of data that used to live or be brought together in arrangements—there would be as little as four- or sixteen-bar sequences; you would then take those sequences and combine them into a song mode. Gaming is very similar to that but it uses actual audio. Not only is it using audio but it's using multitracks, a lot like what Ableton Live is doing—sort of. So for instance, you would compose a motif or section of music that when created can be comprised of rhythm, pads, ear candy, and melody, but they are all split out, like music pre-dubs. Then they can be rearranged in any order, in any number of tracks. A composer can deliver numerous stereo-streamed tracks that could be broken down into their different pre-dubs. So what happens is the music is being rearranged by the computer's AI [artificial intelligence] based on the way the music programmer or music editor deems fit. The strategy is to decide, how do we transition between cues? Do we use stingers during transitions? How do we want to transition on the beats and phrases? There's many, many different techniques to be able to do that and a lot of times composers don't have the technological desire or want to go that far into the music integration process. Some do, some don't—it really depends on each composer. Many composers in gaming are very technological, or sometimes they hire "a person" to handle those tasks while they continue composing. Is that the new role of the music editor, maybe? So once the music gets recorded it's going to need to be put into a game in some way. In gaming, Pro Tools isn't the device to be used for integration. There are programs like Wiise, F-mod … . Some developers have created their own proprietary toolset to be used for audio and music integration.

7. **Do you have staff or assistants dealing specifically with music editorial?**

Well, I mean … let me first say that a lot of what I am saying is on the interactive side of the game—audio during gameplay. The linear side, which is referred to as cinematics—it's very similar to the other formats, like animated films. A composer's team may have a staff member who integrates the music into the game. It could be the composer themselves, the mixer, or a programmer at the developer. I think that the new term or job coming into the music world for gaming is the title of "integrator". It could be thought of as a combination of editing and mixing. The blending of sonic elements and choices as to when a sound, motif or section of audio is played, and where it is panned, is done based on the dynamics of the game and gameplay. It all needs to be programmed. It's all based on how the integrator decides to control the material.

8. **How does a music editor's work relate to your role? Particularly in terms of their technical, musical or interpersonal skills, or any other qualities they may have? What are the workflows between director, producer, video editor, and music editor? What are the things to watch out for? What skill sets are crucial to success in this industry?**

Well I think the role of the music editor in games … outside of a linear format it's very different. I think music editors had to evolve from the world of mag to DAWs—if a music editor wants to go into music integration they would then have to learn another toolset and another way of working. Whether it's a music sound designer, a music programmer, or the mixer that does the job, it's a job that needs to be done—it's not an exact one-to-one fit between those two positions. What happens, I think, in technology, we are all finding out, is that new positions are created and old positions cease to exist. The role of a traditional music editor in gaming … again, there are things that they do that are similar and other things that are totally unique. They would have to have a certain amount of technological savvy and learn the new toolset.

So it really depends … music for mobile games tends to be a little bit of music that is looped to give you a taste and a feel for the game. Many times composers are in-house employees. The audio director—the guy that's in charge of the audio—happens to also be the composer. I think that the emotional arcs of gaming are very much in line with the emotional arcs of movies.

9. **What are some of the technical or communication issues that you as a game sound designer come across with regard to the music? Has a music editor helped resolve any of these?**

I think it's very simple and this is where the mediums are similar: audio is like playing with a color palette. One creative group uses these colors and another creative team uses another set of colors, and then we are going to put them together and see what happens. I think it's the same thing with audio. There's only so much audio spectral space that's out there and the challenge is to figure out how to use all of our audio assets to create an immersive soundtrack using dialogue, music, or sound design—no one element owns all the spectral real state. It's like writing for an orchestra, knowing how to create an arrangement that contains clarity with emotion. It's just too easy for it to become a car wreck. The more communication that happens between all of the areas the better the soundtrack will be.

10. **Is there a story or two relating to your working relationships with composers, music editors, or directors, whether about positive or difficult situations, which you can share as something we might learn from?**

What can be learned? I have been working 22 years in gaming and 30 years in movies. What can be learned is actually very simple, and that is communication. For those projects that I have participated on, whether it be actual games or movies, the more that everybody understands the roles that everybody else is playing the better. Not theoretically but exactly—we have to ask, "What are we doing in this area?" So if music can provide the sound designers with the kind of music they are putting in, if the sound designers could be giving a snippet of audio that the composer can hear and how that's going to play, the better off everyone will be because it allows everybody to look at their palette of colors that they utilize and [to] come up with intelligent choices to figure out how to put this puzzle together. And that's really what it is—it becomes an audio puzzle that a composer can't write the same way they would like on an album. An album is only an all-musical experience and there's nothing else happening other than that. When musicians and sound designers and actors all start working within a multimedia format, they always have to take into account how the other audio mediums are interacting, in the same way that a lead character designer has to understand what the backgrounds are doing, [what's] visually happening, as well as other characters and how they are going to work. Same thing in audio—everybody needs to be understanding and have that knowledge. In the past they haven't had the opportunities of knowing what each other are doing and a product does come out … and it's okay. But to make something special, to make something that really raises the bar and gives the audience a great experience—which ultimately all of us want to do because that why we do what we do—is to enhance the experience of the viewer or player. The more we communicate with each other and have intellectual spectral and audio design, meaning the big-picture design of how things are going to play at any given moment, the better the experience for the audience—and at the end of the day that's what it's all about.

Index